Connecting the Nineteenth-Century World

By the end of the nineteenth century the global telegraph network had connected all continents and brought distant people into direct communication 'at the speed of thought' for the first time. Roland Wenzlhuemer here examines the links between the development of the telegraph and the paths of globalization, and the ways in which global spaces were transformed by this technological advance. His groundbreaking approach combines cultural studies with social-science methodology, including evidence based on historical GIS mapping, to shed new light on both the structural conditions of the global telegraph network and the historical agency of its users. The book reveals what it meant for people to be telegraphically connected or unconnected, how people engaged with the technology, how the use of telegraphy affected communication itself and, ultimately, whether faster communication alone can explain the central role that telegraphy occupied in nineteenth-century globalization.

ROLAND WENZLHUEMER is a research group leader with the Cluster of Excellence 'Asia and Europe in a Global Context' at Heidelberg University. His previous publications include *From Coffee to Tea Cultivation in Ceylon, 1880–1900: An Economic and Social History* (2008) and *Global Communication: Telecommunication and Global Flows of Information in the Late 19th and early 20th Century* (as editor, 2010).

Connecting the Nineteenth-Century World

The Telegraph and Globalization

Roland Wenzlhuemer

CAMBRIDGE
UNIVERSITY PRESS

University Printing House, Cambridge CB2 8BS, United Kingdom

Published in the United States of America by Cambridge University Press, New York

Cambridge University Press is part of the University of Cambridge.

It furthers the University's mission by disseminating knowledge in the pursuit of education, learning and research at the highest international levels of excellence.

www.cambridge.org
Information on this title: www.cambridge.org/9781107025288

First published 2013

A catalogue record for this publication is available from the British Library

Library of Congress Cataloguing in Publication data
Wenzlhuemer, Roland.
Connecting the nineteenth-century world : the telegraph and globalization / by Roland Wenzlhuemer.
p. cm.
Includes bibliographical references and index.
ISBN 978-1-107-02528-8 (hbk.)
1. Telegraph – History – 19th century. 2. Telegraph – Social aspects – History – 19th century. 3. Globalization – History – 19th century. 4. Technological innovations – Social aspects – History – 19th century. 5. Telecommunication systems – History – 19th century. 6. Social networks – History – 19th century. I. Title.
HE7631.W46 2013
384.109′034–dc23

2012016540

ISBN 978-1-107-02528-8 Hardback

Meinen unverbesserlichen Eltern
Meiner unvergleichlichen Frau
Meinen unvernünftigen Töchtern

Contents

Figures

Maps

Tables

Acknowledgements

From the initial idea to the submission of the final manuscript, the theme of this book has in some form or other accompanied me for the last ten years. During this long time, a great number of people have lent me their ears, offered their thoughts and provided a helping hand. Without their support the pages in this book could never have been filled.

My curiosity about the subject was first aroused during a most stimulating discussion with Erwin Giedenbacher in a coffee shop in Salzburg's Kaigasse. From then on, the idea gradually developed into a fully fledged research project, the pursuit of which became possible thanks to the generous financial support of the German Research Foundation (DFG) and the German Academic Exchange Service (DAAD). I am also grateful to the directors and staff at the Centre for Modern Oriental Studies, the Centre for British Studies at Humboldt University in Berlin and the Cluster of Excellence Asia and Europe in a Global Context at Heidelberg University, who have always encouraged my work on the subject and created an extraordinarily pleasant work environment.

Over the years, research on the book took me to numerous libraries and archives, where I have always been treated with the utmost kindness and willingness to help – despite the huge amount of extra work that I have caused. At the British Telecom Archives in London, Ray Martin, Mike Cole, Scott Barlow and David Hay have been of invaluable help. At the Cable & Wireless Archives in Porthcurno, Alan Renton has sacrificed much of his time for me. At the ITU archive and library in Geneva, my particular thanks go to Heather Heywood. At the Historical Archive and Library PTT in Berne, Ronny Trachsel has provided most valuable support – as has Kevin Greenbank at the archives of the Centre for South Asian Studies at the University of Cambridge. I am also grateful to the enthusiastic and most helpful staff at the National Archives at Kew, the British Library, Guildhall Library and the London Metropolitan Archives.

A substantial part of the material unearthed in these archives is of a quantitative nature. I could not have handled and interpreted the vast amount of this data without the help of Karolina Golimowska in Berlin and Daniel Beeker and Michael Offermann in Heidelberg.

Many people have commented on my work at very different stages of progress and have thus helped to shape the present book. I am particularly grateful to (in alphabetical order) Amelia Bonea, Gita Dharampal-Frick, Jessica Fischer, Paul Fletcher, Antje Flüchter, Erwin Giedenbacher, Graeme Gooday, Frank Grüner, Daniel Headrick, Madeleine Herren, Peter Hugill, Yrjö Kaukiainen, Christoph Kirchengast, Deep Kanta Lahiri Choudhury, Isabella Löhr, Thomas Maissen, Simone Müller, Richard Noakes, Norbert Ortmayr, Johannes Paulmann, Corinna Radke, Gerrit Schenk, Kilian Schultes, Rudolf Wagner, Dwayne Winseck and three anonymous reviewers. It goes without saying that all remaining shortcomings of this book are entirely my responsibility.

Finally, I want to thank my family for bearing with me over a long time of vague ideas, endless archive visits and empty manuscript pages. You never seemed to doubt that all of this would eventually lead somewhere.

1 Introduction

1.1 An address in global space

On Monday 9 October 1933, the London firm Agile (Electrodes) Limited submitted a memorandum of complaint to the General Post Office (GPO). Over the weekend, two telegrams dispatched in Berlin and addressed to the overseas telegraphic address Agile London had been received at the company's office. Alas, both telegrams had not been intended for Agile (Electrodes) Limited but for another London firm which happened to be a direct competitor. This raised suspicion with the managing director, Mr Simonis, and he wrote to the Postmaster:

> Over the weekend the enclosed two telegrams have arrived here, which are not in our opinion intended for us. We are not aware that any other telegraphic address Agile exists, for we applied for such several years ago and could not get it. On the other hand, the word 'Agile' is our registered trade mark and that being so we do not think that anybody else can be allowed to use the word for any purpose whatsoever. We shall be glad if you will make an investigation into the position forthwith and let us know what the explanation of the instance is. We may add that on the only other occasions that telegrams addressed Agile have reached us, they have been properly intended for us.[1]

Indeed, in an internal communication the controller at the Central Telegraph Office revealed that the two telegrams 'were erroneously sent for trial to that firm [i.e. Agile (Electrodes) Limited], owing to the fact, that through an unfortunate oversight the registration "AGILE" had not been recorded at all the necessary circulation points in the Central Hall at this Office'.[2] This means that at one of the relay points, through which the

[1] British Telecom Archives, POST 33/2000, 'Registered Telegraphic Addresses. Firms with Similar Names or Businesses, etc. Memorandum Agile (Electrodes) Limited to General Post Office', 9 October 1933.

[2] British Telecom Archives, POST 33/2000, 'Registered Telegraphic Addresses. Firms with Similar Names or Businesses, etc. Letter from the Controller Central Telegraph Office to the Secretary General Post Office', 17 November 1933.

telegrams from Berlin had to go, the overseas telegraphic address in question had not been registered and linked with the postal address of the actual addressee, A. Arc Limited. Following the principle of trial and error, the messages had then been directed to Agile (Electrodes) Limited as the telegraphic address and the company name matched perfectly. Replying to their enquiries, the General Post Office had to reveal to Agile (Electrodes) Limited that the address Agile London had in the meantime been granted to another company. With obvious indignation, Mr Simonis replied,

> We believe that in reply to our memo of the 9th October you informed us that some firm in Barnes used the word 'Agile' as telegraphic address. Will you please answer our letter in writing and give us correct information on the subject? The writer understands from the telephone conversation that you are aware of the fact that we originally applied for 'Agile' as our telegraphic address and that it is an ordinary English word, but that the regulations have been eased, of which we have not been aware. If, indeed, it were possible with a competitive firm to use our Trade Mark as their telegraphic address, it would be a very serious matter to us against which we would have to strongly protest.[3]

In fact, so serious a matter was it for Mr Simonis that, when he did not receive immediate clarification from the General Post Office, he sent only a few days later another no less indignant memo, stating that 'we shall be obliged by your reply by return as this matter is of some importance to us'.[4] The matter now being investigated in some more detail, an intricate situation unfolded. Although they could not find any papers on the subject, the General Post Office conceded that Agile (Electrodes) Limited had, indeed, applied for the telegraphic address Agile at an earlier date. The address, however, had been refused on the grounds that it was too similar to the already existing address Facile. The required difference of three letters was not fulfilled. These regulations were later changed to the effect that a difference of only two letters sufficed for addresses of up to eight letters. Under these new conditions, the competitor A. Arc Limited had successfully applied for Agile London – and to add to the confusion, Agile had not been a registered trademark at that point in time. What to do? Everyone's claims somehow seemed understandable and justified. Owing to the hard fact of the trademark registration by Agile (Electrodes) Limited, it was eventually decided to withdraw the telegraphic address

[3] British Telecom Archives, POST 33/2000, 'Registered Telegraphic Addresses. Firms with Similar Names or Businesses, etc. Memorandum Agile (Electrodes) Limited to General Post Office', 8 November 1933.

[4] British Telecom Archives, POST 33/2000, 'Registered Telegraphic Addresses. Firms with Similar Names or Businesses, etc. Memorandum Agile (Electrodes) Limited to General Post Office', 17 November 1933.

Agile London from A. Arc Limited, and the controller at the Central Telegraph Office sent the respective letter to the firm on 8 December 1933.[5] Unsurprisingly, this led to some consternation on the part of Arc's managing director, Mr Neumann. His request to 'reconsider this matter', however, yielded no fruit.[6] Bitterly accepting the withdrawal of the telegraphic address, the other director of A. Arc Limited, E. W. H. Fairbairn, wrote to the Central Telegraph Office on 22 December 1933:

> We however, make this request, that this address is not registered by any other firm for foreign telegrams, particularly as we have already explained that this is our trade-mark throughout the world with the exception of the United Kingdom. In the meantime, as you will understand that it is necessary for us to register an address, we suggest that the word 'Agile' should be transformed and that this address should read 'ELIGA' instead of 'Agile'.[7]

The General Post Office complied in both cases. A. Arc Limited was assigned the address Eliga – simply the anagram of Agile and, therefore, still carrying old associations – and Agile (Electrodes) Limited was refused the address Agile, London on the grounds that outside the United Kingdom this was the trademark of A. Arc Limited. However, the General Post Office was not immediately able to close the file. Among other things, Agile (Electrodes) Limited filed a complaint against the continued use by A. Arc Limited of the old telegraphic address on their stationery and tried again (and were again refused) to register the old address for themselves. The matter was finally resolved when Mr Simonis 'purposely sent a telegram from Copenhagen addressed "Agile London" and this was duly returned as insufficiently addressed, proving to our satisfaction that the address "Agile London" has now been cancelled'.[8] Grudgingly, Agile (Electrodes) Limited finally accepted the GPO's decision, stating, 'We are unable to follow [the GPO's] argument ... However, we have been looking for a satisfactory alternative ... and make application for the registration of our telegraphic address [of] the

5 British Telecom Archives, POST 33/2000, 'Registered Telegraphic Addresses. Firms with Similar Names or Businesses, etc. Letter from Controller Central Telegraph Office to A. Arc Limited', 8 December 1933.

6 British Telecom Archives, POST 33/2000, 'Registered Telegraphic Addresses. Firms with Similar Names or Businesses, etc. Letter from A. Arc Limited to Controller Central Telegraph Office', 12 December 1933.

7 British Telecom Archives, POST 33/2000, 'Registered Telegraphic Addresses. Firms with Similar Names or Businesses, etc. Letter from A. Arc Limited to Controller Central Telegraph Office', 22 December 1933.

8 British Telecom Archives, POST 33/2000, 'Registered Telegraphic Addresses. Firms with Similar Names or Businesses, etc. Letter from Agile (Electrodes) Limited to the Telegraph & Telephone Department General Post Office', 13 September 1934.

word "Agilerods" or alternatively "Agiletrode".'[9] The latter address was eventually assigned to the firm and the file was closed.

From the middle of the nineteenth century, a global telegraph network had come into existence that linked places and people all over the world via an elaborate system of cables, wires and relay stations. The dispute over Agile London and the many similar cases archived by the General Post Office illustrate how important it was for internationally operating businesses to be visible and reachable in the global telecommunication network. Although the cases that survive in the archives usually date from the 1930s, it can safely be assumed that businessmen in preceding decades shared similar notions as to the recognizability of their telegraphic addresses. After all, it was this very combination of letters that rendered their businesses reachable by telegraph from all over the world, and therefore reserved them a permanent and easy-to-remember place in the global communication network. Securing the company name as one's telegraphic address avoided such confusion as in the example above. Correspondence could simply be addressed to the company name. But more than that: matching telegraphic addresses were symbols of status. Due to the strict regulations guarding the assignment of addresses, which were meant to secure accurate delivery in case of a faulty transmission, boasting the company's name as telegraphic address implicitly signified that the bearer had been internationally active for a long time and had applied for the address early on. Carrying the fitting telegraphic tag was, therefore, a matter of appearance, status and pride just as much as it secured easy recognition. This was the motivation behind Agile (Electrode) Limited's complaint against A. Arc Limited's still carrying the old address on their stationery.

Interestingly, the emergence of the World Wide Web in the early 1990s and its rise to importance for businesses later in that decade led to very similar conflicts. A good number of companies had been a little too slow in realizing the potential of the Internet for both self-representation and customer contact and had not registered a suitable second-level domain in time,[10] while other entrepreneurs – who had been quicker on the uptake – had secured many internationally recognized brands as domain names and now wanted to capitalize on this by selling these domains to the

9 British Telecom Archives, POST 33/2000, 'Registered Telegraphic Addresses. Firms with Similar Names or Businesses, etc. Letter from Agile (Electrodes) Limited to the Telegraph & Telephone Department General Post Office', 5 October 1934.

10 In what is colloquially called an Internet address, a second-level domain is usually the part between the two dots. For example, in www.companyname.com, 'companyname' is the second-level domain.

respective companies and brand-name holders. So widespread was this practice and so pronounced was the interest of the companies to hold suitable domains – or, more colloquially, Internet addresses – that many cases have been taken to court. Trademark, name and competition law all apply in such disputes over domain names and safeguard established companies or individuals against the registration of their names or trademarks by third parties. While, with the help of World Wide Web search engines, it makes little practical difference whether a company's website can be found at www.companyname.com or at some variation of the name, it remains a question of status to own the one perfectly fitting second-level domain name. In short, practicability and recognizability have long ceased to be the principal considerations in selecting a call sign in global telecommunication space. So important has this space become since the late nineteenth century that the status of the placeholder reflects the status of its owner. There is no better signifier for the transformative impact of telecommunication technology – in our case, of telegraphy – on processes of globalization.

1.2 Functions and structures

Globalization thrives on the expansion of global trade and migration and, therefore, on the increasing global movement of goods and people. The effortless movement of information and knowledge, however, might have grown even more important as the example of domain names suggests. The emergence of the Internet as a near-universal telecommunication medium has become a prime symbol of globalization and has pushed forward the global division of labour with hitherto unprecedented force. It has done so by connecting computers across the globe and, thereby, allowing for the exchange of all sorts of digitized information, most of which had previously been transferred via material carriers. While the Internet is not the first telecommunication technology to detach long-distance information flows from the physical movement of a carrier medium, it has pushed such dematerialized information exchange to new extents. This is primarily due to the fact that almost every piece of information can now be digitized (or at least digitally represented) and transmitted via the Internet, with considerations of data volume becoming less and less an issue. Global communication space has thus been transformed in such an incisive way that entirely new spaces anticipated by early observers – such as *cyberspace*,[11] *virtual space*

[11] The term was first introduced by author William Gibson in his science fiction novel *Neuromancer*, published in 1984. William Gibson, *Neuromancer* (New York: Ace, 1984).

or the *space of flows*[12] – have in the meantime actually come into existence in one way or another. The social, economic and cultural impact of these new spaces has been so pronounced (at least in the well-connected regions of the world) that in the eyes of many a prominent researcher they have given rise to a new form of social organization – the so-called information society.

Manuel Castells, who coined the term 'information society' in the closing years of the last millennium,[13] emphasizes the uniqueness of the information revolution that has allegedly transformed many (mostly Western) societies since the 1970s. He argues that three initially unrelated developments – 'the crisis and restructuring of industrialism . . .; the freedom-oriented, cultural social movements of the late 1960s and early 1970s; and the revolution in information and communication technologies'[14] – had to coincide and combine forces in order to allow for an information revolution to unfold. To Castells, this is an unprecedented development. But he concedes that there have been historical precursors when he states that the ability

> of networks to introduce new actors and new contents in the process of social organization, with relative independence of the power centers, increased over time with technological change, and more precisely, with the evolution of communication technologies. This was particularly the case with the possibility of relying on a distributed energy network that characterized the advent of the industrial revolution: railways, ocean liners, and the telegraph constituted the first infrastructure for a quasi-global network with self-reconfiguring capacity.[15]

The journalist Tom Standage also acknowledged the continuities between the emergence of a nineteenth-century global telegraph network and the Internet revolution, when he titled his book on the former subject *The Victorian Internet*. Of course, Standage's book was written for a general audience and needed a catchy title to attract readership, but the author is explicit about the similarities between telegraphy and the Internet beyond the book cover. In the preface he writes,

[12] The concept of the *space of flows* is employed in several of Manuel Castells's works. For instance, Manuel Castells, *The Informational City: Information Technology, Economic Restructuring, and the Urban-Regional Process* (Oxford: Basil Blackwell, 1989); Castells, 'Epilogue: Informationalism and the Network Society', in *The Hacker Ethic and the Spirit of the Information Age*, ed. Pekka Himanen (New York: Random House, 2001); Castells, 'Informationalism, Networks, and the Network Society: A Theoretical Blueprint', in *The Network Society: A Cross-Cultural Perspective*, ed. Manuel Castells (Cheltenham and Northampton: Edward Elgar, 2004).

[13] Manuel Castells, *The Rise of the Network Society* (Malden: Blackwell 1996); Castells, *The Power of Identity* (Malden: Blackwell, 1997); Castells, *End of Millennium* (Malden: Blackwell 1998).

[14] Castells, 'Informationalism, Networks, and the Network Society', 15.

[15] Ibid., 5.

Today the Internet is often described as an information superhighway; its nineteenth-century precursor, the electric telegraph, was dubbed the 'highway of thought.' Modern computers exchange bits and bytes along network cables; telegraph messages were spelled out in dots and dashes of Morse code and sent along wires by human operators. The equipment may have been different, but the telegraph's impact on the lives of its users was strikingly similar.[16]

The historian's urge to find precursors and continuities even in the most unlikely corners can easily lead to the construction of similarities and straight lines of evolution where ruptures and discontinuities should actually be emphasized and made visible. What Standage discounts as a mere difference in equipment is not irrelevant at all. Much of the working logic of a particular technological system stems from the machinery and the techniques accordingly employed. Therefore difference in equipment can often lead to discrepancies in the socioeconomic and cultural significance of a technology as well. In the case at hand, differences that immediately spring to mind revolve around public access to the network, the cost of transmission, the nature of the transmitted content or the need for specialized mediators between the customer and the technology. While Internet access is still far from being evenly distributed around the globe,[17] within well-connected countries it has become affordable for almost everyone and is, therefore, fairly pervasive. Sending a private telegram, on the other hand, for a long time remained the privilege of the well-to-do. Also, distance did still matter in telegraphy. A telegram from London to India took longer to be delivered than a telegram from London to Manchester. And, what is more, it was much more expensive to send. In modern email communication, the time difference in delivery has been reduced to seconds (or less) and there is no difference in cost whether an email is sent to a next-door neighbour or the business partner at the other side of the globe, whether it is sent to one addressee or several

[16] Tom Standage, *The Victorian Internet: The Remarkable Story of the Telegraph and the Nineteenth Century's On-Line Pioneers* (New York: Walker and Co., 1998), viii.

[17] See, for instance, Matthew Zook, 'Old Hierarchies or New Networks of Centrality? The Global Geography of the Internet Content Market', *American Behavioral Scientist* 44, no 10 (2001); Zook, 'Being Connected Is a Matter of Geography', *Networker* 5, no 3 (2001); Zook, 'Hubs, Nodes and Bypassed Places: A Typology of E-commerce Regions in the United States', *Tijdschrift voor economische en sociale geografie* 93, no 5 (2002); Zook, 'Cyberspace and Local Places: The Urban Dominance of Dot.Com Geography in the Late 1990s', in *The Cybercities Reader*, ed. Stephen Graham (London: Routledge, 2004); Matthew Zook et al., 'New Digital Geographies: Information, Communication, and Place', in *Geography and Technology*, ed. Stanley Brunn, Susan Cutter and James W. Harrington (New York: Kluwer Academic Publishers, 2004); Martin Dodge and Rob Kitchin, *Mapping Cyberspace* (New York: Routledge, 2000); Dodge and Kitchin, *Atlas of Cyberspace* (Harlow: Addison-Wesley, 2001). Edward Malecki, 'The Economic Geography of the Internet's Infrastructure', *Economic Geography* 78, no 4 (2002).

thousand recipients at once. Furthermore, digitization and high-capacity connections allow Internet users to exchange much more than just brief text-based messages. Pictures, sounds or videos can all be converted into binary code and then transmitted via electric or fibre-optic lines. Telegraphy only allowed for brief and to-the-point messages that were often transmitted separately from longer and more detailed information sent by post. Also, people who wanted to send telegrams depended on trained specialists to encode, transmit and decode their messages. They had only human-mediated access to the global network, while Internet users today need only basic computer skills (and a computer) in order to send and receive information. The most fundamental difference, however, probably rests in the on-demand nature of the World Wide Web. Although the terms 'Internet' and 'World Wide' *Web* are often used synonymously, they do not signify the same thing. In simple words, the Internet is a network of computers and enables the exchange of information between them (and their users). The World Wide Web, on the other hand, is an application of the Internet that turns some of the computers into data storage devices that can be accessed from other computers in the network. While telegraphy – similar to email today – only enabled the transmission of a message from a sender to a recipient (or several recipients, in the case of email), the World Wide Web stores information and makes it accessible on-demand at any time and from any (connected) place. No matter how hard we look, there is no nineteenth-century equivalent for this killer application of modern telecommunication.[18]

These eclectic differences and discontinuities between nineteenth-century and current telecommunication networks illustrate how hard both systems are to compare and how cautiously such diachronic comparisons have to be handled. In many regards, the essential qualities of the systems differ so pronouncedly that their study does not allow for the same guiding questions – a prerequisite for meaningful comparison. This is, however, not to say that the two telecommunication systems had nothing in common and that nothing can be learned from analytically putting the two next to each other. There are, of course, continuities between the two technologies as the similarity of interests informing both the telegraphic address case and the domain example already suggests. While Standage detects a comparable 'impact on the lives of users', one could also say that telegraphy and current communication technologies fulfil very similar functions in the context of globalization in their respective times. Both network technologies in varying degrees detach the flow of information

[18] The term 'killer application' refers to a specific application for an already existing but not particularly successful technology that brings the breakthrough for this technology.

from the physical movement of people or goods, and therefore foster the dematerialization of information flows. As shall be seen in the following chapter, dematerialization creates a number of new global spaces and significantly transforms others. All these spaces share their actors and objects with customary space, but put them in very different relations to each other – generally attaching less importance to questions of geographical distance. In doing so, dematerialization contributes essentially to the creation of a global sphere through the connection of innumerable locales. In practice, both the telegraph and the Internet (representing all telecommunication media of the day) allow for a closer integration of global markets and the further expansion of capitalism around the globe. Both transform the collection and reporting of news and the participation of those connected in distant affairs. And, of course, both networks were and are of great strategic and administrative value for all those who need to control far-flung territories, remotely stationed troops or globally operating merchant ships. Both networks were and are also used for entertainment purposes. While this is self-explanatory in the case of the Internet, which offers all sorts of digital distractions, it might be less well known that the telegraph has often been used for entertainment purposes as well – for instance, in betting on horses (see Chapter 7) or to allow for telegraphic chess matches, amongst other things, between members of the House of Commons and the Australian Commonwealth House of Representatives.[19]

Both systems thus share a good number of functional similarities in the way that they are or have been used to similar ends and fulfil comparable functions in the globalization processes of their day – mainly thanks to the power over geographic space that the dematerialization of information flows provides. And, of course, both telecommunication systems are based on networks. Networks have a particular logic of working – a particular rationale – that has a strong influence on the nature of relations between those connected in the network. In the case of technology-based networks, to which both the telegraph and the Internet belong, the particular working logic of the mediating technology has also to be considered in this regard and becomes part of the network rationale. The functional similarities as well as the shared network rationale are to a large extent mirrored in the structure of both networks. This means that the functions that a global telecommunication system has to fulfil impact on the structure of its network just as this structure in turn facilitates some courses of

[19] British Telecom Archives, POST 33/1997, 'Anglo-Australian Beam Service. Proposal Chess Match between House of Commons and Australian Commonwealth House of Representatives', 25 June 1926.

action within the system and makes others harder to follow. Following Castells, 'structures do not live by themselves; they always express, in a contradictory and conflictive pattern, the interests, values, and projects of the actors who produce the structure while being conditioned by it'.[20] In other words, the symmetry or asymmetry, the tightness or looseness, the inclusiveness or exclusiveness – to name but a few network dichotomies – of a network are shaped by the tasks and functions that a network has been designed to fulfil, while the network structure, on the other hand, preselects the ways in which any given function is fulfilled. In addition, the network rationale – combining the working logic of networks in general and that of the specific network technology in particular – also impacts on the network structure and vice versa. For instance, the pull to become a member of a network usually grows with the number of other members (remember the growing pressure to own a mobile phone in the 1990s or the insurmountable urge to join Facebook or MySpace in the late 2000s). Also, contrary to Manuel Castells's views,[21] networks do have centres[22] – but they also have an in-built tendency to connect their members in more than one way in order to provide alternative routes and backups. Such inherent qualities and requirements become visible in the physical structure of a network – just as the qualities and requirements of the technology behind the network do. If, for instance, proper insulation against seawater is difficult to achieve, electric telegraphy will be confined to landlines and the network structure will mirror this. Or if – after the insulation problem has been solved – even the biggest ships available can only transport a certain length of submarine telegraph cable, the production of such cables is expensive and the electric signal weakens with the length of cable, then the choice of cable landing sites will reflect this technological need for short submarine connections. The network structure reflects the network rationale (of which the technological rationale is part and parcel). The structural analysis of a network, therefore, tells us more than just which connection – in our case which cable, which wire – went from where to where and how much capacity it had. If done with the right questions in mind, it provides an entry point for the in-depth analysis of the functions, the usage and the rationale of a particular network – issues that are otherwise hard to get an analytical hold on.

[20] Castells, 'Informationalism, Networks, and the Network Society', 24. [21] Ibid., 3.

[22] See, for instance, Roland Wenzlhuemer, 'London in the Global Telecommunication Network of the Nineteenth Century', *New Global Studies* 3, no 1 (2009); Wenzlhuemer, 'Metropolitan Telecommunication: Uneven Telegraphic Connectivity in 19th-Century London', *Social Science Computer Review* 27, no 3 (2009).

Looking at the structures of the nineteenth-century global telegraph network and of today's fibre-optic connections that form – among other things – the backbone of Internet communication, we find that both are surprisingly similar – for instance, in their asymmetries. It seems that today's digital divide resembles the asymmetrical pattern of the nineteenth-century telecommunication network in both structure and actual information flow.[23] With the very notable exception of the economic boom regions of East and South-East Asia, the two are practically alike. The same world regions stand at the centre of the network and feature an extremely high connectivity, while other regions remain at the fringes of the Net and have not been able to utilize the technological advances of the twentieth century to place themselves more centrally. Even the main routes and pathways of information flow have changed but little and in a number of cases the landing sites of the fibre-optic cables are still located at the very same places at which the submarine telegraph cables of the nineteenth century emerged from the sea. This supports the point that the evolution of the global information network shows a certain degree of continuity both in its structure and in its usage patterns. Similar continuities can be identified in the development of telecommunication structures in regional or national contexts as well. Elsewhere I have tried to show how the United Kingdom (and especially London) has managed to maintain its position at the core of a global telecommunication network since the middle of the nineteenth century despite its relegation from world power to secondary geopolitical and economic importance. Here we can find continuities in a number of different contexts: in the position of the United Kingdom in the global information network, in London's position in the latter, in London's position within the United Kingdom domestic network,[24] and finally in the uneven distribution of global connectivity within the metropolis.[25] All this supports Standage's notion that continuity and path-dependence played a significant role in the development of modern informational structures and usage patterns. While it is well known that path-dependence is an important and recurring factor in the historical evolution of many technologies,[26] a path-dependent

[23] Benjamin M. Compaine, *The Digital Divide: Facing a Crisis or Creating a Myth?* (Cambridge, MA and London: MIT Press, 2001).

[24] Wenzlhuemer, 'London in the Global Telecommunication Network of the Nineteenth Century'.

[25] Wenzlhuemer, 'Metropolitan Telecommunication'.

[26] Paul A. David, 'Clio and the Economics of QWERTY', *American Economic Review* 75, no 2 (1985); David, 'Path Dependence: A Foundational Concept for Historical Social Science', *Cliometrica: The Journal of Historical Economics and Econometric History* 1, no 2 (2007).

approach to the history of informationalization runs counter to most common assumptions about information societies. In particular, it challenges the widespread notion that modern information technologies and their infrastructural networks are highly dynamic and evolve largely without historical baggage.

1.3 The purpose of this book

In the preceding section it was established that the global telegraph network of the nineteenth century and the Internet of today share a number of essential traits regarding their functions and structures, while at the same time they are remarkably different in other aspects. These differences go far beyond the question of technical equipment acknowledged by Standage, and reach deep into the socioeconomic and cultural significance of the two systems. So pronounced are these differences that an analytical diachronic comparison is extremely difficult should it produce further insights regarding the role of either the telegraph or the Internet in processes of globalization. But why, then, open this book by juxtaposing and then connecting the two systems in the first place? Because the initial questions that triggered the research behind this book emerged from the ambivalent relation between old and new telecommunication systems. Given the newness of modern telecommunication technology, the extremely high pace of technological change and the transformative impact that global telecommunication exerts on all spheres of society, how can there actually be so many obvious continuities and similarities (structural or otherwise) between global telegraphy and modern telecommunications? Which forces are giving rise to these similarities and what are the mechanisms behind them? A first answer proved to be simple enough to come up with – but on second glance it turned out to lead on to the far more complicated and multilayered problem that this study now looks into.

This preliminary answer suggested that these similarities and continuities principally stem from how people put information technologies to use. The intentions of those who invent, build and use such technologies have not changed much – and this is reflected in the structure as well as in other traits of the systems. This is, for all practical purposes, a socio-determinist view of the interactions between people and technology that pictures technology as a mere instrument that does nothing except fulfil the will of its human users. While such a perspective offers several useful insights and is more convincing than the technological-determinist belief that technologies exclusively shape their carrier societies, it has several shortcomings and eventually proves unsatisfactory as well. It overlooks the fact that technologies – even if purposefully used as instruments to achieve a certain goal – have a particular rationale that cannot be left out of the equation. While technologies help us to achieve a particular goal they also propagate a particular way of doing things that often entails unwanted by-products or unnecessary detours.

Here is a simple example: a hammer is a useful tool if one wants to drive a nail into a piece of wood. It makes this task very easy and efficient. But at the same time, the use of the hammer causes a loud noise – an unwanted and, regarding the task, unnecessary by-product that might be harmless or might just as well annoy the neighbours and, in extreme cases, jeopardize a good neighbourly relationship. It is true that it is not the hammer that *makes* (in the sense of actively producing something) the noise. It is the user who knew it would be loud but decided to hammer away nevertheless. The decision, the action, therefore, seems to rest exclusively in the human actor. And yet, as will be argued in more detail in the next chapter, the matter is a little more complicated than this. By offering an easy way to get the job done, the hammer impacts on the choices human actors have. It makes some choices more desirable, more efficient, than others. The hammer does not force itself upon the user. The final decision rests with the latter. But it offers convincing arguments for being put to use – arguments that more often than not will make the actor accept the noise as an unpleasant by-product. Of course, this example is a very simple one, just as the hammer is a comparatively simple technology. It has been chosen here for reasons of clearness rather than of comprehensiveness. More complex technological systems feature more complex working rationales that might not be immediately obvious. While it is generally well known that hammering produces noise, the side effects and unintended consequences of more complex technological systems are often practically unpredictable.

This brings us back from the hammer to information technologies, which tend to be among the more complex technological systems – also due to the fact that it is their very purpose to connect a great number of people, thereby making them part of the system. In such a complex and interconnected system, it becomes almost impossible for inventors, engineers, policy-makers and users alike to predict how exactly a technology will interact with its environment. By involving so many different system components – many of them humans – the rationale of the technology becomes so complicated that it effectively develops into a *black box*.[27]

[27] For a discussion of blackboxing in the context of actor-network theory, see Bruno Latour, *Pandora's Hope: Essays on the Reality of Science Studies* (Cambridge, MA and London: Harvard University Press, 1999), particularly Chapter 6.

The technology seems to gain a life of its own. It influences the choices of the people involved in the technology in ways that are not immediately discernible. This is the reason why humans involved in a technology usually do not have full control over it. This unpredictability and lack of control has often been mistaken for agency on the side of the technology. While the black-box character of an input–output relation does not automatically mean that independent agency is involved, it nevertheless renders the sociodeterminist models of explanation incomplete and unsatisfactory. Such reasoning proves to be oversimplistic and fails to explain the continuities as well as the discontinuities between nineteenth-century and current information technologies. While humans might have particular uses and purposes when deploying a technology, the rationale of the technology has a bearing on issues such as how exactly a certain goal is reached or which unintended side effects are caused in the course of reaching it.

The initial search for a quick and simple explanation for the diachronic similarities between two actually very different technological systems thus eventually led away from the original problem and pointed to more general questions about the relationship between actors and network technologies in a historical context. How do the functions that such technologies fulfil for their users and the ways in which they are applied shape the network structure? And, in turn, how do these structural conditions then feed back into the rationale of the technology? In combination, these guiding questions acknowledge the social shaping and cultural construction of technologies as well as the impact that technologies can have on the courses of human action. And they lead on to further issues: is it at all possible to historically unravel the rationale of a complex technological system? How exactly does such a rationale unfold and how exactly can it limit and expand human choices? Did such bearing on choices of action entail unintended consequences which could in turn abet technological inertia or lead to frictions between old and new technologies and the cultural practices associated with them? Finally, how did human actors perceive and weigh the impact of such technologies on their lives, choices and freedom of action?

This study looks at these questions in the context of global telegraphic communication and its role in nineteenth-century processes of socioeconomic and cultural globalization. In this context, I understand the term 'globalization' in a way that permits applying it as an analytical tool in hands-on empirical research, while at the same time providing a level of abstraction that allows for a more general diagnosis of modern sociocultural trajectories. Thus globalization comprises all processes that lead to a gradual detachment of patterns of sociocultural interaction from geographical proximity. Globalization processes add more and more global connections to the mix of personal and institutional relations that constitute the networks of historical actors. However, globalization does not evolve in a deterministic fashion with a fixed trajectory. Rather, it should be thought of as a bundle of individual processes which usually overlap and interact strongly but which can also develop along completely different lines at other times. The detachment of patterns of human communication from geographic proximity is one such process that stands at the centre of attention in this work.

This book seeks to shed new light on the interactions of human protagonists with and within the emerging global telegraph network. In this regard, the general questions above culminate in the principal issue of how telegraphy helped to shape processes of globalization by providing new possibilities and new choices to local and global actors while the network was at the same time shaped by the intentions, demands and actions of those very actors. The study is interested in the interplay between the functions and the structures of global telegraphy. In plain words, it wants to establish to which ends people used the telegraph and what exactly it meant for them to be telegraphically connected – or unconnected.

Examining this problem closer, at least three different angles of investigation emerge. First, in what particular contexts and for which purposes did protagonists of nineteenth-century globalization processes resort to telegraphic communication? What were their intentions, goals and requirements and what principal benefits could they gain by using the telegraph? To what extent were these intentions and demands mirrored by the emerging structure of the global telegraph network, by the routes that telegraph lines took or did not take and by the traffic that these structures facilitated? Second, what real or perceived consequences did it have for historical actors to be connected with other, physically removed people? How did the technological rationale of telegraphy transform their action and event horizons? How did it reshape perceptions of space and time and impact on various cultural practices such as the use of language or the production and consumption of news? What was the role of the structural network conditions in this regard? Did frictions occur between established sociocultural necessities and the limited ability of the new communication technology to fulfil these necessities? And third, how can the technological rationale of the telegraph and its transformative potential best be conceptualized? What were the essential new characteristics of the technology and what new choices did they offer to the actors? How did they relate to traditional concepts of space and time? And where do the telegraph and its applications belong in ongoing discussions about globalization?

1.4 The focus of this book

If we accept that globalization is essentially a bundle of processes of the detachment of sociocultural interaction from geographical proximity, it follows that its study necessitates a clear focus on its processual character but not on a particular region or group of actors. Therefore all of the above questions can be investigated in a great number of different historical settings and case studies. An analysis that primarily rests on empirical historical research, however, needs to concentrate on particular units of observation. The present study has a strong focus on Great Britain and the British Empire in this regard. As will be demonstrated in more detail in Chapter 5, by far the biggest share of international telegraph cables was operated by British companies or government departments in our period of observation. As a consequence, the development of a global telegraph network was closely enmeshed in British domestic and imperial interests. On a global level, a focus on British actors, therefore, is almost unavoidable in order to guarantee a fairly valid and representative perspective on the subject matter.

However, as regards the selection of the national case studies in Chapters 7 and 8, other choices – such as, for instance, the United States, France or Germany, to name but a few – would have been possible and no less instructive. Great Britain and British India now feature in these chapters for at least three different reasons: first, especially in the case of Great Britain, the nationalization of the inland telegraph system and the organizational challenges arising from it provide historians with a number of sources of a very rare depth and quality. To my knowledge, no historical sources of comparable scope are available for other countries at this time. To a much more limited extent, this is also true for British India where British administrators have thoroughly evaluated the structure and usage of the system at several points in time. Second, as the global telegraph system of the late nineteenth century was shaped by British imperial interests to a great extent, Britain and British India occupy central positions in the network. Focusing on these two territories provides us with a link between the global and local dimensions of the network. And third, very practically, British and British imperial history is where I have some expertise. I very probably could not have written a book with a substantially different regional focus. This concentration on British and British imperial case studies should, however, not be taken to mean that there was only British-propelled globalization in the nineteenth century. On the contrary, many other actors have, of course, been deeply involved in different processes of globalization for a long time. The

British Empire is only one, admittedly very handy, framework within which to investigate the research questions of this book.

Before coming to the contribution that this book can make to answering some of these questions, let us briefly look at a concrete historical example that directly connects to many of the above issues and might help to illustrate some of the more abstract points made so far. Light and slightly amusing, this case is nevertheless indicative of how a specific technology – in this case submarine telegraphy – can impact on and eventually modify cultural practice. On 23 June 1870, a multitude of illustrious guests gathered at the London residence of John Pender, then, among other things, chairman of the British Indian Submarine Telegraph Company that had just successfully laid a submarine telegraph cable from Europe via the Red Sea to India. The festivities were held to celebrate the opening of the cable. Accordingly, a fully functional telegraph had been erected at Pender's house and at the celebration

> messages were sent to India and the answers received under five minutes; and it was shown that even this interval, short as it is, could be materially curtailed by further practice. Long messages of fifty words and upwards were transmitted to the agents of the Company in Calcutta and Bombay, and acknowledged in a quarter of an hour, while a congratulatory telegram graciously forwarded by H.R.H. the PRINCE OF WALES to the GOVERNOR GENERAL was replied to by LORD MAYO at Simla, the acknowledgement from the Company's Agent at Bombay reaching Arlington Street in eleven minutes from the time at which the original message commenced leaving London.[28]

Before the Prince of Wales sent his message to the viceroy and Governor-General, Lady Mayo, who had not accompanied Lord Mayo to India and who was also present at the party, had the opportunity to send some words to her husband. At exactly 10.34 p.m. she had the following message telegraphed to Simla: 'In availing myself of the Submarine Cable I feel the obligation which science imposes upon the world. Not only does it serve political interests, but assists domestic relations in thus enabling me to send you almost instantaneously an affectionate greeting from your wife and family.' Unfortunately, Lord Mayo's reply arrived only one hour and thirty-seven minutes later, because 'Lord Mayo had arranged to be in his office at 5 a.m., and her Ladyship's message arriving at 4.7 a.m., found his Lordship still in bed'. His telegram said, 'Thankful for your message. I send you affectionate greeting from your two boys, and all here.'[29]

[28] British Library, General Reference Collection, shelfmark 8761.b.62, 'Souvenir of the Inaugural Fête [Held at the House of Mr John Pender], in Commemoration of the Opening of Direct Submarine Telegraph with India', 23 June 1870, 5.

[29] Ibid., 19.

This brief exchange is illustrative in several ways. It shows how established conceptions of time and space are reaching their limits when transcontinental telegraphic communication is involved. Through electric signal transmission, London at night is brought into direct contact with Simla in the early morning. The people at both ends of the wire find themselves in completely different contextual settings but share time with each other. Furthermore, the telegrams indicate how the regular use of the telegraph has already impacted on Lord Mayo's language and co-produced an abbreviated and grammatically incorrect message in typical telegram style. While in the particular situation telegrams were transmitted free of cost and considerations of length and style were, thus, no issue, Mayo had formulated his reply in the usual telegraphic way. The fact that he was dictating a telegram sufficed to change his choice of words and grammar even when there was no technological or economic necessity to do so. Lady Mayo's message, on the other hand, resembled the elaborate style in which contemporary letters were written habitually and, of course, also reflected how distinguished women were expected to express themselves in Victorian society. Her choice of words was completely unaffected by any real or perceived requirements of telegraphic signal transmission.

The messages between Lord and Lady Mayo constitute but one of many telegraphic communications taking place that night. Congratulations were exchanged between businessmen, colonial officials and telegraph administrators alike. And in many cases, the tone and style of the messages was significantly lighter than it would probably have been in a comparable letter. Sir Charles Forbes, for instances, telegraphed to the representative of Sir Charles Forbes & Co. in Bombay, 'We congratulate you all on the opening of Submarine communication, equally important to the imperial as well as the commercial interest.' Twelve minutes later he received the good-humoured reply: 'Salaam Sahib. Reciprocate your congratulations heartily.'[30] And the Prince of Wales dispatched a message to the king of Portugal offering him 'congratulations on the completion of direct Telegraphic communication between England and the East, by way of Portugal', and thanking him for his government's support in the matter. The Prince of Wales received the following reply: 'Thanks for the good wishes you expressed me in your telegram. Equally I congratulate myself for the completion of the Telegraph.' The telegram was simply signed 'LUIZ'.[31] While the festiveness of the occasion might have contributed as well, it was the use of a new

[30] Ibid., 20. [31] Ibid., 21–2.

and less-formal means of communication that made such a temporary suspension of protocol possible.

This is just a brief example of how the use of a specific technology can transform cultural practices. In order to better understand the dynamics between actors and the technologies that they use, we must have a good knowledge of both elements involved in the interaction. So far, whenever historians or communication scientists have talked about the connection between telegraphy and modernization or globalization, they have usually done so without a sound knowledge of the structural conditions of the telegraph network or of its use. Most studies that considered telegraph network structures at all have been based on the superficial interpretation of telegraph maps or late nineteenth-century texts celebrating the success of the new communication technology. It has rarely been attempted to look beyond the surface of these contemporary maps or descriptive texts which have not been designed to inform the work of researchers but rather to provide information to an interested public. While such information is, of course, useful and provides an easy overview regarding the development of the global telegraph network, it is by no means detailed and refined enough to let us identify centres and peripheries, well-connected and unconnected places, in the late nineteenth century beyond the very obvious. The information that has so far been made available allows at best for the visualization of the major international telegraph routes and the principal places that they connected. A structural analysis with more refined statistical instruments has only rarely been pursued for lack of sufficiently detailed data on lines, circuits and connections, despite the fact that it promises hitherto unavailable insights. Elsewhere I have shown in a case study of the European telegraph network of the early twentieth century how the use of more detailed connection data and its statistical interpretation allows us to assess the centrality or non-centrality of a place in a communication network beyond the obvious fact that the metropolises of the day occupied central positions in it.[32] Different places can have different roles and functions within a network and thus exhibit very different forms of centrality. For instance, while not being very centrally positioned itself, a place can be situated on a major connecting circuit as a through-station. In other cases, places that are not at all geographically central themselves can be well connected to nearby communication centres. These are forms of centrality that can often not be revealed by the visual study of a map or circuit diagram. In short, if we want to trace the structure of the global information network of the nineteenth century

[32] Roland Wenzlhuemer, 'The Dematerialization of Telecommunication: Communication Centres and Peripheries in Europe, 1850–1920', *Journal of Global History* 2, no 3 (2007).

in a way that allows for a qualified examination of the guiding questions, it is necessary to find, prepare and analyse detailed statistical data. Only in this way can historical network structures and conditions be traced and reconstructed.

However, analysing the infrastructure of a network alone always produces information about an ideal case. For instance, the insights so gained about the design and structure of the global telegraph network of the late nineteenth century say little about the actual use of the system. Relying on infrastructural data alone, it is not possible to make any secure assumptions about how much of the actual capacity has been used and how much demand there was for different telegraphic services. A good understanding of the relationship between structural preconditions and realized use is, however, essential if telegraphic communication is to be embedded in an actor-centred approach to processes of socioeconomic and cultural globalization. In his influential article 'From Innovation to Use: Ten Eclectic Theses on the Historiography of Technology', David Edgerton remarks, 'To say that the study of the relations of technology and society should be the study of technology in use is a mere truism'.[33] But, as he then elaborates, most of the work done by historians of technology still centres on the history of invention and innovation rather than on the history of technology in actual use. Two of the most interesting theses that Edgerton offers in his article confront this shortcoming. His second thesis reads, 'The histories of innovation and of technology-in-use are remarkably different, in terms of geography, chronology, and sociology.'[34] In his fourth thesis he continues, 'The innovation-orientation of most studies of technology makes difficult a serious engagement between general history and the history of technology. Conversely, an engagement with general historical problems has produced histories of technology-in-use.'[35] If most accounts of the history of a particular technology focus on the time and circumstances of its first invention rather than on the period when it came into widespread use, meaningful exchange with social, economic or cultural historians is jeopardized. Many inventions never came into significant use; in other cases it took decades until a new technology was eventually adopted – and often it took even longer until it finally supplanted its predecessor. An innovation introduces a new way of doing something. Whether potential users will eventually follow this new way is, however, an entirely different matter.

[33] David Edgerton, 'From Innovation to Use: Ten Eclectic Theses on the Historiography of Technology', *History and Technology* 16 (1999), 112.
[34] Ibid., 115. [35] Ibid., 119.

Applied to the case of telegraphic communication, David Edgerton's argument has to be taken one step further. At the beginning of the period of observation of this study, telegraphy is already past the stages of invention and innovation. The technology had long left the inventors' workshops. It was actively endorsed by most national governments, domestic telegraph networks were busily being built and expanded and several groups of people already made good use of the new administrative and business opportunities that it opened up. But typically for a network technology, telegraphy derived much of its value from its potential reach, which depended on the number of people in other, often far-flung, places that could be contacted via the network. In other words, the attractiveness of telegraphy grew with the size of its network, which was accordingly extended in all directions – in the case of the inland telegraph often along railway lines. The fact that infrastructure was put into place, however, did not necessarily mean that such infrastructure always found willing (or capable) users or that it was put to the same use everywhere. Studying the structural characteristics of the telegraph network is an important and necessary endeavour. It tells us much about the thinking of the people planning and building this global network. The structure of the network in many cases mirrored contemporary demand for global connectivity – or at least where such demand was assumed to exist and where it was not. It also reflected the requirements of a particular set of global actors planning and financing the connections – of merchants, businessmen, newsmen, military strategists and administrators. And, of course, adequate structures were a necessary precondition for the exchange of information in the first place. But wherever information about the actual use of the available infrastructure is accessible, it must be carefully studied as only such data carries information about how the structural potential was realized. The analysis of use data renders a second set of actors more visible – the people sending and receiving telegrams, the people who were now globally connected. This study, therefore, seeks to include and interpret information on the actual use of the nineteenth-century global telegraph network whenever such data is available and reasonably reliable. Whenever such a course of action is not feasible, it looks at the network structure and tries to unearth data as detailed as possible in order to allow for a more refined structural analysis. Only in this way does it become possible to assess the position and the function of a particular place in the global network and, hence, to shed some more light on the opportunities, and also the limitations, that historical actors located at such places experienced. Only such an integrated perspective will produce enough knowledge about all the components involved to allow for a better understanding of the interplay of people and technologies, actors and structures, in nineteenth-century globalization.

1.5 Methods and sources

This study is concerned with actors and structures alike. Most of the structures examined are technological infrastructures. They are shaped by the intentions, decisions and actions of humans and in turn influence human actions by facilitating some choices and hindering others. Therefore I propose that meaningful statements about the relationship between human actors and technologies can only be made if an actor-centred approach is applied that nevertheless recognizes the actors' embeddedness in a larger structure or larger structures. While these structures are, of course, of different relevance to different people and are accordingly perceived differently by every individual actor, they themselves are objectifiable. Actors differ in their relationships to the structures while the structures themselves remain stable in the moment of observation. Therefore the perceptions and experiences of a given historical actor depend on the individual situation, the sociocultural context and the structural prerequisites. In the context of the present study, this means that the position that contemporary actors occupied in late nineteenth-century globalization and the transformation of space and time that they experienced depended both on their personal situation and sociocultural context and on the general structure of the evolving global telegraph network.

This constitutes a significant scholarly challenge as both objects of study require different conceptual and methodological approaches. In Chapter 2 the particular application of the terms 'space' and 'network' in this study are presented in detail. The concept of space used here is a dynamic and strictly relational one. Putting the historical actor at the centre, the real and perceived relations that such an actor maintains create his or her space. In this way, it becomes possible to look at the world through the historical actor's eyes and trace an individual person's position in nineteenth-century globalization processes. But then, the relations that constitute an actor's space also need a practical facilitator in the form of a network of objectifiable connections. As similar as they might seem, spaces and networks, relations and connections are not the same. Spaces emerge from a sum of relations that are shaped by the network of connections that facilitates them. As will become clear in the following chapter, this study uses the concepts of 'space' and 'network' in order to grasp both the personal position of an actor in the globalizing world and the structural preconditions of this position.

Reconciling an actor-centred with a structural approach also poses a methodological challenge. It necessitates a mix of qualitative and quantitative historical methods tuned to the specific research questions revolving around actors, structures and the relation between the two. In order to trace the position of one or more historical actors in global communication processes, a variety of different source material has been analysed qualitatively. In this respect, the goal is to trace the vantage point of the individual person and its perspective on and relation to telegraphic communication. Usually, the study's interest rests on changing cultural practices, the perception of global spaces, attitudes towards telegraphy and so on. The perceptions, thoughts, actions and interpretations of the actors stand at the centre of attention here. Among the primary material consulted are private letters, diary entries and autobiographies, popular anecdote collections, newspaper reports, cartoons and satirical articles, petitions and official government documents. All of these different sources have been used with the necessary caution, acknowledging the different contexts of their production.

The study also wants to reconstruct nineteenth-century communication networks in a way that allows for a detailed interpretation of their structures. And these network structures are contrasted with the actual use of the network. In this way, a lens on the interplay of the structures and the actors can be provided. In order to reconstruct both the structure and the use patterns of nineteenth-century telegraph networks, quantitative methods need to be employed. Aiming at the provision of a reasonably complete and solid pool of data, statistical material has been located in various forms. Aggregate data, usually gathered at the national level, has been retrieved from official reports assembled by either government departments, international organizations or private companies. Beyond this, however, in some cases detailed circuit and connection data has been discovered that allows for the meticulous reconstruction of contemporary networks. So far, this has not been done beyond the level of superficially describing contemporary network maps that depict the routes of telegraph lines and cables. Especially for the case of the British national telegraph network, almost complete data on its internal structure has been unearthed. Similar data has been located regarding the structure of the British Indian telegraph network. For both Great Britain and British India, information on network use was also available in the same sources. In other cases, structural information has been produced from known sources such as network maps or circuit lists.

In a second step, the often voluminous quantitative material retrieved from archival sources has been prepared, arranged and interpreted with the help of advanced statistical methods. In the case of structural data, this encompassed social network analysis methods. As the name suggests, social network analysis was originally designed to examine the functioning of social networks. The mathematical methods and calculations on which it builds can, however, be directly applied to technology-mediated networks in the sense of this study as well.[36] In the context of this book, only so-called centrality measures have been calculated. These compute the centrality of the nodes in a network according to different parameters, such as the number of connections they maintain, their mediating role in the network and their proximity to other important nodes. The UCINET software has been employed to conduct these analyses regarding the *degree*, *closeness*, *betweenness* and *eigenvector* of the network nodes.[37] What exactly these measures can reveal about a network and its structure will be explained in greater detail in the appropriate sections. If useful and applicable, the results of quantitative analysis have been visualized in charts and maps. To this end, historical GIS methods have been employed in order to link statistical with geographical data. The MapWindow GIS[38] and fGIS[39] software have been used for this purpose.

The quantitative historical data used in the network analyses in this study is exceptionally detailed and comprehensive, but still the data is not perfect. In some instances, information about particular parts of the network is missing; in other cases networks had to be truncated at some point in order to allow for a detailed analysis. Therefore network analysis results can be slightly distorted at times. The aggregate statistical data has usually been collected on a national level by national administrations or private companies. Even if submitted to an international body and then standardized in the process, different national data sets might have been assembled with different goals and standards in mind. They are thus of varying scope and quality. Whenever the validity and explanatory power of a data set suffers from any such limitations, this is explained in the appropriate section and has been taken into account in the interpretation of the data. Despite such limitations, information on network structures has been easier to locate than information on the actual network use. This is especially true when looking beyond the aggregate national level. As mentioned above, it has in some rare cases been possible to use primary sources that contain both structural and use information in a compatible way. The comparison of structures and use often reveals frequent and significant differences between the ideal and the actual network usage. Analysing the infrastructure of any given network means analysing an

[36] Boris Holzer, *Netzwerke* (Bielefeld: transcript, 2006), 34.

[37] UCINET for Windows: Software for Social Network Analysis Version 6.288, Analytic Technologies, Cambridge, MA.

[38] MapWindow GIS: Open Source Programmable Geographic Information System Tools Ver. 4.8 RC1, Idaho State University, Pocatello.

[39] Forestry GIS (fGIS) Ver. 2005.09.13, University of Wisconsin.

ideal condition that represents a theoretical maximum. For instance, the existence of a brand-new high-capacity connection between two places does not necessarily mean that there is heavy traffic on the route. In most cases, network planners and investors will have responded to an existing or perceived demand when commissioning the building of the new line. And yet, various factors such as prohibitive pricing, the opening of alternative routes or changing economic conditions may prevent the full utilization of the available capacity. In other cases, demand might have been overestimated, or calculated according to standards that did not apply in this particular setting. And in some instances, public demand might have played little role in the planning process in the first place. These examples serve to illustrate that the study of infrastructures can provide an approximation to demand and actual usage, but often not more than that. However, whenever there is no usage data accessible, looking at structural data is the best alternative.

The present book aims at studying the actors of late nineteenth-century processes of globalization embedded into global communication structures. It puts great effort into letting these two objects of study speak with each other. This is achieved by connecting the objectifiable results of the quantitative structure and use analyses with the experiences of the historical actors involved in such structures. To this end, in every chapter statistical findings are brought into correspondence with the individual horizons, perceptions and demands of nineteenth-century protagonists of globalization. This can be done either by looking at existing, non-fictitious persons who have left direct traces of their role in and position on globalization or, in other instances, by interpreting anecdotes, satirical writings or newspaper reports as second-level signifiers of contemporary issues and concerns. It is important to note that the case examples used here come from many different backgrounds and refer to people with significantly different positions and requirements. They are not in-depth case studies that follow one or more actors for a longer time and in microscopic detail. They have been selected in order to communicate with the structural findings. By putting individual experiences and structural conditions next to each other, their mutual interdependence becomes discernible and allows for the fruitful examination of this study's guiding questions.

1.6 The structure of this book

It is the purpose of this introductory chapter to explain both the origin of and the motivation behind the research that informs this book. The chapter opened with a well-documented dispute over a particular telegraphic address. It thus highlighted the importance of being telegraphically connected during the period of observation and provided a first example of the striking continuities between nineteenth-century and more current means of telecommunication. The chapter argued that the similarities between the technologies of the telegraph and the Internet are mostly functional and structural. It is the examination of these similarities in a wider socioeconomic and cultural context that leads on to a more general set of research questions regarding the interaction between people and technologies. With the specific case of the nineteenth-century global telegraph network in mind, the chapter then identified the principal research questions guiding this study and provided a first practical example that connects to many of these questions. Eventually, the methods and sources employed and the methodological challenges arising from the research focus on actors and structures alike were discussed.

Chapter 2 provides the conceptual and analytical framework of the study. It discusses the concepts of globalization, space and networks, with a particular focus on how they relate to each other. As such, it is intimately connected with the creation and transformation of global spaces. The chapter isolates and discusses the key quality of the technology of telegraphy – the dematerialization of information flows – and then moves on to propose an understanding of space that accommodates the impact of dematerialization while steering clear of the notion of an alleged annihilation of time and space through telecommunication. In the concluding section, the chapter focuses on the question of technological agency. It introduces the terms ‘technological rationale’ or ‘network rationale’ in order to offer a balanced and analytically rewarding alternative to techno- or sociodeterminist accounts of the interplay between actors and technologies.

Chapter 3 gives a brief introduction to the technological history of telegraphy. After illustrating the close relationship between the railway and the telegraph with the help of a contemporary example, it then moves on to introduce a definition of the term ‘telecommunication’. It provides a quick overview of the development of optical telegraphy in and outside France. The chapter then goes on to discuss the practically parallel invention of electric telegraphy in the United Kingdom and the United States in the 1830s and its common roots in advances in the understanding of electricity and previous developments in electric signal transmission. It is shown how, in several instances, technological inertia – a term coined by Joel Mokyr[40] – hindered early success of the new technology. Only in the late 1840s and 1850s did electric telegraphy become a

[40] Joel Mokyr, ‘Technological Inertia in Economic History’, *Journal of Economic History* 52, no 2 (1992).

technology-in-use, in David Edgerton's sense,[41] due to successful and economically interesting demonstrations of its potential on both sides of the Atlantic. The chapter explores the origin and working logic of both the American and the British systems, traces alternatives and eventually shows how the technologies involved matured in order to make long-distance submarine telegraphy possible.

In Chapter 4, telegraphy is embedded in four different contexts of application, and thus of research: empire, commerce, news and cultural practices. The chapter highlights the interconnections between imperial expansion and control, the world of trade and finance, and global telegraphy. It shows how much of the historical writing on the telegraph and its uses has focused on these principal fields. The telegraph has, however, also had great ramifications in global news gathering and reporting, and thus contributed to the transformation of global space in terms of knowledge about other places. While this news context is gradually receiving more attention from historians, the connection between telegraphy and social and cultural practices has only rarely been studied in a systematic manner. The selection of these four contexts is, of course, eclectic but can nevertheless structure existing approaches to the field in a way that is useful for the purpose of this book and highlights where this study can provide new impetuses to research.

Chapter 5 starts by highlighting the implications that being globally connected had for actors of globalization, for instance in the City of London, their perceptions of global space and their action and event horizons. The chapter then moves on to trace the expansion of a global cable network between 1865 and 1903 on the basis of capacious cable lists published by the Bureau international des administrations télégraphiques. The principal focuses of the 'wiring of the world', as well as several distinct phases in the development of the system, are identified. In a second step, the growth of the cable system is brought into correspondence with shifts in global communication space. These shifts are traced and visualized by looking at the transmission times of international shipping information published in *The Times* of London between 1850 and 1900. Eventually, a tentative analysis of the correlation between the telegraphic connection of particular world regions and their integration in the world economy is undertaken by looking at British trade statistics and relating those to the expansion of the cable network.

Chapter 6 looks for centres and peripheries in the global telegraph network of the nineteenth and early twentieth centuries. While first

41 Edgerton, 'From Innovation to Use'.

attempts in this direction are already made in Chapter 5, more sophisticated tools are employed here. In three independent case studies, social network analysis methods are applied to uncover the structure of the European and the global communication networks of the day. The first such analysis works with circuit data from the 'Liste des communications télégraphiques internationales directes du régime européen' published by the Bureau international in 1906. The second case study is based on information taken from the 'Carte schématique des grandes communications télégraphiques internationales du régime européen' also published by the bureau in the year 1923. Both these studies look only at the European part of the global telegraph network and focus on comparatively late periods of observation. They do, however, have the advantage of examining circuit data that reflects the direct connections between network nodes. A third case study expands the focus to the entire globe and introduces a chronological element. The telegraph lines depicted in the 'Cartes des communications télégraphiques du régime extra-européen' of the years 1881, 1892 and 1902 are extracted and interpreted with social network analysis tools. In a concluding section, the insights of these structural analyses are contrasted with the results of a study on the international telegraphic traffic handled by different European and non-European countries between 1860 and 1910.

Chapter 7 examines in some more detail the role of telegraphy in Great Britain – the country that not only sported one of the best-developed national telegraph networks of the late nineteenth century but also stood at the centre of global telegraphic information flows. The chapter first uses the intimate connection between the telegraph and 'the turf' as one example to highlight how deeply embedded in social and cultural practices telegraphy had already become in mid-nineteenth-century Britain. It then goes on to discuss the origins of British telegraphy as a private, profit-seeking endeavour and its gradual movement towards becoming a public good. In the following two sections, the chapter draws on a rare and valuable source of information on the structure and use of the British telegraph network. In 1868, in preparation for the nationalization of the system, a full-scale survey of the British network was undertaken, collecting data on existing telegraph circuits and the traffic that they carried. A large part of this survey has survived in the archives and provides the raw material for a detailed social network analysis and a study of the use patterns of the British network in 1868. Both these studies confirm London's central position in the system. Therefore the concluding section of the chapter zooms in on the metropolis and examines its role in the telegraph network, as well as the distribution of telegraphic connectivity within the city.

Chapter 8 applies a similar close-up perspective to the case of British India. In marked difference to the origins of telegraphy in Great Britain, the British Indian telegraph system came into existence primarily on the instigation of the colonial government. The Indian Uprising of 1857–8 and the British trauma resulting from the events gave great impetus to the expansion of the system and significantly shaped its structure. The chapter first discusses the military and administrative origins of the network and the early system's inherent deficiencies regarding service to the public. It then moves on to document how the Indian Telegraph Department network grew from the 1860s to the end of the century and improved in terms of the quality of services rendered to the public. The following two sections, however, show that this public consisted of a very small administrative and commercial elite located in the principal cities of the subcontinent. The structural analysis of the state telegraph network in 1871–2 shows that the system – while not centred at a single decisive node like, for instance, London in the British network – focused almost exclusively on the urban centres of British India. Actual telegraphic traffic was even more concentrated on only a handful of important Indian cities. In a concluding section, the flow of telegraph messages between Europe and India is briefly discussed and it is shown how British India, with the expansion of the global submarine telegraph system to East Asia and Australia, became a central hub in the global communication network.

The concluding Chapter 9 picks up the different threads spun on previous pages and seeks to weave them into one conclusive pattern. To this end, it identifies three principal fields of knowledge about telegraphy to which this study contributes. First, it highlights and summarizes how the new communication technology impacted on the relationship between information and knowledge, and thus in many cases on established cultural practices. Second, it recapitulates the most important findings regarding the structure and traffic of nineteenth-century telegraph networks and, of course, the relationship between both. In a third section, the chapter subsumes the connection between telegraphy and the transformation of global space(s) witnessed in the second half of the nineteenth century. The chapter closes by highlighting the necessity of further, more detailed studies and by sketching possible themes for future research projects.

2 The telegraph and globalization

2.1 Globalization and dematerialization

As Yrjö Kaukiainen has shown in his groundbreaking work, global information transmission massively increased in speed many decades before a global submarine telegraph network started to emerge.[1] This can be attributed to various coinciding factors, the most important of which are the increasing tightness of a global maritime transport network and the rise of steam shipping. Furthermore, European postal systems had already reached a high degree of speed and efficiency, and more costly (and rare) means of communication such as carrier pigeons also achieved astonishing transmission speeds. Nevertheless, the telegraph was celebrated by contemporaries mainly for its swiftness in information transmission. And in the light of current progress, in this regard it has to be asked whether the changes brought about by telegraphy were merely quantitative in nature. Did the telegraph only add some extra speed to a process that had already been accelerating for decades and did it introduce next to no qualitative changes?

Yes and no. Of course, the increase in communication speed further intensified globalization processes. But conceptually it is far more important to look at the development that made this increase possible in the first place – the dematerialization of long-distance information flows. The telegraph made it possible to encode information in electric impulses that could then be sent along a conductor – usually a wire or a set of wires. The transmission of information had eventually been detached from the movement of people, animals or things, all of which consist of matter and, therefore, adhere to certain rules of material movement. The immediate consequence of this is an increased speed of communication in absolute terms. In plain words, it took less time than ever before to transmit a message from a place *A* to another place *B*. This is the quantitative

[1] Yrjö Kaukiainen, 'Shrinking the World: Improvements in the Speed of Information Transmission, c.1820–1870', *European Review of Economic History* 5, no 1 (2001).

improvement that dematerialization brought about. The even more significant change, however, rests in the aforementioned detachment from material carriage, and thus in the relative increase of transmission speeds in relation to material carriers. The flow of information was separated from the flow of people or goods and now worked along a completely new logic. It is one essential constituent of this logic that wherever the telecommunication network reached, dematerialized information outpaced material transport and could, therefore, be used to efficiently co-ordinate, control and command such material movement.[2] This, of course, impacted pronouncedly on the nature and intensity of nineteenth-century globalization. The following brief examples will illustrate the qualitative changes that were brought about by dematerialization.

Telegraphs and railways

One of the factors behind telegraphy's swift expansion in Great Britain was its early symbiosis with the railway (see also the beginning of the next chapter). Charles Wheatstone and William Fothergill Cooke, the British inventor–entrepreneur couple behind the needle telegraph, successfully convinced railway company managers to let them erect telegraph lines along sections of railway track. While it seemed immediately obvious how the telegraph system would benefit from the railway's right of way, it initially took some time and effort to demonstrate the potential use to the railway companies of the telegraph. The technology first had to reach a certain degree of maturity, affordability and reliability. Being successfully employed on the lines of the Great Western Railway and the London & Blackwall Railway, the telegraph eventually proved incredibly useful for the management of 'ancillary single lines where traffic did not justify double track, by enabling them to be operated safely and efficiently'.[3] In other words, as the railway itself in many cases was the fastest means of communication available at the time, it had been next to impossible to manage single-track railway lines for use in both directions in a way that would ensure both efficiency and safety. The special virtue of telegraphic information transmission from the perspective of the railway manager rested in its detachment from material transport (which had reached its contemporary practical apogee in the form of the railways). Telegraphs

[2] Among the first scholars to acknowledge this particular quality of telegraphic communication was James Carey in James W. Carey, 'Technology and Ideology: The Case of the Telegraph', *Prospects, An Annual of American Cultural Studies* 8 (1983).

[3] Jeffrey L. Kieve, *The Electric Telegraph: A Social and Economic History* (Newton Abbot: David & Charles, 1973), 33.

were useful not because they allowed the railway operators to communicate fast but because they allowed them to communicate faster than the fastest-moving means of material communication (excluding, of course, impractical means such as carrier pigeons or horse couriers in relay).

The Salt Hill murder and other crimes

The famous and often-cited case of the murderer John Tawell and his capture by the police also exemplifies the changing relation between railway transport and communication brought about by telegraphy and works along the same logic outlined in the previous subsection. However, while the first example demonstrated merely how the railways internally benefited from the new communicative qualities ushered in by the telegraph, the case of John Tawell shows how a wider public could be affected by the detachment of information from material flows. On the evening of New Year's Day 1845, Tawell poisoned his mistress, Sarah Hart, with prussic acid at her house in Salt Hill near Slough. Witnesses saw him leave the house after the murder dressed like a Quaker. On 3 January 1845, *The Times* of London reported on the murder, including several statements of people involved in the case:

> The Rev. E. T. Champnes, vicar of Upton-cum-Chalvey, examined. – Hearing of the suspicious death of the deceased, and that a person in the dress of a Quaker was the last man who had been seen to leave the house, I proceeded to the Slough station, thinking it likely he might proceed to town by the railway. I saw him pass through the office, when I communicated my suspicions to Mr. Howell, the superintendent at the station. He left for London in a first-class carriage. Mr. Howell then sent off a full description of his person, by means of the electric telegraph, to cause him to be watched by the police upon his arrival at Paddington.
>
> Mr. Howell, of Slough station, deposed as follows: – The prisoner left for town last night by the 7 42 train. I despatched orders by the telegraph to have the prisoner watched on his arrival at Paddington. A few minutes afterwards an answer was returned, stating that the suspected party had arrived, and that sergeant Williams had left the terminus in the same omnibus for the city.[4]

John Tawell was later apprehended at a London coffee house. He was brought to trial, convicted of murder and publicly hanged on 28 March 1845.[5] The murder case caused a public stir in London for a variety of reasons – not the least of which can be found in Tawell's unusually colourful life, which lent itself readily to the purposes of the tabloids. Another factor, however, can be identified in the particulars of his

[4] 'Suspected Murder at Salt-Hill', *The Times*, 3 January 1845, 7.
[5] 'The Salt-Hill Murder. Execution of John Tawell', *The Times*, 29 March 1845, 5–6.

apprehension that would not have been possible (at least not so quickly and smoothly) without the telegraph. Once on the train to Paddington, Tawell would usually have had a considerable head start against his pursuers as no signal could have been given to the train or to Paddington Station. Travelling by the fastest possible means of transport, he would have reached London long before anyone there could have heard of his crime. Only dematerialized information transmission through the telegraph allowed for the message to actually overtake its train-travelling subject.

On the one hand, the dramatic details of Tawell's capture contributed to the sapidity of the story. On the other hand, the extensive reporting in the press popularized the new qualities of the telegraph which seemingly annihilated space and time. And yet Tawell was not the first criminal to be apprehended with the help of the 'electric constable'.[6] In a collection of railway anecdotes published in 1884, Richard Pike devoted a brief section to the role of the telegraph for police work. According to Pike, 'The first application of the telegraph to police purposes took place in 1844, on the Great Western Railway, and as it was the first intimation thieves got of the electric constable being on duty it is full of interest'.[7] Pike then went on to describe how the telegraph was applied between Paddington and Slough stations to catch thieves operating on the trains. He cited extracts from the Paddington Station telegraph book: 'Paddington, 10.50 a.m. – Special train just left. It contained two thieves; one named Oliver Martin, who is dressed in black, *crape on his hat*; the other named Fiddler Dick, in black trousers and light blouse, Both [*sic*] in the third compartment of the first second-class carriage.'[8] At least the latter of the two was then accordingly welcomed on his arrival at Slough. '"Fiddler Dick, you are wanted", was the immediate demand of the police officer, beckoning to the culprit, who came out of

[6] And he would not be the last one caught with the help of some newish piece of telecommunication technology. In 1910, for instance, Dr Hawley Harvey Crippen and his lover Ethel Le Neve were arrested immediately on their arrival in Canada by steamer. Crippen's wife Cora had disappeared earlier in the year. Her friends had not accepted the doctor's explanations for the sudden disappearance and had informed Scotland Yard. Chief Inspector Walter Dew had then interviewed Crippen. Returning for a second interview, Dew found that Crippen and Le Neve had absconded. Indeed, they had escaped to Belgium and booked passage to Canada on the steamer *Montrose*, which they boarded disguised as father and son. When the *Montrose* was already on its way across the Atlantic, the ship's captain, Henry Kendall, recognized the odd couple as Crippen and Le Neve, whose picture he had seen in a newspaper. He sent a wireless telegram to the Yard informing them of his discovery. Chief Inspector Dew then boarded a faster ship to Montreal and apprehended the couple while they were still on board of the *Montrose* in Montreal harbour. See Julie English Early, 'Technology, Modernity, and "the Little Man": Crippen's Capture by Wireless', *Victorian Studies* 39, no 3 (1996).

[7] Richard Pike, ed., *Railway Adventures and Anecdotes: Extending over More than Fifty Years* (London: Hamilton, Adams and Co., and Nottingham: J. Derry, 1884), 92.

[8] Ibid., 92, italics in original.

the carriage thunder-struck at the discovery, and gave himself up, together with the booty, with the air of a completely beaten man.'[9] Several months before the reports about the Salt Hill murder would popularize the capabilities of telegraphic communication as regards the co-ordination of railway transport, apprehended perpetrators were naturally stunned about the new speed of information flow along a telegraph line.

Tramp shipping

In the realm of international shipping, the telegraph had an impact very similar to what we have already heard about railway co-ordination. Once a ship had left its European home harbour and was heading for the Americas, Africa, Asia or Australia, it was out of reach and thus out of the control of its owners. This was of particular concern in tramp shipping when ships do not have a fixed route (like liners) but respond flexibly to market opportunities and thus visit ports of call in a region. In a paper delivered at the Cross-Connexions conference in London in 2005, Birgitte Holten compared three examples of trade transactions between European or North American merchant houses and Brazilian coffee exporters, focusing on their organization and efficiency. The first case took place in 1845, before the time of intercontinental telegraph links.

Holten explained that after dispatching the ship, 'the merchant had little other choice than to sit patiently down and wait for news of its return. . . . This was an expensive, time-consuming and unsophisticated manner of trading.' Agents or exporting firms operating in the Brazilian ports helped with the purchase of goods. However, at times – for instance after a bad harvest or when heavy rains hindered inland transport – even they could not procure the desired product in the necessary quantity or quality. The ship could either lie idle and wait for new stocks to arrive. Or, if that was not feasible, the master of the ship could decide to deviate from the original plan and to load the ship with other goods that were at hand. In other cases, the master would direct the ship to another port in order to fetch a cargo of some sort there and avoid going back to Europe with ballast. Holten confirmed that references to such unplanned and unwished-for deviations from the planned route existed at least until the mid-1860s.[10]

9 Ibid., 93.

10 Birgitte Holten, 'Telegraphy and Business Methods in the Late 19th Century', paper presented at the Cross-Connexions Conference, London, 11–13 November 2005, 3–4.

The only control that the owner or merchant house could exert over the ship in pre-telegraphic times rested in equipping the captain or sometimes an accompanying supercargo with detailed instructions covering every imaginable eventuality. Holten's other two cases stem from the years 1874 (with a transatlantic cable in place but no direct link between Europe and South America) and 1893 respectively. While by 1874 headquarters' control over their ships had improved only marginally but general information on world markets and business conduct was more widely available, South America had by 1893 long been directly linked to the global telegraph network. Information about local market conditions could reach the European merchant house headquarters within days or even hours, rendering it feasible to make decisions centrally and to cut into the leeway of both captain and supercargo present *in situ*. Within less than half a century, international trading methods had changed profoundly. Eventually, each single operation in the commodity chain had become separated, divided out to a smoothly shifting series of minor actions. What made this change possible was the telegraph.[11]

These three examples illustrate the qualitative changes in global communication brought about by the dematerialization of information flows. Of course, several terminological and semantic difficulties arise from the use of the word 'dematerialization'. Neither from a purely philosophical nor from a natural-scientific viewpoint is the use of the term sufficiently exact, as it implies complete escape from the realm of matter as such. This, however, is not how the term is used in the context of this study. Neither does it refer to the philosophical concept of materialism, nor does it desire to withstand scrutiny from post-Newtonian physicists. It is used for the very reasons for which Newtonian physical laws and calculations are still employed in everyday life: because it is exact and yet simple enough to describe what happened to information transmission from the viewpoint of a historian. It stands for the translation of information into acoustic, optical or electric impulses instead of using tangible material carriers. That telegraph lines, for instance, are also quite tangible does not invalidate this definition, as the line (or the cable) itself, once put in place, does not move in order to convey a message but merely provides the path along which information travels. In this respect, the telegraph line is to communication what roads or railway tracks are to transport: not the message, only the medium.[12]

[11] Ibid., 19.

[12] The use of the term 'dematerialization' in several earlier publications has led to discussion about the material and non-material components of telecommunication. In such

Technically, dematerialization merely frees information transmission from a number of (Newtonian) physical constraints from which all material movement suffers. The carrier of dematerialized information does not have a mass (if we ignore the infinitesimal mass of moving electrons for now). It is thus not limited by physical inertia. There are, of course, other limitations. Electric current needs a conductor through which it can travel. And such a conductor has to be put in place before any information can be transmitted. Accordingly, criteria such as geographical distance or topography at least initially still played a role in dematerialized telecommunication.[13] Electric current also encounters electrical resistance – a fact that was a substantial problem in long-distance submarine telegraphy.[14] But the limitations arising from these spheres are different from the limitations of material movement.

It is important to see that the information flows involved in the earliest and still essential forms of communication between humans were non-material in character: sounds, signs, speech. Especially the former two also lend themselves to a certain degree to being used for long-distance communication. Sounds such as drumming or whistling can cover longer distances. Smoke signals or chains of fire beacons, for instance, can also be used to that end. In all these and many more possible examples, information is carried over considerable distances in non-material form. All of these systems, however, were inflexible and suitable only for the transmission of simple, prearranged messages. They were useful and

discussions, the materiality and tangibility of telegraph apparatus, telegraph cables and – not least – telegraph operators have often been used as an argument against the concept of dematerialization. Of course, the materiality of these components of telegraphic communication and its substantial bearing on the communication process is not disavowed. Quite the contrary, as the engagement of this study with network structures underlines. Nonetheless the flow of information itself is of a non-material nature and works along a different set of rules – even if it travels along a material structure. Admittedly, I myself might have contributed to this confusion by referring in previous publications to the 'dematerialization of telecommunication' (of which, however, the material structures are part and parcel) instead of to the 'dematerialization of information flows'. See, for instance, Roland Wenzlhuemer, 'The Development of Telegraphy, 1870–1900: A European Perspective on a World History Challenge', *History Compass* 5, no 5 (2007); Wenzlhuemer, 'The Dematerialization of Telecommunication: Communication Centres and Peripheries in Europe, 1850–1920'; Wenzlhuemer, 'Telecommunications', in *Encyclopedia of the Age of the Industrial Revolution, 1700–1920*, ed. Christine Rider (Westport, CT: Greenwood, 2007); Wenzlhuemer, 'Editorial: Telecommunication and Globalization in the Nineteenth Century', in *Historical Social Research – Historische Sozialforschung. Global Communication: Telecommunication and Global Flows of Information in the Late 19th and Early 20th Century*, ed. Roland Wenzlhuemer (Cologne: Center for Historical Social Research, 2010); Wenzlhuemer, 'Globalization, Communication and the Concept of Space in Global History', in ibid.

13 Carey, 'Technology and Ideology', 304.

14 See, for instance, Edward O. Wildman Whitehouse's involuntary contribution to the destruction of the 1858 transatlantic cable as briefly described in Chapter 3.

efficient in their own right but existed in functional niches. The transmission of reasonably complex information, without prearrangement, over larger stretches of time and space made the materialization of information necessary – for instance, as paintings or engravings, as images or script.[15] The invention and diffusion of telecommunication technologies in the late eighteenth and early nineteenth centuries finally rendered the dematerialization of complex long-distance information flows possible. As will be seen in Chapter 3, the optical telegraph can be considered the first telecommunication system proper. Only with the electric telegraph, however, were many of the problems of optical telegraphy overcome, and only then did the principle of dematerialized information flows reach the maturity necessary for the emergence of first national and then international telecommunication networks.[16] It is in this way that new global spaces mirroring the different logics of their constituting connectors come into existence and transform the way in which people and objects in these various parallel spaces relate to each other. In the following, a strictly relational concept of dynamically emerging and changing spaces will therefore be proposed that provides a conceptual framework for studying, among other things, the impact of dematerialization.

2.2 The annihilation of time and space?

Communication takes place in time and space – like any other social activity. It is the process of transmitting information between two or more participants. As a process, it takes a certain amount of time. It has a speed and a duration. The participants in the communication process occupy specific positions in space. They maintain different relations to each other, and have different distances between each other. In most cases of material communication, the time it takes to transmit information between two participants is a function of their geographic distance (which is in turn the principal constituent of geographic space). As a

[15] I owe this valuable insight to David Christian, who has pointed out to me that human communication first had to go through materialization before it could eventually be dematerialized again.

[16] In this context, maturity means that the technology reached a degree of manageability, reliability and cost efficiency that made it appeal to potential users beyond the state. In this respect, electric telegraphy offered a number of distinct advantages over its optical counterpart. The distance between relay stations could be much longer and extend beyond human sight. There was no need for a line of sight between relay stations and, therefore, the electric telegraph would work in impractical terrain, at night or during periods of bad weather. The electric telegraph also had a higher information throughput than the optical telegraph. All this drastically reduced the personnel and the costs involved in telecommunication and made telegraphy a more reliable and affordable affair.

rule of thumb, communication times will be larger the further the two communicators are positioned from each other. There are, of course, many exceptions to this rule. Natural obstacles, such as mountains, rivers, forests or different climate zones, or artificial boundaries such as unevenly integrated communication networks, state borders, language barriers, tolls or immigration laws, to name but a few, can distort the relation between communication times and geographic space. And yet, as a general rule, distance and communication time in most cases grow proportionally as long as the act of communicating involves materially transporting something.

The dematerialization of information flows profoundly changed this relation. Still, telegraphic communication over large distances had to rely on more relay stations, involved more instances of decoding/encoding and, therefore, generally took longer than transmitting a message to a nearer place. But the influence of geographic distance as a multiplying factor for communication times was severely diminished by the sheer speed with which a message was sent through the wire. While distance still was a factor in the equation, communication time had ceased to be primarily a function thereof. Something had changed in the traditional relationship between time and space, it seemed.[17] Contemporary observers have found a number of terms to refer to this perceived shift. To some the change seemed dramatic enough to let them claim that the telegraph had brought about the 'annihilation of time and space'.[18] Karl Marx made a related but essentially different observation in 1857. He stated in *Grundrisse*,

[17] This is not to say that geography and topography had no more bearing on long-distance communication. In many cases, telegraph lines followed established routes of communication, which in turn acknowledged geographic realities. Referring to landline telegraphy, James Carey therefore remarked that the telegraph 'twisted and altered but did not displace patterns of connection formed by natural geography: by the river and primitive foot and horse path and later by the wooden turnpike and canal'. Carey, 'Technology and Ideology', 304.

[18] Iwan R. Morus, 'The Nervous System of Britain: Space, Time and the Electric Telegraph in the Victorian Age', *British Journal for the History of Science* 33 (2000), 456–63; Jeremy Stein, 'Reflections on Time, Time–Space Compression and Technology in the Nineteenth Century', in *Timespace: Geographies of Temporality*, ed. Jon May and Nigel Thrift (London and New York: Routledge, 2001), 108. The telegraph was, however, not the first technology to which such miracle powers were ascribed. As Wolfgang Schivelbusch has shown in his seminal study on the railway journey, the 'annihilation of space and time' was also closely associated with railway travel. Wolfgang Kaschuba further extends this technological and chronological focus and traces the connection between time–space perceptions and technological change throughout the nineteenth and twentieth centuries. Wolfgang Schivelbusch, *Geschichte der Eisenbahnreise: Zur Industrialisierung von Raum und Zeit im 19. Jahrhundert* (Munich and Vienna: Hanser, 1977); Wolfgang Kaschuba, *Die Überwindung der Distanz: Zeit und Raum in der europäischen Moderne* (Frankfurt a. M.: Fischer Taschenbuch Verlag, 2004).

> Thus, while capital must on one side strive to tear down every spatial barrier to intercourse, i.e. to exchange, and conquer the whole earth for its market, it strives on the other side to annihilate this space with time, i.e. to reduce to a minimum the time spent in motion from one place to another.[19]

Marx made no explicit reference to particular transport or communication technologies in this passage, but he also perceived the shift in time–space relations which he characterized as the annihilation of space *by* time.

It comes as no surprise that today – in times of almost instant global communication via the Internet and rapid global transport (triggered by containerization and the accessibility of air travel) – many observers share a similar impression of geographic space being annihilated. Scholars talk about the 'convergence of time and space'[20] or 'time–space distanciation',[21] about an ongoing 'time–space compression'[22] or, indeed, the '*Entmachtung des Raums*'[23] (the disempowerment of space) – all of which were also witnessed in the second half of the nineteenth century, especially in those world regions which were then penetrated by new transport and communication technologies.[24] Arguably, this allegedly changing relationship between time and space in the context of globalization has attracted some scholarly attention in recent years – and yet it is still

[19] Karl Marx, *Grundrisse: Foundations of the Critique of Political Economy (Rough Draft)* (Harmondsworth: Penguin Books, 1973), 538–9. The original German: 'Während das Kapital also einerseits dahin streben muß, jede örtliche Schranke des Verkehrs, i.e. des Austauschs niederzureißen, die ganze Erde als seinen Markt zu erobern, strebt es andrerseits danach, den Raum zu vernichten durch die Zeit; d.h. die Zeit, die die Bewegung von einem Ort zum andren kostet, auf ein Minimum zu reduzieren.' Karl Marx and Friedrich Engels, *Ökonomische Manuskripte 1857/58* (Berlin: Akademie Verlag, 2006), 438.

[20] Donald G. Janelle, 'Spatial Reorganization: A Model and Concept', *Annals of the Association of American Geographers* 59 (1969).

[21] Anthony Giddens, *A Contemporary Critique of Historical Materialism. Volume 1: Power, Property and the State* (London: Macmillan, 1981); Giddens, *The Constitution of Society* (Cambridge: Polity Press, 1984).

[22] David Harvey, 'Between Space and Time: Reflections on the Geographical Imagination', *Annals of the Association of American Geographers* 80, no 3 (1990). Stein, 'Reflections on Time, Time–Space Compression and Technology', 106.

[23] Ulrich Sonnemann, 'Die Ohnmacht des Raums und der uneingestandene Fehlschlag der Zeitentmachtung: Zur Aporetik des Staus', in *Zeit-Zeichen: Aufschübe und Interferenzen zwischen Endzeit und Echtzeit*, ed. Georg Christoph Tholen and Michael Scholl (Weinheim: VHC, Acta Humanioria, 1990), 21. Quoted in Dieter Läpple, 'Essay über den Raum: Für ein gesellschaftswissenschaftliches Raumkonzept', in *Stadt und Raum: Soziologische Analysen*, ed. Hartmut Häußermann et al. (Pfaffenweiler: Centaurus-Verlag, 1991), 162.

[24] See, for instance, a recent study by Regine Buschauer that looks at the recurrence of discourses on 'annihilated' (German: *vernichtet*), 'dead' (*getötet*), 'disappeared' (*verschwunden*) or 'lost' (*verloren*) space in the context of several technological transformations. Regine Buschauer, *Mobile Räume: Medien- und diskursgeschichtliche Studien zur Tele-Kommunikation* (Bielefeld: transcript, 2010), 17.

worthwhile to look into it systematically. Is it possible to isolate how exactly globalization is reconfiguring time and space and their relation? Can we build a conceptual framework in order to instruct and systematize empirical work on this subject?

The catchy notions about the relation of time and space enumerated above all in one way or another draw on a single-layered definition of space that implicitly ascribes precedence to geographic space – despite the fact that the social production of space is not doubted by most of their authors. Their central argument is that the time it takes to communicate (or travel) between two places in geographic space has in many cases decreased dramatically. For the study of complex processes of global communication, transfers and interactions it is, however, necessary to employ a multilayered and relational concept of space that goes beyond such a unidimensional approach and acknowledges the social production of spaces just as it is able to accommodate the particularities of geographic space.[25] Globalization takes place in a plurality of spaces. And this

> plurality of spaces can be confounding … First, it increases the confusion. And yet, it brings back a hint of the world's complexity to our image of the world, to our simplifying representations of the world. One could sweepingly say: there are as many spaces as there are fields of study, topics, media or historical agents.[26]

This diagnosis, taken from Karl Schlögel's book *Im Raume lesen wir die Zeit*, should be amended: there are, indeed, as many spaces as there are different forms of relation between objects. Reflecting the geographer's perspective, Peter Gould put it like this: 'In fact, for many spaces of great geographic importance the very notion of metricity may not be pertinent. What may be much more important is the simple fact of how people and things are connected together. It is the sheer connectivity of things that creates many spaces of interest to a geographer'.[27]

[25] For a brief description of the concept of relative space and Leibniz's views on this, see Martina Löw, *Raumsoziologie* (Frankfurt a. M.: Suhrkamp, 2001), 27–8. Markus Schroer, *Räume, Grenzen, Orte: Auf dem Weg zu einer Soziologie des Raums* (Frankfurt a. M.: Suhrkamp, 2006), 40.

[26] Karl Schlögel, *Im Raume lesen wir die Zeit: Über Zivilisationsgeschichte und Geopolitik* (Munich: Hanser, 2003), 69. My translation. The original German: 'Die Pluralisierung der Räume hat etwas Verwirrendes an sich … Sie steigert zunächst die Unübersichtlichkeit. Und doch bringt sie in unser Bild von der Welt, unsere ohnehin zur Simplifikation verurteilten Repräsentationen von der Welt, eine Ahnung von der Komplexität zurück, die die Welt ist. Man könnte summarisch sagen: es gibt so viele Räume, wie es Gegenstandsbereiche, Themen, Medien, geschichtliche Akteure gibt'.

[27] Peter Gould, 'Dynamic Structures of Geographic Space', in *Collapsing Space and Time: Geographic Aspects of Communications and Information*, ed. Stanley D. Brunn and Thomas R. Leinbach (Hammersmith: HarperCollinsAcademic, 1991), 10.

In order to master the challenges that the study of globalization processes holds as regards the transformation of global space(s), an understanding of space is proposed here that revolves around the following five general assumptions based on some of the general arguments postulated in the 'spatial turn':[28] space is socially and culturally produced; space is the sum of the relations of its actors and objects; there is not one space, but as many spaces as there are kinds of relations; for analytical purposes, space is best conceived as an actor-centred concept; and, finally, only some spaces are shaped by time, while others are not. In the following, these propositions will be discussed in more detail.

In the 1970s and 1980s, 'critical' or 'radical' geographers were among the first to acknowledge that space is not an objective or objectifiable given, but that it is socially and culturally produced and constantly reconfigured and adapted – a position that has in the meantime become well established in postmodernist thought.[29] Spaces emerge through social action, through ascriptions of meaning and position and through the acceptance and reproduction of those. In this context, geographic space is but one – admittedly sensory very present – form or construction of space.[30] Just as any other space, it is the sum of relations between its

[28] See, for instance, Matthias Middell and Katja Naumann, 'Global History and the Spatial Turn: From the Impact of Area Studies to the Study of Critical Junctures of Globalization', *Journal of Global History* 5, no 1 (2010); Jörg Döring and Tristan Thielmann, eds., *Spatial Turn: Das Raumparadigma in den Kultur- und Sozialwissenschaften* (Bielefeld: transcript, 2008).

[29] See, for instance, Henri Lefebvre, *Le production de l'espace* (Paris: Gallimard, 1974); Edward W. Soja, *Postmodern Geographies: The Reassertion of Space in Critical Social Theory* (London: Verso, 1989); Soja, *Thirdspace: Journeys to Los Angeles and Other Real-and-Imagined Places* (Oxford: Basil Blackwell, 1996); David Harvey, *Social Justice and the City* (Baltimore: Johns Hopkins University Press, 1973); Harvey, *The Condition of Postmodernity: An Enquiry into the Origins of Cultural Change* (Cambridge, MA and Oxford: Blackwell, 1990); Doreen Massey, *Space, Place and Gender* (Minneapolis: University of Minnesota Press, 1994); Massey, *For Space* (London, Thousand Oaks and New Delhi: Sage, 2005).

[30] Sure enough, one could reasonably argue that geographic space emerges from the sum of distances between its objects and is, therefore, not 'imagined' or 'relative' but strictly 'real' and 'absolute'. Mind, however, that what we think of as geographic space is fundamentally different from what we could call physical space. It is the product of projecting our three-dimensional globe on a two-dimensional backcloth. Maps, for instance, do not correctly represent physical space. Depending on the particular form of projection they distort distances, angles or areas to varying degrees. Beyond this well-known form of distortion, our internal vision of geographic space is also different from physical space. If we think of the distance between, say, London and New Delhi, we think of the distance along the surface of the Earth (according to Google Earth roughly 4,180 miles). In physical space, however, the actual distance is much smaller as it would cut right through the Earth (very approximately 3,990 miles). While this example is of little practical purpose, it nevertheless shows how even this most 'real' of spaces is merely a product of projection and imagination.

objects. But in this particular case, geographic distance is the sole measure of relationship. In forming our image of space, geographic space is privileged. The majority of human sensory impressions in some way or other relate to geographic space. Most of our sensory input provides us with information on geographic location – of ourselves as well as of other people or objects. Therefore our individual images of space are massively shaped or influenced by geographic space – but not exclusively. Martina Löw explains that everyday experiences such as using telephones or computers, watching television or partaking in cyberspace, also shape children's perceptions of space beyond the geographic dimension.[31] Since the publication of Löw's book in 2001, access to 'new spaces' has tremendously increased through, for instance, the expansion of mobile telephony, the emergence of multiplayer online games, the further proliferation of email communication and the cheapening of airfares. These technologies or practices provide different impressions of space and mix with everyday perceptions of geographic space to create an individual idea of space in every person, depending on personal habits, needs, practices and experiences. It is against the background of this image or idea of space that the social production of space – which can be, and often is, completely detached from geographic space – takes place. In short, how we visualize space before our inner eyes is often shaped by our sensory impressions, while the actual spatial patterns are socially produced and, in practice, override this sensory image of space.

In *For Space*, Doreen Massey makes three propositions about how we should think about space. The first proposition says that space 'is a product of interrelations. Space does not exist prior to identities/entities and their relations . . . identities/entities, the relations "between" them, and the spatiality which is part of them, are all co-constitutive'.[32] Building on this relative, relational concept of space – and in concordance with Massey's second proposition that '[i]f space is indeed the product of interrelations, then it must be predicated upon the existence of plurality'[33] – this study suggests thinking of space as a theoretically infinite number of spaces. The nature of relations between the individual objects defines the nature of space – and there are as many possible spaces as there are potential sorts of relationship. From this perspective, geographic space is but one variety of space in which objects are arranged according to their geographic distance.

All these spaces are in some form socially and culturally constructed. While some are defined by quantifiable relations or structural conditions

[31] Löw, *Raumsoziologie*, 93–4. [32] Massey, *For Space*, 10. [33] Ibid., 9.

such as distance, cost or duration, other spaces are produced along categories such as ethnicity, class, language or gender – to name but a few – or depend on the horizons and imaginaries of the actors. Actors and objects serve as interfaces between the different spaces. From the perspective endorsed here, space is relative and created only through the relations between the actors and objects arranged in space. Our intellectual understanding of space can work only through them. On the one hand, the multitude of possible relations between actors and objects makes a multitude of different spaces necessary. On the other hand, both actors and objects allow us to intellectually handle the confounding abundance of spaces. They are the focal points in which spaces touch. And accordingly they are the interfaces through which different spaces can interact with each other, impact on each other and influence our perception or concept of space. The understanding of space put forward here is, therefore, a subjective one looking from the inside through the eyes of an actor or a group of actors. Such an actor-centred perspective on space is the only viable way of practically dealing with the confounding complexity of space resulting from the first three propositions made above. In mathematical terms, it would certainly be possible to represent all connections of a given group of actors and objects regarding a particular (and ideally rather narrow) nature of relations in an *n*-dimensional model of interrelations. This would be the outside perspective on relational space. Alas, even with a limited number of actors and a narrowly defined sort of relation, the model would be far too complex and multidimensional for an interpretation in a cultural-studies context. By taking the position of one particular actor (or a group of actors occupying the same relational position), a distinct part of this complex whole is highlighted. It becomes discernible how different spaces converge in the actor to form his or her space.

Manuel Castells has developed the idea of the *space of flows*, in which he criticizes the disconnected treatment of time and space. His concept of the space of flows provides an alternative to the *space of places* (meaning geographic space). The space of flows constitutes itself around practices of time-sharing made possible by advanced communication technology and detached from concerns of geographic proximity. The space of flows is an example of a version of space with an extremely pronounced time dimension. It is closely related to what has here been called communication space, but differs in the details as long-distance time-sharing depends on communication while communication does not always lead to time-sharing. Castells provides us with an alternative model of space in information societies that drops geographic distance in favour of time as the prime relational factor. And yet, as Castells himself acknowledges, the space of flows is only one of many relevant spaces.[34] In the understanding of space outlined here, time is connected with space only if the defining question is time-related. The first two of the above examples have a time dimension. The relations between objects in communication space or transport space mirror how long it takes to communicate or transport something between them. There is an obvious time–space relation. Instances of time define space. In other cases, however, time is not directly connected with space – telephone cost space and transport cost space serve as examples. These spaces are formed without time or duration playing any part in the process. Importantly, geographic space belongs in this category as well. In the perspective suggested here, geographic space is defined solely by the distance between objects. There is no dimension of time. Sure enough, people or things can move through geographic space and, in doing so, change their relations and therefore space itself – but this is not a time dimension in our sense of the word. It merely says that geographic space exists in time – but it is not shaped or transformed by time itself but rather by movements, by changing positions and distances. As processes, these movements have speed and duration and, therefore, produce their own time-related spaces (e.g. transport space, travel space).

In the understanding of space advocated here, space is the sum of a particular set of relations. Some such sets are defined by instances of time and accordingly some spaces are shaped by time. Beyond this, however, it is argued that time and space should be thought of as separate concepts that should not be collapsed into one (at least) four-dimensional model of time–space. Einstein's work has shown that in physics time and space are fundamentally entangled and cannot be thought of separately. And while such a physical concept of time and space does not need to be reproduced by the humanities and social sciences, time and space here are also interwoven through the actors and objects that they of course share. Actors and objects not only have spatial relations but also temporal ones. Arguing that 'the notion of space as *only* systems of simultaneous relations, the flashing of a pinball machine, is inadequate', Doreen Massey deduces from the parallel existence of spatial and temporal relations that a

> temporal movement is also spatial; the moving elements have spatial relations to each other. And the "spatial" interconnections which flash across can only be constituted temporally as well . . . Space is not static, nor time spaceless. Of course spatiality and temporality are different from each other, but neither can be conceptualized as the absence of the other.[35]

[34] Castells, 'Informationalism, Networks, and the Network Society', 36–7.

[35] Doreen Massey, 'Politics and Space-Time', *New Left Review* 1, no 196 (1992), 80, italics in original.

This is certainly true. Space and time should not (indeed cannot) be thought an exclusive dichotomy. But in order to understand both concepts and, above all, their relation to processes of globalization, they need to be treated as distinct. Strictly speaking, a particular person is not 'the same' in 1880 and in 1900. Not only has, of course, the person changed, grown older, matured, maybe, but position in society, the ascriptions and perceptions associated with this person, have all changed over time. Nevertheless, we would colloquially speak of 'the same' individual, use the same name and identify the two temporally removed actors as instances of one person. We do not think of actors or objects that are spatially related in the same manner at all. Therefore collapsing space and time into one multidimensional model of time–space, while mathematically perfectly viable, runs counter to human strategies of ordering knowledge and thus cannot serve us well in the analysis of social processes and cultural practices taking place in time and in space. Spatial as well as temporal relations between actors and objects exist and both need to be understood without ascribing precedence to one or the other. Accordingly, space and time are here treated as separate forms of relations that share actors and objects with each other. Only some particular spaces that are shaped by time in the manner described above maintain a relationship with time that goes beyond this.

Space cannot be annihilated – neither together with time nor by time itself.[36] The popular phrase 'the annihilation of space and time' by new transport or communication technologies cannot hold true. And the same goes for Marx's 'annihilation of space with time'. Quite on the contrary, new technologies as well as new economic systems have created their very own spaces in which common objects are arranged and connected according to new criteria. These new spaces do not replace existing spaces (such as geographic space) but represent a new form of connectedness or interaction between actors and objects in space. A new form of space is created that is entangled with other spaces through its actors and objects. The realm of transport can serve as an example to elaborate further. Geographic space remains fully untouched by the expansion of transport networks. Cities, people, things keep their geographic relations to each other – unless they move (or are moved). If they move, they change their relative positions and, therefore, the structure of geographic space. This is all that geographic space is concerned with – the positions of its objects in relation to each other. Movement itself, however, takes place according to factors represented by other spaces. All these spaces influence the process

[36] See Massey, *For Space*, 90–9.

of moving but should be treated as separate layers that represent connections of different sorts between the moving object, its point of departure and its destination.

While space has not been annihilated, telecommunication technologies have, however, diminished communication time between many objects in geographic space. Does this then mean that time has somehow been annihilated and that at least the second part of the popular statement is correct? Again, no. Two principal arguments can be given to counter this assumption. First, the shrinking of communication times does not annihilate the factor time. Quite on the contrary, it emphasizes the importance of time differences and requires ever faster and more immediate handling of information or tasks. The time allocated to processing and applying information shrinks proportionally with communication times to avoid bottlenecks. In an environment of immediateness, time is not annihilated – it is critical. Archetypical contemporary examples include stock markets and exchanges in which global transfers are made in seconds – and in which, accordingly, seconds can decide whether you buy, sell or hold prematurely or too late. But there are earlier examples as well. In the nineteenth century, new transport and communication technologies brought shrinking communication times and, therefore, made the standardization of time a necessity. The International Meridian Conference in the year 1884 marks '[o]ne of the first dialogues about international standards of communication'[37] and led to the establishment of international time zones. Timekeeping was standardized in order to avoid confusing differences in local times. The shorter communication times became, the more important even minor differences could be. During the Telegraph General Strike in India in the year 1908, for instance, the signallers on strike chose to omit the time and date of telegrams, thereby rendering the messages worthless for many purposes.[38] As can be seen, time became a globally critical factor, and Lewis Mumford therefore absolutely correctly said that 'the clock, not the steam-engine, is the key-machine of the modern industrial age'.[39]

[37] Allen W. Palmer, 'Negotiation and Resistance in Global Networks: The 1884 International Meridian Conference', *Mass Communication & Society* 5, no 1 (2002), 7.

[38] Deep Kanta Lahiri Choudhury, 'Treasons of the Clerks: Sedition and Representation in the Telegraph General Strike of 1908', in *Beyond Representation: Colonial and Postcolonial Constructions of Indian Identity*, ed. Crispin Bates (Oxford and New York: Oxford University Press, 2006), 312.

[39] Lewis Mumford, *Technics and Civilization* (San Diego, New York and London: Harcourt Brace & Company, 1963), 14.

Second, in all those spaces which are formed through time-related connections, time structures space. The emergence of a telecommunication network in the nineteenth century impacted massively on communication space and diminished communication times between many places and people. At the same time, however, other regions were not linked up and, relative to better-connected places, communication times between such peripheries and the centres even increased. While it might seem that within the well-connected parts of the world communication time had shrunk to such an extent that it had become practically insignificant (or 'annihilated'), other regions were left unconnected. Enforced by the increasing gap between the communication centres and the peripheries, time had become one crucial factor of inclusion or exclusion. Again, the increasing relative difference between fast and slow information flows elevated the importance of time rather than making it irrelevant.

Briefly summing up what has been said so far, this study proposes that, when examining global communication and transfers, researchers should operate with a theoretically infinite number of different spaces which flexibly constitute themselves around specific interests or research questions. Some of these spaces have a direct relation with time beyond the fact that they share actors and objects with each other – others (such as geographic space) have not. The crucial advantage of the proposed model is its focus on connections and interactions between actors and objects in space. A particular space is the abstract sum of the relations between its actors and objects. When the pattern of relations changes, the structure of space changes as well. The dematerialization of information flows and its impact on the structure of global communication space provides an excellent example. This development (as well as its modern-day equivalent encapsulated in technologies such as the Internet or mobile telephony) has traditionally been referred to as a classic example of 'time–space compression'. This is, however, an inaccurate or at least highly incomplete description of the process. Space has not been compressed. At best, one particular form of space – communication space – has been restructured, and in the course of this some actors and objects have moved closer together (or have been compressed) while others have moved further apart. The same is true for time as only some spaces are functions of time. At best, we can conclude that *some* spaces – for instance global communication space – have been *partially* compressed, while others have not.

Chapter 5 will explore in some depth how, with the emergence of the submarine telegraph network, global communication space moved further and further away from geographic space in the late nineteenth century. It will be seen that, from a relative perspective, the so-called 'compression of time and space' applied only to certain well-connected parts of the world, while other parts remained relatively remote. If, however, we want to fully understand the socioeconomic and cultural significance of the transformation of communication space, the structures of other spaces must be borne in mind and related to this process. Below, a very brief example is provided to illustrate exactly how different spaces can interact with each other. It will be shown how the understanding of space put forward in this book can help in analysing the effects of changing connectivity patterns on different levels.

After several aborted attempts, a transatlantic telegraph cable eventually connected the United Kingdom and Newfoundland in August 1858. The connection did not last long, but among the messages sent and received were two that cancelled the transhipment of two British regiments stationed in British North America. The telegrams stated concisely, 'The thirty-ninth Regiment is not to return to England' and 'The sixty-second Regiment is not to return to England'.[40] The troops had initially been ordered back by letter due to strategic requirements connected with the Indian Uprising. In the meantime, however, the sepoy insurrection had been put down and the troop movement had become unnecessary. The telegraphic just-in-time cancellation saved the British Crown an impressive sum of money and allegedly was instrumental in advertising the advantages of shrinking intercontinental communication times.[41] While communication space around the United Kingdom, India and North America had been 'compressed', the actual shipping of the troops would have taken place in global transport space. Here technologies such as the railway or steam shipping brought structural changes as well, but intercontinental transport was still a lengthy and costly affair. In other words, the particular structures of transport space and the space created by transport costs made investments in telecommunication technology attractive. Accordingly, the different spaces were closely entangled and impacted on each other.

Brief and sketchy as it may be, this example illustrates that a number of different spaces describe or symbolize the complex relation(s) between two (or more) actors or objects. Often, shifts occur only in one or more particular spaces while others remain unchanged. The understanding of space

[40] Richard Hennig, *Überseeische Telegraphie und auswärtige Politik* (Berlin: Carl Heymanns Verlag, 1919), 4.

[41] Andrew M. Odlyzko, 'History of Communications and Its Implications for the Internet' (AT&T Labs, 2000), 38; Daniel R. Headrick, *The Invisible Weapon: Telecommunications and International Politics, 1851–1945* (New York: Oxford University Press, 1991), 18; Lars U. Scholl, 'The Global Communication Industry and Its Impact on International Shipping before 1914', in *Global Markets: The Internationalization of the Sea Transport Industries since 1850*, ed. David J. Starkey and Gelina Harlaftis (St John's: International Maritime Economic History Association, 1998), 200.

proposed here allows for the isolated analysis of such changes on the very level on which they occur. When examining processes of globalization, this practice holds several distinct advantages. First, most historians will not be interested in shifting relations and connectivity patterns simply for the sake of it. Informative as this might be, their key interest should rest on how such spatial transformations impact on culture, society, economy or the individual. Questions relating to, for instance, the case of communication could be: how do mutual perceptions or flows of information over a great distance change? To what extent do individual horizons broaden or shrink? How do changing connectivity patterns bring about new forms of inclusion and exclusion in a global public sphere, in world trade or in international politics? Second, the model recognizes all sorts of different co-existing spaces. Established perceptions of space are not 'annihilated' or overthrown. They are incorporated in the model and retain their validity and usefulness. Geographic space, for instance, has not been rendered irrelevant. Many forms of interaction between objects in space depend on geographic factors. The concept of the *space of flows*, for instance, can also be incorporated. The model is strictly complementary and not exclusive. Third, this spatial concept allows for a non-elitist analysis of transformations in space. Jeremy Stein has rightly pointed out that 'interpretations of time–space compression typically rely on accounts of privileged social observers, and are thereby elitist'.[42] Even if this concept of space does not recognize a compression of space and/or time, Stein's observation holds true from his perspective. Only a very small privileged group of mostly Western administrators, businessmen and travellers really witnessed a transformation of global communication space in the nineteenth century. By far the biggest part of the world's population had no access to or even knowledge of new communication technologies. In indirect ways, ordinary people's lives would sooner or later be affected by newly defined global relations, but their perceptions of space were essentially different from those of the privileged group. The proposed model allows for an individual, non-elitist treatment of space and acknowledges that each group or person has a unique perception of global space in which different relational spaces play different roles. Fourth, the concept also offers a new perspective on the relation between the global and the local (meaning a particular object or group of objects in space). When shifts in a particular space occur, the relation between the global and the local also changes on a certain level. The focus on one set of relations at a time and the relative nature of the concept can help to visualize these changes. It emphasizes the multitude of different

[42] Stein, 'Reflections on Time, Time–Space Compression and Technology', 107.

connections between the local and the global. A fifth advantage can be found in the universal applicability of the model across all subfields or fashions in history. It can be applied in economic or social history, cultural history, the history of technology or any other such field. It lends itself to positivist views of history just as readily as it can provide a framework for constructivist or post-structuralist studies.

2.3 Actors of globalization and their networks

Following the definition provided above, space is the sum of relations, defined by a specific question or research interest, between its constituents – be they actors or objects. What, then, is the difference between spaces and networks? The two can easily be confused. After all, both have to do with connections, relations and exchanges between their constituents. As mentioned at the beginning of Chapter 2, space is what becomes discernible through the eyes of the actors. It is the stage on (or within) which they act. Such spaces have no agency, no rationale, no function of themselves. They are the sum of particular relations between actors and objects – relations that are created, shaped or severed by, for instance, networks. Networks consist of connections, spaces of relations. And as similar as they might seem, connections and relations are not the same thing. Connections shape and define relations. Within one particular space, connections between two constituents might (or very likely do) exist in the plural, while there is only one resulting relation as a consequence of these multiple connections. Spaces are representations of relational patterns, some of which are created by networks and their network rationales.[43]

[43] The term 'network' is used situatively in this study. In some cases the term has – in Bruno Latour's words – a 'common technical meaning'. It denotes an organizational form that describes the system of interconnections between telegraph apparatuses in countless places around the globe. The apparatuses themselves are part of the network, as are the wires and cables connecting them or the human operators handling them. It is the purpose of this network to encode, send and decode telegraphic messages. At other instances, the term 'network' focuses on the customers of telegraphic services. Of course, both networks interact with and depend on each other and together form yet another (meta)network in the sense of a large technological system. It will be clear from the specific context in which particular way the term 'network' is employed in the following. See Thomas Hughes, 'The Evolution of Large Technological Systems', in *The Social Construction of Technological Systems*, ed. Wiebe E. Bijker, Thomas P. Hughes and Trevor J. Pinch (Cambridge, MA: MIT Press, 1993). It is important to note that the term 'network' is used in a different way in actor-network theory. 'Network' here stands neither for 'common technical' networks nor for social networks. Actor-network theory 'aims at accounting for the very essence of societies and natures'. And it is in this context that the term 'network' is used to describe the fundamental form of organization of the human and non-human world. Bruno

The term 'network rationale' has already been introduced as the particular working logic of a network. The following paragraphs take a closer look at the concept in order to show how the term conceptualizes the relations and mutual influences between networks, network technologies and the human actors connected in these networks. This will forgo a great amount of confusion stemming from the sometimes obfuscating use of the word 'agency'. The best-known debate about whether objects (meaning something non-human) can actually have agency in themselves took (and occasionally still takes) place in the realm of the history and sociology of technology. In a nutshell, the debate revolves around the central question whether that which happens through or because of technology has to be credited to human (because humans design, build and run machines) or to technological agency. While this book examines the impact of telegraphy on globalization and therefore accepts technology as a contributory factor in historical processes, it does not intend to reopen the debate whether technology itself has agency. The two essentialist positions in this debate – technological determinism and sociological determinism – have in their extreme forms long been vitiated.[44] Much of the remaining disagreement stems from varying definitions of and notions about the term 'agency'. Of course, if agency is defined as depending on conscious (or subconscious) decisions and intentions, it must remain a human prerogative.[45] If, however, agency is simply seen as a force that does something or makes something happen – as, for instance, in actor-network theory[46] – it can rightfully be attributed to any person or object that is somehow involved in an action.

Latour, 'On Actor-Network Theory: A Few Clarifications', *Soziale Welt*, 47 (1996), 369–71. Ingo Schulz-Schaeffer, 'Akteur-Netzwerk-Theorie: Zur Koevolution von Gesellschaft, Natur und Technik', in *Soziale Netzwerke: Konzepte und Methoden der sozialwissenschaftlichen Netzwerkforschung*, ed. Johannes Weyer (Munich: Oldenbourg, 2000), 187–8.

44 See, for instance, Merritt Roe Smith and Leo Marx, eds., *Does Technology Drive History? The Dilemma of Technological Determinism* (Cambridge, MA and London: MIT Press, 1994). Or see the principal ideas of actor-network theory laid out in – among many other publications – Bruno Latour, *Science in Action: How to Follow Scientists and Engineers through Society* (Cambridge, MA: Harvard University Press, 1987); Latour, *Reassembling the Social: An Introduction to Actor-Network-Theory* (Oxford: Oxford University Press, 2005); John Law, 'Notes on the Theory of the Actor-Network: Ordering, Strategy, and Heterogeneity', *Systems Practice* 5, no 4 (1992); John Law and John Hassard, eds., *Actor Network Theory and After* (Oxford: Blackwell Publishing, 1999).

45 We leave the philosophically even trickier question of animal agency aside for the moment as it has no relevance in the context of this study.

46 See, for instance, the concise surveys in Andréa Belliger and David J. Krieger, 'Einführung in die Akteur-Netzwerk-Theorie', in *ANThology: Ein einführendes Handbuch zur Akteur-Netzwerk-Theorie*, ed. Andréa Belliger and David J. Krieger (Bielefeld: transcript, 2006); Nina Degele, *Einführung in die Techniksoziologie* (Munich: Wilhelm Fink Verlag, 2002), 126–35.

Neither of the two positions is very helpful in the context of this study. This book seeks to establish how enhanced telecommunication networks changed existing and created new global spaces, how they linked different locales and the people in these locales, and thereby impacted on processes of globalization. In these locales and in these spaces people lived and acted. The networks that we look at consist of connected people. Therefore, does a network's potential for transformation and thus for action rest in the people it connects (and who have designed and built the network) or in the network itself? As mentioned above, the answer depends on one's definition of agency. Fully viable arguments can be found for both positions. For the purposes of this study, however, their extreme notions are not helpful for the following reasons. On the one hand, to extend the term 'agency' to cover the role of every person and object somehow connected to a particular action (as the otherwise very helpful and insightful actor-network theory does) derives the concept of any practical meaning. It loses analytical usefulness, if it is applied in an all-encompassing way. As the principal interest of social historians (or researchers in the humanities and social sciences in general) should always rest with people and their forms of organization, the concept of agency will analytically help best if exclusively applied to human doings. This is not to ascribe any special or 'higher' (in a spiritual sense) quality to humans and their actions. Defining agency as something exclusively human simply gives the social and anthropological sciences a sharper analytical tool for asking and answering their questions about the actions and behaviours, the perceptions and beliefs, of humans.

On the other hand, defining agency as exclusively human and, therefore, occupying a principally sociodeterminist position negates the influence that structures (such as telecommunication networks) or technologies (such as the telegraph) can have on human actions. Reserving agency exclusively for humans practically means proposing that the influence and transformative potential that rests in such structures or objects is merely 'stored' human agency that the human designers, builders and users have inscribed in (and ascribe to) the object. While, in an abstract theoretical sense, this notion is interesting, comprehensible and probably true, it is analytically just as useful as the all-encompassing use of agency propagated by actor-network theory. It is an analytical dead end. In many cases the 'stored' actions of designers, builders and users of such structures or objects become so numerous, so entangled and, therefore, so complicated that they produce unforeseeable and, indeed, unintended consequences. From a purely theoretical–mathematical viewpoint (and in knowledge of all the variables and operators involved), it might still be possible to predict which output a particular combination of inputs will produce. In practice, however, most variables and operators must remain obscure. In plain words, this means that reasonably complex organizational structures or technological systems involve so many people, so many human inputs, so many operational factors of their own that their effects on human actions cannot be pre-established. For any practical purposes, such structures and technologies develop a kind of life of their own. Is it, then, not justified in such cases to speak of structural or technological agency?

These caveats show that there is no simple answer to the question whether non-humans can have agency or not. And this study will not be tempted to provide one. Rather, it steers clear of the problem by defining agency very narrowly as exclusively human and at the same time introducing the term 'rationale' in order to do justice to and to conceptualize the transformative potential of structures and technologies. In short, in the context of this book, neither networks nor the technologies that power these networks have agency, but they do have particular rationales – network rationales as well as technological rationales, where the latter is usually an important constituent of the former. But what exactly is meant by rationale and why is it analytically more useful than the concept of agency? Whenever the word is used in this book, rationale means the particular working logic of an organization or structure (e.g. a network), an instrument or technology (e.g. the telegraph). In combination, the many different human inputs, together with the inner workings of a structure or technology, give rise to a characteristic functioning pattern. This pattern might or might not be discernible for its designers, builders and users, but it will usually have bearings on their decisions and actions – consciously or subconsciously. Let us briefly come back to the hammer example of the introductory chapter. Of course, the user of the hammer knows that the hammer will not only help to drive in a nail but that it will also produce a loud noise that might be unpleasant and disturbing. When using the hammer, the user makes a conscious choice to accept the acoustic by-product for the greater benefit of driving in the nail. Therefore the technological rationale of the hammer (or at least a part thereof) is pretty much out in the open. While the hammer itself does not drive the nail and produce the noise, it is much more likely that the availability of a hammer will 'seduce' the human actor to reap the benefits it promises (to get work done fast and easily) and put up with the drawbacks (noise and angry neighbours). It is part of the rationale of the hammer to make some choices (to use the hammer) more desirable and appealing to a human actor than others, even if the prospective user is in full knowledge of the benefit–drawback balance.

Returning to the case of telecommunication networks, there are both the technological rationale and the network rationale, where the former is part of the latter. Almost all forms of network share a number of characteristics. For instance, networks become more and more attractive for non-members the larger they get. Networks necessitate at least a certain degree of standardization between members. A common protocol of communication is necessary. Digression from such a protocol becomes more difficult the larger the network is. These are just a few examples to illustrate that the particular form of organization called 'network' already gives rise to a particular rationale that influences the choices of both the people organized in the network and those outside it. If, however, the network and the connections between the network nodes depend on a specific technology, the rationale of this technology becomes part of the network rationale. For our case, this means that the technological rationale of telegraphy became a very great and important part of the general network rationale of the global telegraph system.

But what exactly is the technological rationale of telegraphy and how does it imprint itself on the network rationale? These are two of the central questions that inform this work and which it can only start to answer. The rationale of a technology is not immediately discernible in all its details when first examined. Some features might be obvious and all too easy to discover, others might be well hidden and only be revealed by asking specific research questions and tracing the role of the technology in corresponding situations. In the case of telegraphy, some of the features that spring to mind include that it sped up communication; that it employed a specific code system; and, maybe, that it gave rise to a particular style of communication full of abbreviations and grammatical reductions. While all of these aspects are certainly correct, they remain superficial descriptions of the effects of altogether more complicated causes. As has already been established, it is one of the essential traits of telegraphy that it dematerializes long-distance information flows. Electric current travelling along wires now carried the information. The efficiency of telegraphy, therefore, always depended on the contemporary understanding of electricity. Also, this particular form of transmission initially introduced the necessity of a binary telegraph code best embodied in what came to be known as Morse code. Either there was a current on the wire or there was not. Other codes, such as Wheatstone's five-needle code, were just variations on the binary that employed more signal-carrying wires. The binary code made commonly transcribed messages long and expensive to send. As a remedy, elaborate systems of abbreviation were employed in business communication and the proverbial telegram style developed. Specially trained telegraphists were needed to encode and decode telegraphic messages and in many cases specialized code books were necessary to give meaning to the seemingly arbitrary letter combinations emerging from the decoding. All this forms part of the rationale of telegraphy. While the technology was originally devised to speed up long-distance communication, it also introduced, among other things, a need for brevity and specialized mediation that became essential features of telegraph networks.

Furthermore, the global telegraph network, like many technology-based networks, exhibited a strong structural continuity despite the fact that the mediating technology matured and overcame previous limitations. For instance, there was a good reason why the first successful telegraphic connection across the Atlantic connected not the two important metropolises, London and New York, but rather the western tip of Ireland and Newfoundland. Submarine cable laying was still in its infancy and the length of the cables was an important issue. A couple of years later, in 1870, Porthcurno in the very west of Cornwall was chosen as the British landing site for a submarine telegraph connection to Carcavelos, Portugal, which was to form the first leg of the submarine telegraph line to British India. Both remote places served as principal cable-landing sites for a long time – in the case of Porthcurno for exactly a hundred years – despite rapid improvements in electric signalling and cable laying that had quickly made considerations of distance largely obsolete. But the network structure conserved itself due to the step-by-step evolution of the network's mediating technology. When new cables with higher capacities were laid, these cables still depended on the infrastructure in place on the shore, on the availability of trained personnel or on the existence of connecting lines. This interdependence of the network components exerted a strong conserving power on the structure of the nineteenth-century telegraph network. And together with many other factors, they shaped the particular rationale of global telegraphy.

In combination with the actions of humans, such rationales shape the interplay between people and structures, society and technology. Employing the concept of network rationales in this study allows observers to acknowledge the transformative power of technologies and structures but does not at the same time sever the connection between human agency and such concepts as intention, responsibility and meaning. Agency is defined here to rest only in human actors. From the viewpoint of the humanities and social sciences, actions cannot be separated from the intentions behind them, the feelings in them or the perceptions of them. Doing this would deprive actions of any meaning and make it impossible to understand them – which, after all, is one of the researcher's most important aims. It is in this point that this study digresses pronouncedly from the ideas of actor-network theory.[47]

The principal way in which technology influences human actions is that it alters the array of choices and possible courses of action open for someone. Investigating the feedback that the use of technologies has on society therefore revolves around the key question of how, and by what means or mechanisms, specific technologies alter the choices of their users, open up new ways or make traditional ways more laborious and cumbersome. The rationale of a particular technology in most cases comes as a package of factors and influences that cannot be disentangled by the user. If one factor of this package proves to be particularly advantageous and becomes a strong incentive for the use of a technology, the rest of the rationale unfolds as well in the application of the technology and often alters an actor's array of choices in areas that would have seemed highly unlikely to be affected at all. The fact that only parts of the working rationale of a technology are obvious, while other parts become clearly discernible during and after (long-term) use, makes technological impact assessment a complicated endeavour and renders the historical study of the use of technologies all the more necessary.

Regarding the case of nineteenth-century telegraphy, we have already touched upon several examples that illustrate how the application of a technology for a particular reason (such as fast communication with a

[47] On the expansion of the term 'agency' beyond humans, John Law has written the following:

> Let me be clear. Actor-network theory is analytically radical in part because it treads on a set of ethical, epistemological, and ontological toes. In particular, it does not celebrate the idea that there is a difference in kind between people on the one hand, and objects on the other. It denies that people are *necessarily* special. Indeed it raises a basic question about what we *mean* when we talk of people. Necessarily then, it sets the alarm bells of ethical and epistemological humanism ringing. What should we make of this? A clarificatory point, and then an argument.
>
> The clarificatory point is this. We need, I think, to distinguish between ethics and sociology. The one may – indeed should – inform the other, but they are not identical. To say that there is no fundamental difference between people and objects is an analytical stance, not an ethical position. And to say this does not mean that we have to treat the people in our lives as machines. We don't have to deny them the rights, duties, or responsibilities that we usually accord to people. Indeed, we might use it to sharpen ethical questions about the special character of the human effect – as, for instance, in difficult cases such as life maintained by virtue of the technologies of intensive care.

Law, 'Notes on the Theory of the Actor-Network', 383, original emphasis. I share Law's notion that the distinction between ethics and sociology is not problematic as long as the two inform each other. I do, however, also believe that analytically leveling the differences between humans and objects hinders rather than furthers our understanding of their interaction, of which an understanding of the feelings, intentions and perceptions involved is part and parcel.

distant other) entailed the limitation of choices in another field. The use of the telegraph as a medium of transmission impacted directly on the nature and structure of its content. Due to the high investment and maintenance costs involved, the satisfactory demand and the limited competition, telegrams were usually expensive to send – especially in the early days of telegraphy. Furthermore, the transmission of messages was time-consuming and laborious. Accordingly, the price of a telegram was usually based on its length – a practice that gave the sender every incentive to be concise and eventually led to the evolution of what has become known as telegram style. This need for brevity made it sensible for the sender to be very selective concerning the topics that should be communicated by telegraph (often leaving more elaborate background information to be sent by traditional post) as well as to be generous as regards the use of proper grammar and style. The rationale of telegraphy, therefore, not only rendered long-distance communication fast and efficient, it also transformed the choices that users had regarding their topics and their ways of expression.

The choice, however, finally remains with the actors. In circumstances where money or time is not of the essence or when telegrams are conveyed free of charge, more elaborate messages might well be sent. The different telegrams exchanged between England and India at John Pender's telegraphic soirée, to which reference has already been made in the introductory chapter, illustrate this. The managing director of the British Indian Submarine Telegraph Company, for instance, sent a message to the manager in Bombay asking, 'How are you all?' He received the brief reply 'All well' and then proceeded to demand, 'Please ask gentlemen of the press, Bombay, to send a message to gentlemen of the press, New York.' The fitting reply amounted to 'Will do so when here'.[48] The communicators in this exchange were well-versed in telegraphy and used concise and abbreviated language even on an occasion when messages were sent free of charge. As has been seen in the introduction, Lord Mayo's reply to the greetings sent by his wife was similarly brief and inornate. The original message from Lady Mayo, however, reflects her customary way of expressing herself rather than the requirements of the technological system of telegraphy.[49] In its elaborate style it lives up to what is expected from Lady Mayo socially rather than technologically. It is a message that would have been written in exactly the same manner had it

[48] British Library, General Reference Collection, shelfmark 8761.b.62. 'Souvenir of the Inaugural Fête [held at the house of Mr John Pender], in commemoration of the opening of direct submarine telegraph with India', 23 June 1870, 17–18.

[49] Ibid., 5.

been sent by letter. And, of course, the telegram could be transmitted to India successfully even if it ignored the technological rationale of the telegraph. Another example for acting against the ways seemingly prescribed by technology can be found in the transmission of the king of Prussia's 1866 speech from the throne. The speech was read to the Prussian parliament by Otto von Bismarck and then telegraphically transmitted word by word via the newly opened transatlantic cable. Legend has it that the transmission of this single message alone cost the Prussian state 29,000 marks.[50]

These examples show that the choice ultimately remains with the actor. It is certainly possible, under the right circumstances, to send an elaborate and grammatically correct message to India or across the Atlantic via telegraph. The technology is perfectly capable of facilitating this even if the overall rationale of the technology makes other decisions more likely and less costly. Agency as such, however, stays with the people – the inventors, maintainers, entrepreneurs and users of telegraphy. Therefore researchers should be interested in how the agency of these people interacted with the particular qualities, the rationale, of the telegraph and how it impacted on the structure of global space, on globalization and, therefore, eventually on contemporary society.

[50] Hennig, *Überseeische Telegraphie und auswärtige Politik*, 5.

3 The technological history of telegraphy

3.1 Petitioning for network access

Late in the year 1867, the following memorandum – composed and signed by numerous inhabitants of the Lincolnshire village of Tattershall – was submitted to the directors of the Great Northern Railway Company:

> We the undersigned Inhabitants of Tattershall and neighbourhood being informed that it is the intention of the Great Northern Railway Company to establish a Telegraph Station at Dogdyke on the loop line of the Great Northern Railway beg to suggest to the Directors that it would be more advantageous to the Company and a greater benefit to the Public to give telegraph communication to Tattershall instead of Dogdyke, considering the short distance between the two places, and Tattershall being a first-class Station and in direct communication with the large villages of Coningsby and Billinghay we therefore urge the Directors to give the matter their earnest consideration.[1]

On 7 October, the Great Northern's general manager, Seymour Clarke, wrote a rather short and plain letter to James Banks Stanhope, the Member of Parliament for North Lincolnshire, in which he reacted to the petition and made it very clear that the company would not reconsider its decision:

> I am very sorry that the convenience of the working of the loop line has induced us to put up the Telegraph at Dogdyke rather than at a more important station. The Telegraph has been added intermediately between the Stations where it was originally placed, for the purpose of Telegraphing the running trains in foggy weather and at night, and with every desire to meet the convenience of yourself and your neighbours, I cannot overlook the facts I have had the pleasure of giving you above.[2]

[1] National Archives, RAIL 236/718/22, 'Inhabitants of Tattershall for Installation of Telegraph Communication at Tattershall instead of Dogdyke. Memorial', 1867.

[2] National Archives, RAIL 236/718/22, 'Inhabitants of Tattershall for Installation of Telegraph Communication at Tattershall instead of Dogdyke. Letter Seymour Clarke to James Banks Stanhope', 7 October 1867.

The memorandum and the Great Northern Railway Company's reaction to it are today held at the British National Archives in Kew. From these documents, it is not entirely clear how exactly the petition was submitted to the company in the first place. It can only be suspected that the Earl Fortescue, who owned a large estate in and around Tattershall, attached it to a letter he had written to the company directors. This would explain why Fortescue received a much more elaborate reply and statement on the issue. Francis Cockshott, Superintendent of the Line, wrote on 2 October,

My Lord.

I have the honour to acknowledge receipt of your Lordships letter of yesterdays date.

By reason of our through Coal traffic being now sent over the Loop Line it has been found necessary to open several additional Signal Stations on the Line between Lincoln and Boston and Peterboro and an intermediate Station between each existing telegraph Station has been selected.

The arrangement has to do with the working of the Line alone and it is believed that the safety of the Line will be best secured by opening Bardney, Dogdkye [*sic*], Algarkirk, and St. James Deeping as the additional Signal Stations above referred to.

It is quite true that the opening of these stations for traffic purposes will really make them telegraphic Stations and will admit of telegrams being sent to and from these places, but the safety of the Line being of the chief importance, all other questions have been considered as of secondary.

The question has had the very careful consideration of the Directors and I trust your Lordship will consider this as sufficient explanation why Dogdyke should have been selected in preference to Tattershall.

I would further remark that Dogdyke is situated on a sharp curve and at a level Croping [*sic*] of considerable importance and these considerations coupled with the fact that Dogdyke is the most central Station between the existing telegraph Stations of Kirkstead and Boston have led to the selection of Dogdyke as being one of the new Signal Stations. Tattershall is 3¾ miles from Kirkstead and 12 miles from Boston so that it could not under any circumstances be made an intermediate Signal Station.

I have the honour to be
My Lord
Your most obedient Servant
Francis P. Cockshott[3]

As these letters indicate, the memorandum brought no immediate benefit to the inhabitants of Tattershall. The England-wide evaluation of

[3] National Archives, RAIL 236/718/22, 'Inhabitants of Tattershall for Installation of Telegraph Communication at Tattershall instead of Dogdyke. Letter Francis P. Cockshott to Earl Fortescue', 2 October 1867.

telegraph stations conducted in June 1868 includes neither a station at Dogdyke nor one at Tattershall.[4] Several years later, in 1876, the infrequently compiled 'List of Codes and Telegraph Stations in the United Kingdom' contains a telegraph station at Dogdyke, open Monday to Saturday for the collection of messages only.[5] Tattershall is not to be found in this list or in those for 1882 and 1885, but eventually shows up in the corresponding publication for the year 1889.[6] The village had eventually been telegraphically connected sometime between 1885 and 1889.

While the memorandum had no immediate effect on the policy of the Great Northern Railway Company, it is instructive as to the importance of getting telegraphically connected in the second half of the nineteenth century. In the 1850s and 1860s, even the inhabitants of small and rather remote English villages seem to have felt the need to get access to the new technology. Thus the Tattershall example shows that the telegraph did not exclusively belong to an elusive global sphere, but that it was a very real concern for the local public – or parts thereof as the list of signatories of the memorandum shows. And the correspondence also illustrates the pivotal but often ambivalent role of the railway companies in providing access to telegraphic communication. Private railway companies – as the letters of both Clarke and Cockshott leave little doubt – cared mainly about the co-ordination of their trains and not so much about the real or perceived needs of a village population. Nevertheless, railways became the principal vehicle through which telegraphy could spread. As will be discussed below, the technology behind the telegraph had been developed and

[4] British Telecom Archives, POST 81/51, 'Electric and International Telegraph Co Circuit Returns – Metropolitan and "A" and "B"', 1868; British Telecom Archives, POST 81/52, 'Electric and International Telegraph Co Circuit Returns, "C" to "H"', 1868; British Telecom Archives, POST 81/53, 'Electric and International Telegraph Co Circuit Returns, "I" to "O"', 1868; British Telecom Archives, POST 81/54, 'Electric and International Telegraph Co Circuit Returns, "P" to "T"', 1868; British Telecom Archives, POST 81/55, 'Electric and International Telegraph Co Circuit Returns, and Scotland "U" to "Y"', 1868; British Telecom Archives, POST 81/12. 'British and Irish Magnetic Telegraph Co (formerly the English Telegraph Company) Circuit Returns – Metropolitan and "A" to "M"', 1868; British Telecom Archives, POST 81/13, 'British and Irish Magnetic Telegraph Co (formerly the English Telegraph Company) Circuit Returns "N" to "Z" and Scotland and Ireland', 1868; British Telecom Archives, POST 81/77, 'United Kingdom Electric Telegraph Company, Circuit Returns from Offices in the Metropolitan, English and Scottish Districts', 1868.

[5] British Telecom Archives, POST 82/70, 'List of Codes and Telegraph Stations in the United Kingdom', 1876.

[6] British Telecom Archives, POST 82/71, 'List of Codes and Telegraph Stations in the United Kingdom', 1882. British Telecom Archives, POST 82/72, 'List of Codes and Telegraph Stations in the United Kingdom', 1885. British Telecom Archives, POST 82/73, 'List of Codes and Telegraph Stations in the United Kingdom', 1889.

refined for decades before the railways eventually created a significant demand for telegraphic communication.

3.2 Telecommunication

The word 'telecommunication' was first used by Edouard Estaunié (1862–1942), director of the Ecôle supérieure des postes et télégraphes de France,[7] in his *Traité pratique de télécommunication électrique* published in the year 1904. Composed of the Greek τηλε (*tele*) for 'distant' and the Latin *communicatio* for 'connection', the term, in the literal sense of the word, denotes the conveyance of information over a great distance. Estaunié himself had a somewhat narrower meaning in mind. To him, telecommunication depended on electric transmission and encompassed telegraphy, telephony and wireless telegraphy only. This study, however, suggests widening the definition of the term slightly in order to encompass all technologies of distance communication that rely on the dematerialization of information flows and are able to convey complex messages.

The basic forms of human communication rely on non-material information flows. Signs and sounds do not need a material carrier. They travel courtesy of light and sound waves. In order to convey information across time and space detached from the actual communicator, the information had to be attached to a material carrier first – the flow of information had to be materialized. The emergence of drawing, painting or writing serves as the principal but certainly not the only example here. Material information storage is, however, subject to certain physical limitations. The carrying materials can be lost or destroyed, or simply wither away. Often, space is limited. And in terms of transport, many materials do not lend themselves readily to being moved over great distances. Even lighter and more flexible storage material, such as paper, had to be physically transported and were, therefore, limited in their transmission speed. This, of course, also applies in the case of information travelling attached to people themselves.

Early techniques of dematerializing information flows soon freed long-distance communication from some of its limitations. Fire beacons or drum signals, to give but two prominent examples, made use of optical or acoustic information transmission but could carry information further than the human voice. The transmission capacity of such early technologies, however, was modest. In many cases, only simple pre-arranged messages could be transmitted. These systems were later improved and extended. In ancient Greece, at least two different technologies were known and

[7] Anton A. Huurdeman, *The Worldwide History of Telecommunications* (New York: John Wiley & Sons, Inc., 2003), 3.

employed to convey more complex messages over distances – hydraulic telegraphy and torch telegraphy.[8] Both systems worked, but the transmission rate was low, the distance covered was small and, of course, both depended on good weather conditions and clear sight.

The principle of information transmission employed, however, was largely the same as in the optical telegraph systems of the eighteenth and nineteenth centuries, which – following the definition of the term provided above – qualify as the first telecommunication system that worked satisfactorily and was employed over a reasonably large network.[9] Clearly visible optical signals were given at one station and then reproduced at another station. Thanks mainly to the invention of the telescope, however, the distance between the stations could be increased in the case of optical telegraphy. And the complex signalling system could be operated by only two persons per station – one on the lookout and one on the signal mechanics. These technological advances increased the functionality of optical signal transmission and, for the first time, rendered it possible to erect a larger network of stations. The invention of the optical telegraph is usually credited to the French clergyman Claude Chappe (1763–1805). Supported by his four brothers, Chappe had been working on an apparatus for optical signal transmission since 1790. His first attempt used two large clocks with different symbols on the dial. The movement of their hands was synchronized. When the hand of the sending clock reached a symbol that should be transmitted, two copper pans produced a loud sound in order to inform the observers at the other clock. This system proved cumbersome to operate and Chappe revised it to build what he called a *tachygraphe*. Again, a large clock with different symbols on the dial was installed on a tall structure. From below, the hand of the clock could be manipulated in order to point at a specific symbol. At another such clock in the distance, an observer with a telescope could read this symbol and adjust the hand of his clock accordingly. In this fashion, messages could be passed on along a line of such *tachygraphe* stations.

[8] Laszlo Solymar, *Getting the Message: A History of Communications* (Oxford: Oxford University Press, 1999), 14; Volker Aschoff, *Aus der Geschichte der Nachrichtentechnik* (Opladen: Westdeutscher Verlag, 1974), 17–18.

[9] On the history of optical telegraphy see, for instance, Klaus Beyrer and Birgit-Susann Mathis, eds., *So weit das Auge reicht: Die Geschichte der optischen Telegrafie* (Karlsruhe: Braun, 1995); Klaus Beyrer, 'Die optische Telegraphie als Beginn der modernen Telekommunikation', in *Vom Flügeltelegraphen zum Internet: Geschichte der modernen Telekommunikation*, ed. Hans-Jürgen Teuteberg and Cornelius Neutsch (Stuttgart: Franz Steiner Verlag, 1998); Alexander J. Field, 'French Optical Telegraphy, 1793–1855: Hardware, Software, Administration', *Technology and Culture* 35, no 2 (1994); Patrice Flichy, 'The Birth of Long Distance Communication: Semaphore Telegraphs in Europe (1790–1840)', *Réseaux* 1, no 1 (1993).

The system functioned but suffered from the limited visibility of the symbols and the low number of signal variations.[10] Therefore Chappe further improved the signalling works and eventually came up with a solution that would be in use in France in almost unchanged form for the next fifty years. A large wooden pole was mounted on each station. At the upper end of the pole, a movable beam about 4.5 metres in length was attached. And at each end of this beam, another shorter movable beam was mounted.[11] The position of all three beams could be manipulated from below via a system of wires and cranks. At the receiving station, the configuration of the beams could be read, reproduced and passed on to the next station in the relay chain. This system became known as the semaphore, or as optical or aerial telegraphy. Thanks to the telescope and the better general visibility of the large beams, the distance between stations could be considerably enlarged. On the first non-experimental line, over more than 200 kilometres between Paris and Lille, opened in 1794, the stations were between four and fifteen kilometres apart.[12] The line was inaugurated with a message from the front line stating that Condé had been retaken. The message was received at Paris only an hour after the actual event. In the face of the administrative and strategic challenges it faced, the young republic had a great demand for such swift communication. 'By the time Napoleon came to power, a further line linked Paris with Strasbourg in the east, another with Brest to the west, and the Lille line had been extended (in 1798) as far as Dunkirk. It was by no means far enough, in Napoleon's view.'[13] The French optical telegraph network was further expanded under Napoleon and thereafter. It developed into the largest and best-integrated system worldwide and remained operational well into the 1850s.[14]

In the United Kingdom, the first optical telegraph stations were erected only two years after the inauguration of the Paris–Lille line. A connection from London to Portsmouth was opened in 1796 and another one from London to Plymouth followed in 1805.[15] These lines were operated under the auspices of the British Admiralty and served purely military purposes.[16] One reason for their erection was the fear of a French invasion

[10] Huurdeman, *The Worldwide History of Telecommunications*, 20.

[11] Beyrer, 'Die optische Telegraphie als Beginn der modernen Telekommunikation', 14.

[12] Huurdeman, *The Worldwide History of Telecommunications*, 24.

[13] Andy Martin, 'Mentioned in Dispatches: Napoleon, Chappe and Chateaubriand', *Modern and Contemporary France* 8, no 4 (2000).

[14] Huurdeman, *The Worldwide History of Telecommunications*, 37. [15] Ibid., 41.

[16] For a detailed description of the British optical telegraph lines between London and the Norfolk harbours, see John F. Fone, 'Signalling from Norwich to the Coast in the Napoleonic Period', *Norfolk Archaeology* 42 (1996); H. V. James, 'The London–Yarmouth Telegraph Line 1806–1814', *Norfolk Archaeology* 37 (1978).

across the Channel. Instead of copying Chappe's design, the stations on these lines employed a shutter system. Mounted on a tall structure was a frame with six shutters that could be opened or closed. The different combinations of open and closed shutters stood for different letters that could then be passed along the line of stations.[17] Both in France[18] and in Britain at this point in time, the optical telegraph networks were reserved exclusively for administrative and military purposes. Answering to the existing demand for the transmission of private messages, a commercial optical telegraph line was opened between Liverpool and Holyhead in 1827. Another line from Hull to Spurn Head followed in 1839.[19] In France, a private stockholder-funded line between Paris and Rouen had been opened in 1831. It was financially unsuccessful and closed only a year later. To safeguard the government monopoly on telegraph communication, the French government prohibited the further establishment of private lines in 1837.[20]

During the early nineteenth century, optical telegraph lines were erected in other countries as well. A line from Berlin via Cologne to Koblenz was opened in 1834,[21] and several other mostly coastal connections were established in the United States, Australia and India.[22] Especially over shorter distances – for instance from a port to a nearby administrative centre – these lines worked reasonably well. Nevertheless, communication via optical telegraph did suffer from several severe drawbacks. First of all, swift and accurate communication depended on clear sight. The fall of night or adverse weather conditions impeded the working of the system.[23] Second, the transmission capacity and the speed of the system were limited due to the many relay stations involved. Third, a reasonably large network of optical telegraph stations needed a large

[17] Aschoff, *Aus der Geschichte der Nachrichtentechnik*, 24–5.

[18] Patrice A. Carré, 'From the Telegraph to the Telex: A History of Technology, Early Networks and Issues in France in the 19th and 20th Centuries', *Flux* 11 (1993), 22.

[19] Huurdeman, *The Worldwide History of Telecommunications*, 41.

[20] Flichy, 'The Birth of Long Distance Communication', 97.

[21] Beyrer, 'Die optische Telegraphie als Beginn der modernen Telekommunikation', 24.

[22] Gunakar Muley, 'The Introduction of Semaphore Telegraphy in Colonial India', in *Webs of History: Information, Communication and Technology from Early to Post-colonial India*, ed. Amiya Kumar Bagchi, Dipankar Sinha and Barnita Bagchi (New Delhi: Manohar, 2005).

[23] Gunakar Muley reproduces an anecdote that has long been circulating in substantially different versions in popular-history discussions of the semaphore. 'There is an interesting story about the Duke of Wellington, Arthur Wellesley, when in 1809, he was engaged in a war with the French troops in Spain. One day when the semaphore message "Wellington defeated" arrived in London, the city was soon plunged into gloom. Because of fog the last two words – "the French" – of the message were not clearly seen at that time. It was only after some time that the full message was received – "Wellington defeated the French", and then the gloom turned into joy.' Ibid., 169.

number of operators and was, therefore, costly both to erect and to maintain. Furthermore, if the semaphore code employed in communication was known, it was very easy to listen in. Finally, the optical telegraph could not be used to cross larger bodies of water or other natural obstacles to clear sight between the stations. Due to these shortcomings of optical signal transmission, outside France the technology was employed on individual routes only that never grew into communication networks in the full sense of the word. Only the emergence of electric telegraphy would eventually fill this gap.[24]

3.3 Inertia

In a well-known article published in 1967, Robert Heilbroner asked whether machines made history, and answered at least partially in the affirmative. One of the arguments he provided was the simultaneity of invention that can be observed in so many cases of scientific discovery or breakthroughs in engineering. Heilbroner put forward that the 'phenomenon of simultaneous discovery' in his view 'argues that the process of discovery takes place along a well-defined frontier of knowledge rather than in grab-bag fashion'.[25] Why this argument should in some way or another support the notion of technological determinism or the creed that machines indeed do make history remains entirely unclear. The observation itself, however, is absolutely accurate and applies, among many other examples, also to the case of electric telegraphy. Usually, the invention of the electric telegraph is credited to Samuel Finley Breese Morse and Alfred Vail in the United States, as well as to William Fothergill Cooke and Charles Wheatstone in the United Kingdom. Both pairs came up with slightly different solutions to the problem of electric information transmission at almost exactly the same time. Morse, originally a painter and from 1832 a professor at the University of the City of New York, had started to experiment with electric telegraphy in 1835. By 1837 his prototype had improved so much that it could be publicly demonstrated in his

[24] For a more detailed description of the technological evolution of telegraphy and wireless telegraphy than will be provided in the following pages see, for instance, Huurdeman, *The Worldwide History of Telecommunications*; Ken G. Beauchamp, *History of Telegraphy*, IEE History of Technology Series (London: Institution of Electrical Engineers, 2001); Lewis Coe, *The Telegraph: A History of Morse's Invention and Its Predecessors in the United States* (Jefferson and London: McFarland, 1993); Lewis Coe, *Wireless Radio: A Brief History* (Jefferson and London: McFarland, 1996).

[25] Robert Heilbroner, 'Do Machines Make History?', *Technology and Culture* 8, no 3 (1967), 337.

New York classroom.[26] In the same year, Cooke and Wheatstone obtained a patent that secured them the rights to exploit electric telegraphy in the United Kingdom. They demonstrated their version of the telegraph on a stretch of railway track between Euston and Camden Town stations in London that was operated by the London and Birmingham Railway.[27] Cooke had only come in touch with telegraphy a year earlier during a university lecture at Heidelberg, where Georg Wilhelm Muncke had discussed Paul Schilling von Canstatt's latest advances in the field of electric signal transmission.[28] The simultaneity of developments on both sides of the Atlantic, as well as the inspiration Cooke owed to Muncke and Schilling von Canstatt, illustrates that the electric telegraph was, indeed, not stumbled upon.

The very idea that information could be conveyed with the help of electricity had first been publicized in 1753. An anonymous author signing with the initials C. M. only described an 'expeditious method of conveying intelligence' in the *Scots' Magazine*. The method proposed built on the knowledge of the day: electricity could be produced by frictional machines and it was well known that electrostatic forces attracted very light objects such as pieces of paper. 'C. M. thus proposed using the electricity of a frictional machine, channelling it through the appropriate wires, and letting it attract the corresponding pieces of paper with the letter of the alphabet selected on the receiving side.'[29] This method never caught on due to its many impracticalities and its general unreliability. However, the idea had come at a time when the scientific understanding of electricity and its characteristics started to improve continuously through the contributions of such scientists as Ewald Jürgen von Kleist, Luigi Galvani, Alessandro Volta and – a little later – Michael Faraday.[30] And with greater knowledge and better instruments (such as the battery) at their disposal, a relatively large number of people started to look into other possibilities of using electricity to communicate. Among those were

[26] Huurdeman, *The Worldwide History of Telecommunications*, 56–7.

[27] Ibid., 67. James E. Brittain, 'Scanning the Past: Morse and the Telegraph', *Proceedings of the IEEE* 79 (1991), 591.

[28] Iwan R. Morus, 'The Electric Ariel: Telegraphy and Commercial Culture in Early Victorian England', *Victorian Studies* 39, no 1 (1995), 350.

[29] Huurdeman, *The Worldwide History of Telecommunications*, 48.

[30] For a discussion of Michael Faraday's contribution to the understanding of electricity and its connection to the telegraph industry, see Bruce J. Hunt, 'Michael Faraday, Cable Telegraphy and the Rise of Field Theory', in *History of Technology*, ed. Graham Hollister-Short and Frank A. J. L. James (London and New York: Mansell, 1991); Bruce J. Hunt, 'Doing Science in a Global Empire: Cable Telegraphy and Electrical Physics in Victorian Britain', in *Victorian Science in Context*, ed. Bernard Lightman (Chicago and London: The University of Chicago Press, 1997), 126–7.

Samuel Thomas von Soemmering in Munich and Francis Ronalds in London. The former constructed an electric telegraph that conveyed messages by causing a galvanic reaction and producing bubbles of hydrogen in an electrolytic liquid.[31] The latter, a London merchant, adapted and improved C. M.'s system in the garden of his house in Hammersmith.[32] There he erected two wooden structures connected by a wire of a total length of almost 13 kilometres. Ronalds connected a frictional machine to one end of the wire and a pair of pith balls to the other. When electric current was applied, the extremely lightweight pith balls would move apart. On the structures two synchronized dials with rotating hands were mounted. The sender would discharge the electric load when the hand at his dial indicated the letter he wanted to transmit. And at the receiving end, movement of the pith balls would prompt an observer to read his dial in precisely that moment.[33] Jeffrey Kieve mentions that this design would probably have failed in everyday use over longer distances due to the fact that high-voltage static electricity was used.[34] The showpiece in Ronalds's garden, however, worked nicely.

Indeed, the system functioned so satisfactorily that Francis Ronalds felt obliged to write to the Admiralty in order to advertise his apparatus. The reply, however, was unambiguous: the Admiralty had no need for any new form of telegraphic communication as its own optical telegraphs were working just fine.[35] This is a classical case of technological inertia. The term has been coined by Joel Mokyr and denotes the resistance to technological progress that stems from the 'built-in stability' of technological systems.[36] Despite the fact that Ronalds's apparatus (or a future improvement thereof) was superior to the existing solution, the Admiralty did not show even the slightest interest in the innovation. Prior investments had to be safeguarded. A winning team should not be changed. The possible gains from employing Ronalds's design were not yet great enough to overcome the inertia of the prevailing system. The same logic was at work in France. It was there that the optical telegraph network was densest and investments in the technology had been greatest. Accordingly, the

31 Keith Dawson, 'Electromagnetic Telegraphy: Early Ideas, Proposals, and Apparatus', *History of Technology* 1 (1976), 119.

32 More on Francis Ronalds and his apparatus can be learned from Volker Aschoff, *Nachrichtentechnische Entwicklung in der ersten Hälfte des 19. Jahrhunderts. Volume 2: Geschichte der Nachrichtentechnik* (Berlin, Heidelberg, New York, London, Paris and Tokyo: Springer, 1987), 29–43.

33 Huurdeman, *The Worldwide History of Telecommunications*, 49–50.

34 Kieve, *The Electric Telegraph*, 15.

35 Huurdeman, *The Worldwide History of Telecommunications*, 50; Kieve, *The Electric Telegraph*, 16.

36 Mokyr, 'Technological Inertia in Economic History', 327.

electric telegraph had a very slow start in France as the inertia of the established system was considerable.[37] Only in the 1850s could a real change of systems finally take place. And, as shall soon be seen, this was not the only instance of technological inertia seriously hampering the spread of electric telegraphy.

In 1820, Hans Christian Oersted discovered the principles of electromagnetism and thus placed a new method at the disposal of engineers working on electric signal transmission. In the following years, three different parties started to construct their own electric telegraphs. At the University of Göttingen, Carl Friedrich Gauss and Wilhelm Eduard Weber used an induction transmitter and a mirror-galvanometer to send (and detect) electric current over a wire. They erected an experimental line between Weber's astronomical observatory and Gauss's laboratory. They also developed an alphabetic code for their machine. But while their design worked very well, the two scientists had no inclination to exploit the system beyond its use for their experiments with electricity.[38] In 1835, Gauss and Weber were visited by Carl August von Steinheil, a professor of mathematics and physics at the University of Munich. They introduced him to their telegraph, and back in Munich Steinheil started to develop the apparatus further. Most notably, he reconfigured the machine so that the moving needles would leave marks on a paper strip on which the telegraphic message was recorded as a series of dots on two separate lines.[39] Steinheil also recognized the potential of a symbiosis between the emerging railways and the telegraph. Experimenting with a railway telegraph, he discovered the Earth's electrical conductivity, and thus greatly facilitated all further experiments in the field. Unfortunately, Steinheil's telegraph was never employed on any larger scale because, 'divided into some 100 autonomous states, territories, and towns, Germany was not, however, mature enough for electrical telegraphy: The first long optical telegraph line (Berlin–Coblenz) had only started to operate three years earlier',[40] in 1832.

Besides Gauss, Weber and Steinheil, Paul Schilling von Canstatt also worked on an electric telegraph in the 1820s and early 1830s.[41] Schilling

[37] See, for instance, Pascal Griset, 'France and the Adoption of the Electric Telegraph: An Achievement without a Real Future', in *Communication and Its Lines: Telegraphy in the 19th Century among Economy, Politics and Technology*, ed. Andrea Giuntini (Prato: Istituto di studi storici postali onlus, 2004).

[38] Huurdeman, *The Worldwide History of Telecommunications*, 50–2.

[39] Volker Aschoff, *Aus der Geschichte der Telegraphen-Codes* (Opladen: Westdeutscher Verlag, 1981), 26.

[40] Huurdeman, *The Worldwide History of Telecommunications*, 53.

[41] Volker Aschoff, *Paul Schilling von Canstatt und die Geschichte des elektromagnetischen Telegraphen* (Munich, Oldenbourg and Düsseldorf: VDI-Verlag, 1977).

von Canstatt had become acquainted with telegraphy while assisting Soemmering with his experiments in Munich between 1809 and 1811. After hearing about Oersted's findings, he started to use electromagnetically deflected needles to display the presence of electric current. In 1832, Schilling von Canstatt demonstrated his apparatus to Alexander von Humboldt in Berlin. And in 1835 he presented it to members of the Physikalische Verein in Frankfurt am Main in the presence of the aforementioned Georg Wilhelm Muncke. After a long time of official neglect, Schilling von Canstatt's telegraph eventually attracted the attention of both the British government and Tsar Nicholas I of Russia. Unfortunately, Schilling von Canstatt died in 1837 before his telegraph could be employed in practice. A copy of his original apparatus, however, had remained with Muncke, who used it in his lectures at Heidelberg – some of which were eventually attended by William Fothergill Cooke.[42]

Building on these advances in the understanding of electricity and on previous developments in electric signal transmission, the electric telegraph was then quickly brought to technological maturity on both sides of the Atlantic. Cooke and Wheatstone, as well as Morse and Vail (whose work also relied 'on artfully combining elements that had been anticipated by others'[43]), had demonstrated the potential of their machines in 1837. But initially nothing much happened. Morse found it difficult to convince Congress to support an experimental line between Washington and Baltimore and had wrestled with the difficulties of getting his patent acknowledged. In London, Cooke – like Steinheil before him – had recognized the potential of a symbiosis between the railways and the telegraph. A successful demonstration had taken place on a stretch of track of the London and Birmingham Railway. But the company would not adopt the telegraph even on this short stretch as it was found 'that the whistle is more advantageous and suitable at every respect' for the transmission of signals.[44] Until 1839, Cooke and Wheatstone could not convince a single railway company of the benefits of their apparatus. The spread of electric telegraphy, then, was slow – hampered by a shortness of funds and a general sense of mistrust towards 'the wires' on the part of the railway companies.[45] Once again, technological inertia and the stability of

[42] Huurdeman, *The Worldwide History of Telecommunications*, 54–5.

[43] Maury Klein, 'What Hath God Wrought?', *American Heritage of Invention and Technology* 8 (Spring 1993), 34.

[44] *Guide to the London and Birmingham Railway*, quoted in Kieve, *The Electric Telegraph*, 28.

[45] Steven Roberts, 'Distant Writing: A History of Telegraph Companies in Britain between 1838 and 1868' (2007), http://distantwriting.co.uk/default.aspx, 4; Kieve, *The Electric Telegraph*, 36.

existing technological systems delayed the expansion of telegraphy both in the United States and in the United Kingdom – albeit for slightly different reasons and with different means.

3.4 Technology-in-use

In 1842, Congress finally agreed to fund Morse's experimental line between Washington and Baltimore. Two years later, it went into operation and proved a success. At almost exactly the same time, Cooke eventually managed to convince the Great Western Railway Company to let him expand his telegraph lines along their tracks to the town of Slough near Windsor. He paid all expenses out of his own pocket and was gratified with the public and financial success of the line (see Chapter 7). Based on these successes in the United States and the United Kingdom, electric telegraphy gradually caught on and the first small networks started to emerge. Eventually the railway companies recognized the benefits that the telegraph brought to railway management and started to erect telegraph lines along their tracks. Finally, the telegraph left the phase of invention behind and became a technology-in-use in David Edgerton's sense of the term.[46]

In the early days of telegraphy, several different systems existed parallel to each other.

> The basic principle of the telegraph was quite straightforward. The apparatus consisted of a galvanic battery, a circuit breaker and some means of registering the presence of electricity in the circuit – in other words any one of the wide variety of instruments devised by the electricians to make the power of the battery visible.[47]

It was here and in the corresponding code systems that the prevailing apparatuses differed most. Morse's original design featured a device with a pencil that drew a flat line on a strip of moving paper when there was no current in the circuit. Whenever the circuit was closed, the pencil was deflected and the flat line was interrupted by an indentation (sometimes called a 'V'). The combination of several such indentations of different lengths and intervals allowed for the transmission of numbers and letters with the help of a still rather cumbersome counting code.[48] This system worked but was made significantly more efficient by two improvements devised by Alfred Vail, Morse's assistant and later associate. Vail changed

[46] Edgerton, 'From Innovation to Use'.
[47] Iwan R. Morus, 'Telegraphy and the Technology of Display: The Electricians and Samuel Morse', in *History of Technology*, ed. Graham Hollister-Short and Frank A. J. L. James (London and New York: Mansell, 1991), 31.
[48] Aschoff, *Aus der Geschichte der Telegraphen-Codes*, 29.

the writing mechanism in such a way that in default mode the pencil did not mark the paper. Only when current was applied did the pencil touch the moving paper strip. Depending on how long the circuit was closed, either a short dot or a longer dash appeared on the paper. Perhaps even more importantly, Vail also came up with a new code system using these dots and dashes to transmit the alphabet. Before developing the code, Vail had visited a print shop in order to find out which letters appeared most frequently in the English language. These letters were to be transmitted with shorter combinations of dots and dashes, while rarer letters were assigned more complicated combinations.[49] Thus the efficiency of the code improved significantly.

Cooke's and Wheatstone's original design worked differently. The so-called five-needle telegraph needed six different wires – one for each needle and another one for the alarm. On the receiving end, the needles were arranged along an axis from left to right. When no current was applied, the needles were at right angles to this axis. Each needle could be deflected individually either to the left or to the right. To transmit a symbol, current was applied to two wires and two needles were deflected in such a way as to point at a specific intersection on the board on which they were mounted. Every such intersection was associated with a letter of the alphabet. As only twenty different combinations were possible, the letters C, J, Q, U, X and Z had to be omitted.[50] The five-needle telegraph had the advantage that messages could be sent and received without the knowledge of a specific code. Letters could simply be read from the board. On the other hand, however, the design was expensive and relatively unreliable due to the many wires involved. Therefore Cooke and Wheatstone in a further step reduced the number of wires and needles. They developed both a single-needle and a double-needle telegraph and devised different codes for these systems. Again, the needles could be deflected either to the left or to the right. Different combinations of movements of either one or two needles were assigned letters of the alphabet. In the case of the single-needle telegraph, the resulting code contained twenty-three letters, omitting J, Q and Z.[51] The single-needle design was very straightforward, cheap and reliable. It was preferred by the railway and, for instance, employed on the line to Slough in 1843.[52]

49 Huurdeman, *The Worldwide History of Telecommunications*, 58–9.

50 Morus, 'Telegraphy and the Technology of Display', 31; Huurdeman, *The Worldwide History of Telecommunications*, 67.

51 Huurdeman, *The Worldwide History of Telecommunications*, 67–8.

52 On the Paddington–Slough line the single-needle telegraph was also used to send the message that led to the capture of the murderer John Tawell (see Chapter 2). Apparently, the omission of the letter Q had caused some confusion when the message was decoded at

The double-needle design, however, was more efficient and was used increasingly on commercial lines.

Cooke and Wheatstone also developed different versions of a pointer telegraph. Letters and numbers were arranged around a dial. When a button associated with a particular symbol was pressed by the sender, the pointer at the receiving end would move until it indicated the chosen symbol. While technically much improved, this design resembled some of the early telegraph prototypes involving synchronized dials.[53] In addition to the Morse system and the needle telegraphs, other inventors came up with their own designs. In Britain, Alexander Bain developed an electrochemical telegraph that exhibited two innovations. First, information input occurred through punched paper tape that was fed into the machine. Whenever punched dots and dashes occurred, the electric circuit was closed. Second, at the receiving instrument, a conducting pen glided over a strip of paper treated with potassium. Whenever a current was applied, the potassium ferric cyanide decomposed and left discoloured marks on the paper.[54] In the United States, Royal E. House developed a printing telegraph that recorded the received message in plain text. It was first used commercially in 1850.[55] Seven years later David Hughes got his own design patented. The Hughes teleprinter was efficient and easy to operate and produced a printed message at the receiving end. It was, however, a delicate piece of machinery and needed skilled mechanics for maintenance.[56] All these and many other designs by inventors such as Louis-François Breguet and others found their individual fields of application. For quite some time, all these systems were used in parallel, with the Morse and Cooke–Wheatstone designs clearly enjoying the widest use. Over the course of time, however, the necessary national and international standardization of telegraphy favoured the more widespread systems. Internationally, the Morse system and its various improvements started to emerge as the dominant design.[57] At the first international conference concerned with the standardization of international telegraphy in Paris in 1865, it was decided that only Morse telegraphs should be used in international

Paddington Station. Tawell had boarded the train dressed as a Quaker and could be easily identified by his attire. However, 'Quaker' had to be transmitted as 'Kwaker' – a newly created word that was not immediately understood at Paddington.

53 Huurdeman, *The Worldwide History of Telecommunications*, 69–70.

54 Morus, 'Telegraphy and the Technology of Display', 31.

55 Huurdeman, *The Worldwide History of Telecommunications*, 65. 56 Ibid., 103–4.

57 Franz Pichler, 'Die Einführung der Morse-Telegraphie in Deutschland und Österreich: Die konstruktive Entwicklung der Apparate', *Elektrotechnik und Informationstechnik* 9 (2006).

traffic.[58] At the follow-up conference in Vienna three years later, the convention was amended to allow Hughes apparatuses as well.[59] This, of course, provided a boost to the spread of both Morse and Hughes systems. Only in the United Kingdom and some smaller countries did the needle telegraphs prevail on any significant scale.

From the 1850s onwards, the desire to bridge large bodies of water telegraphically posed new technical challenges to telegraph engineers.[60] The conducting wire had to be insulated against salt water. At the same time, it had to withstand considerable forces stemming from ocean currents or ships' anchors. Furthermore, great distances had to be covered in one leg without the possibility of relay stations. Cables, therefore, were extraordinarily long and heavy and could only be put in place with special ships. The length of the wire also required a good understanding of the characteristics of electricity.[61] After several failed attempts, proper insulation became available in the form of gutta percha – a natural latex from tropical trees.[62] Unlike rubber, gutta percha 'retains its plasticity over time as well as under the extreme pressure and low temperatures that characterize the seafloor'.[63] The submarine telegraph cable that connected England and France across the Channel in 1851 was insulated with two layers of gutta percha per wire and worked satisfactorily for many decades.[64] After the successful Channel crossing, it was soon tried to cover greater distances. Bridging the Atlantic with a telegraph cable became the foremost goal in the field. Here, the sheer length of the cable created a number of entirely different problems. First, methods had to be developed to transport and eventually lay such big and heavy loads of cable. Also, some knowledge about the topography of the seafloor was necessary when laying cables in the deep sea. The development of ocean sounding greatly

[58] *Documents diplomatiques de la Conférence télégraphique internationale de Paris* (Paris: Imprimerie impériale, 1865), 9, Art. 3.

[59] *Documents de la Conférence télégraphique internationale de Vienne* (Vienna: Imprimerie impériale et royale de la cour et de l'état, 1868), 6, Art. 3.

[60] For an overview of technological innovations relating to submarine cable telegraphy, see Gillian Cookson, *The Cable: The Wire That Changed the World* (Stroud: Tempus, 2003); Cookson, 'Submarine Cables: Novelty and Innovations 1850–1870', *Transactions of the Newcomen Society* 76, no 2 (2006).

[61] Bernard Finn, 'Submarine Telegraphy: A Study in Technical Stagnation', in *Communications under the Seas: The Evolving Cable Network and Its Implications*, ed. Bernard Finn and Daqing Yang, Dibner Institute Studies in the History of Science and Technology (Cambridge, MA and London: MIT Press, 2009), 11.

[62] John Tully, 'A Victorian Ecological Disaster: Imperialism, the Telegraph, and Gutta-Percha', *Journal of World History* 20, no 4 (2009).

[63] Peter J. Hugill, *Global Communications since 1844: Geopolitics and Technology* (Baltimore: Johns Hopkins University Press, 1999), 29.

[64] Finn, 'Submarine Telegraphy', 11.

facilitated submarine cable laying in this respect.[65] And, of course, crossing such a large body of water did not allow for relay stations. The electric signal had to travel the entire distance in one leg. This created new problems as electric resistance increased with the length of the cable and so did the retardation of telegraphic signals that could easily render messages unintelligeable. The well-known story of Edward O. Wildman Whitehouse, the self-trained chief engineer on one of the first transatlantic cable expeditions, illustrates that contemporary understandings of the laws of electricity still needed improvement. The cable put in place by this expedition in 1858 was very short-lived. It failed for a number of reasons; one of them was that Whitehouse tried to overcome resistance and signal retardation by applying high voltage to the cable. Instead of getting signals through, this course of action practically roasted the cable.[66] The work of scientists such as William Thomson (later Lord Kelvin) and Michael Faraday,[67] however, contributed to a more profound understanding of the theory of electricity and soon made the exact transmission of signals possible – for instance, along the Persian Gulf cables of 1865 or the functioning transatlantic cable of 1866.

Peter Hugill divides the history of submarine telegraph cables into five distinct phases. In the experimental period lasting until 1858, most of the problems mentioned above had not been completely solved and cables over longer distances would not work beyond a few weeks. Hugill calls the

[65] For more information on ocean sounding and its connection with submarine telegraph cables, see, for instance, Sabine Höhler, 'Depth Records and Ocean Volumes: Ocean Profiling by Sounding Technology, 1850–1930', *History and Technology* 18, no 2 (2002); Höhler, 'A Sound Survey: The Technological Perception of Ocean Depth, 1850–1930' (paper presented at Transforming Spaces: The Topological Turn in Technology Studies, Darmstadt, 2003); Anita McConnell, *No Sea Too Deep: The History of Oceanographic Instruments* (Bristol: Hilger, 1982); McConnell, 'The Art of Submarine Cable-Laying: Its Contribution to Physical Oceanography', in *Ocean Sciences: Their History and Relation to Man. Proceedings of the 4th International Congress on the History of Oceanography, 23–29 September 1987*, ed. Walter Lenz and Margaret Deacon (Hamburg: Bundesamt für Seeschiffahrt und Hydrographie, 1990).

[66] See, for instance, Vary T. Coates and Bernard Finn, *A Retrospective Technology Assessment: Submarine Telegraphy – The Transatlantic Cable of 1866*, ed. Program of Policy Studies in Science and Technology (San Francisco: San Francisco Press, 1979), 30; Bruce J. Hunt, 'The Ohm Is Where the Art Is: British Telegraph Engineers and the Development of Electrical Standards', *Osiris* 9 (1994), 53; Hunt, 'Scientists, Engineers and Wildman Whitehouse: Measurement and Credibility in Early Cable Telegraphy', *British Journal for the History of Science* 29, no 101 (1996); Donard De Cogan, 'Dr E. O. W. Whitehouse and the 1858 trans-Atlantic Cable', *History of Technology* 10 (1985). De Cogan especially emphasizes that after the failure of the cable Wildman Whitehouse was a ready scapegoat and took most of the blame for the disaster. Indeed, however, many other factors, such as the poor quality of the material or rough handling of the cable, also contributed to its fast demise.

[67] Hunt, 'Michael Faraday, Cable Telegraphy and the Rise of Field Theory'.

second phase the 'successful but short-lived period, 1865–1869'. Preliminary solutions to most of the pressing problems had been found, but cable manufacturing, laying and operating had not yet been perfected. In the third 'period of low-speed lines, 1873–1882', the cables were reliable and long-lived but they were still limited in speed and capacity. The principal challenges of submarine cable laying, however, had been solved by this time. What followed in Hugill's final two phases from 1894 to 1910 and from 1923 to 1928 was merely an increase in speed and traffic.[68] Much of this general increase in speed and capacity (in submarine as well as in landline telegraphy) was connected with the constant improvement of input and output devices and with the development of *duplex* and later *quadruplex* telegraphy. Duplex telegraphy had first been patented by Joseph Stearns in 1872 in the United States. It rendered it possible to use one wire for signal transmission in both directions at the same time and thus doubled its capacity. Only a little later, Thomas Edison developed *diplex* telegraphy – a system that allowed for sending two messages simultaneously over the same line in the same direction. The combination of duplex and diplex became known as quadruplex telegraphy as it quadrupled the original capacity of a line.[69]

[68] Hugill, *Global Communications since 1844*, 29–35.

[69] Frank Hartmann, *Globale Medienkultur: Technik, Geschichte, Theorien* (Vienna: WUV/ UTB, 2006), 109.

4 Telegraphy in context

4.1 The telegraph as a tool of empire

In its issue of 10 December 1892, *Punch* published a caricature drawn by Edward Linley Sambourne which would soon become a classic (Figure 4.1). The caricature entitled 'The Rhodes Colossus Striding from Cape Town to Cairo' depicts Cecil Rhodes standing on the continent of Africa – his right foot in South Africa and his left in Egypt.[1] Today, it is reproduced in almost every textbook passage or historical study on the so-called Scramble for Africa in particular or British imperialism in general. Usually, it is used to illustrate Rhodes's Cape-to-Cairo idea that propagandized the acquisition of a continuous territory under British colonial control from South Africa to Egypt. In this context, the envisaged Cape-to-Cairo Railway is often mentioned as an instrument to establish and maintain control in the British colonies in Africa. What is mostly overlooked, however, is the fact that in the caricature Rhodes – in a gesture that could be interpreted as measuring distance – holds in his hands a telegraph wire that connects Cairo and the Cape. Actually, this wire is the central element in the drawing, which, together with the accompanying poem,[2] is a satirical reply to an article published in *The Times* of 30 November 1892. The piece reported a reception given for Rhodes at a London hotel, summarized the principal points of Rhodes's speech and climaxed with

> the most interesting and original part of MR. RHODES'S speech – the little surprise that he had prepared for the meeting. Dissociating himself for the moment from the Chartered Company, he announced that it was his intention, either with the help of his friends or by himself, to continue the telegraph northwards, across the Zambesi, through Nyassaland, and along Lake Tanganyika to Uganda. Nor is this all. A wire once carried to Uganda, said MR. RHODES, could not stop short of Wady Halfa. In other words, this colonial MONTE CRISTO means to cross the

[1] 'The Rhodes Colossus Striding from Cape Town to Cairo', *Punch, or the London Charivari* 103 (10 December 1892), 266.
[2] Ibid., 267.

Figure 4.1 *Punch* cartoon showing Cecil Rhodes, telegraph wire in hand.

Soudan, not to fight but to 'deal with' the MAHDI, and to complete the overland telegraph line from Cape Town to Cairo; that is, from England to the whole of her possessions, or colonies, or 'Spheres of influence' in Africa. The prospect is dazzling; for, as MR. RHODES says, with the telegraph there we would hear very little more of the abandonment of Uganda, and, of course, if the further and more serious extensions of the line were really made, our hold upon Egypt would be greatly strengthened.[3]

For Rhodes and many of his contemporary imperialists, the telegraph was primarily an instrument of imperial control that served administrative and strategic purposes. It facilitated communication between the different echelons of colonial rule and, in times of crisis, made the efficient movement of troops so much easier. In short, it strengthened Britain's grip on its far-flung territories. The telegraph was a prime *tool of empire.*[4] Especially regarding the uses of submarine cables (although Rhodes in the above case has been talking about a landline connection), these are some of the principal associations that contemporaries made when thinking of the worldwide telegraph network, so much of which

[3] 'The Enthusiastic Meeting Which Yesterday', *The Times*, 30 November 1892, 9.

[4] Daniel R. Headrick, *The Tools of Empire: Technology and European Imperialism in the Nineteenth Century* (New York: Oxford University Press, 1981).

was under British control. Therefore it is not surprising that much of the historical research on telegraphy has also chosen to look at the technology in the context of imperial control and territorial expansion. In general, after the Second World War, historians were relatively slow to identify the telegraph as a possible topic of their work. And when they did so, their focus either rested on the history of the transatlantic connection[5] – this feat of engineering that even Stefan Zweig chose to

[5] Among the early historical works on the transatlantic cable are Bern Dibner, *The Atlantic Cable* (Norwalk, CT: Burndy Library, 1959); Walter D. Freezee, 'The First Trans-Atlantic Cable', *Journal of the Washington Academy of Science* 68 (1978); F. Scowen, 'Transoceanic Submarine Telegraphy', *Transactions of the Newcomen Society* 48 (1978); Coates and Finn, *A Retrospective Technology Assessment*. Interest in the subject, however, remains unbroken. Among the newer works are the following: James R. Chiles, 'The Cable under the Sea', *American Heritage of Invention & Technology* 3 (Fall 1987); Donard De Cogan, 'Ireland, Telecommunications and International Politics, 1866–1922', *History Ireland* 1 (1993); Colin Hempstead, 'Representations of Transatlantic Telegraphy', *Engineering Science and Education Journal* 4, no 6 (1995); Pascal Griset, *Entreprise, technologie et souverainité: Les télécommunications transatlantiques de la France, XIX–XXe siècles*, ed. Institut d'Histoire de l'Industrie (Paris: Éditions rive droite, 1996); Donald R. Tarrant, *Atlantic Sentinel: Newfoundland's Role in Transatlantic Cable Communication* (St John's: Flanker Press, 1999); Gillian Cookson, 'The Transatlantic Telegraph Cable', *History Today* 50, no 3 (2000); Cookson, *The Cable*; Menahem Blondheim, '"Slender Bridges" of Misunderstanding: The Social Legacy of Transatlantic Cable Communications', in *Atlantic Communications: The Media in American and German History from the Seventeenth to the Twentieth Century*, ed. Norbert Finzsch and Ursula Lehmkuhl (Oxford and New York: Berg, 2004); John Steele Gordon, *A Thread across the Ocean: The Heroic Story of the Transatlantic Cable* (London: Simon & Schuster, 2002); Donard De Cogan and Dominic De Cogan, 'Private Enterprise and State Control in Trans-Atlantic Telegraph (The Early Period)', in *Communication and Its Lines: Telegraphy in the 19th Century among Economy, Politics and Technology*, ed. Andrea Giuntini (Prato: Istituto di studi storici postali onlus, 2004); Norbert Finzsch and Ursula Lehmkuhl, eds., *Atlantic Communications: The Media in American and German History from the Seventeenth to the Twentieth Century* (Oxford and New York: Berg, 2004); Jürgen Wilke, 'The Telegraph and the Transatlantic Communications Relations', in *Atlantic Communications: The Media in American and German History from the Seventeenth to the Twentieth Century*, ed. Norbert Finzsch and Ursula Lehmkuhl (Oxford and New York: Berg, 2004); Chester G. Hearn, *Circuits in the Sea: The Men, the Ships, and the Atlantic Cable* (Westport, CT: Praeger, 2004); Christian Holtorf, 'Die Modernisierung des nordatlantischen Raumes: Cyrus Field, Taliaferro Shaffner und das submarine Telegraphennetz von 1858', in *Ortsgespräche: Raum und Kommunikation im 19. und 20. Jahrhundert*, ed. Alexander C. T. Geppert, Uffa Jensen and Jörn Weinhold (Bielefeld: transcript, 2005); Christopher Hoag, 'The Atlantic Telegraph Cable and Capital Market Information Flows', *Journal of Economic History* 66, no 2 (2006); Pascal Griset, 'Je t'aime, moi non plus: The Development of Atlantic Submarine Cables and the Complexity of the French–American Dialogue, 1870–1960', in *Communications under the Seas: The Evolving Cable Network and Its Implications*, ed. Bernard Finn and Daqing Yang, Dibner Institute Studies in the History of Science and Technology (Cambridge, MA and London: MIT Press, 2009); Simone Müller, 'The Transatlantic Telegraphs and the *Class of 1866*: the Formative Years of Transnational Networks in Telegraphic Space, 1858–1884/89', in *Historical Social Research – Historische Sozialforschung. Global Communication: Telecommunication and Global Flows of Information in the Late 19th and Early 20th Century*, ed. Roland Wenzlhuemer (Cologne: Center for Historical Social Research, 2010).

commemorate as one of twelve (later fourteen) *Sternstunden der Menschheit*[6] – or on submarine and landline telegraphy as a means of power in an imperial world order.[7] Explicitly or implicitly, such research has certainly been influenced by Harold Innis's sweeping survey – first published in 1950 – on the relationship between empire and communications.[8]

Among the first studies discussing telegraphy in an imperial context were Christina Phelps Harris's article on the laying of the Persian Gulf submarine cables to India in 1864,[9] and Paul Kennedy's piece on cable communications and imperial strategy.[10] The former was written by a political scientist and published in a geographical journal. It is basically a description of the events leading to the establishment of the first submarine telegraph connection between Europe and India. The latter looked at the geostrategic significance of cable communication in the late nineteenth and early twentieth centuries and discussed British policy in this respect. Together with articles by Kenneth Inglis (examining telegraphic communication between England and Australia[11]) and Mel Gorman (looking at the establishment of a telegraph network in British India[12]) these two already set the tone for much of the historical research on telegraphy that was to come in the following decades. A larger-scale interest in the subject, however, was only triggered by the publication of Daniel Headrick's influential study *The Tools of Empire* in 1981.[13]

[6] Stefan Zweig, *Sternstunden der Menschheit: Vierzehn historische Miniaturen* (Frankfurt a. M.: S. Fischer, 2009) (translated in 1940 as *The Tide of Fortune: Twelve Historical Miniatures*).

[7] Since the late 1990s, several historical studies have also started to focus on the relationship between empires and imperial control on the one hand and information access, information gathering and information transmission on the other. See, for instance, Christopher A. Bayly, *Empire and Information: Intelligence Gathering and Social Communication in India, 1780–1870* (New York: Cambridge University Press, 1996). Renate Pieper, *Die Vermittlung einer neuen Welt: Amerika im Nachrichtennetz des Habsburgischen Imperiums 1493–1598*, ed. Heinz Durchhardt, Veröffentlichungen des Instituts für europäische Geschichte Mainz, Abteilung für Universalgeschichte (Mainz: Philipp von Zabern, 2000). Arndt Brendecke, *Imperium und Empirie: Funktionen des Wissens in der Spanischen Kolonialherrschaft* (Cologne, Weimar and Vienna: Böhlau, 2009).

[8] Harold A. Innis, *Empire and Communications* (Toronto: Dundurn Press, 2007).

[9] Christina Phelps Harris, 'The Persian Gulf Submarine Telegraph of 1864', *Geographical Journal* 135, no 2 (1969).

[10] Paul. M. Kennedy, 'Imperial Cable Communications and Strategy, 1870–1914', *English Historical Review* 86, no 341 (1971).

[11] Kenneth Stanley Inglis, 'The Imperial Connection: Telegraphic Communication between England and Australia, 1872–1902', in *Australia and Britain: Studies in a Changing Relationship*, ed. A. Frederick Madden and Wyndraeth Humphreys Morris-Jones, Studies in Commonwealth Politics and History (Sydney: Frank Cass, 1980).

[12] Mel Gorman, 'Sir William O'Shaughnessy, Lord Dalhousie, and the Establishment of the Telegraph System in India', *Technology and Culture* 12, no 4 (1971).

[13] Headrick, *The Tools of Empire.*

Here, Headrick examined a number of technological innovations, such as steamships, guns and railways, in terms of their role in expanding and maintaining European imperialism in the nineteenth century. The book contained only a relatively short and survey-style chapter of eight pages on submarine cables, but it embedded the subject in a larger context of technological innovation and imperialism, and thus triggered much scholarly interest in telegraphy. The author himself also chose to stay with and expand the subject and published a number of monographs and articles in this field.[14] The issue of global communication, imperial control and geopolitical supremacy was, among others, also taken up by Peter Hugill, Jill Hills and Peter McMahon in their monographs.[15] Robert Boyce traced the role of submarine cables in Britain's rise as a world power and looked at the discrepancies between the global and the local in the context of the Pacific telegraph cable.[16] In 2005, Duncan Bell discussed the connection between time, space and empire in British political thought, using submarine telegraphy and its impact on perceptions of time and space as one case

[14] For instance, Daniel R. Headrick, *The Tentacles of Progress: Technology Transfer in the Age of Imperialism, 1850–1940* (New York and Oxford: Oxford University Press, 1988); Headrick, *The Invisible Weapon*; Headrick, 'Radio versus Cable: International Telecommunications before Satellites' (1991), http://history.nasa.gov/SP-4217/ch1.htm; Headrick, *When Information Came of Age: Technologies of Knowledge in the Age of Reason and Revolution, 1700–1850* (Oxford and New York: Oxford University Press, 2000); Headrick, 'Strategic and Military Aspects of Submarine Telegraph Cables, 1851–1945', in *Communications under the Seas: The Evolving Cable Network and Its Implications*, ed. Bernard Finn and Daqing Yang, Dibner Institute Studies in the History of Science and Technology (Cambridge, MA and London: MIT Press, 2009); Headrick, 'A Double-Edged Sword: Communications and Imperial Control in British India', in *Historical Social Research – Historische Sozialforschung. Global Communication: Telecommunication and Global Flows of Information in the Late 19th and Early 20th Century*, ed. Roland Wenzlhuemer (Cologne: Center for Historical Social Research, 2010); Daniel R. Headrick and Pascal Griset, 'Submarine Telegraph Cables: Business and Politics, 1838–1939', *Business History Review* 75, no 3 (2001).

[15] Hugill, *Global Communications since 1844*; Hugill, 'The Geopolitical Implications of Communication under the Seas', in *Communications under the Seas: The Evolving Cable Network and Its Implications*, ed. Bernard Finn and Daqing Yang, Dibner Institute Studies in the History of Science and Technology (Cambridge, MA and London: MIT Press, 2009). Jill Hills, *The Struggle for Control of Global Communication: The Formative Century*, The History of Communication (Urbana: University of Illinois Press, 2002). Peter McMahon, *Global Control: Information Technology and Globalization since 1845* (Cheltenham: Edward Elgar, 2002); McMahon, 'Early Electrical Communications Technology and Structural Change in the International Political Economy: The Cases of Telegraphy and Radio', *Prometheus* 20, no 4 (2002).

[16] Robert Boyce, 'Submarine Cables as a Factor in Britain's Ascendancy as a World Power, 1850–1914', in *Kommunikationsrevolutionen: Die neuen Medien des 16. und 19. Jahrhunderts*, ed. Michael North (Cologne: Böhlau, 1995); Boyce, 'Imperial Dreams and National Realities: Britain, Canada and the Struggle for a Pacific Telegraph Cable, 1879–1902', *English Historical Review* 115, no 460 (2000).

study.[17] In a recent monograph, Deep Kanta Lahiri Choudhury focused on the relationship between imperialism, the control of communication and telegraphy using the example of British India.[18] The telegraph has also been discussed in the context of non-British colonial settings – for instance by Allain, Friedewald, Silva, Márquez, Shahvar and, most notably, Daqing Yang.[19] The technology has also been examined as an instrument of power in nineteenth-century China.[20] And exchanging the imperial for a more general international setting, the telegraph has also been recognized as an instrument of cross-government

[17] Duncan S. A. Bell, 'Dissolving Distance: Technology, Space, and Empire in British Political Thought, 1770–1900', *Journal of Modern History* 77, no 3 (2005).

[18] Deep Kanta Lahiri Choudhury, *Telegraphic Imperialism: Crisis and Panic in the Indian Empire, c.1830–1920* (Basingstoke: Palgrave Macmillan, 2010).

[19] Jean-Claude Allain, 'Strategic Independence and Security of Communications: The Undersea Telegraph Cables', in *Nationhood and Nationalism in France: From Boulangism to the Great War, 1889–1918*, ed. Robert Tombs (London and New York: HarperCollinsAcademic, 1991). Michael Friedewald, 'Funkentelegrafie und deutsche Kolonien: Technik als Mittel imperialistischer Politik', in *Kommunikation in Geschichte und Gegenwart: Vorträge der Jahrestagung der Georg-Agricola-Gesellschaft 2001 in München*, ed. Kai Handel (Freiberg/Sachsen: Georg-Agricola-Gesellschaft, 2002), 51–68. Ana Paula Silva, 'Portugal and the Building of Atlantic Telegraph Networks', *Journal of History of Science and Technology* 2 (2008); Silva, 'Shaping the Portuguese Empire in the 20th Century: The Telegraph and the Radio', *ICON* 7 (2001). Javier Márquez Quevedo, 'Telecommunications and Colonial Rivalry: European Telegraph Cables to the Canary Islands and Northwest Africa, 1883–1914', in *Historical Social Research – Historische Sozialforschung. Global Communication: Telecommunication and Global Flows of Information in the Late 19th and Early 20th Century*, ed. Roland Wenzlhuemer (Cologne: Center for Historical Social Research, 2010). Soli Shahvar, 'Concession Hunting in the Age of Reform: British Companies and the Search for Government Guarantees; Telegraph Concessions through Ottoman Territories, 1855–8', *Middle Eastern Studies* 38, no 4 (2002); Shahvar, 'Tribes and Telegraphs in Lower Iraq: The Muntafiq and the Baghdad–Basrah Telegraph Line of 1863–65', *Middle Eastern Studies* 39, no 1 (2003); Shahvar, 'Iron Poles, Wooden Poles: The Electric Telegraph and the Ottoman–Iranian Boundary Conflict, 1863–1865', *British Journal of Middle Eastern Studies* 34, no 1 (2007). Daqing Yang, *Technology of Empire: Telecommunications and Japanese Expansion in Asia, 1883–1945* (Cambridge, MA: Harvard University Asia Center, 2010); Yang, 'Submarine Cables and the Two Japanese Empires', in *Communications under the Seas: The Evolving Cable Network and Its Implications*, ed. Bernard Finn and Daqing Yang, Dibner Institute Studies in the History of Science and Technology (Cambridge, MA and London: MIT Press, 2009); Yang, 'Telecommunication and the Japanese Empire: A Preliminary Analysis of Telegraphic Traffic', in *Historical Social Research – Historische Sozialforschung. Global Communication: Telecommunication and Global Flows of Information in the Late 19th and Early 20th Century*, ed. Roland Wenzlhuemer (Cologne: Center for Historical Social Research, 2010).

[20] Erik Baark, *Lightning Wires: The Telegraph and China's Technological Modernization, 1860–1890*, Contributions in Asian Studies (Westport, CT: Greenwood Press, 1997); Yongming Zhou, *Historicizing Online Politics: Telegraphy, the Internet, and Political Participation in China* (Stanford, CA: Stanford University Press, 2006). For Korea, see Ung Kang, 'The Development of the Telegraph in Korea in the Late 19th Century', *Kagakusi Kenkyu* 30 (1991).

communication and international diplomacy[21] – on the nature of which the new technology made a significant impact.

All these studies have contributed significantly to our understanding of the relationship between empires and global communication. They show how politicians and colonial administrators alike were keen to benefit from swift communication between far-flung parts of the world and how global communication networks were thus formed by imperial interests. Only rarely, however, do most of these studies question this all-too-simple relationship between imperialism, globalization and communication in which technologies are reduced to mere instruments of empire and imperial control. Dwayne Winseck and Robert Pike were among the first to balance this approach by suggesting that the role of government interest might have been overstated in previous examinations of the emergence of a global telegraph network. In their work, they have shown that the global cable network was formed by a powerful and not always easy alliance between private corporations and governments,[22] in which the companies every so often were in the driving seat.[23] And recently, Paul Fletcher has shown that the employment of the telegraph by the imperial administration has not been as purposeful and outcome-oriented as suggested by most of the historical work in the

[21] David Paull Nickles, *Under the Wire: How the Telegraph Changed Diplomacy* (Cambridge, MA and London: Harvard University Press, 2003); Nickles, 'Telegraph Diplomats: The United States' Relations with France in 1848 and 1870', *Technology and Culture* 40, no 1 (1999); Nickles, 'Diplomatic Telegraph in American and German History', in *Atlantic Communications: The Media in American and German History from the Seventeenth to the Twentieth Century*, ed. Norbert Finzsch and Ursula Lehmkuhl (Oxford and New York: Berg, 2004); Nickles, 'Submarine Cables and Diplomatic Culture', in *Communications under the Seas: The Evolving Cable Network and Its Implications*, ed. Bernard Finn and Daqing Yang, Dibner Institute Studies in the History of Science and Technology (Cambridge, MA and London: MIT Press, 2009). Laszlo Solymar, 'The Effect of the Telegraph on Law and Order, War, Diplomacy, and Power Politics', *Interdisciplinary Science Reviews* 25, no 3 (2000). Jack Nicholls, 'The Impact of the Telegraph on Anglo-Japanese Diplomacy during the Nineteenth Century', *New Voices* 3, no 1 (2009). Keith Neilson, 'For Diplomatic, Economic, Strategic and Telegraphic Reasons: British Imperial Defence, the Middle East and India, 1914–1918', in *Far-Flung Lines: Essays on Imperial Defence in Honour of Donald Mackenzie Schurman*, ed. Greg Kennedy and Keith Neilson, Naval Policy and History (London and Portland: Frank Cass, 1997).

[22] Dwayne R. Winseck and Robert M. Pike, *Communication and Empire: Media, Markets, and Globalization, 1860–1930* (Durham, NC and London: Duke University Press, 2007); Dwayne R. Winseck, 'Back to the Future: Telecommunications, Online Information Services and Convergence from 1840 to 1910', *Media History* 5, no 2 (1999); Robert M. Pike and Dwayne R. Winseck, 'The Politics of Global Media Reform, 1907–23', *Media, Culture & Society* 26, no 5 (2004).

[23] Recently, the emergence of a nationwide telegraph and telephone network in the United States of America has been described along similar lines. See Richard R. John, *Network Nation: Inventing American Telecommunications* (Cambridge, MA and London: The Belknap Press of Harvard University Press, 2010).

field.[24] In plain words, Winseck and Pike primarily ask how the global telegraph network of the late nineteenth and early twentieth centuries came into being in the first place and how it developed its specific form. Fletcher, on the other hand, examines how colonial administrations use such a new technology and infrastructure once they become available. Both these strains of research emphasize the influence of economic interests on the structure and use of global communications in the nineteenth century – and thereby link the imperial setting of telegraph expansion with that of global trade and finance.

4.2 The telegraph in trade and finance

Returning to the opening example of this chapter, it should be added that Cecil Rhodes probably thought himself more the businessman than the colonial administrator or statesman. In practically all his actions, economic deliberations were present. The above quote from *The Times* states that Rhodes announced his intentions '[d]issociating himself for the moment from the Chartered Company'.[25] Rhodes was one of the directors of the British South Africa Company, which had been founded to propagate economic interests in southern and central Africa. The company had received a royal charter in 1889 and it has been said that '[n]o other chartered company appealed so strongly to the cupidity of the gamblers in the stock exchange'.[26] Of course, Rhodes's dissociation from his directorship was rhetorical only. The telegraph was as much an instrument of imperial control as it fostered business in the region and made hitherto hard-to-reach areas accessible to British produce and capital. In an imperial setting, it is almost impossible to separate territorial and economic interests, administrative and financial purposes. Therefore, as Winseck and Pike have shown, communication systems in the British Empire – across the oceans and on land – were usually shaped by a coalition of businessmen and politicians.

That is to say that from its very inception, the telegraph was intimately connected with the world of business, finance and trade – even when it

24 Paul Fletcher, 'The Uses and Limitations of Telegrams in Official Correspondence between Ceylon's Governor General and the Secretary of State for the Colonies, circa 1870–1900', in *Historical Social Research – Historische Sozialforschung. Global Communication: Telecommunication and Global Flows of Information in the Late 19th and Early 20th Century*, ed. Roland Wenzlhuemer (Cologne: Center for Historical Social Research, 2010).

25 'The Enthusiastic Meeting Which Yesterday', 9.

26 John S. Galbraith, *Crown and Charter: The Early Years of the British South Africa Company* (Berkeley, Los Angeles and London: University of California Press, 1974), x.

seemed that other interests were more important. Already in the days of optical telegraphy, several private lines had been built in the United Kingdom – e.g. from Holyhead to Liverpool or from Spurn Head to Hull[27] – to quickly bring information on arriving ships to the commercial centres. In France, where optical telegraphy was first a de facto and from 1837 also a de jure state monopoly, two bankers from Bordeaux bribed their way into the system in 1836 and paid signallers to convey hidden commercial information for them.[28] As will be discussed in more detail in Chapter 7, the British domestic telegraph network grew almost entirely out of business interests and saw practically no government involvement in its early days. The same can be said for the United States system. Even in British India, where the earliest telegraph lines were installed under government control as an answer to the events of 1857–8, commercial considerations were not completely absent (see Chapter 8). The benefits that telegraphic communication offered to merchants, bankers, investors or shipowners rested both in the speed and in the regularity of information flows. An article published in *The Times* on 4 April 1857 makes this point very well. The piece is not concerned with telegraphy – which in terms of a global network was still in its infancy[29] – but celebrates the arrival of the Peninsular & Oriental steamship *Simla* at Marseilles bringing 'dates from Sydney of February 11, from Melbourne of February 15, from Mauritius of March 1, and from Suez of March 26'.[30] The timely arrival of the *Simla* had proved the practicability of the route via Mauritius and established regular communication with Australia within about fifty days. Acknowledging this satisfactory result, *The Times* then goes on to

> congratulate the public, and in especial the mercantile community. Nothing could have been more injurious to the operations of trade than the extreme uncertainty which has too long characterized our communications with our Australian Colonies. Had there simply been tediousness and delay, so long as the delay and the tediousness were of regular occurrence the inconvenience, deplorable enough in all cases, might have been borne; but, with dates, varying from three months and a half to two months, it was well-nigh impossible to use forecast for the future . . . Our merchants must acquire the satisfactory conviction that they are not venturing

27 Huurdeman, *The Worldwide History of Telecommunications*, 41.

28 Flichy, 'The Birth of Long Distance Communication. Semaphore Telegraphs in Europe (1790–1840)', 96.

29 The network was, however, already tight enough in the Mediterranean to convey the news of the *Simla*'s arrival in Suez to London. In the same issue, *The Times* reprinted a telegram, dispatched in Alexandria on 28 March, saying, 'The Simla arrived at Suez on the 26th, bringing 48 passengers and 85,000 oz. of gold. Her dates are – Sydney, February 11; Melbourne, February 15; King George's Sound, February 22; the Mauritius, March 1; and Ceylon, March 10.' 'Australia', *The Times*, 4 April 1857, 10.

30 'The Arrival of the Simla at Marseilles Presents', *The Times*, 4 April 1857, 9.

their fortunes on a mere hazard when they engage in Australian operations, or else the trade will fall into the hands of mere speculators. Regularity, and then speed, are the necessary conditions of commercial intercourse.[31]

The article closes by asking, 'Is it a dream to suppose that ten years hence a man may be standing one day in London, and in forty days afterwards transacting business at our Antipodes?'[32] Reality distinctly outperformed this daring dream. Only fourteen years after the publication of the piece, Australia was incorporated into the global telegraph network and communication with London took no more than a few hours, or days at most. The benefit to the business community was the same as with regular steamship communication before. Swift and reliable flows of information made investments more predictable and thus safer. They opened up new markets for both capital and produce. And, of course, quick and accurate information itself developed into a commodity which had its very own value.

In the nineteenth-century world of business, the telegraph was employed in a number of different ways and with different effects. In 1978, the economists Kenneth Garbade and William Silber were among the first to examine systematically the impact of telegraphy on the performance of financial markets in the second half of the nineteenth century. They found that both domestic and intercontinental telegraphy led to an almost instant integration of financial markets.[33] In a case study on the functioning of the Buffalo agricultural commodity market published only one year later, geographer John Langdale showed that a reliable telegraphic connection to New York 'reduced the level of uncertainty and led to a more regular operation of the [Buffalo] market'.[34] Emphasizing the role of the London Stock Exchange, Ranald Michie also traced market integration through telegraphic information flows.[35] Mette Ejrnæs, Karl Gunnar Persson and Søren Rich recently highlighted the same mechanism regarding post-Corn Laws grain trade.[36] Stefano Baia Curioni and Luca Fantacci amended the view that telegraphy almost automatically

[31] Ibid., 9. [32] Ibid., 9.

[33] Kenneth D. Garbade and William L. Silber, 'Technology, Communication and the Performance of Financial Markets: 1840–1975', *Journal of Finance* 33, no 3 (1978).

[34] John Langdale, 'Impact of the Telegraph on the Buffalo Agricultural Commodity Market: 1846–1848', *Professional Geographer* 31, no 2 (1979), 169.

[35] Ranald C. Michie, 'The London Stock Exchange and the British Securities Market, 1850–1914', *Economic History Review*, New Series 38, no 1 (1985); Michie, 'Friend or Foe? Information Technology and the London Stock Exchange since 1700', *Journal of Historical Geography* 23, no 3 (1997).

[36] Mette Ejrnæa, Karl Gunnar Persson and Søren Rich, 'Feeding the British: Convergence and Market Efficiency in the Nineteenth-Century Grain Trade', *Economic History Review* 61, no. S1 (2008). Mette Ejrnæa and Karl Gunnar Persson, 'The Gains from Improved Market Efficiency: Trade before and after the Transatlantic Telegraph', *European Review of Economic History* 14, no 3 (2010).

entailed the integration of markets by observing that 'the relationship between development of the communications sector and development of markets therefore does not display univocal traits, but produces different solutions according to institutional and cultural conditions which are typical of the different markets'.[37] Furthermore, Alexander Field examined the effect of the telegraph on the transmission of financial asset and commodity prices as well as its consequences for economic growth.[38] More recently, David Hochfelder has shown how telegraphic flows of market information made it easier for the general public to participate in financial markets in the closing decades of the nineteenth century.[39]

More concerned with general market structures than with purely financial products are several contributions by such researchers as Richard Du Boff or JoAnne Yates.[40] Du Boff makes the interesting point that telegraphy 'improved the functioning of markets and enhanced competition, but it simultaneously strengthened forces making for monopolization'.[41] He thus showed that new technologies can have very different, sometimes seemingly contradictory, impacts in different social, economic and cultural settings. Examining the ramifications of improved steamship and telegraphic communication between London and Japan, as well as with British West Africa, Peter Davies demonstrated that swift transport and communication lowered the capital requirements of merchants and generally facilitated long-distance

[37] Stefano Baia Curioni and Luca Fantacci, 'Telegraphy and New Financial Procedures', in *Communication and Its Lines: Telegraphy in the 19th Century among Economy, Politics and Technology*, ed. Andrea Giuntini (Prato: Istituto di studi storici postali onlus, 2004).

[38] Alexander J. Field, 'The Magnetic Telegraph, Price and Quantity Data, and the New Management of Capital', *Journal of Economic History* 52, no 2 (1992); Field, 'The Telegraphic Transmission of Financial Asset Prices and Orders to Trade: Implications for Economic Growth, Trading Volume, and Securities Market Regulation', in *Research in Economic History*, ed. Alexander J. Field (Stamford and London: JAI, 1998).

[39] David Hochfelder, '"Where the Common People Could Speculate": The Ticker, Bucket Shops, and the Origins of Popular Participation in Financial Markets, 1880–1920', *Journal of American History* 93, no 2 (2006). For a related argument, see also J. Peter Ferderer, 'Advances in Communication Technology and Growth of the American over-the-Counter Markets, 1876–1929', *Journal of Economic History* 68, no 2 (2008).

[40] Richard B. Du Boff, 'Business Demand and the Development of the Telegraph in the United States, 1844–1860', *Business History Review* 54, no 4 (1980); Du Boff, 'The Telegraph in Nineteenth-Century America: Technology and Monopoly', *Comparative Studies in Society and History* 26, no 4 (1984); Du Boff, 'The Rise of Communications Regulation: The Telegraph Industry, 1844–1880', *Journal of Communication* 34, no 3 (1984). JoAnne Yates, 'The Telegraph's Effect on Nineteenth Century Market and Firms', *Business and Economic History* 15 (1986).

[41] Richard B. Du Boff, 'The Telegraph and the Structure of Markets in the United States, 1845–1890', in *Commercial and Financial Services*, ed. Ranald C. Michie (Oxford and Cambridge, MA: Basil Blackwell, 1994), 253.

trade.[42] Mika Kallioinen explored the same context by looking at the concrete case of a Finnish merchant house and its worldwide correspondence.[43] Both Jorma Ahvenainen[44] – who has written extensively on the history of telegraphy[45] – and Yrjö Kaukiainen have analysed the increasing speed of the flow of shipping information from ports all over the world to London throughout the nineteenth century.[46] Also focusing on the connection between intercontinental shipping and telegraphy, Lars Scholl, Birgitte Holten and Byron Lew and Bruce Cater have demonstrated that global telegraphy also placed new means of control into the hands of merchants and shipowners who could now co-ordinate their tramp ships from European headquarters.[47] All these studies have revealed and often requalified the intimate relationship between the telegraph and commerce – a relationship that impacted in many ways on the form and the applications of the global telegraph network.

4.3 The telegraph and the news

By November 1914, the SMS *Emden* had already built a reputation. Since the outbreak of the First World War, the German light cruiser had been very successfully engaged in independent raids on Allied – mostly

[42] Peter N. Davies, 'The Impact of Improving Communications on Commercial Transactions: Nineteenth-Century Case Studies from British West Africa and Japan', *International Journal of Maritime History* 14, no 1 (2002).

[43] Mika Kallioinen, 'Information, Communication, Technology, and Business in the Nineteenth Century: The Case of a Finnish Merchant House', *Scandinavian Economic History Review* 102, no 1 (2004).

[44] Jorma Ahvenainen, 'Telegraphs, Trade and Policy: The Role of the International Telegraphs in the Years 1870–1914', in *Commercial and Financial Services*, ed. Ranald C. Michie (Oxford and Cambridge, MA: Basil Blackwell, 1994).

[45] Jorma Ahvenainen, *The Far Eastern Telegraphs: The History of Telegraphic Communications between the Far East, Europe and America before the First World War* (Helsinki: Finnish Academy of Science and Letters, 1981); Ahvenainen, 'The Role of Telegraphs in the 19th Century Revolution of Communications', in *Kommunikationsrevolutionen: Die neuen Medien des 16. und 19. Jahrhunderts*, ed. Michael North (Cologne: Böhlau, 1995); Ahvenainen, *The History of the Caribbean Telegraphs before the First World War* (Helsinki: Finnish Academy of Science and Letters, 1996); Ahvenainen, *The European Cable Companies in South America before the First World War* (Helsinki: Finnish Academy of Science and Letters, 2004); Ahvenainen, 'The International Telegraph Union: The Cable Companies and the Governments', in *Communications under the Seas: The Evolving Cable Network and Its Implications*, ed. Bernard Finn and Daqing Yang, Dibner Institute Studies in the History of Science and Technology (Cambridge, MA and London: MIT Press, 2009); John A. Britton and Jorma Ahvenainen, 'Showdown in South America: James Scrymser, John Pender, and United States–British Cable Competition', *Business History Review* 78 (2004).

[46] Kaukiainen, 'Shrinking the World.

[47] Scholl, 'The Global Communication Industry'. Holten, 'Telegraphy and Business Methods in the Late 19th Century'. Byron Lew and Bruce Cater, 'The Telegraph, Co-ordination of Tramp Shipping, and Growth in World Trade, 1870–1910', *European Review of Economic History* 10, no 2 (2006).

British – vessels and other strategic targets in the Indian Ocean. On 9 November, the *Emden* was approaching Direction Island – one of the Cocos Islands – which housed an important cable and wireless relay station of the Eastern Telegraph Company. It was Captain Karl von Müller's plan to destroy the station and thus cripple British communication in the Indian Ocean region. A landing party led by Lieutenant Commander Hellmuth von Mücke was sent ashore to carry out this business. The *Emden* had, however, been spotted when approaching and the telegraph crew on Direction Island had dispatched a wireless call for help to which the HMAS *Sydney* responded. The *Sydney* reached the island while the *Emden*'s landing party was still ashore, engaged the German ship in a sea battle and hit it so severely that von Müller had to run it aground in order to avoid sinking. The *Emden* eventually surrendered. In the meantime, the landing party seized the schooner *Ayesha* anchored at Direction Island and managed to escape. Under the command of von Mücke, they avoided capture and in an odyssey via Sumatra, the Arabian Peninsula and Constantinople returned to Germany where they received a hero's welcome. Back at home, von Mücke wrote two books about his adventures called *The Emden* and *The Ayesha*. The latter opens with von Mücke and his party landing on Direction Island – and the *Sydney* not yet a problem.

With our machine guns and firearms ready for action, we landed at a little dock on the beach, without meeting with resistance of any kind, and, falling into step, we promptly proceeded to the wireless station … We quickly found the telegraph building and the wireless station, took possession of both of them, and so prevented any attempt to send signals. Then I got hold of one of the Englishmen who were swarming about us, and ordered him to summon the director of the station, who soon made his appearance, – a very agreeable and portly gentleman.

'I have orders to destroy the wireless and telegraph station, and I advise you to make no resistance. It will be to your own interest, moreover, to hand over the keys of the several houses at once, as that will relieve me of the necessity of forcing the doors. All firearms in your possession are to be delivered immediately. All Europeans on the island are to assemble in the square in front of the telegraph building.'

The director seemed to accept the situation very calmly. He assured me that he had not the least intention of resisting, and then produced a huge bunch of keys from out his pocket [*sic*], pointed out the houses in which there was electric apparatus of which we had as yet not taken possession, and finished with the remark: 'And now, please accept my congratulations.'

'Congratulations! Well, what for?' I asked with some surprise.

'The Iron Cross has been conferred on you. We learned of it from the Reuter telegram that has just been sent on.'[48]

[48] Hellmuth von Mücke, *The 'Ayesha': Being the Adventures of the Landing Squad of the 'Emden'* (Boston, MA: Ritter & Company, 1917), 3–6.

The press was among the first regular customers of telegraphic services in a national as well as in an international context and usually enjoyed special rates for press telegrams. A quick and constant inflow of information from all parts of the world enabled the newspapers to present their readers with the most up-to-date and accurate news and was, therefore, very much in their interest. Already in the early days of telegraphy, the telegraph companies in the United Kingdom, for instance, started to provide time-critical information about race results and stock-market prices to the papers on a regular basis.[49] In France and Germany, Agence Havas and Wolffs Telegraphisches Bureau[50] started to collect and distribute stock market information and other news via the telegraph in the late 1840s.[51] Even before the foundation of Associated Press in 1846 in the United States, a privately organized wire service had started to provide upstate New York newspapers with telegraphic information.[52] In England, Paul Julius Reuter was among the first to recognize the economic potential of the increasing desire for quick news from abroad.[53] Shortly before the opening of the first cable across the English Channel in 1851, he set up an office in London and negotiated the right to exchange stock-market prices between Paris and London. Soon, Reuter's company also sent other reports and news as well and developed into a fully fledged news agency relying on a worldwide network of correspondents and the services of the telegraph.[54] 'Following the progress of the cable, Reuters opened offices in Alexandria in 1865, Bombay in 1866, Melbourne and Sydney in 1874 and Cape Town in 1876.'[55] Paul Julius Reuter's motto was, indeed, 'Follow the Cable',[56] and this he did so successfully that Havas was

[49] Roberts, 'Distant Writing', 55.

[50] Dieter Basse, *Wolff's Telegraphisches Bureau 1849 bis 1933: Agenturpublizistik zwischen Politik und Wirtschaft*, Kommunikation und Politik (Munich and New York: K. G. Saur, 1991).

[51] Jürgen Wilke, *Grundzüge der Medien- und Kommunikationsgeschichte* (Cologne, Weimar and Vienna: Böhlau, 2008), 245.

[52] Richard Schwarzlose, 'The Nation's First Wire Service: Evidence Supporting a Footnote', *Journalism Quarterly* 57 (1980); Schwarzlose, 'Early Telegraphic News Dispatches: Forerunners of the AP', *Journalism Quarterly* 51 (1974).

[53] For an interesting assessment of Reuter's idea of information, news or intelligence, see Toni Weller and David Bawden, 'Individual Perceptions: A New Chapter on Victorian Information History', *Library History* 22, no 2 (2006), 145–8.

[54] For a comprehensive history of Reuters, see Donald Read, *The Power of News: The History of Reuters* (Oxford: Oxford University Press, 1999).

[55] Terhi Rantanen, 'The Globalization of Electronic News in the 19th Century', *Media, Culture & Society* 19, no 4 (1997), 613; Rantanen, *When News Was New* (Malden, Oxford and Chichester: Wiley-Blackwell, 2009), 51.

[56] Donald Read, 'Reuters: News Agency of the British Empire', *Contemporary British History* 8, no 2 (1994), 202. Jeremy Tunstall and Michael Palmer, *Media Moguls* (London and New York: Routledge, 1991), 51.

compelled to remark in 1909, 'Thanks to the English telegraphic cable installations connecting every world centre, London easily dominates all the news agencies'.[57] During the second half of the nineteenth century, newspapers and governments alike had become dependent on a cartel of four news agencies (Reuters, Havas, Wolff and Associated Press), which controlled the global flow of information.[58] These agencies' reliance on the global telegraph network impacted on the nature of news flows, which were also shaped by the rationale of the network. Important news travelled along telegraph lines. And wherever there were such lines, there was also the latest news, as the above episode of Lieutenant Commander von Mücke and the Iron Cross aptly illustrates. With the help of telegraphic transmission, news could outpace its protagonists, geographical peripheries could become information centres and vice versa. The association of news distribution and telegraphy contributed significantly to the ongoing transformation of global space.

Reuters maintained close connections to the British government and the principal cable companies. It has, therefore, rightly been described as a 'semi-official institution' of the British Empire.[59] Accordingly, the flow of telegraphic news was intimately connected not only with the structure of the cable network but also with imperial policies. Therefore news and telegraphy have often been discussed in the context of the British Empire – for instance, by Chandrika Kaul, Simon Potter, Denis Cryle and Ross Harvey[60] – and thus in a global context. But news agencies and other news services were also active on a national scale and made use of telegraphic information transmission in this setting as well. And within both a global and a national framework, news transmission by telegraph had a decisive impact not only on the

[57] Havas-Paris to its London correspondent, Mercadier, 14 May 1909, quoted in Tunstall and Palmer, *Media Moguls*, 51.

[58] Alex Nalbach, '"Poisoned at the Source"? Telegraphic News Services and Big Business in the Nineteenth Century', *Business History Review* 77, no 4 (2003).

[59] Read, *The Power of News*.

[60] Chandrika Kaul, 'A New Angle of Vision: The London Press, Governmental Information Management and the Indian Empire, 1900–22', *Contemporary British History* 8, no 2 (1994); Kaul, *Reporting the Raj: The British Press and India, 1880–1922* (Manchester: Manchester University Press, 2003). Simon J. Potter, 'Communication and Integration: The British and Dominions Press and the British World, c.1876–1914', *Journal of Imperial and Commonwealth History* 31, no 2 (2003); Potter, *News and the British World: The Emergence of an Imperial Press System, 1876–1922* (Oxford: Oxford University Press, 2003). Denis Cryle, 'Peripheral Politics? Antipodean Interventions in Imperial News and Cable Communication (1870–1912)', in *Media and the British Empire*, ed. Chandrika Kaul (Basingstoke and New York: Palgrave Macmillan, 2006). Ross Harvey, 'A "Sense of Common Citizenship"? Mrs Potts of Reefton, New Zealand, Communicates with the Empire', in *Media and the British Empire*, ed. Chandrika Kaul (Basingstoke and New York: Palgrave Macmillan, 2006).

issues of from which regions news reached its consumers and within what time frame, but also on the content and the nature of the news.[61] Already in 1967, Donald Shaw demonstrated that the growing reliance on telegraphic news led to a decline of bias in reports about presidential campaigns in the late nineteenth-century United States.[62] And more recently, Amelia Bonea has examined how reliance on telegraphic news flows conditioned the contents and scope of reports on the Austro-Prussian War of 1866 in the *Times of India*.[63]

4.4 Society and culture

On 21 February 1880, *Chambers's Journal of Popular Literature, Science and Arts* printed a collection of anecdotes and memorable stories concerned with mishaps in the everyday use of the telegraph. Among the stories related was the following:

> A noble lord, as proud and fond as a man should be of his beautiful young wife, was just about rising to speak in a debate, when a telegram was put into his hands. He read it, left the House, jumped into a cab, drove to Charing Cross, and took the train to Dover. Next day he returned home, rushed into his wife's room, and finding her there, upbraided the astonished lady in no measured terms. She protested her ignorance of having done anything to offend him.
>
> 'Then what did you mean by your telegram?' he asked.
>
> 'Mean? What I said of course. What are you talking about?'
>
> 'Read it for yourself,' said he.
>
> She read: 'I flee with Mr — to Dover straight. Pray for me.'
>
> For the moment words would not come; then after a merry fit of laughter, the suspected wife, quietly remarked: 'O those dreadful telegraph people! No wonder

[61] For an introduction to pre-telegraphic and telegraphic news gathering (primarily in the United States and British North America), see Richard B. Kielbowicz, 'News Gathering by Printers' Exchanges before the Telegraph', *Journalism History* 9 (1982); Kielbowicz, 'News Gathering by Mail in the Age of the Telegraph: Adapting to a New Technology', *Technology and Culture* 28, no 1 (1987). Peter G. Goheen, 'The Impact of the Telegraph on the Newspaper in Mid-Nineteenth Century British North America', *Urban Geography* 11, no 2 (1990); Menahem Blondheim, *News over the Wires: The Telegraph and the Flow of Public Information in America, 1844–1897* (Cambridge, MA: Harvard University Press, 1994); Blondheim, 'Rehearsal for Media Regulation: Congress versus the Telegraph-News Monopoly, 1866–1900', *Federal Communications Law Journal* 56, no 2 (2004).

[62] Donald L. Shaw, 'News Bias and the Telegraph: A Study of Historical Change', *Journalism Quarterly* 44 (Spring 1967).

[63] Amelia Bonea, 'The Medium and Its Message: Reporting the Austro-Prussian War in the *Times of India*', in *Historical Social Research – Historische Sozialforschung. Global Communication: Telecommunication and Global Flows of Information in the Late 19th and Early 20th Century*, ed. Roland Wenzlhuemer (Cologne: Center for Historical Social Research, 2010).

you are out of your mind, dear. I telegraphed simply: "I tea with Mrs — in Dover Street. Stay for me."'[64]

Of course, it is doubtful – although not entirely impossible – that this episode had taken place in exactly the described way. The very existence of this – and several other – anecdote collections concerned mainly with the telegraph in everyday, life situations is in itself testimony to the fact that telegraphic communication had quickly become a feature of daily routine for certain groups of people in the late nineteenth century. And as such, the technology had a transformative impact on many established cultural practices outside the more obvious realms of imperial control, global business or news delivery. In the above story, the telegram had become a means of household communication used for the conveyance of the apparently most trivial information. The triviality of the message is satirically reinforced by the delivery of the telegram at the exact moment when its recipient 'was just about rising to speak in a debate'. And the punchline, of course, thrives on the changes in grammar and style that telegraphic communication so often entailed, the decontextualization of information and the misunderstandings that can arise from this.

James W. Carey has been among the first to notice (and to write about) the transformation of cultural practices and its connection with what he has called 'ideology'. In 1983, Carey stated in his essay 'Technology and Ideology: The Case of the Telegraph', 'The effect of the telegraph on modern life and its role as a model for future developments in communications have scarcely been explored . . . I take the neglect of the telegraph to be unfortunate for a number of reasons.'[65] While the first two reasons which Carey gives are still close to established ways of thinking about the technology, his third point broke new ground:

> Third, the telegraph brought about changes in the nature of language, of ordinary knowledge, of the very structures of awareness. While the telegraph in its early days was used as a toy – as was the computer, which it prefigured – for playing long-distance chess, its implications for human knowledge were the subject of extended, often euphoric, and often pessimistic debate.[66]

In the course of the essay, as well as in a revised and amended version he published as part of his 1989 book *Communication as Culture*,[67] Carey presents a *tour de force* of telegraph history and 'treat[s] the transformation

[64] 'Tales of the Telegraph', *Chambers's Journal of Popular Literature, Science and Arts*, no 843 (1880), 127.

[65] Carey, 'Technology and Ideology', 303. [66] Ibid., 304.

[67] James W. Carey, *Communication as Culture: Essays on Media and Society*, ed. David Thorburn, Media and Popular Culture: A Series of Critical Books (Boston: Unwin Hyman, 1989).

of time, space, ideology, language, markets, journalism, and the Sabbath in supple and elegant ways'.[68] While it might be going slightly too far to say that *Technology and Ideology* 'all but single-handedly rescued the telegraph from scholarly neglect, raising it to its current status as the canonical fountainhead of electronic media',[69] it did draw attention to the role of telegraphy in more mundane but certainly not less rewarding contexts.

Building on many of Carey's thoughts and suggestions, research on the sociocultural significance of telegraphy has increased in both quantity and quality since the publication of Carey's writings in the 1980s. For instance, the impact of telegraphic communication on language has started to receive attention from linguists, historians and literature studies scholars alike.[70] Other researchers examined not so much the functioning of the technology itself, but rather its perception and representation. Iwan Morus and Yakup Bektas have looked at the ways in which the telegraph was presented and put on display by its inventors and their agents.[71] Elsewhere, Bektas has also examined the cultural construction of the technology in the Ottoman Empire.[72] Colin Hempstead has worked on newspaper representations of the transatlantic telegraph,[73] and Richard Noakes has touched upon contemporary expectations of the telegraph that literally transcended its known purposes.[74] Telegraphic

[68] John Durham Peters, 'Technology and Ideology: The Case of the Telegraph Revisited', in *Thinking with James Carey: Essays on Communications, Transportation, History*, ed. Jeremy Packer and Craig Robertson (New York, Washington, Bern, Frankfurt a. M., Berlin, Brussels, Vienna and Oxford: Peter Lang, 2006), 137.

[69] Ibid., 37–8.

[70] Ellen L. Barton, 'The Grammar of Telegraphic Structures: Sentential and Nonsentential Derivation', *Journal of English Linguistics* 26, no 1 (1998). Deep Kanta Lahiri Choudhury, 'Of Codes and Coda: Meaning in Telegraph Messages, circa 1850–1920', in *Historical Social Research – Historische Sozialforschung. Global Communication: Telecommunication and Global Flows of Information in the Late 19th and Early 20th Century*, ed. Roland Wenzlhuemer (Cologne: Center for Historical Social Research, 2010). Jerusha Hull McCormack, 'Domesticating Delphi: Emily Dickinson and the Electro-Magnetic Telegraph', *American Quarterly* 55, no 4 (2003); Marc Föcking, 'Drei Verbindungen: Lyrik. Telefon. Telegrafie 1900–1913 (Liliencron. Altenberg. Apollinaire)', in *Die schönen und die nützlichen Künste: Literatur, Technik und Medien seit der Aufklärung*, ed. Knut Hickethier and Katja Schumann (Munich: Fink, 2007).

[71] Morus, 'Telegraphy and the Technology of Display'. Yakup Bektas, 'Displaying the American Genius: The Electromagnetic Telegraph in the Wider World', *British Journal for the History of Science* 34, no 2 (2001).

[72] Yakup Bektas, 'The Sultan's Messenger: Cultural Constructions of Ottoman Telegraphy, 1847–1880', *Technology and Culture* 41, no 4 (2000).

[73] Hempstead, 'Representations of Transatlantic Telegraphy'.

[74] Richard J. Noakes, 'Telegraphy Is an Occult Art: Cromwell Fleetwood Varley and the Diffusion of Electricity to the Other World', *British Journal for the History of Science* 32, no 4 (1999).

communication was also a relatively frequent element of nineteenth- and early twentieth-century fiction – for instance, in *The Count of Monte Cristo*, several Sherlock Holmes stories or Henry James's *In the Cage*.[75]

The widespread use of the telegraph also brought with it changes in the social fabric. Nevertheless, 'the social consequences of the new communication medium have been neglected almost completely' by historians.[76] To date, only a handful of studies in this regard exist. In 1988, Edwin Gabler studied the new professional group of telegraphers in an American, mostly Western Union, context.[77] Almost a decade later, Annteresa Lubrano published a book that promised to examine 'how technology innovation caused social change' but which fell considerably short of this goal.[78] Only five years later, however, Gregory Downey presented a compelling study of telegraph messenger boys and thus traced how telegraphy led to the emergence of a new social group.[79] In 2003, Downey and Aad Blok edited a volume that put the same theme of information technology and labour into a wider context.[80] And, of course, the role of women in the telegraph offices and general questions of gender in the telegraph industry have also started to receive attention from historians.[81]

[75] Geoffrey Winthrop-Young, 'The Informatics of Revenge: Telegraphy, Speed and Storage in *The Count of Monte Cristo*', *Weber Studies: An Interdisciplinary Humanities Journal* 14, no 1 (1997). Robert N. Brodie, '"Take a Wire, Like a Good Fellow": The Telegraph in the Canon', *Baker Street Journal: An Irregular Quarterly of Sherlockiana* 41, no 3 (1991). Tomas Pollard, 'Telegraphing the Sentence and the Story: Iconicity in *In the Cage* by Henry James', *European Journal of English Studies* 5, no 1 (2001); Richard Menke, 'Telegraphic Realism: Henry James's *In the Cage*', *Modern Language Association* 115, no 5 (2000); Andrew J. Moody, '"The Harmless Pleasure of Knowing": Privacy in the Telegraph Office and Henry James's "In the Cage"', *Henry James Review* 16, no 1 (1995).

[76] English-language abstract in Michael Mann, 'Telekommunikation in Britisch-Indien (ca. 1850–1930). Ein globalgeschichtliches Paradigma', *Comparativ: Zeitschrift für Globalgeschichte und vergleichende Gesellschaftsforschung* 19, no 6 (2009), 86.

[77] Edwin Gabler, *The American Telegrapher: A Social History, 1860–1900* (New Brunswick: Rutgers University Press, 1988).

[78] Annteresa Lubrano, *The Telegraph: How Technology Innovation Caused Social Change* (New York: Garland, 1997).

[79] Gregory Downey, *Telegraph Messenger Boys: Labor, Technology, and Geography, 1850–1950* (New York: Routledge, 2002).

[80] Aad Blok and Gregory Downey, eds., *Uncovering Labour in Information Revolutions, 1750–2000* (Cambridge: Cambridge University Press, 2003). In this context, see also Charles Craypo, 'The Impact of Changing Corporate Structure and Technology on Telegraph Labour, 1870–1978', *Journal of the American Statistical Association* (1997).

[81] Anna Davin, 'Women Telegraphists and Typists', in *Women in Industry and Technology: From Prehistory to the Present Day*, ed. Amanda Devonshire and Barbara Wood (London: Museum of London, 1996); Thomas C. Jepsen, 'Women Telegraph Operators on the Western Frontier', *Journal of the West* 35 (1996); Jepsen, 'Women Telegraphers in the Railroad Depot', *Railroad History* 173 (1995); Shirley Tillotson, '"We May All Soon Be 'First-Class Men'": Gender and Skill in Canada's Early Twentieth Century Urban

Only recently have the first prosopographical studies on telegraph history appeared. These studies are usually concerned with historical actors belonging to the business community, to the political establishment or to both. They could therefore also have been mentioned in the first two sections of this chapter. However, their focus is usually less on explaining the role of the telegraph in a national, imperial or business context than on illuminating the social ties and group dynamics among the people active in the telegraph industry. They have, therefore, great explanatory potential regarding the role of formal and informal groups in shaping the global telegraph network. In addition to its discussion of telegraphy in an imperial context, Winseck and Pike's *Communication and Empire* is among the first studies to contain prosopographical elements.[82] Simone Müller explicitly uses prosopographical methods in her work on the transatlantic telegraph.[83]

Telegraph Industry', *Journal of Canadian Labour Studies* 27 (1991); Melodie Andrews, '"What the Girls Can Do": The Debate over the Employment of Women in the Early American Telegraph Industry', *Essays in Economic and Business History* 8 (1990).

82 Winseck and Pike, *Communication and Empire*.

83 Müller, 'The Transatlantic Telegraphs and the *Class of 1866*'.

5 The global telegraph network

5.1 Towards a worldwide web

On 7 December 1870 – in the very year in which the British domestic telegraph system had been nationalized and handed over to the General Post Office and in which both the submarine cable connection and the so-called Siemens line between Europe and India had been inaugurated – a half-humorous and half-complaining letter to the editor was published in *The Times* of London. The letter was written on a light note but is nevertheless instructive about the various problems that international telegraphy customers faced at that time. It shall be quoted here in its full length:

The Post Office and the Telegraphs.

To the Editor of the Times.

Sir, – I observe that the Post Office clerks who have charge of the telegraphs have been holding a meeting to suggest improvements in the conduct of the service. To judge by my experience, there are some improvements they might contrive to introduce without any such ceremony; and it may be useful if you will let me give your readers an instance of the manner in which telegraphic business is now conducted in the City of London.

I had occasion to telegraph to Calcutta between 9 and 10 in the evening. I was in doubt what offices would be open at that hour, but I thought it would be safe to apply at Head-Quarters, so I went straight to the General Post Office. It was closed; but there was a plate on the door stating that between 8 and 12 p.m. messages were received at the telegraph office in Cornhill, after that hour until the morning at the office in Telegraph-street. I confess I thought it odd that in the centre of the heart of the British Empire a man should thus be sent from pillar to post, according to the hours of the night, in order to find the right end of the electric wire which is now the very nerve of the social body. But we are becoming drilled into submission to such circuitous regulations, and I proceeded without a murmur to Cornhill.

Here, at the central telegraphic office of the City of London for the first four hours of the night, the whole apparent force of the department consisted of one clerk. This gentleman was civil, but not vigorous, and looked, indeed, as if he might with benefit to himself have been one of the clerks at the General Post Office who go to bed so early. I asked him the price of a telegram to Calcutta. 'Calcutta!' he said, and looked very much as if I had asked to telegraph to Fernando Po.

He turned, however, to a book on the counter, which he searched very deliberately. Now, Sir, Calcutta is not an unknown place. I thought it was the capital of British India, and that it was in close and constant communication with the City of London. The clerk in charge at the central office might have expected to know the cost of telegraphing thither, and the best way of doing so, without a special search. However, he found Calcutta in his Directory, and told me the charge would be 1l. 17s. for ten words, but what it would be for more than ten words he could scarcely say. I asked if I should write my message on the usual form. 'No,' he said, 'you must write it on a Falmouth and Gibraltar form.' Where were the Falmouth and Gibraltar forms? Again he had to search, and he searched high and low, and right and left, in order to find me the form for telegraphing from Cornhill to Calcutta. He lighted a paper torch, and peered into a dark cupboard; but it was no good. The means did not exist at Cornhill of sending a message to Calcutta. At last he said, 'Do you know where the Falmouth and Gibraltar office is? You may as well go there. We should have to turn the message over to them.' And then he directed me with easy politeness to Broad-street.

I was more concerned at that moment to get my message off than to criticize the ways of the Post Office, so I went one step further, to Broad-street. There, upon saying that I wanted to telegraph to Calcutta, a gentleman stepped forward, and again, in the old tone of surprise, said, 'Calcutta!' I began to think I must, after all, be doing something very strange in telegraphing to Calcutta that the proposal should be so perplexing to the telegraph clerks. But this gentleman had reason for his surprise. He was at least as polite as the gentleman on Cornhill, and there was an absence of official languor about him which was refreshing. He informed me that the Falmouth line was broken between Lisbon and Gibraltar, that it would consequently take five or six days to telegraph to Calcutta, and that his company advised the public for the present to send their messages through Persia by the Indo-European Company, whose office was in Telegraph-street. When I said I had just been sent to him from the postal office in Cornhill, he replied that the Post Office had been duly informed of the break in the line, and that they ought to have sent me at once to the other company. I was of the same opinion.

So I went, as a fourth attempt, to Telegraph-street, and there, in the office of the Indo-European Company, I found – wonderful to state – not only one, but two clerks, who received my message, and said it would probably be in Calcutta in three hours. I told them of my pursuit of Calcutta under difficulties, and they said the Post Office seemed to have some prejudice against them, and that other persons had made the same complaint of being sent on a fruitless errand to Broad-street.

Now, Sir, the whole thing was so very free and easy that I feel more amusement than vexation at my experience. That a Government official should prosecute a languid search at 10 o'clock in the evening to discover the means of communication between the City of London and the capital of British India, and should be, after all, unsuccessful; that a customer of the department should be asked to 'turn over' his message for himself to the Colonial Company because the Department would have to do it if he didn't; that he should have to go to four places before sending the message, and, after all, should owe no thanks to the Post Office for sending it; all this seems to me so singularly out of the common way as to have a touch of the humorous. But I should think this method of administration was not conducive to the success of the Post Office telegraphs. It is certainly not business, and no private firm who wished to encourage custom would allow their work to be done in such fashion. Mr. Scudamore seems, in short, to have enough to do at present without troubling himself to preside over official Parliaments.

I am, Sir, yours faithfully,

W.

London, Dec. 6.[1]

The to-and-fro described in the letter is not particularly unusual in highly bureaucratized systems. The writer seems to have been aware of this and neither took himself nor the trouble inflicted on him too seriously. But despite the lightness of tone – or maybe just because of it – the anonymous writer managed to point his finger directly at several of the problems that someone who wanted to send an international telegram had to face around the time of writing.[2] In addition, the letter also conveys a new perception of time and space that had already started to take root in these early years of global telegraphy. Apparently, the matter about which the anonymous author needed to telegraph to Calcutta was so urgent that it could not wait until the next morning. As has already been argued in the opening chapters of this book, time was not annihilated by the new communication technologies – quite on the contrary, it became ever more important. And the writer also hints at another development touched upon in Chapter 2 – the separation of geographic and communication space – when he remarks that the clerk 'looked very much as if I had asked to telegraph to Fernando Po'. Fernando Po is an island off the coast of Equatorial Guinea that today is called Bioko. It might not be the centre of the world, but as the crow flies it is about 2,500 kilometres closer to London than Calcutta. Before the opening of the Suez Canal little more than a year before the letter was written, ships to India had to circumnavigate Africa and in doing so would come very close to Fernando Po. The island was, therefore, not as remote as the statement in the letter suggests. As the capital of British India, however, Calcutta occupied a central position in the world as seen from London. Reasons for contact and exchange between the two cities were abundant and communication accordingly frequent. From a vantage point in the City of London, Calcutta, therefore, seemed to be much nearer and easier to reach than some island off the African coast. Never exactly identical, communication space had been further separated from geographic space.

1 'The Post Office and the Telegraphs', *The Times*, 7 December 1870, 6.

2 See Roland Wenzlhuemer, '"I had occasion to telegraph to Calcutta": Die Telegrafie und ihre Rolle in der Globalisierung im 19. Jahrhundert', *Themenportal europäische Geschichte* (2011), www.europa.clio-online.de/2011/Article=513.

The necessity to send the telegram at once, as well as the reference to Fernando Po, therefore, hints at shifting perceptions of time and space by those who have access to telecommunication technology. But, as already referred to, the anonymous letter also unerringly points out the inconveniences and complexities of international telegraphy in the first decades of its existence that could at times render the system utterly obscure for both customer and telegraph operator. The first issue was somewhat peculiar to the British telegraph system. In the United Kingdom, several private companies had managed the domestic telegraph network until the nationalization of the system in 1870. As these companies competed for customers, there were many overlaps between their individual networks in business centres, while outside these centres there was often little connectivity. Jeffrey Kieve gives the following example:

> Under the companies, 'town offices' had been opened only in large towns. These tended to be in the business centre, with the offices of the three major companies close together, often only a few yards apart – in Edinburgh all telegraph offices were within about half a mile of each other, the rest of the city having none.[3]

In the City of London, for instance, all of the bigger telegraph companies would maintain a multitude of offices at strategic places. Before nationalization, the GPO conducted a thorough survey in order to identify such overlaps and avoid doublings as far as possible. Many telegraph offices in the City of London were closed as a consequence.[4] Still, so short a time after nationalization, there was some confusion as to the location of the principal offices. The General Post Office headquarters on St Martin's Le Grand seemed a natural choice for the writer, but the Central Telegraph Office moved there only in 1874. Until then, the former headquarters of the Electric & International Telegraph Company (usually called the Electric) at Telegraph Street (servicing the second part of the night) remained the best-connected telegraph station in town. That the former Electric station on Cornhill – a few hundred metres' walking distance from Telegraph Street – was open for service during the first part of the night was, however, surely not common knowledge even among regular customers.

The writer's wanderings through the City of London also highlight the problems occurring at the touching points of domestic and international telegraphy. In most countries, the inland telegraph system was run by either a government department or a quasi-monopolist company in close co-operation with the authorities. A situation like in Great Britain before

[3] Kieve, *The Electric Telegraph*, 176.
[4] British Telecom Archives, POST 82/181, 'Re-arrangement of the Metropolitan Telegraph System', 1869.

1870, where several private companies competed in a free market, was the exception rather than the rule as regards domestic telegraphy. International trunk connections, however, were in almost all important cases handled by private companies – sometimes with public involvement but usually without it. The Falmouth, Gibraltar & Malta Telegraph Company, for instance, was one of four companies formed by John Pender in the late 1860s in order to establish a direct submarine telegraph connection between Great Britain and British India. After some years of successful working, these four companies were merged in 1872 to create the Eastern Telegraph Company[5] – 'the company that would tower over the industry for the next half century'.[6] The Indo-European Telegraph Company, with its head office in Telegraph Street, ran an overland telegraph line via Prussia, Russia and Persia (the so-called Siemens line) that connected with the lines and cables of the Indo-European Telegraph Department. Pender's companies (and ultimately the Eastern) and the Indo-European had close relations with the big British inland telegraph companies and benefited from the nationalization of the domestic system.

[5] Winseck and Pike, *Communication and Empire*, 37–8. Headrick, *The Invisible Weapon*, 35–6. While the Eastern and its preceding companies had been formed to provide a submarine link between Europe and India, John Pender soon started to expand his business. In 1873, he merged the British Australian Telegraph Company, the British-Indian Extension Company and the China Submarine Telegraph Company to create the Eastern Extension, Australasia and China Telegraph Company. Together with the Eastern Telegraph Company, it laid the foundations for Pender's Eastern and Associated Telegraph Companies, which, from its inception in 1873, started to incorporate many smaller telegraph companies to service the Caribbean, Central and South America, and Africa. In other cases, the enlarged Eastern entered into arrangements with competitors and formed so-called cable cartels – for instance, with the Great Northern Telegraph Company regarding the telegraphic traffic to the Far East. It thus became the dominant cable company for many decades. In an effort to retain British control over global communications, the Eastern and Associated Telegraph Companies and Marconi's Wireless Telegraph Company were merged in 1928 to create Imperial and International Communications Limited. In 1934, after a series of further acquisitions, the new company's name was changed to Cable & Wireless Limited. See Kurt Jacobsen, 'Small Nation, International Submarine Telegraphy, and International Politics: The Great Northern Telegraph Company, 1869–1940', in *Communications under the Seas: The Evolving Cable Network and Its Implications*, ed. Bernard Finn and Daqing Yang, Dibner Institute Studies in the History of Science and Technology (Cambridge, MA and London: MIT Press, 2009); Jacobsen, 'The Great Northern Telegraph Company and the British Empire', in *Britain and Denmark: Political, Economic, and Cultural Relations in the 19th and 20th Centuries*, ed. Jørgen Sevaldsen, Bo Bjørke and Claus Bjørn (Copenhagen: Museum Tusculanum Press, 2002); Robert Boyce, 'The Origins of Cable and Wireless Limited, 1918–1939: Capitalism, Imperialism, and Technical Change', in *Communications under the Seas: The Evolving Cable Network and Its Implications*, ed. Bernard Finn and Daqing Yang, Dibner Institute Studies in the History of Science and Technology (Cambridge, MA and London: MIT Press, 2009); Cable & Wireless Archive, DOC/I&IC/1/9, 'Imperial and International Communications Ltd., Report of the Directors. 1929 to 1933', 1929–33.

[6] Winseck and Pike, *Communication and Empire*, 38.

The expansion of a global telegraph network, therefore, received a massive boost from surplus capital that swelled the coffers of the Electric and the English & Irish Magnetic Telegraph Company (the Magnetic) after the 1870 GPO takeover. The General Post Office also assured the private telegraph companies that it would not itself partake in international telegraphy.[7] The global and the local parts of the evolving telegraph network had de facto been divided up – with national governments and a few quasi-monopolist private firms in charge of the domestic networks and a handful of international companies running the trunk connections. Co-operation between these parties, however, was not free of friction, as the above letter indicates. Public telegraph departments had different priorities than did their private counterparts. Information exchange was often imperfect and could lead to delays in message handling as telegrams had to be transferred between the domestic and the trunk network.

Another problem that becomes apparent in the letter can be identified in the frequent interruptions of international telegraph lines and cables. These occurred regularly, both on submarine and overland lines, and could have a number of different causes. In the Administration Report of the Indo-European Telegraph Department for 1882–3, Director-in-Chief John Underwood Bateman-Champain related the following:

> 4. Owing to military operations in Egypt, the Eastern Company's section was out of order from 10th July 1882 till the 28th September, the result being a great additional amount of business by way of the Persian Gulf . . . 31. The Suez route was either partially interrupted or defective in one or more of its cable sections for nearly the entire official year . . . 38. The main cause of this extraordinary rise in the traffic over our system was of course the long continued interruption of the Suez route referred to in para. 4 of this letter, but it was not only while the war lasted that more than the normal proportion of messages were transmitted *viâ* the Persian Gulf. In fact, for several months both before and after the war in Egypt, the working of the Red Sea system was more or less defective and thousands of despatches were, during the year, transferred by the Eastern to the Indo-European route for transmission to their destination.[8]

The overland routes between Europe and India experienced similar problems and frequently saw their lines interrupted due to vandalism or a local interest in the copper that the lines were made of.[9] And of

[7] Ibid., 37.

[8] British Library, Oriental Collections, IOR/V/24/4289, 'Administration Report of the Indo-European Telegraph Department for 1882–83', 1883, paras. 4, 31, 38.

[9] See, for instance, Thomas E. Ewing, '"A Most Powerful Instrument for a Despot": The Telegraph as a Transnational Instrument of Imperial Control and Political Mobilization in the Middle East', in *The Nation State and Beyond*, ed. Isabella Löhr and Roland Wenzlhuemer (Heidelberg: Springer, forthcoming).

course, natural disasters also often brought about line breakdowns, as this extract from the Administration Report of the Indian Telegraph Department for 1880–1 illustrates:

33. The interruptions during the year due to extraordinary causes … were as follows: – July 1880. – Between Ngathineyoung and Bassein, lasting 139 hours. Country flooded, line broken in several places and submerged. Great flood in the Irrawaddy River. The whole country below the embankment under water to a considerable depth for a mile on either side of the river … November 1880. – Between Bangalore and Bellary, lasting 136 hours. Both wires caught in branches of a tree which was floating down the river during heavy floods near Jogunhally Tank, 87 miles from Bangalore: two posts washed down and a portion of the line imbedded in the river, also carried away.[10]

But despite all these issues and challenges that international telegraphy had to face, a global network started to develop – carefully at first but with more momentum after the successful laying of a transatlantic connection in 1866 and the financial boost courtesy of the General Post Office. And most of the time, sending a message between two places connected through the telegraph network caused far less trouble than in the example described in the anonymous letter. On 17 February 1869, for instance, a letter from the London-based firm Schuster, Son, and Co. to the editor was published in *The Times* stating,

Sir, – As an instance of the excellent working of the telegraph between here and Calcutta, we beg to bring to your notice the following case, viz.: – We sent yesterday, the 15th inst., at 11 35 a.m., a message consisting of 30 words to our Calcutta correspondents, and at 6 50 p.m. last night we received a telegram from Calcutta acknowledging our message of the morning, and answering in detail. The time thus occupied between the transmission of our message and the receipt of the Calcutta reply was within 7½ hours, and we firmly believe the shortest on record.[11]

Of course, other messages needed a longer time to receive an answer as indicated by a second note, signed with the acronym E.I.L.C.F.C. and published in *The Times* two days later as a direct reply to the Schuster note: 'As we yesterday, the 17th, 10 55 a.m., received a telegram, dated Calcutta, the 11th, 4 30 p.m., we are at a loss to know why we are so much less favoured than your correspondents, that while their messages and reply took but half one day, our single message was near six days on the road.'[12] Such extended delivery times were not uncommon between Europe and India in the late 1860s and early 1870s, but compared to pre-telegraph communication times

[10] British Library, Oriental Collections, IOR/V/24/4286, 'Administration Report of the Indian Telegraph Department for 1880–81', 1881, 9.

[11] 'The Calcutta Telegraph', *The Times*, 19 February 1869, 8. [12] Ibid., 7.

they still constituted a major achievement. Accordingly, international telegraphy was immediately put to use by globally active merchants and businessmen. A good example of such immediate use can be found on the transatlantic route in the year 1858. The first lasting transatlantic telegraphic connection was opened only in 1866, but there had been several previous attempts to install a transatlantic cable. In 1858, a cable had worked for approximately three weeks before it ceased to transmit. In this short span of time, however, *Lloyd's List* in London already started to receive shipping information from North America via the cable. On 24 August 1858 the ship news rubric of *The Times* (based on information from *Lloyd's List*) announced that the ship *Heinrich von Gagern* on her way from New Orleans to Bremen 'has put in [at Norfolk, United States] for hands, seven of her crew being dead with fever, and others sick with the fever'. The note was dated 'Norfolk, United States, Aug. 23'.[13] Similarly, when the first extremely short-lived cable connection between Suez and Karachi was opened in early 1860, the business community was first in line to make good use of the new, enhanced communication between Europe and India. *The Times* reported on 17 March 1860 that the first private telegram sent via the newly opened route had been received in London. The telegram reads, 'Calcutta, March 10. – Ship Red Gauntlet, bound to London, burnt and scuttled. Some cargo will be saved.'[14] Only a few days after this message had been sent, the cable link fell prey to 'the heat of tropical waters, their deadly teredo borer, sub-surface hot springs,

[13] 'Ship News', *The Times*, 24 August 1858, 9. During the three weeks of a working transatlantic cable in 1858, no other piece of ship news from North America was published in *The Times* that shows a similarly short transmission time. The note itself is unusually confusing and inexact. In full, it reads, 'Norfolk, United States, Aug. 23. – The Heinrich, Bremen ship, from New Orleans, has put in here for hands, seven of her crew being dead with fever, and others sick with the fever. The Heinrich V. Gagern, Reimers, cleared at New Orleans, July 10, for Bremen.' A short notice in *The Times* of the next day clarified that the *H. Von Gagern* had previously been reported as the *Heinrich*. 'Shipping Intelligence', *The Times*, 25 August 1858, 7. This, however, seems to be incorrect as well. *Lloyd's List* of 25 August 1858 states that the *Heinrich von Gagern* has left New Orleans for Bremen on 9 August – 'and not the *Hinuch* as before reported.' *Lloyd's List*, 25 August 1858, 3. The original note in *The Times*, therefore, related two pieces of news about the same ship with parts of the message untypically garbled for the standards of the ship news columns. The *Lloyd's List* passage even mentioned a third ship name and gave a different date for the ship's departure at New Orleans than *The Times* clarification. The jumbled chronology of the statements – reporting first about the stopover at Norfolk due to disease and only later about the ship's departure at New Orleans – is testimony to possible confusions arising from the application of the telegraph. It could, of course, be speculated that the unusual garbling of the message and the general confusion regarding the *Heinrich von Gagern* were in general a consequence of the transmission by telegraph via an only partially working cable. But at the moment there is no evidence available that could add substance to such a speculation.

[14] 'Telegraph between England and India', *The Times*, 17 March 1860, 10.

"mud volcanoes" and numberless jagged coral reefs in the Red Sea',[15] and went out of operation.[16]

5.2 The structure of the global submarine telegraph network

Being administered by government departments or companies operating mostly in a national context, different domestic telegraph networks worked according to different technological and operational standards. While there was a desire to establish border-crossing telegraph connections from very early on, such problems of standardization often rendered the exchange of messages between different domestic systems complicated and painstakingly slow – and thereby deprived telegraphic communication of its principal advantage. The harmonization of the different systems, therefore, became highly desirable, especially for European countries with many neighbouring networks. Only a few years after the first non-experimental telegraph lines had been built in continental Europe, early initiatives aiming at system standardization emerged. Within the German Confederation, the multitude of different state systems made unification all the more pressing. In July 1850, representatives of Prussia, Austria–Hungary, Bavaria and Saxony met at Dresden to discuss the harmonization of telegraphic communication between them. They founded the Deutsch-Österreichischer Telegraphenverein (DÖTV)[17] – the Austrian–German Telegraph Union – and agreed on standardization in three regards: technical, operational and tariff-related. These efforts bore fruit and quickened international communication between the signatories.[18] Right from its inception, the DÖTV aimed at attracting new members. In 1851 Württemberg joined the union and in 1854 Baden and Mecklenburg-Schwerin followed. Furthermore, a number of bilateral treaties harmonizing telegraphic exchange with other European countries were signed. In 1855, the Western European Telegraph Union was founded by France, Belgium, Spain, Sardinia and Switzerland. Both unions co-operated closely from the

[15] Harris, 'The Persian Gulf Submarine Telegraph of 1864', 170.

[16] J. M. Adams, 'Development of the Anglo-Indian Telegraph', *Engineering Science and Education Journal* 6, no 4 (1997), 141.

[17] For a comprehensive history of the Deutsch-Österreichischer Telegraphenverein, see Josef Reindl, *Der Deutsch-Österreichische Telegraphenverein und die Entwicklung des deutschen Telegraphenwesens 1850–1871* (Frankfurt a. M.: Peter Lang, 1993).

[18] Josef Reindl, 'Partikularstaatliche Politik und technische Dynamik: Die drahtgebundene Telegraphie und der Deutsch-Österreichische Telegraphenverein von 1850', in *Vom Flügeltelegraphen zum Internet: Geschichte der modernen Telekommunikation*, ed. Hans-Jürgen Teuteberg and Cornelius Neutsch (Stuttgart: Franz Steiner Verlag, 1998), 34–5.

beginning.[19] Eventually, in 1865, representatives of twenty European states met at the Conférence télégraphique internationale in Paris and adopted a convention that regulated international telegraphic exchange between the signatories.[20]

These concerted efforts at least partially harmonized European telegraphy early in its history. Given that dematerialized communication unfolds its greatest benefits over long distances, the desire to build an international network is not surprising. Within a European context, this could be achieved by connecting the existing national networks of neighbouring countries. However, should two systems be connected which were geographically further removed, long-distance trunk routes had to be erected. And while several overland trunk routes were, of course, built (for instance the Indo-European line), most of these connections ran through submarine telegraph cables. Especially in intercontinental telegraphy, many places could only be reached by crossing open water, and thus depended on submarine connections. But even in cases where there was a continuous landmass between the points to be connected (for instance between Europe and Asia, Africa or North and South America) submarine cables were usually given preference over landlines once technical problems had been solved and the technology worked satisfactorily. Submarine cables had a number of advantages over landlines: while cable landing rights needed to be negotiated with the countries at both ends of the wire, there were no problems of right of way; cables between, for instance, a colonial power and its colonies did not have to pass through foreign (and potentially unstable or even hostile) territory;[21] once the problem of long-distance signal transmission had been solved, relay stations could be very far apart and few in number; and in times of conflict it was more difficult (although not impossible) for other parties to interrupt submarine cable connections or to listen in when not near the shore ends.[22]

19 Ibid., 42.

20 *Documents diplomatiques de la Conférence télégraphique internationale de Paris.*

21 For the role of submarine telegraph cables in British imperial administration and strategy, see Kennedy, 'Imperial Cable Communications and Strategy, 1870–1914'.

22 In 1902, the Inter-departmental Committee on Cable Communications brought its second report before the Houses of Parliament. The committee also commented on the danger of cable cutting in times of warfare and had the following opinion on the matter: '9. The experience of the Spanish–American War, while it brings into prominence the important influence which submarine cable telegraphy exercises in maritime warfare, also shows how large a part is played by chance in cable-cutting operations. We are convinced, however, that there is no serious physical difficulty in cutting cables, and that on the outbreak of war cables may be cut either in shallow water without, or in deep water with, special appliances. While, therefore, it is generally advisable that cables should be landed at fortified positions, where such exist, in order that the instruments and operating stations may be under protection, we would point out that the importance of

After several years of testing in harbours or across rivers, the first successful open-water cable connection was established between Dover and Calais in 1850 by the Submarine Telegraph Company – and was cut by a fishing boat's anchor almost immediately after its opening. A year later, another attempt was made and this time the connection proved to be a lasting one.[23] Stimulated by this success, the Submarine Telegraph Company laid more cables connecting Great Britain with mainland Europe. In 1852, a cable between Boulogne, France, and Folkestone, England, took up service. A year later, a connection between Middlekerke, Belgium, and Ramsgate, England, was inaugurated. In the meantime, the Magnetic – in its capacity of one of the private telegraph firms running the United Kingdom domestic network – managed to connect Portpatrick in Scotland with Donaghadee in Ireland in 1853. Many more cables between Great Britain and the Continent, within Scandinavia or criss-crossing the Mediterranean followed in the 1850s and early 1860s,[24] most of which worked very well.[25] The successful functioning of these cables also fuelled the desire to connect Europe and North America telegraphically. Attempts to put a transatlantic cable in place started in the mid-1850s as a US–UK joint venture, but encountered many unexpected technical problems, most of which had something to do with the sheer length of the cable. As the laying of the transatlantic cable has attracted most of the historical research on submarine telegraphy and is comparatively well researched (see Chapter 4), the story need not be retold here. It shall suffice to say that in 1858 a transatlantic cable was for the first time successfully put in place, but ceased to work after approximately three weeks of on–off service. It took another eight years, until 1866, to establish a lasting and dependable connection between the two continents. Together with the Persian Gulf cables, which had been

fortifying the shore ends may easily be exaggerated, because the attempt to break the cable will probably be made at a convenient distance from the shore, beyond the range of guns.' House of Commons Parliamentary Papers, Cd. 1056, 'Cable Communications Report of the Inter-departmental Committee on Cable Communications', 1902, 15. Britain itself, on the other hand, was well prepared for cable cutting and censorship, as became obvious with the outbreak of the First World War. See Cable & Wireless Archive, DOC/E&ATC/7/1, 'Correspondence regarding censorship. 1914 to 1918', 1914–18.

23 Headrick, *The Tools of Empire*, 158.

24 See Andrea Giuntini, 'The Power of Cables: Submarine Communication in the Mediterranean', in *Communication and Its Lines: Telegraphy in the 19th Century among Economy, Politics and Technology*, ed. Andrea Giuntini (Prato: Istituto di studi storici postali onlus, 2004).

25 See, for instance, 'Nomenclature des cables formant le réseau sous-marin du globe dressée d'après des documents officiels par le Bureau international des administrations télégraphiques', *Journal télégraphique* 3, no 29 (1877).

opened a year earlier covering one leg of the route to India,[26] the success of the 1866 transatlantic cable gave an unprecedented boost to the cable-laying business. Submarine cable laying and operating had reached a stage of technological maturity rendering the endeavour profitable and the risks at least roughly calculable. In combination with the availability of huge amounts of capital caused by the nationalization of the British inland network, this brought about a dramatic expansion of the global submarine telegraph network from the late 1860s and early 1870s onwards. The following paragraphs will take a closer look at the structural pattern of this expansion and try to identify the core as well as the peripheral regions in the telegraphic development of the world.

In Article 61 of the convention issued by the Conférence télégraphique internationale taking place in Vienna in June 1868, the signing parties decided to found a Bureau international des administrations télégraphiques which would mainly be concerned with standardization and compatibility in European telegraphic transmissions.[27] In the Règlement de service international attached to the convention, the Swiss telegraph administration was authorized to organize the international bureau which was founded in Berne and eventually became the International Telegraph Union (ITU).[28] From 1869 onwards, the bureau published the *Journal télégraphique*, dealing with practically all matters related to international telegraphy. In 1877, the journal for the first time had a supplement, with the title 'Nomenclature des cables formant le réseau sous-marin du globe'.[29] Already two years earlier, an issue of the journal had contained a list of the most important submarine telegraph cables in existence,[30] but the 1877 'Nomenclature' is far more comprehensive and offers detailed information about all cables known to the Bureau international and, therefore, about almost all cables in existence. Its 'Avant-propos' opens, 'Dans cette nomenclature, nous nous sommes attachés à reproduire aussi complètement que possible

26 Harris, 'The Persian Gulf Submarine Telegraph of 1864'.

27 *Documents de la Conférence télégraphique internationale de Vienne*, 86–90.

28 Since 1934, ITU has stood for International Telecommunication Union. In 1947 it was made a specialized agency of the United Nations. A year later it moved from Berne to Geneva, where the ITU still resides today, and it remains the world's oldest international organization. For a comprehensive history of the International Telegraph Union, see George A. Codding and Anthony M. Rutkowski, *The International Telecommunication Union in a Changing World* (Dedham, MA: Artech House, 1982); Andreas Tegge, *Die Internationale Telekommunikations-Union: Organisation und Funktion einer Weltorganisation im Wandel* (Baden-Baden: Nomos, 1994).

29 'Nomenclature des Cables formant le réseau sous-marin du globe dressée d'après des documents officiels par le Bureau international des administrations télégraphiques'.

30 'Les communications sous-marines du globe', *Journal télégraphique* 3, no 12 (1875).

l'ensemble de tous les câbles sous-marins actuellement en exploitation dans les différentes mers du globe, en les rattachant chacun à l'Administration privée ou gouvernementale qui les exploite.' The original text contains a footnote after 'câbles sous-marins' that reads, 'Parmi les câbles sous-marins, nous avons fait figurer ceux des baies et golfes côtiers ainsi que des estuaries des fleuves, mais non ceux des lacs ou cours d'eau intérieurs des terres.'[31] Until 1903, eight more such 'Nomenclatures' were published in the journal in the years 1883, 1887, 1889, 1892, 1894, 1897, 1901 and 1903.[32] Combined with the less comprehensive list of 1875, they enable us to trace in some detail the development of the global submarine telegraph network between the mid-1860s and the first decade of the twentieth century. To this end, almost all cables from these 'Nomenclatures' have been entered into a spreadsheet together with associated data on the cable operator, the length of cable and the length of wire, the year in which the cable went into operation and whether it was run by a governmental department or a private company.[33] The 'Nomenclatures' contain no information as to when certain cables ceased to function. Cables that had stopped working

[31] 'Nomenclature des câbles formant le réseau sous-marin du globe dressée d'après des documents officiels par le Bureau international des administrations télégraphiques', 575.

[32] 'Nomenclature des câbles formant le réseau sous-marin du globe dressée d'après des documents officiels par le Bureau international des administrations télégraphiques', *Journal télégraphique* 7, no 5 (1883); 'Nomenclature des câbles formant le réseau sous-marin du globe dressée d'après des documents officiels par le Bureau international des administrations télégraphiques', *Journal télégraphique* 11, no 4 (1887); 'Nomenclature des câbles formant le réseau sous-marin du globe dressée d'après des documents officiels par le Bureau international des administrations télégraphiques', *Journal télégraphique* 13, no 9 (1889); 'Nomenclature des câbles formant le réseau sous-marin du globe dressée d'après des documents officiels par le Bureau international des administrations télégraphiques', *Journal télégraphique* 16, no 4 (1892); 'Nomenclature des câbles formant le réseau sous-marin du globe dressée d'après des documents officiels par le Bureau international des administrations télégraphiques', *Journal télégraphique* 18, no 10 (1894); 'Nomenclature des câbles formant le réseau sous-marin du globe dressée d'après des documents officiels par le Bureau international des administrations télégraphiques', *Journal télégraphique* 21, no 11 (1897); 'Nomenclature des câbles formant le réseau sous-marin du globe dressée d'après des documents officiels par le Bureau international des administrations télégraphiques', *Journal télégraphique* 25 (1901); 'Nomenclature des câbles formant le réseau sous-marin du globe dressée d'après des documents officiels par le Bureau international des administrations télégraphiques', *Journal télégraphique* 27 (1903).

[33] Due to the sheer amount of short domestic cables in operation towards the end of the nineteenth century, the following cables have not been included in the spreadsheet and thus do not feature in the following analysis: cables across rivers and estuaries in Great Britain and Ireland; cables across rivers in Brazil, Argentina and India; several cables connecting the smaller islands of Japan with the main islands; only in 1903 the cables connecting the myriad islands of the Philippines; and also only in 1903 a number of shorter cables connecting the islands of New Zealand (due to the unreadability of the source). In all these cases, the excluded cables are short domestic connections with mainly national relevance.

for good were simply not listed any more. Therefore for some cables there is no clearly defined endpoint of operation but a time window starting in the year in which the last list that contained the cable was published and ending in the year the first list without the cable was printed. In addition to the information taken directly from the 'Nomenclatures', all cable landing sites and cable routes have been geo-referenced. Maps 5.1 – 5.5 have been produced from this information and visualize the growth of the global submarine cable network between 1865 and 1903. Connections run by government departments are shown as dashed, those managed by private companies as solid lines.

Map 5.1 depicts the global submarine cable network as it existed in the year 1865. In Europe, the cable connections between Great Britain and the mainland run mostly by private companies since the 1850s are visible. Most other coastal connections are parts of domestic telegraph systems operated by government departments. On the other side of the Atlantic, short cables connecting Newfoundland with the North American mainland had been put in place in the 1850s as part of the short-lived transatlantic connection and were now waiting to become useful again. The only long-distance submarine connections in operation in 1865 were the Persian Gulf cables connecting Al-Faw (or Fao), at the northern tip of the Gulf, with Karachi in British India. The cables were managed by the Indo-European Telegraph Department of the British Indian Government and, in combination with the Turkish and Indian telegraph systems, provided the first direct telegraphic link between Europe and India. The Persian Gulf cables went into operation in 1865 and qualify as the first functioning long-distance cables (with individual lengths of up to 369 nautical miles, equalling about 680 kilometres).

The significant time lag between the laying of the first intra-European connections in the early 1850s and the opening of the Persian Gulf cables illustrates the magnitude of both the technical and financial obstacles that had to be negotiated before the submarine cable network could really go global. With these hindrances overcome, however, global telegraphic expansion received a formidable boost. Map 5.2 shows all submarine connections in service in 1870 – only five years after the inauguration of the Persian Gulf cables. The transatlantic link had become a reality, with both Ireland and France in direct telegraphic communication with North America. John Pender's various companies provided a continuous submarine connection between Great Britain and British India and had already started to extend their network towards the east with connections to Penang, Singapore and Batavia. The intra-European communication system had also been further expanded. Apart from the Persian Gulf cables, all major international connections in 1870 were managed by

Map 5.1 Global submarine cable network, 1865. Note: Private cables are shown as solid lines; government cables as dashed lines.

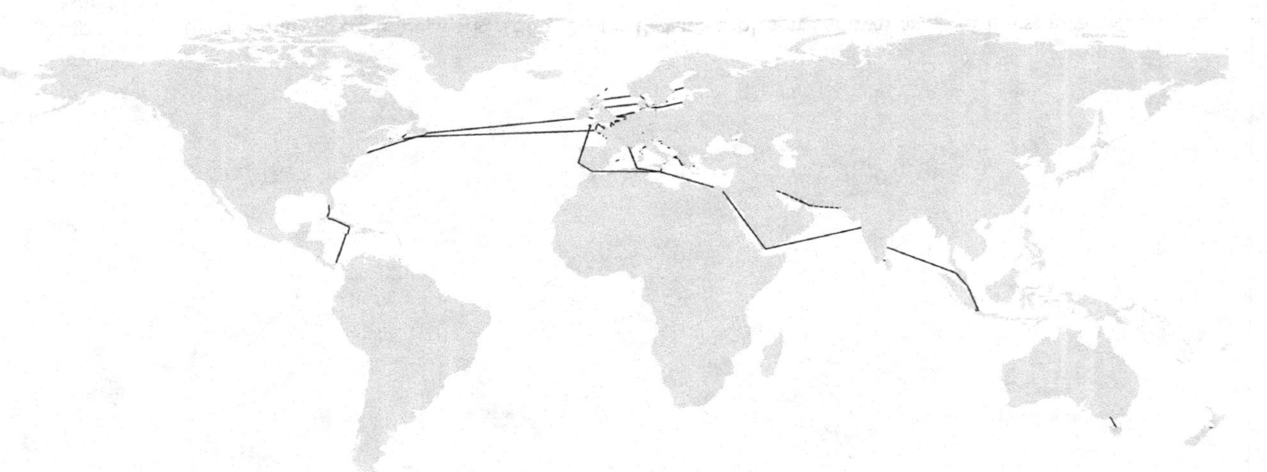

Map 5.2 Global submarine cable network, 1870. Note: Private cables are shown as solid lines; government cables as dashed lines.

private companies operating mostly out of Europe (and there chiefly out of Great Britain) and to a certain extent out of the United States. Their focus in these early years of expansion rested quite clearly on connecting Europe with North America and Asia.

By 1880 (see Map 5.3), the transatlantic and the intra-European cable systems had been further upgraded. Connections across the Atlantic, the North Sea and the Mediterranean had multiplied. In Asia, the network had been extended eastwards to incorporate South East Asia, the Chinese coast and Japan. Port Darwin in Australia had been brought into telegraphic communication with Java, and therefore with the world, in 1871. Five years later another cable connected New Zealand with Australia. Since 1874, Europe had also been in direct communication with South America via Madeira and the Cape Verde Islands. The cable network in the Caribbean had also been extended. And, in 1879, a cable was eventually laid along the African east coast connecting the South African port city of Durban with the submarine cable link between Europe and Asia at Aden, thus bringing global telegraphy to sub-Saharan Africa. As can be seen in Map 5.3, this massive extension of the global submarine cable network was almost exclusively implemented by private companies.

Map 5.4 depicts the submarine cable network in 1890. Again, the network had been further expanded. Cables connecting with the line between Europe and South America now reached down along the African west coast to Port Nolloth in South Africa. And the existing cables along the South American west coast had been linked up with the Caribbean system, thereby establishing another connection between North and South America. Apart from these expansions of the global system, very few new regions had been incorporated into the global network between 1880 and 1890. Rather, the existing communication centres had been further developed. The cable system in and around Europe had, again, been upgraded massively and the same is true for the transatlantic link. Still, the biggest part of the network extension had been carried out by private companies, but Map 5.4 also shows that in several instances gaps in the network were closed by government involvement – for instance between the Canary Islands and Senegal; along the coast of French Indochina; or between Sulawesi, Java and Sumatra in the Dutch Indies.

Map 5.5 eventually shows the situation in 1903. This year is preferred over 1900 for two reasons. First, the last 'Nomenclature' to be considered here stems from 1903 and therefore data is actually available until then. Second, the two transpacific connections were completed in 1902 and 1903 respectively and form a kind of natural endpoint for our analysis as the last remaining ocean had finally been traversed with telegraph cables

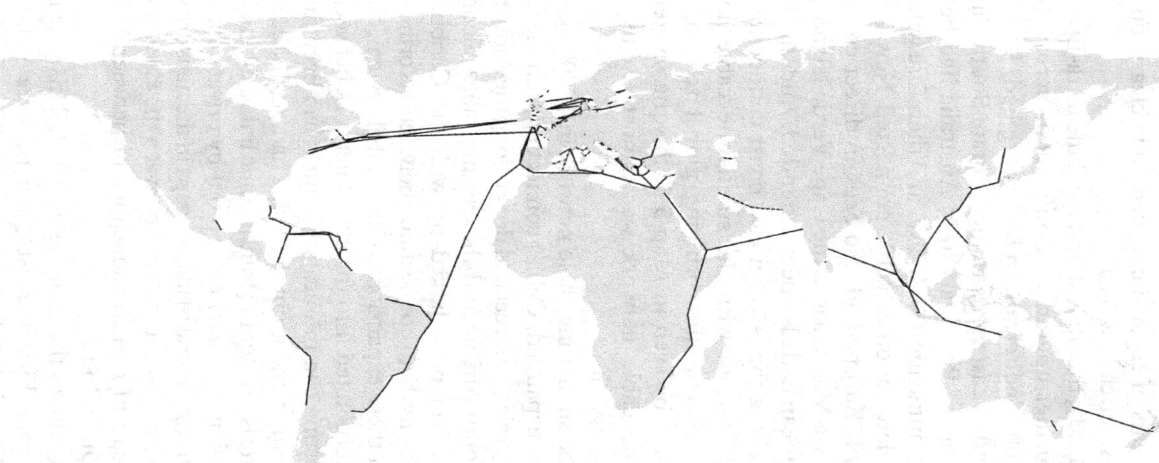

Map 5.3 Global submarine cable network, 1880. Note: Private cables are shown as solid lines; government cables as dashed lines.

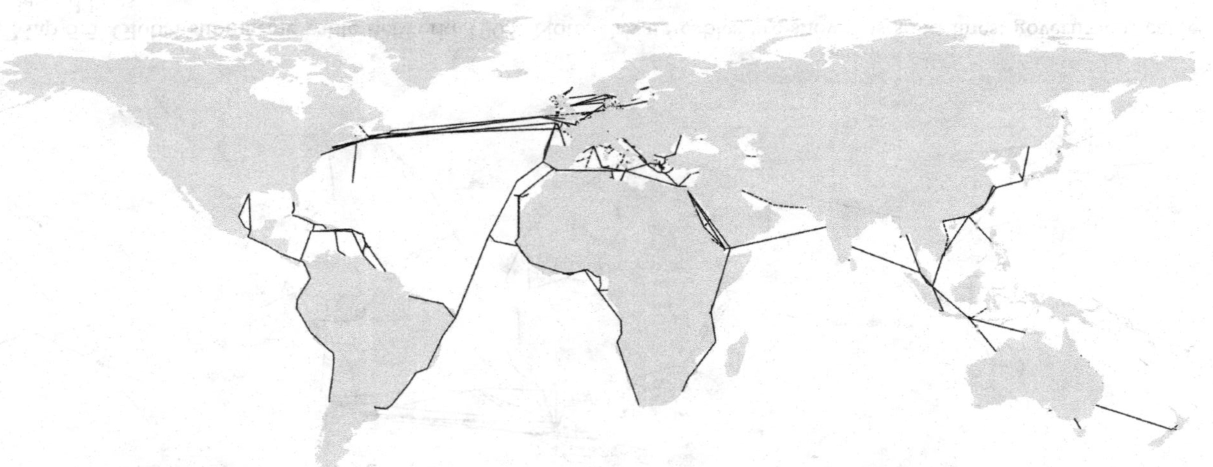

Map 5.4 Global submarine cable network, 1890. Note: Private cables are shown as solid lines; government cables as dashed lines.

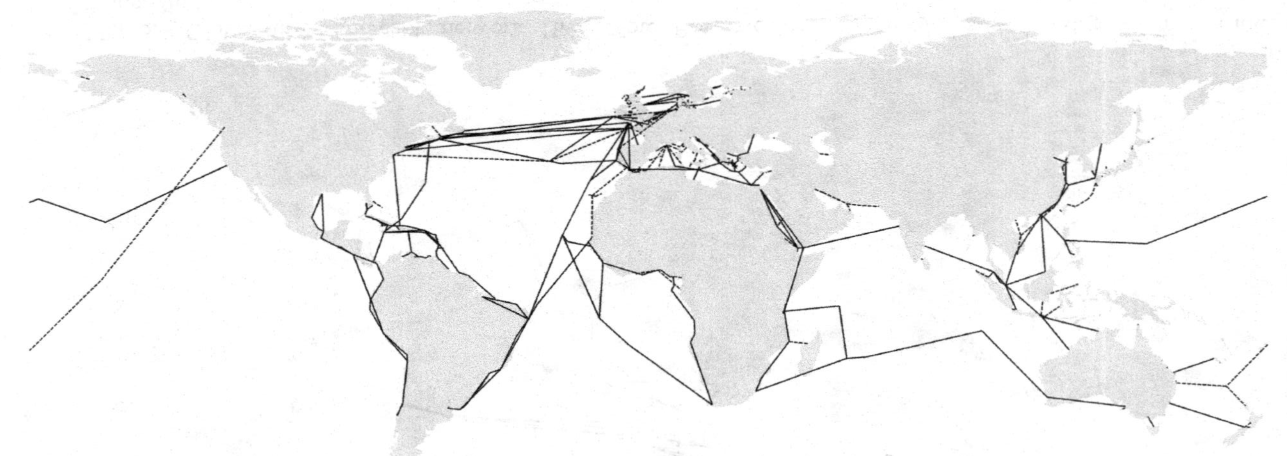

Map 5.5 Global submarine cable network, 1903. Note: Private cables are shown as solid lines; government cables as dashed lines.

as well. Comparing the structure of the global submarine cable network in 1890 and 1903, it becomes discernible that by 1890 most economically or politically important regions of the world had been integrated into the worldwide web of telegraph wires. The last decade of the nineteenth century mainly saw the increasing establishment of cross-connections between the different cable systems – particularly between South America and Africa, Africa and Australia, and eventually across the Pacific. The transatlantic route was further upgraded and the same is true for the intra-European systems in the North Sea, the European Atlantic coast and the Mediterranean. Interestingly, government involvement in cable laying increased during this period of observation. In Asia, along the African west coast and particularly in Europe, many government cables came into operation either to close gaps in the system or to provide for an alternative to the existing connections (which were probably considered unreliable in times of crisis). The biggest public endeavour, however, was the installation of the transpacific cable by the so-called Pacific Cable Board in 1902. The completion of the telegraphic circumnavigation of the globe by laying a transpacific cable had been discussed since the 1870s – often at the instigation of railway pioneer Sir Sandford Fleming. This plan, however, met considerable resistance for a number of reasons and from a number of different parties. The Pacific saw considerably less trade than the Atlantic and, therefore, seemed less lucrative from the perspective of the cable companies. Furthermore, the Eastern and Associated Telegraph Companies – as the quasi-monopolist cable firm of the day – feared that this connection could shift the centre of the global telegraph network unfavourably for itself. Several British politicians shared similar anxieties, culminating in the fear that the United Kingdom could lose its position at the very centre of the web. Giving evidence to the Pacific Cable Committee in 1896, John Lamb, the Secretary of the Post Office, said,

The whole centre [of telegraphic communication] would not move away; but the tendency would be to establish a second centre on the Western coast of America. At present if you look at a map of the world you will find that practically all the telegraphs of the world are centred on England; but under this arrangement [i.e. with a transpacific cable in place] another centre, a rival centre, would be established on the West coast of America . . . I think it would affect the British merchant in this sense: he would be at a disadvantage as compared with the price of telegraphing, whereas now he is at an advantage ... Well, in this way; the British merchant pays 4*s*. 9*d*. a word for his telegram, and the New York merchant pays 5*s*. 9*d*. and the San Francisco pays, I think, 6*s*. . . . If you have this cable made across the Pacific the British merchant will pay 3*s*. and the New York merchant will, I suppose, pay something like 2*s*., or, at the outside, 2*s*. 3*d*. Let us assume the latter figure. He is then 9*d.* better off than the Britisher, whereas now he is 1*s.* worse off. So he will improve his position to the extent of 1*s.* 9*d.*; his relative position.[34]

Despite such concerns and massive delays, two transpacific cables were eventually opened within only two years' time. The Commercial Pacific Cable Company announced its plan to telegraphically traverse the Pacific in 1901. It was supported by the United States government and officially despised by the other principal cable companies – most ardently by the Eastern and the Great Northern Telegraph Company. In 1903, the Commercial Pacific completed a cable from San Francisco via Honolulu to Manila. Only more than twenty years later did it transpire that the Eastern and the Great Northern had since 1896 been scheming to prevent an American company from controlling the transpacific traffic,[35] and in a particularly deceitful act had secretly acquired the majority of shares of the allegedly all-American Commerical Pacific.[36]

This private cable was, however, not the first to traverse the Pacific. Already a year earlier, in 1902, the Pacific Cable Board had laid a cable from British Columbia via Fanning Island, Fiji and Norfolk Island to Australia and New Zealand. Put under pressure by the announcement of the Commercial Pacific's project and the rising international tensions that rendered an all-British connection all the more desirable, the Pacific Cable Board had been formed jointly by Britain, Canada, Australia and New Zealand in 1901.[37] In terms of capacity and transmission speed, however, the public cable could not compete with the commercial connection.[38]

Summarizing the structural development of the global submarine cable network (as partly visualized in Maps 5.1–5.5), the different phases of expansion can be isolated:[39] first, a phase of experimental and short-haul use lasting roughly until 1865. Then a phase of rapid expansion following the boosts received by the successful working of the Persian Gulf and

34 House of Commons Parliamentary Papers, C. 9247, 'Pacific Cable Committee. Report, Minutes of Proceedings, &c.', 1899, 112–13, italics in original.

35 Cable & Wireless Archive, DOC/EEACTC/1/13, Minute Book No 5, 'Eastern Extension Company. Minute Books of the Board', 29 January 1896.

36 Cable & Wireless Archive, DOC/CW/7/15, 'Commercial Pacific Cable Company 1934 to 1935', 1934/35.

37 For a comprehensive study of the developments leading to the establishment of the Pacific Cable Board and the laying of the cable, see Boyce, 'Imperial Dreams and National Realities'.

38 Michael Wobring, *Die Globalisierung der Telekommunikation im 19. Jahrhundert: Pläne, Projekte und Kapazitätsausbauten zwischen Wirtschaft und Politik* (Frankfurt a. M.: Peter Lang, 2005), 198.

39 While Peter Hugill's phases of submarine telegraphy mentioned at the end of Chapter 3 reflect the technological history of submarine cables, these phases focus on the structure of the network. Hugill, *Global Communications since 1844*, 29–35.

transatlantic cables. The pace of expansion slowed down around 1880 when all continents had been incorporated into the evolving global network. In a third phase, lasting roughly from 1880 to 1890, all major world regions were brought into the network. And in a fourth phase, the focus of expansion rested on the establishment of cross-links between the different parts of the system, culminating in the transpacific cables opened in 1902 and 1903. These general phases also become discernible in Table 5.1, which gives the total length of submarine cables existing between 1865 and 1903 as well as the average annual growth rates of the network. The information in the table has been computed on the basis of the data in the 'Nomenclatures', and therefore does not consider several inter-island cables and connections across rivers and estuaries. Also, there may be slight biases due to lack of information on the exact date at which a certain cable went out of operation (as described above). The distortion resulting from these inaccuracies is, however, minuscule and does not influence the validity of the argument, which rests mainly on the growth rates and the proportions of private and government cable lengths. For the sake of comparability, the length of cables has been converted into kilometres from the original data in nautical miles.

Table 5.1 also identifies a phase of rapid expansion between 1865 and 1880, with a peak in the five years before 1870. In this period, the average annual growth rate of the entire global submarine cable network in terms

Table 5.1 *Length of submarine cables under private and government management, 1865–1903.*

	Private		Government		Total	
Year	Abs. (km)	AAG (%)	Abs. (km)	AAG (%)	Abs. (km)	AAG (%)
1865	1,282	n.a.	3,119	n.a.	4,400	n.a.
1870	46,007	104.7	4,858	9.3	50,865	63.1
1880	131,975	11.1	10,762	8.3	142,737	10.9
1890	221,477	5.3	23,852	8.3	245,329	5.6
1903	332,056	3.2	74,250	9.1	406,307	4.0

Note: Length is given in kilometres here. In the sources, nautical miles are used.
Source: 'Nomenclature des câbles formant le réseau sous-marin du globe dressée d'après des documents officiels par le Bureau international des administrations télégraphiques', *Journal télégraphique* 3, no 29 (1877), *Journal télégraphique* 7, no 5 (1883), *Journal télégraphique* 11, no 4 (1887), *Journal télégraphique* 13, no 9 (1889), *Journal télégraphique* 16, no 4 (1892), *Journal télégraphique* 18, no 10 (1894), *Journal télégraphique* 21, no 11 (1897), *Journal télégraphique* 25 (1901) and *Journal télégraphique* 27(1903).

of cable length amounted to more than 63 per cent. In the following decade, growth was still impressive at almost 11 per cent annually. Between 1880 and 1890, the average growth rate reached only half of this figure, dropping to just under 4 per cent in the cross-connections phase from 1890 to 1903. The table also clearly shows how much of the global submarine cable network had indeed been erected and operated by private companies throughout the period of observation. Before this is discussed in more detail, it is interesting to see in Table 5.1 that government involvement in the expansion of the network remained very stable throughout the entire period, while private companies invested massively at the beginning and then reduced their activities in the course of time. The average annual growth rates of the length of government-owned cables vary by less than 1 per cent at all four points of measurement, while private growth rates started at more than 100 per cent annually and then dropped to just over 3 per cent. This supports the point that private telegraph companies in their activities reacted to a real or perceived demand for communication, while government ventures often filled less profitable gaps in the network or provided alternative routes for administrative or strategic purposes.

More detailed information on cable ownership is available for individual years – for instance for the year 1877. Here, the data has been taken directly from the 'Nomenclature' for this year and has not been computed in the manner described above. Table 5.2 shows the proportion of cables and the length of cables operated by private companies and governments in 1877. Out of a total of 569 working cables in place, governments operated 420, amounting to almost three-quarters of the total number. In terms of length, however, only 8,227 kilometres of cable and 10,607

Table 5.2 *Private and government ownership of submarine telegraph cables, 1877.*

	Number of cables		Length of cables		Length of wires	
Ownership	Abs.	%	Abs. (km)	%	Abs. (km)	%
Private	149	26.19	110,282	93.06	121,372	91.96
Government	420	73.81	8,227	6.94	10,607	8.04
Total	569	100	118,509	100	131,979	100

Note: length is given in kilometres here. In the sources, nautical miles are used.
Source: 'Nomenclature des câbles formant le réseau sous-marin du globe dressée d'après des documents officiels par le Bureau international des administrations télégraphiques', *Journal télégraphique* 3, no 29 (1877), 590.

kilometres of wire were in public hands. This amounts to only 6.94 per cent and 8.04 per cent of the total lengths respectively, leaving by far the biggest part to the private companies. These numbers clearly support the point that most private companies concentrated on comparatively few profitable long-distance connections – the trunk routes of global telegraphic communication – while governments provided the often less profitable but equally important local branch routes. The 'Nomenclature' further qualifies this data. All cables in public ownership are displayed as to the various countries operating them and for all private cables the companies are listed (see Tables A.1 and A.2 in the Appendix for detailed information[40]). Apart from the Indo-European Telegraph Department and the British and French governments, no other administration ran cable networks of any significant length. Regarding private cables, altogether twenty-one firms were active in the business in that year. Of these twenty-one companies, seventeen had their main business seat either partially or exclusively in London. The length of cable controlled by firms with a seat only in London amounted to more than 88 per cent of the total length in private hands. While most companies listed here had also attracted international capital and should be seen as transnational rather than British players, the concentration on London nevertheless supports the central role of both the British metropolis and the British imperial (and business) interest in the expansion of the global cable network.

To summarize, in 1877 more than half of the length of all government cables was run by either the British or the British Indian administration. And more than 88 per cent of the length of privately owned cables was run by companies operating out of London. Drawing on a different set of sources, Daniel Headrick and Pascal Griset have shown that this situation remained largely unchanged fifteen years later. They refer to numbers assembled by the United States Department of the Navy stating that 63.1 per cent of the length of all submarine cables in place in the year 1892 were in the hands of British companies (equalling 70 per cent of all private cables). Together with the British government cables, this amounts to 66.3 per cent of the network in British hands.[41] Elsewhere Headrick also

[40] A version of Table A.1 has already been published in an earlier article by the author. Please note that in the process of publication a typographical error slipped into this earlier table. Instead of operating 193 (mostly very short) cables, Norway is attributed only a single cable in the earlier version. Please accept the author's apologies for this mistake which luckily occurred at a position not central to the argument supported by the table. Wenzlhuemer, 'London in the Global Telecommunication Network of the Nineteenth Century', 12.

[41] Headrick and Griset, 'Submarine Telegraph Cables', 560.

notes that 'British firms had laid all British and most non-British cables in the world and owned 24 of the world's 30 cable ships' around the time of the signing of the International Cable Convention in 1885.[42] These figures highlight the central role that Great Britain and the British Empire occupied in global telegraphic communication in the nineteenth century. A combination of several factors had brought this about. The availability of capital and an early symbiosis with one of the key technologies of the Industrial Revolution, the railway, had led to the early emergence of a tight domestic telegraph network in Great Britain. The close business connections across the Atlantic – themselves remnants of British colonialism – and with British India created a demand for instant communication along this east–west axis. This commercial demand was far higher than that created by British imperial administrative and strategic communicational needs. The capital accumulated by successful investments in the transatlantic cable and the nationalization of the British domestic network made it possible for British companies to respond quickly to this demand. And the British government in many ways supported the companies in doing this. Referring to John Pender's cable empire, Headrick and Griset elaborate:

> Although the chancellor of the Exchequer refused to grant subsidies to cable ventures, Pender enjoyed government support in the form of naval surveys of the ocean bottoms and diplomatic pressure on foreign governments to grant landing rights. He maintained close ties with the British government by placing members of the Foreign and Colonial Offices on the boards of directors of his companies.[43]

Therefore it comes as no surprise that the structure and growth patterns of the global cable network to a great extent reflected the changing dynamics of British imperial and business interests. Unfortunately, there is no comprehensive information on the actual use of the submarine cable network and on global information flow patterns. Such data exists only for isolated cases and routes (as will be seen for the telegraphic information flow between India and Europe in Chapter 8) or on an aggregate level regarding the general amount of external traffic of a country (as will be explored in the following chapter).[44] At the moment (and this is unlikely to change soon) the growth patterns of the global submarine cable

[42] Headrick, *The Tentacles of Progress*, 115.

[43] Headrick and Griset, 'Submarine Telegraph Cables', 562. On diplomatic pressure, see also Márquez Quevedo, 'Telecommunications and Colonial Rivalry'.

[44] At the Cable & Wireless Archives at Porthcurno, at least four memoranda can be found that contain some rudimentary information on the traffic that the more important Eastern stations around the globe saw. It seems that these memos – all of which draw from the year 1879 – were sent from the Eastern clearing house in London to Porthcurno as a kind of quality management. They list the percentages of errors that occurred in the telegrams

network can only be traced by examining its infrastructural growth, as has been done in the previous paragraphs. It is, however, possible to trace some of the impact that the expansion of the network had. The following sections will look at the transformation of global communication space by means of the submarine telegraph, as well as at the relation between these changes and British business interests.

5.3 Shifts in global communication space

Since the early modern period, information about international business and shipping has often been gathered and exchanged in coffee houses. One such coffee house was opened by Edward Lloyd in the City of London in the late seventeenth century. It quickly became a meeting point for shipowners, merchants, investors, insurers and other people interested in international trade. Several well-known institutions that still exist today sprang from the informal but regular meetings at Lloyd's coffee house: the Lloyd's of London insurance market, the ship classifiers Lloyd's Register of Shipping and *Lloyd's List*. The latter of the three was originally published by Edward Lloyd himself and contained information on issues such as arrivals and departures at British and international ports, wreckages or maritime casualties. Usually with a day's delay, a selection of the most important pieces of 'ship news' or 'shipping intelligence' was then published in *The Times* of London and circulated beyond the specialist readership of *Lloyd's List*.

The Finnish historian Yrjö Kaukiainen mentions that *Lloyd's List*

> enjoyed favoured treatment from the Royal Mail which meant that very few private information systems were able to produce equally quick, or quicker, communication. Thus we can expect that, in terms of both speed and reliability, *Lloyd's List* commanded the best available flows of information throughout the period in question.[45]

handled by a particular station during a particular month. As a by-product, they also give the total number of messages handled at the stations covered. Judging from this scarce information, it seems that the Eastern stations along the route from London to Aden saw by far the biggest amount of traffic. Cable & Wireless Archive, DOC/ETC/7/15/9, 'Porthcurno Station Correspondence. Return of Number of Errors made during February 1879', 7 July 1879; Cable & Wireless Archive, DOC/ETC/7/15/11, 'Porthcurno Station Correspondence. Return of Number of Errors made during March 1879', 31 July 1879; Cable & Wireless Archive, exhibited in display window at the Porthcurno Telegraph Museum, 'Porthcurno Station Correspondence. Return of Number of Errors made during April 1879', 14 August 1879; Cable & Wireless Archive, exhibited in display window at the Porthcurno Telegraph Museum, 'Porthcurno Station Correspondence. Return of Number of Errors made during May 1879', 18 September 1879.

[45] Kaukiainen, 'Shrinking the World', 3, italics in original.

In Kaukiainen's case, the period in question ranges from approximately 1820 to 1870. By comparing the date of an event (i.e. the arrival or departure of a ship) with the time of its publication in *Lloyd's List*, it is possible to establish the average time of communication between the place of the event and the place of publication in London. Kaukiainen has taken data samples from the *List* at ten-year intervals and has been able to show that the speed of communication between London and practically all world regions covered in *Lloyd's List* increased massively between 1820 and 1870. This is all the more interesting as these are, at least seen from a global vantage point, mostly pre-telegraphic times. In the Appendix to his article, Kaukiainen notes that only in the year 1870 were some of the dispatches on a number of routes already conveyed by telegraph.[46] In all other cases, messages had been transported by traditional means at sea and overland.

Kaukiainen concludes that the 'material drawn from *Lloyd's List* indicates that a major overall improvement [of global communication times] took place between 1820 and 1860; in terms of actual dispatch times, it clearly exceeded that which took place after the introduction of the telegraph in the 1860s and 1870s.'[47] Looking at the absolute speed of communication this is, of course, true. By 1860, the improvements both in shipping and in overland transport occurring in the first half of the nineteenth century had reduced communication times between London and most other regions of the world to less than half, sometimes to a third or a quarter, of what they had been at the beginning of the century. The case of India, however, is particularly significant. India had come into telegraphic contact with Great Britain via the Persian Gulf cables in 1865 and even more directly via the Siemens line or the Red Sea cable in 1870. This is reflected by the significant reduction in communication times from 22 per cent of the 1820 value in 1860 to 4 per cent in 1870. While in absolute terms this might be belittled by the developments between 1820 and 1860, it becomes all the more interesting when put into relation to the communication times of telegraphically unconnected regions in the same year. As has been laid out in Chapter 2, the principal characteristic of telegraphy is the dematerialization of information and its detachment from material transport. Although sea and land transport quickened impressively between 1820 and 1860, communication times mostly remained a function of the geographic (or, better, the navigational) distance between the communicating parties. The telegraph ended this automatism by detaching communication space from geographic or

[46] Ibid., 27–8. [47] Ibid., 21.

navigational space. While the most impressive improvements in absolute communication times have occurred in the pre-telegraphic period, global telegraphy introduced a completely new pattern to global communication. In order to make this pattern visible, Yrjö Kaukiainen's methods have been slightly adapted and his study has been continued for the rest of the nineteenth century.

Unfortunately, Kaukiainen's work and the present study are not directly compatible. Results can be compared, of course, and generally confirm each other, but the methods applied as well as the form of presentation differ in some areas. The data presented here has not been drawn directly from *Lloyd's List* but rather from the 'Ship News' and 'Latest Shipping Intelligence' sections of *The Times* of London. The information originated with *Lloyd's List*, but only a few selected locations and ships were listed in *The Times* of the following day. Looking at *The Times* shipping information, therefore, means looking at a preselected array of information that was perceived as important information for a wider public, and it also means looking at the amount of time it took for shipping information to reach this general public and not a group of *List* subscribers with a highly specialized interest. Furthermore, the amount of data published in *The Times* is easier to handle for a researcher, while it is, of course, far less comprehensive than the material in *Lloyd's List*. Information on individual port cities has been grouped in world regions similar in style to Kaukiainen's procedure but due to the dissimilar source base, the composition of world regions differs slightly.

Samples have been drawn from *The Times* of London for the years 1850, 1860, 1870, 1880, 1890 and 1900 at four different times each year in order to avoid seasonal biases caused, for instance, by the monsoon pattern (see Table A.3 in the Appendix). Depending on the average lengths of *List* extracts published in *The Times*, the annual samples vary in size from 600 to 1,400. The difference in days between the date of an event (usually the arrival or departure of a ship) and the date of the publication of this event in *The Times* has been calculated for each event in the samples. According to the location of the event, these time differences have been grouped geographically and both the average and the median time of communication with London have been computed and displayed in the table. In several cases, it has not been possible to draw representative samples for a particular world region in a particular year. Data is marked as not available (n.a.) in these cases in the table in the Appendix. For some regions, reliable data was not available for the period of observation. In such cases, the region has not been included in the discussion at all. From 1860 onwards, information on the average annual growth of the speed of communication with London during the ten years leading up to the year of observation could be computed. It is important to note that these values relate to the growth of the speed of communication and not to the growth of the time of communication. This means that positive numbers indicate that communication became faster, while negative numbers show that communication slowed down.

The figures for the years 1850 and 1860 generally confirm Yrjö Kaukiainen's analysis of global communication speed in this period. Kaukiainen identifies the period between 1820 and 1850 as that of the fastest 'shrinking of the world' before global telegraphy. Except for the cases of India and the East Coast of the United States, however, only very slow further improvement can be detected for the period between 1850 and 1870. The data from *The Times* of London supports this point and also comes very close to Kaukiainen's values in terms of absolute message-delivery times.[48] The communication times between London and most other parts of the world did shrink between 1850 and 1860, but only at modest rates. The biggest average annual growth of speed can be seen either on the longest routes – for instance between London and ports in southern Africa, Australia or South America – or within Europe where the telegraph already made a crucial impact. Growth rates drop further in the following decade and in some cases even turn into the negative – with the notable exceptions of communication with India and across the Atlantic. Here, a massive reduction of delivery times can be examined. The transatlantic cable, the Indo-European overland route to India and Pender's submarine cable to Bombay had brought communication times between the East Coast of the US and London to an average of 8.1 days (between an event and its publication in *The Times*) and to 9.6 days between London and the South Asian east coast. In terms of communicational proximity, the eastern US was, therefore, about as close to London as, for instance, the European Atlantic coast or the western Mediterranean. And it had already moved closer than the eastern Mediterranean. This transformation of global communication space becomes even more striking if we look at median communication times. Here, the United States has moved as close to London as the North Sea. And the same is true for the Arabian Peninsula and for the South Asian west coast (with the east coast only marginally further away).[49] The infrastructural growth of the global submarine telegraph network,

[48] See the list of individual port cities in ibid., 27.

[49] While the average can be distorted by the prevalence of extraordinarily high or low values, the median is more resistant to such distortions. In the case at hand, the significant difference between average and median values indicates that a certain percentage of messages has still been delivered by traditional means, leading to the prevalence of a few rather high values in the delivery times sampled. These values distort the average value, but not so much the median value.

therefore, immediately impacted on global communication times and started to transform global communication space.

In the previous section, it was shown that the 'wiring of the world' received a particular boost between 1870 and 1880 and moved forward at an impressive pace. Again, global communication times immediately reflected this structural expansion. With the notable exception of the South American north-east,[50] all regions included in our analysis exhibited dramatic growth rates in the speed of communication with London between 1870 and 1880. By the end of the decade, delivery times had dropped to around three, four or five days. Regions such as the Arabian Peninsula (with the important telegraphic hub at Aden), eastern South Asia or even New Zealand in communicational terms moved closer to London than practically all of Europe, with an average of 1.8 days between an event's taking place and its publication in *The Times*.[51] In the following decade, most remaining world regions were integrated in the global telegraph network and existing connections were improved and expanded. Accordingly, by 1890 communication times for all reasonably well-connected regions had long started to converge (see the average and median values for 1890 in Table A.3). Communication

[50] This exception should be attributed to the fact that *The Times* in 1880 contained almost no shipping information from the cities of Pernambuco, Cearà and Para (today Recife, Fortaleza and Belém in Brazil), while there was quite some information from Demerara (today Georgetown, Guyana). A cable connecting Carcavelos in Portugal with Pernambuco via Madeira and the Cape Verde Islands had been put in place in 1874. Several other cables along the South American coast connected Pernambuco with Cearà, Para, Cayenne and Demerara to the north. But the connection between Para, Cayenne and Demerara worked only for about two years until it was abandoned. By 1880, it had not yet been re-established. Therefore information from the latter two places needed to cover at least a good part of the distance to London by ship or overland transport. And because information from Demerara for some reason makes up most of the data sample for north-eastern South America, this is reflected in the data in Table A.3. For information on the Brazilian coastal telegraph network, see Carlos Alves Müller, 'Longa Distância: A Evolução dos Sistemas Nacionais de Telecomunicações da Argentina e do Brasil em Conexão com as Telecomunicações Internacionais (1808–2003)', (PhD thesis, University of Brasília, Instituto de Ciências Sociais, 2007), 265–330.

[51] Median values of 1.5 and two days confirm this dramatic shift in global communication space. It is, however, important to note here that as soon as communication times have reached a value of only a few days, the location of a specific region within the time zone system becomes relevant. The astonishingly low figures for New Zealand in 1880, for instance, must partly be explained by the time difference. According to the modern system of standard time zones, New Zealand time is twelve hours in front of London time. New York, on the other hand, is five hours behind London. Adding this up, in order to produce the same difference of days between an event and its publication in London, information from New Zealand statistically has about seventeen hours more time to travel to London than information from New York. While places such as New Zealand, Australia or Japan might be extreme cases, this time distortion has to be taken into account when comparing communication times of places east and west of London.

with parts of South America and southern Africa, however, seem to have been of variable speed. In both cases, there is an interesting difference between the average and the median values, which means that most messages were conveyed at good speed (median values of around two, three or four days) while some messages took considerably longer (producing average values of around five, six or even seven days). At sixteen days, communication with London took longest for Indian Ocean islands such as Mauritius or Réunion. In 1890, these islands had not yet been telegraphically connected.

By the turn of the century, global communication times had further converged. Most shipping news from most world regions now took between one and three days to travel to London and get published. Only in the case of South America and parts of Africa were delivery times still a little higher, with average and median values converging. The Arabian Peninsula, India and the East Coast of the United States were still closer to London than continental Europe (or at least as close). Several ports in Australia and New Zealand found their way into *The Times* shipping intelligence columns within only a day's delay (not considering the statistical bias generated by the time difference, as described in the footnote above). Interestingly, absolute message delivery times had in many instances grown between 1890 and 1900. At the moment, one can only speculate about the reasons behind this. The massive expansion of global telegraphic demand set against an only moderate expansion of network capacity might provide an explanation, but there is currently no hard evidence to support this.

It is safe to say that by 1900 global communication space had been almost completely detached from geographic or navigational space. Only in very isolated cases (for instance those of remote islands) was communicational distance still a function of geographic distance. A look at the rates for telegrams sent from the United Kingdom to places all over the world further confirms this diagnosis. In the third chapter of the second report of the Inter-departmental Committee on Cable Communications, detailed tables showing such rates are provided.[52] These tables show that the price one had to pay per word in a telegram sent from the United Kingdom depended only very loosely on the distance that such a telegram had to cover. Rather, such factors as available capacity, company competition and imperial interest seem to have informed the emergence of such rate patterns. First, it can be seen that a message sent within the British Empire was on average cheaper than one leaving British territory.

52 House of Commons Parliamentary Papers, Cd. 1056, 'Cable Communications Report of the Inter-departmental Committee on Cable Communications', 1902, 36–9.

By 1902, most British possessions could be reached at a rate of between one and five shillings per word. Only in some cases – for instance West Africa or British Guiana – did higher rates apply. Telegrams to foreign countries, on the other hand, often came at rates considerably higher than five shillings per word and could in exceptional cases even reach rates of 10s 10d. But also within the British Empire, the price of a telegram could vary considerably. From the United Kingdom to British Columbia in the Dominion of Canada a word rate of 1s 6d applied from 1895 onwards. In the same year, a telegram to most British possessions in the West Indies amounted to more than nine shillings. Over the next seven years, the rates for this region would only drop to between four and five shillings a word. A similar pattern exists for the telegraphic traffic between the United Kingdom and foreign countries. A message to the United States cost between one shilling and 1s 8d per word during the last decade of the nineteenth century, while in 1890 a telegram to China amounted to between 7s 1d and 8s 9d per word. Ten years later, 5s 6d was charged. And in 1890 a message to Brazil cost at least six shillings a word. This exemplary data emphasizes that also in terms of communication cost, geographic distance had ceased to be the decisive factor.

However, the studies conducted in the above section and previously by Yrjö Kaukiainen can only draw an incomplete picture of global communication space and of the centres and peripheries therein. They analyse material published in London and interpret data on communication times with London. Accordingly, they can only look at global communication space from a London vantage point. Following the concept of space as outlined in Chapter 2, the space that becomes discernible through our analysis is only generated by asking how long it took for information to reach London. Other perspectives or points of departure cannot be considered in such a study (and accordingly cannot be reflected in the resulting transformation of space). Therefore alternative methods for identifying global communicational centres and peripheries will be introduced and applied in the next chapter. But before coming to this, it shall briefly be tested in the concluding section of this chapter whether global communication space (as seen from London) can be brought into correspondence with world trade (as seen from London).

5.4 Trade routes and cable routes

In 1911, the Standing Sub-committee of the Committee of Imperial Defence submitted a report on submarine cable communications in time of war. This report was chiefly concerned with the question of 'how

Britain would isolate Germany from the world' in case of war.[53] But it also contained some general information on the structure and working principles of the mostly British-run submarine cable network. Paragraph 18, for instance, reads,

> The routes of the cables to British Colonies and Protectorates follow the main trade routes across the Atlantic to North and South America, along the Mediterranean and Red Sea to Bombay, and down the west coast of Africa as far as Sierra Leone, and most of the main trade routes and main cables converge alike on main centres of commerce, many of which are naval bases. On the other hand, the important cables between Vancouver and Australasia, between Australia and Mauritius, and those down the South-West and East Coasts of Africa diverge for considerable distances from the main trade routes, while others, such as those to the West Indies, between India and Singapore and Hong Kong, though they cross or pass near important trade routes, do not follow their course.[54]

The resemblance between major trade and cable routes alluded to in this short passage is all but surprising. The detachment of information flows from material transport brought about by the telegraph is extremely useful for the control and co-ordination of international shipping and for time-critical trading. Therefore business interest produced a demand that rendered cables to particular regions profitable. The cable routes roughly followed the flows of money and commodities. However, the report also refers to other cases – namely those between Vancouver and Australasia as well as Australia and Mauritius – where the pathways of communication digressed from those of commerce. At times, strategic or administrative demands overrode mere economic considerations and led to the laying of cables with little or no business significance. In the end, however, the most insightful question is not why a particular region had been connected but rather what happened as a consequence. Does getting globally connected quasi-automatically lead to a tighter integration into the global market? Or, in more general terms, does progress in one particular sphere of globalization (here: global communication) directly entail the acceleration of other forms of globalization (here: global economic integration)? This is, of course, a complex set of questions that cannot be answered satisfactorily here. Undertaken in some detail and with the necessary care, such a study will in itself fill entire books. Therefore it must suffice here analytically to stay at the surface of both data and methods. In the following, it can only be

53 Jonathan Reed Winkler, 'Information Warfare in World War I', *Journal of Military History* 73 (2009), 848.

54 National Archives, CAB 16/14, 'Standing Sub-committee of the Committee of Imperial Defence. Submarine Cable Communication in Time of War. Report with Table and Appendices', December 1911, 6.

pointed out from where more detailed future studies on these questions could set out.

Again, the perspective of the following brief analysis is a British one. Its findings can, therefore, be directly compared to the shifts in global communication space described in the previous section. Between 1854 and 1921, the statistical office of the Custom House provided the Houses of Parliament with a detailed annual statement of the trade of the United Kingdom of the previous year.[55] These statements contained information on the value of all commodities Britain imported from or exported to foreign countries or British possessions. In the context of this study, British trade volumes with only a few selected regions have been examined (for detailed information see Table A.4 in the Appendix). These regions have been chosen from a capacious list in order to show that in some cases cable communications clearly pushed a region into the international market, while in other cases there is no such indication whatsoever. All the regions examined here were telegraphically connected in the 1860s and 1870s; therefore only trade data for the years between 1863 and 1880 has been evaluated. As the interest of this analysis rests on changes in trade volume rather than on absolute volume, average growth figures have been computed. In order to balance extraordinarily big annual fluctuations, these growth figures are based on five-year moving averages.[56]

Japan was integrated in the global submarine cable network via connections to Russia, China and, further, South East Asia in 1871. For the same year, the data shows a surge of British imports from Japan after a decade of constant decrease. For five years, imports from Japan grew by rates of between 18 per cent and 51 per cent annually. From the mid-1870s onwards, growth rates level off and remained relatively stable for some time. While there seems to be a clear correlation between the advent of

[55] The statements of trade used here are House of Commons Parliamentary Papers, 3723, 'Annual Statement of the Trade and Navigation of the United Kingdom with Foreign Countries and British Possessions in the Year 1865', 1866; House of Commons Parliamentary Papers, C. 437, 'Annual Statement of the Trade and Navigation of the United Kingdom with Foreign Countries and British Possessions in the Year 1870', 1871; House of Commons Parliamentary Papers, C. 1571, 'Annual Statement of the Trade of the United Kingdom with Foreign Countries and British Possessions for the Year 1875', 1876; House of Commons Parliamentary Papers, C. 2920, 'Annual Statement of the Trade of the United Kingdom with Foreign Countries and British Possessions for the Year 1880', 1881.

[56] The five-year moving average for the year 1870, for instance, is calculated by adding up the values for the five years from 1868 to 1872 and dividing this sum by five. For the year 1871, the values for 1869 to 1873 are handled accordingly. While still displaying the development of a particular value over time, moving averages smooth the distorting impact of outliers.

the cable and the rise of British imports from Japan,[57] British exports to Japan do not exhibit any such clearly discernible pattern. The same thing can be said regarding imports from and exports to the United States of America. British imports from the US started to grow continuously (and at quite a high pace) after the laying of the transatlantic cable in 1866. As the growth rates are based on five-year moving averages, growth already begins in 1865. And while there was a growth of imports from the US between 1864 and 1865 in absolute numbers, the moving average smoothens the edges of the process. The absolute figures given in the statements of trade illustrate that the value of imports grew from around £18 million to £21.5 million between 1864 and 1865,[58] but it exploded and reached a value of almost £47 million in 1866.[59] Again, no corresponding pattern can bc detected regarding British exports to the United States. There is a temporary surge for the year 1866 but it is not sustained in the following years.

Aden became an important telegraphic hub in 1870, serving as a relay station on the submarine cable route between Europe and India. British trade with Aden had been minuscule before this point in time, but it received a strong stimulus through the cable. British exports and imports both increase steadily from 1870 (the growth rate of imports of almost 700 per cent from 1868 to 1869 is a consequence of the very small absolute trade numbers). In the case of Australia, only British exports to the Antipodes seem to have been given a boost by improved communication. In the years after the telegraphic connection was put into service in 1871, export value grew to more than £20 million annually. Imports from Australia also grew during the period of observation, but at a steady, linear pace with no extraordinary surges. British Guiana was first telegraphically integrated into a worldwide network in the year 1875. However, as already mentioned in a footnote above, the coastal cables connecting the colony with Para, Pernambuco and, eventually, Europe only worked until 1877. A rise in British imports started only two years before the cable reached Guiana and peaked during the brief period of direct telegraphic connection. Exports to British Guiana, however, seem completely unaffected by the cable and display a rather erratic development.

[57] At this level of investigation, we can only speak of a correlation. The data analysed in this study does not allow for the verification or falsification of a direct causal relationship.

[58] House of Commons Parliamentary Papers, 3723, 'Annual Statement of the Trade and Navigation of the United Kingdom with Foreign Countries and British Possessions in the Year 1865', 1866, 2.

[59] House of Commons Parliamentary Papers, C. 437, 'Annual Statement of the Trade and Navigation of the United Kingdom with Foreign Countries and British Possessions in the Year 1870', 1871, 2.

The eastern parts of British North America came into direct telegraphic communication with Britain thanks to the transatlantic cable of 1866. British trade relations with British North America received a temporary surge in that year that was corrected in the following two or three years. Then, from the end of the 1860s onwards, both imports and exports grew steadily. In the case of British exports, this was only the continuation of an existing trend. Regarding imports, however, 1866 brought a reversal of the downward trend. It seems that the transatlantic cable had a direct and lasting impact here. A similar pattern can be seen for Hong Kong, which received a cable connection in 1871. British exports to Hong Kong had been growing for some time and reached a temporary peak in 1870, but there seems to be no correlation with the advent of the cable a year later. Imports from Hong Kong, however, started to increase massively after 1871, reaching five-year moving average growth rates of between 18 and 56 per cent. In this case, there seems to be a clear correlation. Exactly the same can be said for Singapore and the Straits Settlements. British exports thereto only peak temporarily with the cable connection of 1870, and afterwards develop in a rather erratic fashion. Imports, however, received a clear boost with the telegraph.

In the other cases, there seems to be no connection whatsoever between trade relations with Britain and telegraphic development. No such impact is discernible for Madeira (1874), the British West Indies (1874) or British India (1865 and, again, 1870). Therefore the results of the study of British trade statistics are hard to interpret. There seems to be no clear pattern. Sometimes improved communications – or, more precisely speaking, the dematerialization of information flows from and to a particular region – quite clearly led to a tighter integration into the world economy (of which the British market formed a decisive part during the period of observation). At other times, no such connection seems to exist at all. At the current level of sophistication of the study, it cannot be said why a correlation exists in some regions but not in others. Furthermore, if a correlation becomes discernible it usually affects only the British imports from a particular region. With the exceptions of Australia and, to a degree, Aden, British exports usually remained unaffected by improved communications, it seems. While it is easy to see why better and faster knowledge about the market situation would entail the rise of imports from a particular region, it cannot at the present moment be said why the same does not seem to be true for the export market.

What becomes clear from the preliminary study conducted in this section is that deterministic understandings (no matter of which brand) of the relationship between society and technology cannot hold. Relations and correlations between the communicational and economic globalization of a region are erratic and seem to follow no predeterminable pattern. Therefore this complex interrelationship needs to be researched in considerable detail, focusing on particular case studies and the concrete circumstances of the ongoing processes of globalization and the people involved in these processes. As pointed out, there is a clear correlation in many cases – a correlation that works through and is carried by the historical actors. These actors need to become the focus of more detailed case studies before it will be possible to say anything more meaningful about the causal chains leading (or not leading) to correlation.

6 Global centres and peripheries

6.1 Identifying centres and peripheries

After receiving specialized training at the Royal Engineering College at Cooper's Hill, Surrey, Eustace Alban Kenyon was appointed assistant superintendent in the Indian Telegraph Department on 26 September 1880 and posted to Calcutta. In 1896, Kenyon was promoted to superintendent and by 1905 he had been made superintendent first grade.[1] Right from his arrival in India up to at least 1898, Kenyon frequently wrote letters to his family in England describing both the life of an Englishman in India and his work in the telegraph department. These letters can today be consulted in the archive collection of the Centre of South Asian Studies of the University of Cambridge. Many of Kenyon's letters deal in one form or another with telegraphy and its impact on both personal time and space. On 9 March 1891, for instance, Kenyon wrote a letter to his sister Tizie. He had been posted to Ellore (today Eluru) to supervise the erection of a new telegraph line, and had

> just finished all work up to a little north of this, as far as the route is sanctioned and [I] am now just waiting for a boat – which ought to have been here long ago to take me off to Coconada from where I go on by sea on Friday to Vizagapatam; always supposing that I don't meanwhile get a telegram saying that the remainder of the line is sanctioned & that I am to go on with that. I shall be very annoyed if I do get any such telegram, as I have now broken up my working party and sent the men off to their homes, over 100 miles away.[2]

Before Kenyon could finish the letter, the boat arrived and took him to the city of Coconada (today: Kakinada) on the Indian east coast. All the way from Ellore to Coconada, Kenyon travelled practically along the main telegraph line running down the coast from Calcutta to Madras. And no

[1] *The India List and India Office List for 1905 Compiled from Official Records by Direction of the Secretary of State for India in Council* (London: Harrison and Sons, 1905).

[2] Eustace Alban Kenyon, 'Letter to Tizie', 9 March 1891, Cambridge South Asian Archive, Centre of South Asian Studies, University of Cambridge, Kenyon (E. A.) Papers.

matter where he was on this route, a telegraph message commanding him back to Ellore could reach him at any time outpacing boats, railways or steamships alike. Kenyon's anxiety as to the possibility to be ordered back at any minute transpires through the words of the letter. Being close to a telegraph line meant being reachable. Peripheries could all of a sudden feel very central indeed.[3] The same rationale already became visible in a letter written six years earlier in a telegraph camp somewhere in the Tenasserim Range between Burma and Siam. Kenyon had been posted there when a new telegraph line and road to connect British Burma with the Siamese system were being built.[4] From No 2 Telegraph Camp near the Tenasserim River he wrote to his mother on 1 February 1885: 'No letters arrived yet this week so I have nothing to answer, I hope to get them tomorrow evening as I heard by telegram that they left Myitta yesterday morning.'[5] Even by today's standards, Myitta in Myanmar is still a rather remote town. Kenyon and his party camped somewhere in the jungle-covered hills probably to the south-east of Myitta, but as part of their task they carried a functioning telegraph line with them and accordingly they were telegraphically connected with the rest of the world via Tavoy, Moulmein and Rangoon. While in terms of its geographic position, the telegraph camp remained at the very periphery of the globalizing world, it was central in terms of information access (in this case information about the painstakingly slow movement of letters).

The dematerialization of information flows made possible by the telegraph entailed that wherever there was access to the network, peripheries ceased to be peripheral and spaces were transformed. Measuring the distribution of centres and peripheries in the global telegraph network of the nineteenth century, therefore, essentially means mapping communication

[3] While the letter itself provides no direct evidence of this, it is nevertheless reasonable to assume that Kenyon had learned by telegraph that a boat would pick him up and take him to Coconada. Without the possibility of telegraphic communication, the boat would have arrived without prior notification. Therefore Kenyon's unpleasant wait for the boat and his critical sense of time and punctuality was, very likely, a consequence of connectedness.

[4] During his assignment to the Siamese border, Kenyon had some problems with his health and eventually went on leave to Simla. From there, he wrote a letter to his sister Mary on 9 July 1885 explaining why his party had also built a road through the jungle next to the telegraph line. 'Why should you all persist in thinking the road from Tavoy to Siam must be to enable us to march troops there? Can you not imagine that in such hills and jungles a tolerably good & level path may be absolutely necessary to maintain the telegraph line; also that it may sometimes be a useful thing to open up a new trade route to a neighbouring country; also if we intended to use it for an invasion of Siam, do you think the Siamese would be so compliant as to help us by making their part of the road.' Eustace Alban Kenyon, 'Letter to Mary', 9 July 1885, Cambridge South Asian Archive, Centre of South Asian Studies, University of Cambridge, Kenyon (E. A.) Papers.

[5] Eustace Alban Kenyon, 'Letter to Mother', 1 February 1885, Cambridge South Asian Archive, Centre of South Asian Studies, University of Cambridge, Kenyon (E. A.) Papers.

space. As has been argued in some detail in Chapter 2 and elsewhere,[6] space is understood in this study as an ad hoc construct that constitutes itself as an answer to a specific problem (for instance a research question). This kind of space is seen through the eyes of a particular actor or group of actors. The study of shifting communication times with London presented in the previous chapter, for example, is a survey of global communication space as seen by the business community based in the British metropolis. Space as defined in this study can thus only be examined and measured from a vantage point within. This is different with networks. Networks are not spaces, but they can be vehicles for the constitution of spaces as they provide the connections between the different actors or groups of actors. As structures, networks can be examined and analysed from an outside vantage point that does not need to be anchored at a particular network node. Such an outside perspective on the centres and peripheries in a network allows for a better understanding of the network structure itself.[7] Structures need to be charted and understood because they provide a maximum potential for the constitution of spaces – in the case at hand, communication space. Whether this structural potential is then realized and put to use, however, is another question.

The present chapter will be concerned with the identification of centres and peripheries in the global communication network of the nineteenth and early twentieth centuries and it will do so in four different settings with four different studies. Three of these studies will look at network structures, one at network use. This later study will be based on the 'Statistique générale de la télégraphie', but focuses on the external telegraph traffic of a number of different countries around the world. Apart from data on individual case studies, such aggregate data is the only information on actual global information flows (i.e. the realization of the structural potential) available at the moment. The conclusions that can be drawn from this material alone are limited, but put into the context of the three other analyses conducted in this chapter, global centres and peripheries, as well

[6] Wenzlhuemer, 'Globalization, Communication and the Concept of Space in Global History'.

[7] Manuel Castells holds that '[a] network has no center, just nodes. Nodes may be of varying relevance for the network.' Castells, 'Informationalism, Networks, and the Network Society', 3. Actually, nodes with a high relevance for the network – thanks to the many connections they maintain or the high amount of network traffic they handle – form the centre(s) of a network. While the network as such could still function without at least some of these nodes, this does not diminish the centrality of such nodes in terms of information access or control over information flows. Therefore networks clearly do have centres, just as they do have peripheries. Of course, places or people that are not part of a network are – at least seen from within the network – even more peripheral than a peripheral network node.

as their shifting or non-shifting positions throughout the second half of the nineteenth century, will become clearly discernible. These other three studies will look in some more detail at the underlying network structures. They will do so by means of a social network analysis – a tool designed not only to identify central and less central nodes in networks but also to reveal the specific functions and characteristics of particular nodes.

Social network analysis was originally developed in the social and behavioural sciences in the 1970s (although its roots reach back to the 1930s). 'It is grounded in the observation that social actors are interdependent and that the links among them have important consequences for every individual ... Social network analysis involves theorizing, model building and empirical research focused on uncovering the patterning of links among actors.'[8] The method can be applied to practically any form of network. It does not matter much whether the entities connected in a network are people, institutions, states or something entirely different.[9] And it does not make a difference whether the connections in the network are technologically mediated (as in the case of the telegraph network) or not. Social network analysis simply looks at the pattern of connections in a given network and examines the position of the different network nodes as to their centrality (and function) in the structure. It is, therefore, ideally suited to identify centres and peripheries in a network and also to further qualify which factors contributed to the position of a particular node. Social network analysis software usually provides a great number of analytical tools to establish different forms of centrality in a network. Here, only four of these tools will be applied – *degree*, *closeness*, *betweenness* and *eigenvector* – that are particularly insightful regarding the analysis of centrality in a telecommunication network. What exactly these four values signify will be explained in detail in the actual studies.[10]

[8] Linton C. Freeman, 'Social Network Analysis: Definition and History', in *Encyclopedia of Psychology*, ed. A. E. Kazdan (New York: Oxford University Press, 2000), 350.

[9] Holzer, *Netzwerke*, 34.

[10] For a more detailed introduction to social network analysis and its fields of application, see, for instance, Linton C. Freeman, 'Centrality in Networks: I. Conceptual Clarification', *Social Networks* 1, no 3 (1979); Freeman, 'The Gatekeeper, Pair-Dependency and Structural Centrality', *Quality and Quantity* 14 (1980); Freeman, 'Social Network Analysis'; Freeman, *The Development of Social Network Analysis: A Study in the Sociology of Science* (Vancouver: Empirical Press, 2004); Freeman, *Social Network Analysis*, 4 vols. (London: Sage Publications, 2007); Linton C. Freeman, Douglas R. White and A. Kimball Romney, eds., *Research Methods in Social Network Analysis* (Fairfax: George Mason University Press, 1989); Stanley Wasserman and Katherine Faust, *Social Network Analysis: Methods and Applications* (Cambridge: Cambridge University Press, 1994); Peter J. Carrington, John Scott and Stanley

While the application of social network analysis methods on technologically mediated networks such as the nineteenth-century telegraph network does not raise any procedural problems, the incompleteness (or unavailability) of historical data can be problematic. In order to produce accurate results, the network analysis has to be conducted on the entire network. If parts of the network are truncated (because of missing or inaccurate data, for instance), centres and peripheries tend to shift. Such truncations therefore distort the analysis of the network structure. In the case of historical data, however, incompleteness and inaccuracy are often the rule rather than the exception. Especially regarding such a complex structure as the global telegraph network of the nineteenth century, it is practically impossible to acquire and then prepare data on the entire network structure. In theory, every interconnected telegraph line – from the intercontinental trunk routes to the village level – would have to be considered in a full network analysis. In practice, this is (and will remain) impossible, simply for reasons of missing and incomparable data. Therefore we can only work with incomplete data sets and will have to acknowledge and consider the distortions (some of them slight, others more critical) arising from this incompleteness. It is one way of reducing the impact of such distortions to conduct several network analyses with different sets of data which are all incomplete in different ways. It then becomes possible to look for overlaps as well as contradictions between the analyses, making it easier to account for any distortions arising from the truncation of the network data. Therefore three different data sets will be analysed in the following.

The first study will use the information on telegraphic connections within Europe given in the 'Liste des communications télégraphiques internationales directes du régime européen' published by the Bureau international des administrations télégraphiques in 1906. This list contains all direct connections between places in Europe existing in that year but leaves out intermediary stations in the circuits that were considered comparatively unimportant by the bureau. 'Outre les communications directes du régime européen, la liste mentionne aussi celles des communications internationals du régime extra-européen qui figurent sur la carte

Wasserman, *Models and Methods in Social Network Analysis* (Cambridge: Cambridge University Press, 2005); John Scott, *Social Network Analysis: A Handbook*, 2nd ed. (London: Sage Publications, 2000); Mustafa Emirbayer and Jeff Goodwin, 'Network Analysis, Culture, and the Problem of Agency', *American Journal of Sociology* 99, no 6 (1994); Mark Huisman and Marijtje A. J. van Duijn, 'Software for Social Network Analysis', in *Models and Methods in Social Network Analysis*, ed. Peter J. Carrington, John Scott and Stanley Wasserman (Cambridge: Cambridge University Press, 2005); Han Woo Park, 'Hyperlink Network Analysis: A New Method for the Study of Social Structure on the Web', *Connection* 25, no 1 (2003).

du régime européen.'[11] This means that in addition to the purely European telegraph connections, those starting (or ending) in Europe have also been included, but the parts of the network at the other ends of these lines have been truncated. The second study also focuses on Europe and is based not on a list of connections but on a map. In the year 1923, the Bureau international for the first time published a map showing all direct circuits existing in Europe as well as their wire capacities. The connections are weighed and the social network analysis software can differ between weaker (i.e. fewer circuits between two places) and stronger (more circuits) connections. Extra-European connections with one end in Europe are also considered here, but the network parts at the other end are also truncated. Thanks to the richness of data, both studies are able to clearly identify centres and peripheries in Europe – but only in Europe. No compatible data on direct telegraphic circuits is available for these years outside Europe. The third study tries to remedy this shortcoming and employs a global perspective. It is based on the 'Cartes des communications télégraphiques du régime extra-européen' published by the Bureau international at irregular intervals. These maps depict telegraph connections all around the globe, but of course focus on the most important connections only. The data derived from them is less detailed by far than the data on the European network. In combination, however, these different perspectives will allow for the identification of centres and peripheries in the global telegraph network. As already pointed out above, a fourth study then moves away from social network analysis and looks at the international telegraph traffic data (on the aggregate national level) and its development throughout the second half of the nineteenth century.

6.2 Social network analysis: European telegraph circuits 1906

As laid out above, social network analysis offers valuable instruments for identifying centres and peripheries in a network, but it also needs comparatively large and compatible amounts of data. In historical research, the acquisition of such suitable data often makes a number of compromises necessary. In this first case study, at least two such compromises are necessary – an exclusive focus on Europe and the point of observation in 1906 when an earlier date might have been better comparable to several other case studies in this book. The data that informs the

[11] ITU Archives, Bureau international des administrations télégraphiques, 'Liste des communications télégraphiques internationales directes du régime européen, Annexe a la carte des communications télégraphiques du régime européen – édition 1906', 1906, 2.

following social network analysis comes from the 'Liste des communications télégraphiques internationales directes du régime européen' published by the Bureau international for the first time in 1906.[12] Before this date, comprehensive information on the international telegraph network can only be read from maps compiled by the same institution. These maps are extremely valuable, as they depict the stations and telegraphic connections in place in a given year in some detail and are the only source available that allows for a truly global analysis of the telegraph network (as will be done later in this chapter). Unfortunately, however, no circuit data can be read from these maps (prior to the 'Carte schématique des grandes communications télégraphiques internationales du régime européen' of the year 1923, which does contain circuit data and informs the network analysis conducted in the second case study of this chapter). This means that the 'Liste des communications' is the first source to contain information on communication circuits and, therefore, on existing direct communication between two places. The list clearly shows which stations were in direct telegraphic contact without the need to relay or re-patch. While such communication circuits, of course, depended on the telegraph connections usually depicted in telegraph maps, they are much closer to the practice of communicating telegraphically. A social network analysis drawing on such circuit data, therefore, comes closer to the practical use patterns within the network than a study of mere connections. On an international level, this can only be done for the data from 1906 onwards.

The second compromise has already been discussed in the previous section. In theory, a network analysis can only yield perfectly accurate results when conducted on the entire network. Truncations of parts of the network influence and distort the results of the analysis. In the case of historical networks, however, such distortions can rarely be avoided and must, therefore, be taken into account in the interpretation of the results. In the case at hand, the 'Liste des communications' focuses exclusively on the European telegraph network. Other parts are radically truncated. Sometimes extra-European connections are not considered at all;' sometimes they are truncated halfway. Some transatlantic connections, for instance, terminate at the Azores and the Indo-European line goes no further than Tehran. The submarine connection to Asia via Suez ends in Alexandria. Of course, such truncations decrease the centrality of the gatekeeping places – in our case mostly of London and southern England (transatlantic, Asia, Africa) and Berlin (transatlantic via Emden, Indo-European line). Seen from a global perspective, these

[12] Ibid.

places were certainly more central than becomes discernible from the network analysis.

In the first edition published in 1906, the 'Liste des communications télégraphiques internationales directes du régime européen' contains a thirty-nine-page list of direct telegraph communications between places in Europe. All in all, this list features 632 stations – most of them in Europe and only some of them part of a halfway truncated intercontinental route. Of course, many more telegraph stations were open for public service in Europe in the year 1906. But for both the sheer mass of information and the lack of suitable compatible data, it is not possible to consider every existing station and every existing route in the network analysis. A selection needs to be made. In the case at hand, this selection has already been made by the Bureau international, which has decided to include only 632 stations and the circuits between them in their list. The people conducting this selection were contemporary experts in the field and extremely well placed to do this. It is, therefore, reasonable to assume that the information included in the 'Liste des communications' is much more representative than any such selections made by historians in retrospect. The 632 telegraph stations and their circuit connections have been entered into a spreadsheet and prepared for computation by the social network analysis software UCINET.[13] It is important to note that the connection data given in the 'Liste des communications' is unvalued. There is no additional information on the strength of the connection, which in the case of a telegraph network means the number of wires in a circuit. Each circuit therefore counted for an unvalued connection. If, however, the list contained several circuits between the same two places, this was entered into the spreadsheet as valued information. The social network analysis was accordingly conducted on valued data, and thus acknowledged that some connections between places were stronger than others. Altogether, four different centrality measurements were performed on the data – *degree*, *closeness*, *betweenness* and *eigenvector*.

The calculation of the Freeman *degree* is one of the most widely used centrality measures in social network analysis and simply counts the number of connections that a node has with other nodes. Valued data is recognized by the Freeman degree measure, and therefore multiple circuits between two given places are weighted accordingly. For the same reason, the normalized degree (*nDegree*) has not been included in the table as it should only be calculated for binary data, i.e. for data that does not recognize the different strengths of connections but merely takes into

[13] UCINET for Windows.

account whether there is a connection or not. The comparatively unsophisticated *degree* count shows that the major European capital cities maintained the highest number of direct telegraphic connections with other cities (see Table A.5 in the Appendix for a complete list of the top nodes). London is conveniently in the lead, being directly tapped into forty-five direct circuits. Berlin, Vienna and Paris are very close together, with thirty-seven, thirty-four and thirty-three circuits respectively. After this group of four, there is a sizeable gap until cities such as Hamburg, Budapest, Milan, Antwerp and Cologne follow.[14] This does not come as a surprise and simply confirms that the imperial and national centres of late nineteenth- and early twentieth-century Europe also stood at the core of their respective national and international telegraph networks. The central roles of Vienna and Budapest, however, are slightly more surprising, as Austria–Hungary lagged behind in telegraphic development throughout the nineteenth century and never came close to the structural and traffic denseness of Great Britain, Germany and France.[15] Nevertheless, both cities in the dual monarchy acted as important central European hubs and gateways between Western and Eastern Europe. In Belgium and the Netherlands, no single city could compete with the aforementioned metropolises in terms of degree centrality, but the region as such exhibited an unusually dense web of secondary places. Interestingly, however, the principal Swiss cities did not exhibit the high values one might expect in light of its national telegraph use density. Only Basle did reasonably well in the degree count (thirteen). Geneva was already lagging far behind (nine), and Zurich has a degree centrality of only six.

The Freeman degree analysis merely highlights how many direct connections a specific node maintained with other nodes in the network. While this is, of course, instructive in many ways, it tells us little about the qualitative position of a node in a network. In his categorization of network analysis methods, Linton Freeman presents two other ways of calculating centrality in a network that go beyond the simple degree value: *farness/closeness* and *betweenness*.[16] Both only operate with binary connections and do not recognize valued data. They ignore the strength of the link between two nodes and are only interested in their positions within a network. Farness is the sum of connections that it takes for a node to reach

[14] As a general rule, place names are used in a standardized, usually modernized, form in the text of this study. The tables, however, reproduce place names as used in the original sources.

[15] See the analysis of the development of domestic telegraph networks in Europe in Wenzlhuemer, 'The Development of Telegraphy, 1870–1900'.

[16] Freeman, 'Centrality in Networks: I. Conceptual Clarification'; Freeman, 'The Gatekeeper, Pair-Dependency and Structural Centrality'.

each and every other network node. The higher the number of connections, the less central the node is. Closeness is the reciprocal value of farness. In its normalized form as *nCloseness*, it shows the percentage of the highest possible closeness value. Generally, the best-connected places in terms of degree centrality also feature the highest nCloseness values. This means that from places with many circuit connections it was easiest to reach the rest of Europe – or the rest of the world. Accordingly, Vienna, Berlin, London and Paris exhibit the highest values here (between 0.685 and 0.686). It is, however, far more interesting how close together the individual cities are in terms of closeness centrality. Of the 632 places in the 'Liste des communications', 489 were connected to the main network body. Of course, the remaining 143 nodes were in practice also part of the network, but their connections to the main body were considered to be minor by the Bureau international and were, therefore, not included in the list. Technically, farness for these nodes is infinite, as in the data set at hand they have no connection to the 489 places constituting the main network. Interestingly, within these 489 nodes, the one with the lowest farness value (Vienna, with 92,029) and the one with the highest value (Neisse, with 96,671) are only several thousand steps apart. Translated into normalized closeness, Vienna reaches 0.686 per cent of the lowest (theoretically) possible farness value, while Neisse reaches 0.656 per cent. This accounts for a very small difference in terms of closeness centrality between the most central and the least central node in the network. There were, of course, differences in the farness and closeness of places in the European telegraph network of 1906. From some places – usually the ones with higher degree values – it was comparatively easier and faster to reach all other places in the web. Importantly, however, the diminutiveness of these prevailing differences shows how tightly integrated the telegraph network in Europe was at this point in time.

The third social network analysis measure calculated here – Freeman *betweenness* – produces significantly different results. Betweenness refers to the centrality of a network node in terms of its mediating position in the network. It describes how often the shortest connection between two nodes passes through a certain node and is, therefore, a clear indicator for the importance of a particular city or town as regards the efficient functioning of the entire network. The normalized value *nBetweenness* is the original value divided by the maximum number of node pairs excluding the evaluated node. Nodes with high betweenness values are centrally placed regarding the network traffic and can, therefore, exert control over the flow of information. While there are only small differences in the closeness values, betweenness is very unevenly distributed within the network (see Table A.6 in the Appendix). Only the European metropolises achieve notable values in this category. Vienna (22.374) and Berlin (17.55) lead the table, followed already at some distance by Paris (12.612) and London (8.943). Due to the aforementioned truncation of the telegraphic connection across the Atlantic, to Africa and to Asia, the value for London seems to be distorted. The British capital occupied a crucial gatekeeper position in this regard that is not represented by the data on which the network analysis is based. The case studies conducted in the following sections will clearly illustrate this bias and show that London should rather be seen as on a par with Berlin and Paris here. And all three of them should probably be seen as closer to the leader, Vienna, as the values for Berlin and Paris also partially suffer from the truncation. Berlin and Paris to a certain degree were also gatekeepers to America, Africa and Asia, while Vienna occupied no such role in intercontinental telegraph traffic but rather one as the most important gate to Eastern Europe, which has not been truncated. Taking this into account, the top four nodes should be seen as reasonably close together and a significant gap between them and the other network nodes becomes apparent in terms of betweenness centrality. It seems clear that the role of central traffic hubs in the European and global telegraph network was exclusively filled by the big imperial capitals of the day. Control over the global flow of information rested there. The major cities of Belgium, the Netherlands and Switzerland did not exhibit notable betweenness values and were easily outperformed by secondary nodes such as Budapest, Breslau, Milan, Munich, Sarajevo and several others. In combination with the results of the degree measurement and the findings of the domestic network study, this seems to suggest that these countries featured well-developed networks with high use rates but were not placed centrally in terms of control over the telegraphic information flow.

The results of the fourth network analysis method – the Bonacich *eigenvector* – further confirm this. Here, a node is central when it is connected to other central nodes.[17] London, Berlin and Paris top the ranking, with London in a very commanding lead, despite the various truncations of the network (see Table A.7 in the Appendix). Interestingly, Vienna clearly falls back. While the Austrian capital occupied an important role as a hub and relay station to Eastern Europe, it did not maintain so many direct connections with other centrally placed nodes. In short, this means that London and, to a lesser degree, Berlin and Paris were on the most important circuits together with other important European

[17] Phillip Bonacich, 'Factoring and Weighting Approaches to Status Scores and Clique Identification', *Journal of Mathematical Sociology* 2 (1972); Bonacich, 'Power and Centrality: A Family of Measures', *American Journal of Sociology* 92, no 5 (1987).

cities, while Vienna – despite its many connections and the high betweenness value – found itself on relatively less-important telegraphic routes. Also, several places in Belgium, the Netherlands and Switzerland feature notable eigenvector values. Amsterdam, Antwerp, Rotterdam, Brussels, Zurich and Basle can all be found among the top twenty nodes in this category. Therefore the results of the eigenvector measurement first of all support the central role of London, Berlin, Paris and Vienna in the European telegraph network of the late nineteenth and early twentieth centuries. These were beyond doubt the most important hubs and control centres of telegraphic information flows in the period under study. Furthermore, however, the eigenvector values also confirm the assumption that Belgium, the Netherlands and (by 1906 already, to a lesser degree) Switzerland were placed at privileged positions near these control centres.[18] The major Belgian, Dutch and Swiss cities could, therefore, tap into the information flows rather easily, while they had no controlling power over these flows.

6.3 Social network analysis: European telegraph circuits 1923

The second case study shares some of the limitations of the 'Liste des communications' analysis. It is based on the 'Carte schématique des grandes communications télégraphiques internationales du régime européen' issued by the Bureau international in Berne in the year 1923.[19] As the name of the map already signifies, only European nodes and circuits and intercontinental connections with one end in Europe are shown and can therefore be considered in the network analysis. In comparison to the 'Liste des communications', however, many more transatlantic and transmediterranean cables are included and accordingly the truncations do not weight quite as heavily here – although they do, of course, distort the network analysis results nevertheless. What is more, the 'Carte schématique' is the first available source that actually carries information about the capacity of a circuit. The resulting network analysis can, therefore, work with valued circuit data and will produce more refined results. The map was published in 1923, and thus covers a period somewhat later than that looked at previously. The 1906 and 1923 network analyses can, however, mutually control each other. Statements on the

[18] This was first put forward in Wenzlhuemer, 'The Development of Telegraphy, 1870–1900'.

[19] ITU Archives, Bureau international de l'Union télégraphique, 'Carte schématique des grandes communications télégraphiques internationales du régime européen', 1923.

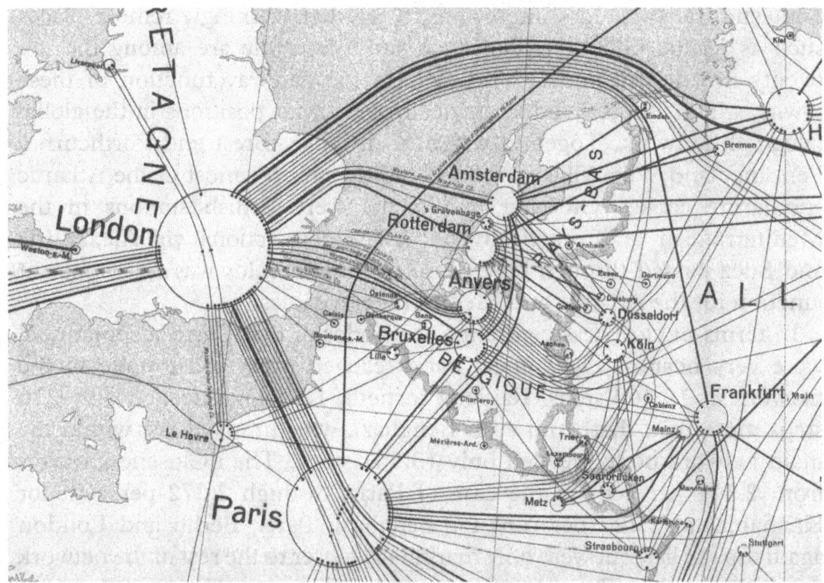

Figure 6.1 Extract of the 'Carte schématique des grandes communications télégraphiques internationales du régime européen'.

centrality and non-centrality of cities and regions in Europe that are confirmed by both case studies will, indeed, have very high accuracy. Figure 6.1 depicts an extract of the 'Carte schématique'. In total, the map shows 289 cities or towns in Europe. Of those, 248 are connected to the main network body and thus exhibit meaningful network analysis results. All in all, 554 circuit connections between these nodes have been considered in the social network analysis that encompasses the same four centrality measures as in the previous section.

The Freeman degree centrality analysis of cities and towns included on the 'Carte schématique' shows that London (69), Paris (58) and Berlin (50) maintained the highest number of direct connections with other places (see Table A.8 in the Appendix). Vienna followed at some distance. Budapest came fifth, before Amsterdam, Antwerp, Brussels and Rotterdam, representing the Belgian–Dutch region that did so well in the domestic telegraph study as well as in the 'Liste des communication' analysis.[20] Zurich and Basle rank twentieth and twenty-first in the list and could not quite live up to the excellent performance of Switzerland in the

20 Wenzlhuemer, 'The Development of Telegraphy, 1870–1900'.

domestic statistics. It is interesting to see that seemingly remote places such as Malta, Gibraltar, Penzance and Waterville are among the top twenty-five degree nodes. This reflects the gateway function of these towns, which all occupied strategically important positions in the global telegraph network. Together with, for instance, Brest and Porthcurno, Penzance and Waterville served as landing sites for most of the Atlantic submarine cables. Gibraltar and Malta were British stations in the Mediterranean and practically all Asian connections via Alexandria and Suez passed through here. Similarly, Carcavelos was an important junction for the Atlantic and Mediterranean cables.

In terms of closeness centrality, the nodes of the 'Carte schématique' were very near to each other. Paris reached every other node in the network in 12,460 steps. Ranking fortieth, Kristiania needed only 216 steps more than that. And even Benghazi, which ranked last within the main network body, needed only 13,541 steps. The nCloseness ranges from 2.311 per cent in the case of Paris, through 2.272 per cent for Kristiania, to 2.127 per cent for Benghazi. Paris, Berlin and London again top the list, but were only marginally closer to the rest of the network than other nodes. The network was very well integrated and all the cities and towns connected to the main network were reasonably easy to reach from any other position in the net. There were marginal advantages for the French, German and British metropolises, but as a matter of fact most places were – telegraphically speaking – almost equally close to each other.

Berlin, Paris and London (all around 20 per cent) clearly ranked highest in terms of betweenness centrality, and thus also in terms of control over the flow of information (see Table A.9 in the Appendix). Vienna followed fourth but reached only around 12 per cent in nBetweenness. Prague and Budapest already lagged far behind with slightly over 8 per cent each. At rank 24, Basle was the first representative of the well-developed countries of Belgium, the Netherlands and Switzerland. Three other Swiss cities – Zurich (rank 28), Geneva (rank 34) and Berne (rank 39) – can be found in the top 40. Rotterdam only comes in twenty-seventh in this category and is the only Dutch city in the top group. At rank 37, Brussels is the only Belgian node in this class. The high betweenness values for Berlin, Paris, London and, to a lesser extent, Vienna emphasize these cities' central positions in the telegraphic information flow. It was highly likely that a message sent between two European places would pass through one of these central junctions. And especially for London, an even higher value could reasonably have been expected had the data set used for the social network analysis included the North American and South Asian networks as well. While marginally more Swiss, Dutch and Belgian cities rank among the top forty betweenness nodes than in the 'Liste des communications' analysis, the results of both studies are very similar. In terms of betweenness and control over the information flow, these places exerted only little influence.

As regards their eigenvector values, Paris, Berlin and London can again be found at the top end of the list – but London interestingly did worse than the other two (see Table A.10 in the Appendix). Vienna comes, as usual, fourth, but then quickly follow such places as Antwerp (fifth), Brussels (eighth), Amsterdam (ninth), Rotterdam (eleventh) and Zurich (twelfth) in the list. Therefore the eigenvector ranking generally supports the findings of the analysis of the 'Liste des communications' in the previous section. Antwerp, Brussels and Amsterdam exhibited normalized eigenvector values of between 30 and 28 per cent. They are, therefore, in the range of Hamburg or Prague and even relatively close to Vienna, while their normalized betweenness values are marginal compared to those of their competitors. A little further down the table, the same holds true for the Swiss cities of Zurich, Basle and Berne. As to their position in the European telegraph network, this means that Belgium, the Netherlands and Switzerland were not central in terms of being situated on the main routes of communication. They were of only limited importance for the actual flow of information between other network nodes. But they enjoyed excellent access to the control centres of the network.

To summarize, the results of the 'Carte schématique' network analysis confirm practically all of the important findings of the 'Liste des communications' study. The only major difference can be found in the position of London within the European telegraph network. In the 1923 study, London occupied an even more central role and was the leading node among the European metropolises. This can mainly be attributed to the inclusion of more intercontinental cable connections in the 'Carte schématique'. While the non-European parts of the global telecommunication network are still truncated and are thus not considered in the network analysis, at least the intercontinental connections feature in the map. In the 1906 'Liste des communications', the truncations are much more radical, and therefore London as a gateway node performed not quite as well as in the second analysis. In all other important aspects, however, the results are very similar and thus mutually affirmative. In both studies, closeness is very evenly distributed within the network, which hints at a high degree of network integration. In all other centrality measures, the European metropolises of London, Paris and Berlin top the tables – usually followed at some distance by Vienna. The major cities of Belgium, the Netherlands and Switzerland – all of which exhibited very impressive structure and use rates regarding the development of their domestic networks – scored reasonably good degree, not quite so good betweenness and very impressive eigenvector values in both studies. As already pointed out, this means that they were well placed within the network and tightly connected to the central nodes, but had little control over the information flow themselves. The similarity of the results of both studies suggests that these general findings have a high degree of accuracy.

6.4 Social network analysis: global telegraph connections 1881 to 1902

Both of the studies above rely on actual circuit data but are confined to Europe in their geographical focus. In the following analysis, this focus is extended to cover the entire globe. Furthermore, data is available for three different years – 1881, 1892 and 1902. Therefore the analysis gains a chronological dimension and allows for interpretations of the structural development of the global telegraph network in the last twenty years of the nineteenth century. However, the study has, of course, some drawbacks. The only available sources on which such an analysis can be based are the global communication maps compiled by the Bureau international in Berne. These maps were published at irregular intervals in the late nineteenth century and showed the telegraph lines of the world – both terrestrial and submarine. While the maps are admirably detailed, they cannot, of course, give micro-level information and are forced to focus on the principal connections. Also, they depict telegraph lines, not circuits. The maps therefore show the practical course of the telegraph lines, but do not contain information about which nodes were directly connected with which other nodes. These two shortcomings impact on the accuracy of the network analysis. This has to be taken into account when interpreting the results. Nevertheless, the maps are the best sources available if telegraphic centres and peripheries and their development over time are to be examined on a global scale.

The network analysis has been based on information taken from three different maps at approximately ten-year intervals. In each case, the connections depicted in the map have been entered into a data matrix, which has then been fed into the network analysis software. The first map shows the global telegraph network in the year 1881.[21] It contains 1,954 network nodes and 2,450 connections between them. The second map depicts the situation in 1892, containing 2,949 nodes and 3,938 different connections.[22] The third map is for the

[21] ITU Archives, Bureau international des administrations télégraphiques, 'Carte des communications télégraphiques du régime extra-européen', 1881.

[22] ITU Archives, Bureau international des administrations télégraphiques, 'Carte des communications télégraphiques de régime extra-européen', 1892.

year 1902.[23] By then, the network covered had expanded to 3,813 nodes and 5,160 connections. This quantitative increase of the information depicted in the maps is already testimony to the fast growth of the network in the last decades of the nineteenth century. The two transpacific cables are already shown as projected routes in the 1902 map but have not been included in the calculations.

As regards degree centrality, London, Paris and Vienna led the ranking in all three years under observation (see Table A.11 in the Appendix). Berlin was always among the top six nodes. This confirms the findings of the previous sections and shows that even on a global scale the greatest number of telegraphic connections converged on these European metropolises.[24] Other nodes at the top end of the list throughout the period of observation include the French cities of Marseilles and Lyon, St Louis in the United States and the Mediterranean island of Malta. Marseilles controlled much of the European traffic with North Africa and other places around the Mediterranean. Malta was a central relay station en route to Alexandria, Suez and thus Asia. And Lyon and St Louis were important mainland hubs in France and the United States. Places such as Cincinnati, Chicago, Brussels, Basle, Munich and Halle – to name but a few – had similar roles. St Pierre and Cape Canso, on the other hand, lay on the transatlantic route and occupied a pivotal relay function there. Havana had already emerged as an important regional hub in the Caribbean by 1881. Taken together, the degree results confirm the findings of previous sections in this chapter. A few big European metropolises stood at the structural centre of the system, followed by a number of regional centres mostly in Europe and the United States. The transatlantic route and the cable network in the Mediterranean – being the telegraphic gateway to the East – also featured important nodes. Only minor variations occurred in this general structural pattern during the period of observation (see the visualization in Maps 6.1–6.3). The most notable of those is probably the rise in importance of South American nodes such as Rio de Janeiro or Recife in Brazil at the turn of the century.

As regards closeness centrality, almost all places featuring high values were port cities with direct access to the submarine cable network. Mediterranean nodes such as Malta, Gibraltar or Alexandria are prominent here – especially those that acted as relay stations on the submarine

[23] ITU Archives, Bureau international des administrations télégraphiques, 'Cartes des communications télégraphiques du régime extra-européen', 1902.

[24] However, it also signifies the extent to which the micro level is missing in the maps that serve as sources. In the degree ranking stemming from the analysis of the 'Liste des communications' of the year 1906, London reached position 45 as compared to only position 15 in the global connections map of 1902.

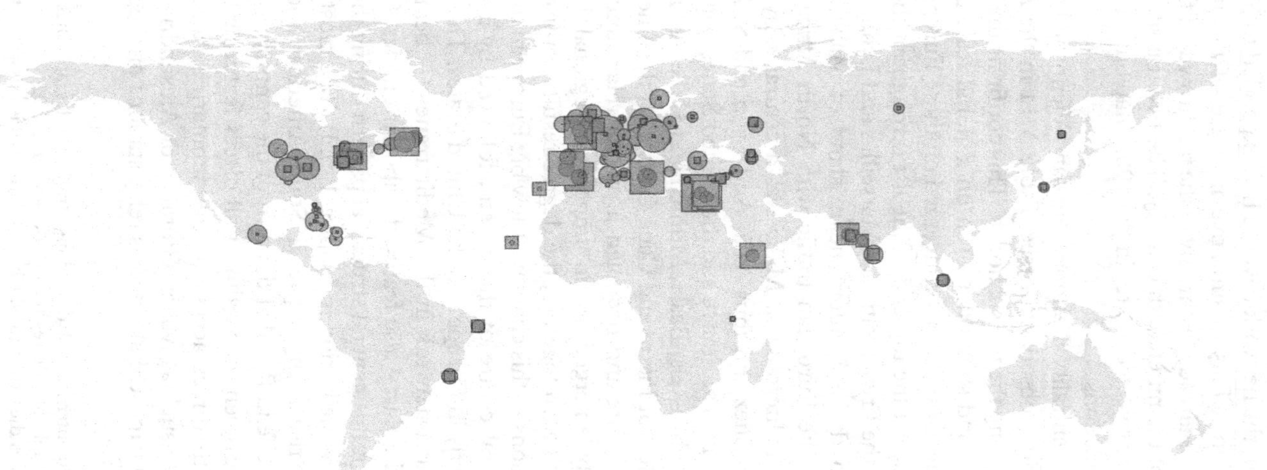

Map 6.1 Freeman degree and betweenness in the global telegraph network, 1881. Note: Circles represent degree; rectangles represent betweenness.

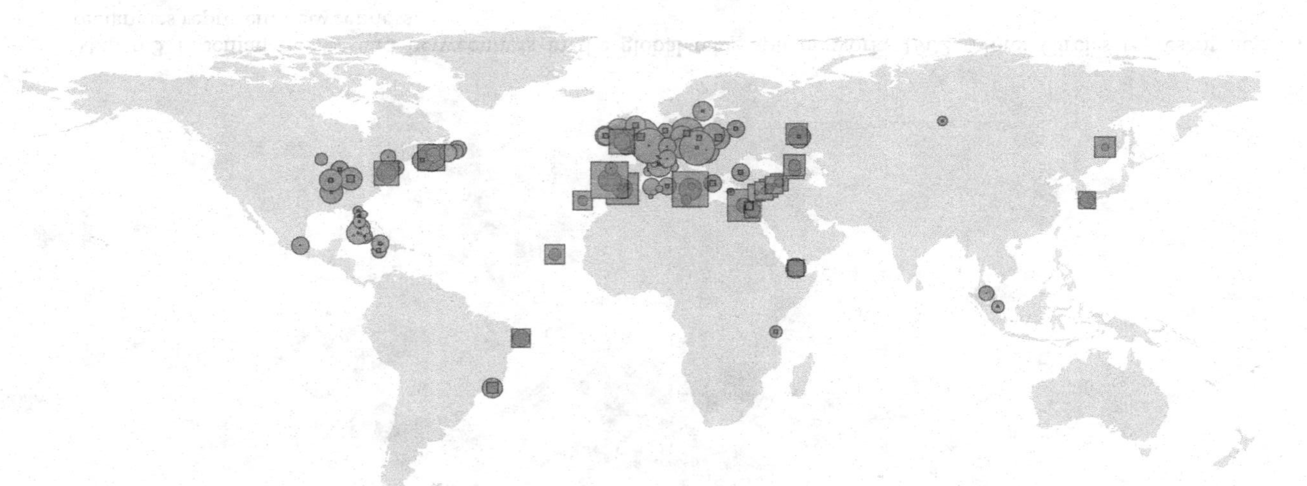

Map 6.2 Freeman degree and betweenness in the global telegraph network, 1892. Note: Circles represent degree; rectangles represent betweenness.

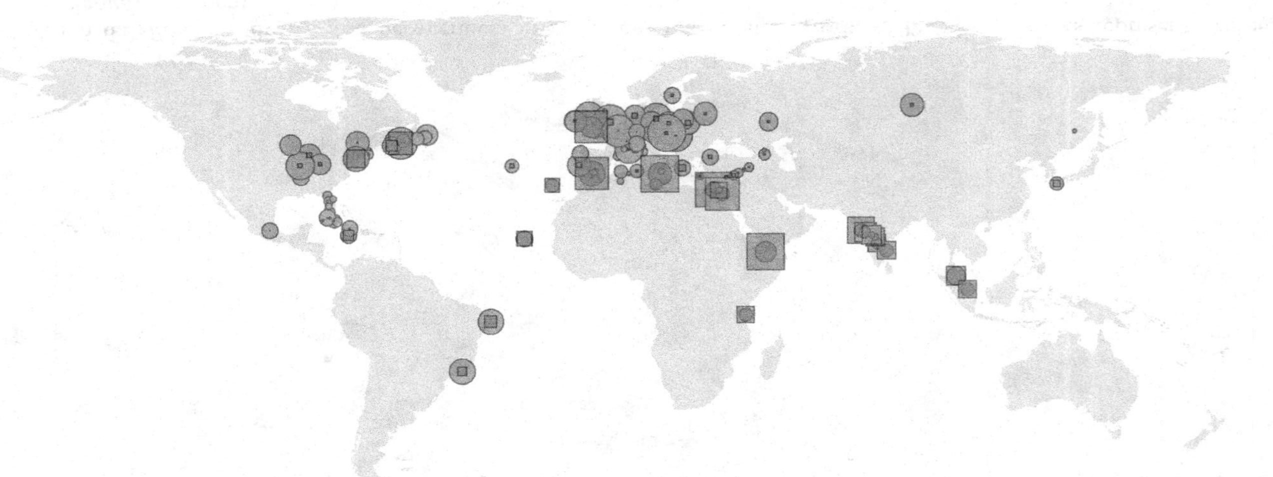

Map 6.3 Freeman degree and betweenness in the global telegraph network, 1902. Note: Circles represent degree; rectangles represent betweenness.

route to Asia (or on its short overland stretch between Alexandria and Suez via Tantah). The same is true for Penzance (practically next to Porthcurno where most Eastern cables landed), Exeter and Dartmouth in England, Vigo in Spain and Lisbon in Portugal. All these places were on the main route from England to Asia. Many Atlantic or Mediterranean stations nearby and connected to this route – such as Coimbra, Lanarca, Sitia, Malaga and Modica – also achieved high closeness values. Places such as Brest, Funchal, St Pierre and Cape Canso, on the other hand, derived their centrality from their positions on the principal transatlantic routes. Interestingly, London is the only metropolis with reasonably high closeness values. This shows how closely London was connected to the central axes of global communication going through port cities. Altogether, three points become discernible from the analysis of closeness centrality. First, the study emphasizes the importance of access to the submarine cable network that carried practically all long-distance communication. Those stations with either direct or secondary access to this part of the network exhibited the highest closeness values. Second, a clear central axis of global telegraphic communication started to emerge from the East Coast of the United States, via the European Atlantic coast, the Mediterranean and the Red Sea, and on to Asia. Third, there was practically no change in these structural focuses throughout the period of observation. At least in terms of closeness, the core region of the global network did not shift in the slightest during this time.

The results of the betweenness analysis largely confirm these findings. As can be seen from the visualization in Maps 6.1–6.3, the same central east–west axis becomes discernible here (see also Table A.12 in the Appendix). Nodes such as St Pierre, Cape Canso, Duxbury, New York, Brest and Funchal saw a considerable portion of the transatlantic traffic pass through them. Similarly, most of the important relay stations en route from England to India also feature high values – such as Penzance, Lisbon, Gibraltar, Malta, Alexandria, Tantah, Suez, Aden and Bombay. For 1902, a number of Indian cities exhibit high values that, together with Penang, prolonged this axis further to the east. This was due to the expansion of the telegraph network in and around South East Asia and Australia towards the end of the nineteenth century. Ten years earlier, a cluster of relatively high betweenness values is visible along a route from the Mediterranean across Turkey and via Tiflis into Russia. There had, indeed, been developing an expansion of the Russian telegraph network since 1881 that rendered the intermediary stations in the Caucasus more important. This structural importance, however, seems to have been short-lived, as by 1902 none of these nodes were among the top hundred any more. While the closeness values show relatively little variance between the top and the bottom values, this is different in the case of betweenness. Here, nodes such as Alexandria, Lisbon, Malta and later Aden and Suez exhibited much higher values than their pursuers. This, again, emphasizes the central role that the Mediterranean (and its western and eastern extensions) played in the global telegraph network of the late nineteenth century.

After the mutually reconfirming results of the degree, closeness and betweenness analyses, the eigenvector measure presents a more or less inconclusive picture. In each year under study, a different cluster of network nodes ranks particularly high in terms of eigenvector centrality. In 1881, western Mediterranean places such as Marseilles, Algiers or Malta and their neighbouring nodes are in the lead. By 1892, they had been supplanted by an exclusively Caribbean cluster arranged around Key West, at the southern tip of Florida, and Havana and several other cities in Cuba. Again ten years later, those in turn were replaced by stations located mostly on the transatlantic route, such as Cape Canso, Waterville, New York, Valentia, Penzance and Heart's Content. Acknowledging the expansion of transatlantic connections towards the end of the century, this shift in focus on the transatlantic route is credible. Regarding the previous two cases, however, the eigenvector clusters in the western Mediterranean and in the Caribbean seem arbitrary and without foundation. The inconclusiveness of these results might stem from two different factors. First, they might originate in the limitations of the sources explained above. The lack of circuit data is especially limiting when calculating the eigenvector as it does not reflect direct circuit connections between major nodes but lists all intermediary stations. Second, the confusing results could also be partially due to the fact that for the eigenvector calculations in this section a faster but less accurate mode of computation has been employed. This was necessary because of the sheer number of nodes and the resulting size of the data matrix and could have impacted on the accuracy of the findings, which should, therefore, be treated with caution.

6.5 Network use: external telegraph messages 1860–1910

The data analysed in the previous three case studies was exclusively of structural origin. It represented the connections between network nodes, not the actual communication. Unfortunately, for analyses as detailed and superregional (or even global) as those in the previous sections, usually only structural data is available. In most cases, it is the only possible means to gauge the centrality of a place (and therefore the communicational preconditions of the people living and working in this place) within a global network. Yet, in order to provide information not just about the possibility of communication but about the actual realization of this potential, structural data needs to be put into perspective. It needs a corrective – ideally in the form of use data. Such data on telegraphic traffic is usually only available in some detail for selected routes (for instance, for the several routes between Europe and India, as shall be seen in Chapter 8) or on the aggregate national level. In the latter case, it is not possible to break information down to the infra-national level and thus to obtain use and traffic data for individual network nodes. The few cases for which this is possible – see, for instance, the case studies discussed in the following two chapters – constitute rare exceptions to the rule and usually work only within a national framework.

In order to facilitate the work of the Bureau international des administrations télégraphiques in Berne, the telegraph administrations of the participating countries provided annual statistics on their telegraphic systems which were then centrally processed, printed and distributed by the bureau. The 'Statistique générale de la télégraphie' is still held by and accessible at the ITU library and archives in Geneva. It contains detailed information on the international telegraphic traffic of the included countries. The total number of telegrams handled is divided into three categories: messages sent, received and transmitted. While the first two categories are self-explanatory, the third features all messages that passed through the country in question on their way between two other countries. Thanks to this detailed breakdown, the data does not merely speak about the quantitative participation of a country in global communication but also about its qualitative role as producer, consumer or transmitter of information. The data compiled in these statistics informs the following analysis.

Despite the bureau's efforts to compile statistical data on telegraphy in the years preceding its own foundation, the available figures become reliable and comparable only in the early 1860s. The year 1860 has, therefore, been chosen as the earliest possible starting date with data of reasonable reliability available. Data samples have then been drawn every ten years until 1910, only years before the onset of the First World War.[25]

[25] ITU Archives, Bureau international des administrations télégraphiques, 'Statistique générale de la télégraphie dans les différents pays de l'ancien continent', 1849–1869 ITU Archives, Bureau international des administrations télégraphiques, 'Statistique générale de la télégraphie dans les différents pays de l'ancien continent', 1870; ITU Archives, Bureau international des administrations télégraphiques, 'Statistique générale de la télégraphie', 1880; ITU Archives, Bureau international des administrations télégraphiques, 'Statistique générale de la télégraphie', 1890 ITU Archives, Bureau international des administrations télégraphiques, 'Statistique générale de la télégraphie', 1900; ITU Archives, Bureau international de l'Union télégraphique, 'Statistique générale de la télégraphie', 1910.

The period of observation thus covers a time span of fifty years and was certainly formative in the development of both national and global telegraphy.

In order to compile its statistics, the Bureau international had to rely on the information submitted by the participating countries. The parameters under which such information had been gathered varied considerably from country to country – as did the accuracy and diligence with which the data were prepared and forwarded to Berne. A flood of explanatory footnotes in the statistics – each one specifying the special circumstances in a particular country – are testimony to the varying standards of the submitted information. While the statisticians at the Bureau international did what they could to make the data comparable, this has to be considered in any contemporary consultation of the statistics. Accordingly, incomplete or obviously inconclusive entries have not been included in the analysis. Only data categories have been selected that are generally comparable – such as length of lines, number of stations or messages sent. Furthermore, all data presented in the following has been indexed with a selected European average in the particular year equalling 100.[26] In combination, these measures guarantee the comparability of the samples and their accuracy at least in relation to each other. In many cases, comprehensive tables containing a large amount of data prepared in this way can be found in the Appendix to this book and further illustrate the interpretation of the data.

As regards external telegraphic traffic in the year 1860, the highest values can be found for countries that also did well in the analysis in the previous sections of this chapter (see Table A.13 in the Appendix). Belgium, Denmark, the Netherlands and Switzerland – for which the 'Statistique générale' gives only transit message figures for 1860 – exhibit the highest per capita values in terms of international telegraphic traffic. In the first two categories, Norway also performs very well. On the other hand, the major European powers – France, Germany and Austria-Hungary – have very little external traffic compared to the European average. France and the dual monarchy have particularly little transit traffic. The values for Germany – which did not yet exist as a political

[26] Eleven European countries have been included in the selected European average: Austria, Belgium, Denmark, France, Germany, Hungary, Netherlands, Romania, Spain, Sweden and Switzerland. In every sample year, the data of these eleven countries in a particular data category has been summed up and an average has been calculated. This average equals 100 in the data index. These countries have been selected for the simple reason that they have been included in the statistics in all sample years. Only in very rare cases were one or two countries dropped from the index for a single category in a single year. If this has been done, it is clearly indicated in the tables.

entity in 1860 – are generally inflated as the traffic between the individual German states counted as external rather than internal here.

In the period from 1860 to 1870, the average annual growth of external traffic was very evenly distributed with practically no runaway values (see Table A.14 in the Appendix). Germany and Norway feature the highest growth rates – which is particularly interesting in the case of the former as the starting value is inflated (see above) but the end value is not. In the year 1870, Germany is the only major European power exhibiting per capita values above the European average regarding sent and received international messages (see Table A.15 in the Appendix). The transit value, however, is considerably below average. While Germany does not seem to have been a central hub for international telegraphic traffic in 1870, the situation is exactly the opposite in Austria. Here, performance in the first two categories is significantly below average, while the transit value is at 124 per cent of the average. France has interestingly low values per head, in the region of those of Austria, as well. The highest international traffic per capita can, as ten years before, be found in Belgium, Denmark, the Netherlands and Switzerland. Norway also did well but handled very little through-traffic. Denmark and the Netherlands, on the other hand, did best in this third category and seem to have been central relay countries. This is surprising as it does not confirm the findings of the structural studies in the previous sections of this chapter that ascribed very little betweenness to nodes in these countries. Outside Europe, the 'Statistique générale' gives meaningful information only for British India, which exhibited minuscule values in all categories. In absolute numbers, the international messages sent and received are in the region of those of Portugal. In the per capita measures, the indexed values accordingly tend towards zero.

Just as in the previous decade, international telegraphic traffic grew rather evenly between 1870 and 1880. There were only a few exceptions to this: Hungary exhibited extraordinarily high growth rates in this period, and both British India and Portugal significantly increased their numbers of transit messages. This mirrors the two countries' position in the global telegraph network. From 1870 onwards, the Portuguese port city of Carcavelos became a relay station on the submarine route to India. And through the eastward extension of the network, British India itself became a through-station for all traffic between Europe and South East Asia, East Asia and Australia. Interestingly, Germany exhibited minuscule growth in external traffic and even negative growth in terms of absolute transit messages handled. The country ceased to perform above the index average (see Table A.16 in the Appendix). Together with the other major European powers, France and Great Britain, it was significantly below average in all categories – especially in the transit category. In the first two categories, Great Britain still did best with values of 87 and 71 per cent of the average. The Netherlands, Belgium and Switzerland (and, to a lesser degree, Denmark and Norway) still had impressive per capita values. In 1880, Denmark was one of the principal international traffic hubs with almost as many through-messages as Great Britain. The Netherlands, on the other hand, had lost their hub position of ten years previously. Outside Europe, Algeria and Tunisia (in 1880 treated as one entity in the statistics) participated very actively in global telegraphic communication with per capita values of 63 per cent and 52 per cent of the European average.

Again, growth values were very evenly distributed across all countries for the decade from 1880 to 1890. The only notable digressions can be found in the growth of transit traffic in France, Hungary, Romania and Portugal. While absolute figures in this category remained rather small in the cases of the former three, Portugal had become an important international transit country by 1890 (see Table A.17 in the Appendix). To an even more pronounced degree, the same is true for Denmark and Switzerland. Both countries handled about 2.7 times the average per capita transit traffic. Interestingly, the Netherlands also partially regained their status as a transit country, which had been lost during the previous decade. German and French performance remained largely unchanged. Both countries exhibited per capita values significantly below average. Among the major European powers, only Great Britain managed to exceed the average in at least one category. Outside Europe, Algerian traffic had collapsed completely by 1890. This is due to the fact that from 1888 onwards, French Algeria and the French protectorate Tunisia were treated as separate entities in the 'Statistique générale'. Through this division, it became apparent that the Tunisian part handled most of the international traffic and participated quite actively in global telegraphic communication. Interestingly, regarding internal messages per capita, the situation was the opposite. Here, French Algeria was well within the European average from 1890 until the end of the period of observation, while Tunisia could not even achieve half of the average.[27] In the case of Japan, there is no broken-down data for the year 1890 but merely aggregate figures for the total external traffic handled. Despite the fact that the number of international messages sent, received or transmitted in Japan grew by an average of 15 per cent annually between 1880 and 1890, with a total number of 98,036 messages the country reached only about 1 per cent of the European per capita average in 1890.

[27] See Wenzlhuemer, 'The Development of Telegraphy, 1870–1900', 14–16.

By the turn of the century, the absolute growth of international telegraphic communication had further levelled off – a tendency that had already become discernible in 1890. While there was, of course, still absolute growth, the average annual values rarely exceeded 3 per cent, 4 per cent or 5 per cent. Japan, for which broken-down data now became available, is a notable exception, with 17 per cent average annual growth in total external traffic. But while, around 1900, Japan was already approaching European per capita values in terms of internal traffic, international traffic was still minuscule in both absolute and relative terms (see Table A.18 in the Appendix). The country reached only 4 per cent of the European average in the first two categories. In terms of messages transmitted, the absolute number was 3,972, amounting to less than 0.5 per cent of the corresponding European average. British India was the only other exception regarding average annual growth. In the decade leading up to the new century, the number of transit messages handled increased by 10 per cent annually, which reflects the growth of the Asian telegraph system and the increasing Euro-Asian and Euro-Australian traffic. Outside Europe, Australia – and in particular New South Wales – started to participate fully in global communication and immediately exhibited very high per capita figures. Tunisia had more than doubled its external traffic between 1890 and 1900 and was now even above the European average in the category of messages sent. Apart from that, the situation had remained fairly unchanged. Switzerland, Belgium, the Netherlands, Norway, Denmark and Luxembourg had the highest per capita traffic with other countries, while the major European powers stagnated in this regard. Denmark, together with Switzerland and Portugal, handled an impressive amount of through-traffic. In absolute numbers, these three small countries each transmitted more than 600,000 messages a year. Interestingly, both Belgium and the Netherlands had, again, lost their hub positions and would not regain them until the end of the period of observation.

Ten years later, in 1910, the established pattern had still seen only minimal change. Overall, growth rates in the first decade of the twentieth century were a little higher than in the previous decade but also rather evenly distributed. Only Romania and Russia showed unusually high average annual growth rates in transit messages. And Japan exhibited 10 per cent annual growth in the number of international messages received. Apart from that, the picture remained mostly unchanged. In Europe, Switzerland and Denmark still occupied central relay positions with per capita transit values of 288 per cent and 320 per cent respectively (see Table A.19 in the Appendix). In 1910, Switzerland transmitted almost as many international telegrams as Great Britain. With a little less than one million transit messages, Denmark was only slightly behind here. The major European powers were still not able to extend their per-capita external traffic and showed little positive or negative development. Outside Europe, Australia gradually came into full swing and participated to an impressive degree in global communication. While further detailed studies of the roles of Australia and New Zealand in the worldwide telegraph network are necessary, it seems safe to say that telegraphy here was seen as a remedy for the disadvantages of geographical remoteness.

Seen over the entire period of observation from 1860 to 1910, there seems to be remarkably little development and change in terms of the international traffic handled by the countries that submitted information to the Bureau international. Changes and shifts, if they occurred at all, took place in individual categories and within very strict limits. Neither did the major European powers catch up with initially very well-connected countries such as the Netherlands, Belgium or Switzerland, nor did these smaller countries level off in their development and lose their leading positions over time. There is no such overall dynamic in international traffic. While it does, of course, grow in absolute terms, its country-wise per capita distribution remained practically unchanged throughout the late nineteenth and early twentieth centuries. The use analysis has also revealed significant differences between the structural make-up of the global telegraph network and its use patterns. The social network analyses in the earlier sections of this chapter have attributed the highest international connectivity to the European metropolises and some other strategically well-placed nodes. Cities in Switzerland, Belgium or the Netherlands, for instance, have generally done well in these analyses, but rather in the degree and eigenvector measures and not at all in terms of betweenness. The analysis of external telegraphic traffic, however, has shown that these and several other smaller countries handled extraordinarily high proportions of international traffic. This discrepancy can partially be explained by the fact that the highest indexed figures are per capita values. Accordingly, these figures merely say that, for instance, the Swiss, the Belgians, the Dutch or the Danes sent, received and transmitted more international telegrams per head than the bigger European powers. These are relative figures that need not necessarily be reflected in the structure of the network, which is absolute. On the other hand, however, external traffic in absolute numbers was quite substantial in these smaller countries as well, even if it could, of course, not reach the dimensions of Great Britain, France or Germany. It could have been expected that this significant telegraphic flow, especially in the transit category, would have had an impact on the network structure as well and might have shifted the nodes in these countries closer to the central axes of international traffic, as revealed in the previous section.

7 The British telegraph network

7.1 The telegraph and the turf

In 1848, a collection of anecdotes was published in London under the title *The London Anecdotes for All Readers*. Part 1: *Anecdotes of the Electric Telegraph*. The stories in this volume dealt eclectically with a number of different fields of application of telegraphy, such as financial speculation, law enforcement, train management and various cases of treachery and fraud. Among the latter, several anecdotes dealt with the uses and abuses of telegraphy in connection with horse-racing under the general heading 'The Telegraph and the Turf'. The opening paragraph reads,

The race-horse was once a favourite symbol of rapidity; now, even Pegasus is outstripped; and the achievement of Flying Childers, who went over the four-mile course at Newmarket in six minutes and forty-eight seconds, or at the rate of thirty-five miles an hour, is thrown into the shade. The result of every meet is known in town, and at Tattersall's, almost before the last horse and jockey are at the goal; thus superseding the fleet posters and pigeons that conveyed the intelligence by the old regime. Well must our readers remember the crowded Strandway, and the rush of race-result-bearing couriers over Waterloo bridge, for publication in the evening newspapers. Now, the news comes silently as a dream, without either pigeon, horse-flesh, or spur; and arrives, in real earnest, before either the horse or its rider, the pigeon or its dispatch, the train or its intelligence, are started![1]

This passage illustrates that even in the early days of telegraphy, ready uses for the new technology had been found beyond the usual fields of administration, business and railway control. Of course, the communication of race results for publication in the newspapers can be seen and treated as part of the press use of the telegraph, but in the subsequent paragraph it was made very clear that the press was not alone with its interest in the races. The *Anecdotes* continues,

It was not to be supposed that the advantages of the exclusive obtainment of intelligence on such topics by its possessor would for a moment be overlooked

[1] New Anecdote Library, ed., *The London Anecdotes for All Readers*. Part 1: *Anecdotes of the Electric Telegraph* (London: 1848), 29.

by the turfites; and accordingly, we have to relate a few instances of the manœuvres of the sporting fraternity, which redound much to their ingenuity, but very slightly to their credit. We should, however, premise, that the railway companies whose telegraphs were then (for it was before the general system of the Electric Telegraph Company was anything like completed) connected with Newmarket, Doncaster, Slough and Ascot, resolved, and very fairly, not to permit the result of a race to be made known by telegraph, though we are afraid this rule was in some instances broken by the payment of a handsome fee – excepting by the ordinary methods, either of pigeon, passenger, or post-horses. The consequence was, that the 'knowing ones' resorted to a variety of *ruses*, one of which, in sporting phraseology, would probably be called – NO GO!"[2]

Under this heading – NO GO! – then follows the first telegraph-and-turf anecdote about the somewhat transparent attempt of a London sports better to obtain telegraphic information about the winning horse at Cup Day at Doncaster:

[T]he turfite thus apostrophized the keeper of the telegraph [at Shoreditch, London]: 'Hangit! I'm heartily glad your're here, for I'm in a most awful fix. A friend I left at Doncaster, first thing this morning, not being able to let me have it when I left him, has promised to transmit by the next train a very valuable parcel, to be placed in one of the first-class carriages. Will you be kind enough to inquire for me the number of the carriage it is placed in . . .' So far so good; but the clerk was too cunning for his customer, and explained to him that the object was rather too transparent for him to be gulled; . . . The fact was, as is known to all sportsmen, the horses when placed are *numbered*: of course, the number to be returned by the correspondent in concert at Doncaster, to the inquiry of the telegraph, would have been the number of the 'winning horse' . . . Added to this, the turfite was informed . . . that the carriages on the Eastern Counties . . . were *not numbered*, though the carriages on other lines were.[3]

As a look at the remaining turf anecdotes reveals, similar (but better-planned) attempts to obtain the race results by telegraph could at times also be successful. About twenty years later, the connection between the telegraph and the turf had further intensified. Most important racecourses now had temporary telegraph offices directly on the premises. And the communication of the results by telegram was now the rule rather than the exception. Anyone with access to the telegraph network could now partake actively in the event. And for the General Post Office, which was running the British domestic telegraph system since its nationalization in the year 1870, this meant good business – as can be seen from the following two communications: a letter from the Postmaster General to the Treasury from 1878 and a passage from Frank Ives Scudamore's

[2] Ibid., 29–30, italics in original. [3] Ibid., 30–1, italics in original.

report about the working of the telegraph system after nationalization from 1871.

The town of Newmarket in Suffolk – widely accepted as the headquarters of British horse-racing[4] – has two principal racecourses: Rowley Mile and the so-called July Course. Like today, in the late nineteenth century most races throughout the season took place at Rowley Mile, which accordingly hosted a permanent telegraph office open during races in order to cater to the press and the 'betting men'. The July Course, however, saw just one important meeting per season and therefore less durable telegraphic structures were available there. In February 1879, this unsatisfactory situation prompted Postmaster General John Manners to write a letter to the Treasury presenting the situation at Newmarket racecourse and stating,

> It has hitherto been the practice to send a tent from London which is erected near the winning post [of the July Course] and used as a temporary Telegraph Office . . . This arrangement is not found to be satisfactory; the tent affords very little security to the Staff and apparatus; the work is done in great discomfort, and when the weather is wet, and boisterous, it is almost impossible to conduct the business properly . . . A letter was, therefore, addressed to Messrs. Weatherby asking them to move the Jockey Club to erect a permanent Telegraph Office on the 'July' Race Course, and a reply was received stating that the Stewards are willing to comply with the wishes of the Department, but only on the understanding that a rent be paid. A further letter was then written expressing the opinion that in consideration of the large sum (£100 a year) paid to the Jockey Club for rent, the additional accommodation ought to be provided free of cost. It was also pointed out that the establishment of a Telegraph Office on the Course, besides being a convenience to the frequenters of the meeting, must be indirectly an advantage to the Jockey Club, because the number of persons paying for admission to the Enclosures would doubtless decrease if telegraphic communication were not provided.[5]

In order to support his request to erect a more adequate telegraph office at the July Course, Manners attached a table giving the receipts and expenses of the GPO in connection with the race meetings at Newmarket. From this table, it becomes clear that in the year 1878 the operation of the telegraph office open only during seven race meetings per year earned the GPO the handy sum of £2,449 17s 1d – all expenses already deducted. During these seven meetings a total of 73,723 telegrams were sent from

[4] House of Commons Parliamentary Papers, C. 304, 'Telegraphs. Report by Mr. Scudamore on the Re-organization of the Telegraph System of the United Kingdom', 1871, 34.

[5] National Archives, T 1/15916, 'Telegraph Service at Newmarket Race Meetings: Transport for Telegraphists and Provision of Improved Accommodation. Letter John Manners, GPO, to Treasury', 5 February 1879.

Newmarket racecourse (including 13,966 press messages), while 21,848 telegrams were received.

Horse-racing and its demand for telegraphic communication had already been an important issue several years before the Postmaster General brought it to the attention of the Treasury. In 1871, Frank Ives Scudamore submitted a detailed report about the nationalization of the British domestic telegraph system to the Postmaster General. Among many other issues, the report also contained a section on 'Race Meetings', opening with the informative statement that

> [t]he telegraphic business done at and in connexion with race meetings is large and lucrative, but troublesome. Special arrangements have to be made for every meeting; the work has to be done under great pressure; and the senders of the messages are more irritable, and, when they are irritated, more free in the use of their tongues than any other class of the community.[6]

Nevertheless, the report went on, various arrangements had been made (among those the improvement of the telegraphic facilities at Newmarket racecourse, which in less than a decade would already be insufficient again) to satisfy the needs of the audience on the spot, the press and the betters, because race meetings produced an immense demand for telegraphic communication and were – as the above passage illustrates – a lucrative business. To underline this point, Scudamore referred to the work of Mr Preece, Mr Kerswell and Mr Johnstone, 'who have superintended the arrangements at the great meetings of the past year'[7] and included several of their findings in his report. Regarding the telegraphic traffic at Newmarket racecourse, they stated,

> As Newmarket shows the heaviest business in the aggregate, so it furnishes the largest results from any single meeting, viz., the 'Cambridgeshire' week, when upwards of 8,000 messages were disposed of. In the 15 days of the October meetings there were, in round numbers, 20,000 messages forwarded and received; and of these, upwards of 2,000 were long press messages containing 120,000 words. Large as are these figures, they become still larger when it is borne in mind that the bulk of this work was performed on the mornings of the race days between 10 a.m. and 1 p.m., and in the evening after 8 p.m. During the 'Cæsarewitch' week, for instance, on Tuesday, the 'Cæsarewitch' day, nearly 1,000 messages were taken in and disposed of at the town office, between 10 a.m. and 1 p.m.; on Wednesday, 800 between 10 a.m. and 12 noon; and on Thursday, 750 between 10 a.m. and 12.30 p.m. Of upwards of 3,500 received messages for the 15 days only about 30 remained undelivered at the close of the

[6] House of Commons Parliamentary Papers, C. 304, 'Telegraphs. Report by Mr. Scudamore on the Re-organization of the Telegraph System of the United Kingdom', 1871, 33.

[7] Ibid., 33.

meetings, which, considering the difficulty of 'localizing' betting men, and the great drawback which has always been experienced on this account is, I consider, a wonderful result.[8]

The numbers both from this report and from the Postmaster General's letter illustrate how lucrative a telegraphic business the race meetings were and how much traffic they produced. Although it is not explicitly mentioned in the text, the numbers given by Preece, Kerswell and Johnstone in the Scudamore report most likely refer to the race meetings of the year 1870, while the table in Manners's letter contains information for 1878. The October meetings in Newmarket produced traffic of around 20,000 telegraphic messages in two weeks in 1870. Eight years later, this had increased to around 34,500. The figures are all the more interesting when compared to the weekly traffic handled in British town offices. In the year 1868, for instance, Liverpool boasted the third-highest telegraphic traffic in the entire United Kingdom (after London and Manchester). Taken together, all Electric offices in the city handled a little less than 10,000 messages – sent, received and transmitted – per week in this year.[9] This means that during race meetings the telegraph station at Newmarket handled just as much traffic as did all Electric telegraph offices in the telegraphically third-busiest city of the country. Extending this comparison to India, Bombay saw the single biggest part of the telegraphic traffic of the subcontinent at the time of observation. According to the Administration Report of the Indian Telegraph Department, the telegraph offices in Bombay handled a total of 236,092 messages throughout the 1870–1 fiscal year.[10] This amounts to an average of a little more than 4,500 telegrams per week and, accordingly, to less than half the number of messages transacted during race meetings at Newmarket.

The mere existence of a whole section of 'Anecdotes of the Electric Telegraph' in the *London Anecdotes for All Readers* published in 1848 is in

[8] Ibid., 33–4.

[9] Elsewhere, I have stated that we no longer have information on the Magnetic's Liverpool traffic. This reflects the contents of the sources I am familiar with from the time, but is incorrect. While a lot of information on Liverpool stations is missing in the 1868 station-by-station survey that informs much of the remainder of this chapter, aggregate traffic information (apparently taken from the 1868 survey) is also available in a station-by-station compilation on telegraph staff, wages and weekly messages. British Telecom Archives, POST 82/303, 'Telegraphs. Return of Persons Employed; Wages; Average Weekly Messages', 1869–1872. The article wrongly claiming that there is no more information on the Magnetic's Liverpool traffic is Wenzlhuemer, 'London in the Global Telecommunication Network of the Nineteenth Century', 15.

[10] British Library, Oriental Collections, IOR/V/24/4284, 'Administration Report of the Indian Telegraph Department for 1867–68 to 1870–71', 1871, 66.

itself already a testimony to the sociocultural significance that the technology had achieved in the United Kingdom very early in its history. In 128 pages, the recounted anecdotes dealt not only with the typical fields of application of the telegraph, but also with its more profane uses and consequences that were already becoming a part of daily life for some classes of the population. The thorough transformation of a deeply rooted and widespread cultural practice such as horse betting between the 1840s and the 1870s is but one particularly illustrative example. From railway travel, to sending for a doctor, to a game of chess – none of these everyday businesses remained unchanged by the new capacities of the telegraph. And the United Kingdom was spearheading this development. The following sections will, therefore, look in some detail at the place of telegraphy in British economy and society.

7.2 From private service to public good

Discussing the history of government involvement in telegraphy in Great Britain, Charles R. Perry identified '[t]wo aspects of the early history of British telegraphy which set it apart from the experience of some other countries'. The first such aspect, according to Perry, is that 'there was never as close a connection made in Britain between the telegraph and military and security purposes as was the case in some continental countries'. And '[s]econdly, Britain differed in the competitive strategy of its firms from the pattern of development in the United States'.[11] The latter point alludes to the fact that in the United States of America Western Union built up a quasi-monopoly in the domestic telegraph business through a series of mergers and takeovers, while 'British market concentration declined almost continually throughout the private enterprise

[11] Charles R. Perry, 'The Rise and Fall of Government Telegraphy in Britain', *Business and Economic History* 26, no 2 (1997), 417. The heading of the current section has been borrowed from Richard John, who – like several others – has dicussed this matter in the context of the United States telegraph system. See Richard R. John, 'Private Enterprise, Public Good? Communications Deregulation as a National Political Issue, 1839–1851', in *Communication and Its Lines: Telegraphy in the 19th Century among Economy, Politics and Technology*, ed. Andrea Giuntini (Prato: Istituto di studi storici postali onlus, 2004); Tomas Nonnenmacher, 'State Promotion and Regulation of the Telegraph Industry, 1845–1860', *Journal of Economic History* 61, no 1 (2001); Nonnenmacher, 'Law, Emerging Technology, and Market Structure: The Development of the Telegraph Industry, 1838–1868', *Journal of Economic History* 57, no 2 (1997); David Hochfelder, 'Constructing an Industrial Divide: Western Union, AT&T, and the Federal Government, 1876–1971', *Business History Review* 76, no 4 (2002); Paul Israel, *From Machine Shop to Industrial Laboratory: Telegraphy and the Changing Context of American Invention, 1830–1920*, ed. Merritt Roe Smith, Johns Hopkins Studies in the History of Technology (Baltimore and London: Johns Hopkins University Press, 1992).

period',[12] or until nationalization in 1870. This is to say that the propagation of telegraphic communication in the United Kingdom was from its very onset in the year 1837 a commercial endeavour following the clear goal of making a profit. Also from very early on, the telegraph business was a highly competitive one in which several substantial companies competed for customers and traffic. Even before the first telegraph line went into operation on British soil, the commercial potential of the technology was of central concern to those involved. William Fothergill Cooke, for instance, had been introduced to electric information transmission during a lecture by the physicist Georg Wilhelm Muncke at Heidelberg University in 1836. 'Within weeks, [Cooke] had constructed a model telegraph and was preparing to return to London to exploit its commercial possibilities.'[13] Back in London, Cooke entered into an uneasy partnership with Charles Wheatstone. In June 1837, one of the last patents signed by William IV secured Cooke and Wheatstone the rights to exploit electric telegraphy in the United Kingdom. The patent protected 'a comprehensive set of claims that left few loop-holes for any challengers'.[14]

The technology behind the telegraph was led to maturity and applicability at the same time in the United States of America and in the United Kingdom. But while Samuel Morse eventually managed to convince Congress in 1842 to finance a test line between Washington and Baltimore that would go into operation in 1844,[15] telegraphy enjoyed no such start-up support on the other side of the Atlantic. Cooke and Wheatstone needed to find investors for their project and started to approach railway companies, advertising the potential benefits of telegraphic communication for train co-ordination. They entered into co-operation with the Great Western Railway and the London & Blackwall Railway companies. Along the tracks of the former company, a telegraph line between Paddington and West Drayton stations was finished in 1839.[16] A much shorter stretch of telegraph wire along the latter's route went into operation the following year. Both endeavours worked satisfactorily and proved to be very useful for railway purposes. Nevertheless, many of the railways themselves 'were lukewarm, some hostile, to what was called a "dangerous experiment". Many refused to be bothered with "the wires". Years were to pass before the natural affinity of wire and rail came to be recognised by the majority of the conservative railway

[12] James Foreman-Peck, 'Competition, Co-operation and Nationalisation in the Nineteenth Century Telegraph System', *Business History* 31, no 3 (1989), 82.

[13] Morus, 'The Electric Ariel', 350. [14] Roberts, 'Distant Writing', 2.

[15] Huurdeman, *The Worldwide History of Telecommunications*, 59–60. [16] Ibid., 67.

managements'.[17] One of the reasons for this reluctance to invest in telegraphy and to buy licenses from Cooke and Wheatstone can be found in the levelling-off of the railway boom in 1841 brought about by a shortness of cheap credit.[18] In Cooke's own words: 'At the beginning of 1843 we were at our lowest point of depression. The patents remained almost unproductive, and we had incurred, in various ways, a considerable outlay.'[19]

Cooke, however, managed to convince the Great Western management to allow him to expand the existing line from West Drayton to Slough, with all expenses payable out of his own pocket. When the line was completed in May 1843, Cooke opened it for public commercial use,[20] and benefited from Slough's proximity to Windsor where the queen's household had a certain demand for swift communication with London. Sending a message cost a uniform charge of one shilling regardless of its length. Visitors who wanted to observe the spectacle at the telegraph office had to pay the same amount as an entrance fee.[21] Also in 1843, Cooke obtained permission to extend the line to Windsor directly. In the following year, this extension made it possible for the telegraph to acquire

> considerable fame by its speedy announcement to the ministers of the Crown and London generally, of the birth of Queen Victoria's second son, Alfred Ernest, at Windsor, on 6 August 1844 . . . Three special trains carrying notables left London for a great banquet at Windsor. The telegraph was soon again in use – the Duke of Wellington's forgotten dress suit being obtained from Apsley House in time for the royal dinner party in the Windsor banqueting hall.[22]

Together with the capture of the murderer John Tawell – to which reference has been made in earlier chapters – these events contributed to the popularization of the new technology and drew the attention of the public (and, of course, the press) to its potential. Accordingly, telegraph lines were gradually erected alongside more and more railway tracks. The breakthrough regarding the acceptance of telegraphy as a reliable and practicable means of long-distance communication came with the assignment to build an eighty-eight-mile connection – the longest so far – between London and Portsmouth for the Admiralty.[23]

17 Kieve, *The Electric Telegraph: A Social and Economic History*, 36.
18 Roberts, 'Distant Writing', 4.
19 Cooke, in the fourth version (published in 1866) of his anti-Wheatstone pamphlet *The Electric Telegraph: Was It Invented by Professor Wheatstone?*, quoted in Kieve, *The Electric Telegraph: A Social and Economic History*, 36.
20 Huurdeman, *The Worldwide History of Telecommunications*, 70.
21 Roberts, 'Distant Writing', 5.
22 Kieve, *The Electric Telegraph: A Social and Economic History*, 36–7.
23 Ibid., 37–8.

Considering that the Admiralty had refused any support for Francis Ronalds's prototype telegraph in the 1810s on the grounds that the existing semaphore system worked satisfactorily (see Chapter 3), the commissioning of the London–Portsmouth line signifies that telegraphy had now reached a degree of technological maturity (going hand in hand with public acceptance) that rendered it fit for use on a large scale. As a consequence, Cooke eventually managed to find investors who were both willing and financially able to purchase the patents that Cooke and Wheatstone held jointly. With capital from John Lewis Ricardo,[24] a member of an influential merchant family, and George Parker Bidder, a railway engineer and partner of Robert Stephenson, Cooke registered the Electric Telegraph Company in September 1845 in order to take over and fully exploit the patents. Wheatstone was bought out and held no share in the newly established company.[25] Partly due to government reluctance to get involved in the propagation of a new and largely untested technology and partly due to William Fothergill Cooke's entrepreneurial vision, domestic telegraphy in Great Britain was, indeed, a thoroughly commercial affair right from the start. And in the mid-1840s, the incorporation of the Electric Telegraph Company served as a temporary high-water mark in this respect. This is, however, not to say that the British government held no interest in telegraphy beyond the London–Portsmouth line and did not recognize its administrative and strategic potential. Quite on the contrary, the Act of Parliament by which the Electric Telegraph Company was incorporated also contained a passage that reserved the right of the government to take over the control of the telegraph system in cases of emergency. Precisely such an emergency came about only two years later in the form of the Chartist riots of 1848. Although published in 1953, Frederick Mather's article on the role of railways and telegraphs during the period of Chartism is still the only systematic study investigating this matter. Unfortunately, the tone of the piece is often tendentious and its analytical value is, therefore, greatly diminished. One of its virtues, however, is that it draws directly on a number of contemporary sources. For instance, Mather quotes from the warrant that Home Secretary Sir George Grey sent to John Lewis Ricardo on 10 April 1848. The warrant opens as follows:

> Whereas by an Act passed in the ninth year of Her Majesty, intituled 'An Act for forming and regulating the Electric Telegraph Company, and to enable the said Company to work certain Letters Patent', it was amongst other things

[24] On the role of Ricardo in this context, see Roger Neil Barton, 'New Media: The Birth of Telegraphic News in Britain 1847–68', *Media History* 16, no 4 (2010).

[25] Kieve, *The Electric Telegraph: A Social and Economic History*, 42–4.

enacted that it should be lawful for one of Her Majesty's Principal Secretaries of State for the time being, in case emergencies might arise in which it might be expedient for the public service that the entire control over the operations of the said company, and the conveyance of signals should be vested in Her Majesty's Government, by warrant under his hand to cause possession to be taken of all the Telegraphs and Telegraphic Apparatus at the various stations of the Company, their Licencees or Assigns, for the space of one week from the date of such warrant, for the purpose of preventing any communication being made or signals given, save such as shall be authorized and directed by such Secretary of State.[26]

Mather claims 'that the government was using its control of the telegraphs not only to prevent communications between the Chartists but to strengthen its own lines of communication',[27] and accordingly benefited greatly from its emergency powers. Nevertheless, this instance remained the only case of direct government interference under the law until telegraph nationalization.

In these first decades of its history, telegraphic communication in Great Britain was, therefore, not seen as a public good – neither by the telegraph companies that were aiming at making a profit, nor by the government, which at that point in time was more concerned with the potential problems that could arise from unlimited access to the telegraph network. While there is evidence that the Electric had severe financial difficulties in the early years of its existence,[28] the long-term prospects of profit seemed bright and started to attract competition in the field. In the early 1850s, several telegraph companies were incorporated. Among the first were, for instance, the British Electric Telegraph Company,[29] the English & Irish Magnetic Telegraph Company[30] and the International Telegraph Company.[31] Through a series of mergers between these and other firms throughout the 1850s, two main rival companies emerged: the Electric & International Telegraph Company (called the Electric, based on the Electric Telegraph Company) and the British & Irish Magnetic Telegraph Company (called the Magnetic, based on the English & Irish

[26] Home Office Warrant to John L. Ricardo, 10 April 1848, quoted in Frederick C. Mather, 'The Railways, the Electric Telegraph and Public Order during the Chartist Period, 1837–48', *Journal of the Historical Association* 38, no 132 (1953), 49.

[27] Ibid., 50–1.

[28] Kieve, *The Electric Telegraph: A Social and Economic History*, 48–9; Roberts, 'Distant Writing', 8.

[29] National Archives, BT 41/88/501, 'British Electric Telegraph Company', 1844–*c.*1860.

[30] National Archives, BT 41/225/1269, 'English and Irish Magnetic Telegraph Company', 1844–*c.*1860.

[31] National Archives, BT 41/321/1847, 'International Telegraph Company', 1844–*c.*1860.

Table 7.1 *Number of inland messages forwarded in the United Kingdom, 1868.*

Type	Company	Messages	%
Telegraph companies	Electric & International	3,137,478	52.3
	British & Irish Magnetic	1,530,961	25.5
	United Kingdom	776,714	12.9
	London & Provincial	183,304	3.1
	Universal Private	27,542	0.5
	Subtotal	5,655,999	94.3
Railway companies	South Eastern Railway	103,386	1.7
	London, Brighton and South Coast Railway	86,937	1.4
	London Chatham Railway	88,418	1.5
	North British Railway	51,032	0.9
	Caledonian Railway	16,262	0.3
	Subtotal	346,035	5.8
Total		**6,002,034**	**100.0**

Source: British Telecom Archives, POST 82/173, 'Estimates of Revenues and Expenditure under the Post Office with Returns of Staff, Accounts, Telegrams, Offices, Etc of Telegraph Companies', 1866–9.

Magnetic Telegraph Company).[32] Until nationalization, the Electric remained the biggest and most important company, followed by the Magnetic. Registered already in 1850, the United Kingdom Telegraph Company (called the UK) eventually managed to raise sufficient capital to start operations in 1860.[33] At some considerable distance behind the Electric and the Magnetic, the UK became the third-biggest telegraph company in Great Britain.

Table 7.1 shows the numbers of messages handled by each of these three companies during the year 1868. With more than half of the entire telegraphic traffic going through the hands of its clerks, the Electric dominated the field. The Magnetic secured about a quarter of the business for itself. About 13 per cent of all messages were transmitted by the UK as the third important company. These proportions confirm that the business was neatly divided among those three competitors, who among themselves handled more than 90 per cent of traffic. The London & Provincial Telegraph Company and the

[32] For a history of the 'brief lives' of the companies that would later be merged to form the Magnetic, see Roger Neil Barton, 'Brief Lives: Three British Telegraph Companies 1850–56', *International Journal for the History of Engineering & Technology* 80, no 2 (2010).

[33] Kieve, *The Electric Telegraph: A Social and Economic History*, 61–2.

Universal Private Telegraph Company occupied specific niches of the business. The former was founded in 1859 as the London District Telegraph Company (called the District). It was closely linked to the Magnetic and 'was to develop telegraphic communication within the radius of 4 miles from Charing Cross, with provisions to extend to 20 miles, thus exploiting the potential of the London traffic without extending the system to unprofitable areas'.[34] The District, as will be seen later in this chapter, had an exclusive focus on London. The Universal Private Telegraph Company filled a different niche by providing direct telegraphic connections for private subscribers.[35] Regarding their share of the British telegraphic traffic, both companies were marginal. The railway companies that make up the lower half of Table 7.1 are those which had not entered into contracts with the major telegraph companies and for which the data has, therefore, not been included under the Electric, Magnetic or UK headings.

These figures show that domestic telegraphy in Britain was dominated by only three companies with nationwide operations, amongst which one company clearly occupied a leading role. Accordingly, the actual competition between these companies, and as a consequence the correspondence between demand and supply, remained limited – as did the quality of public service in the eyes of many contemporary observers.[36] Therefore calls for a reform of the telegraph system started to be voiced from about the mid-1850s onwards. As David Hochfelder points out, three different methods of reform seemed viable at that point and were discussed by contemporaries: a merger of the existing companies and the creation of a private telegraph monopoly under close governmental scrutiny, the cultivation of more competition in the field through the easy granting of the right of way along public highways, or the nationalization of the entire industry.[37] However, none of these plans could initially enlist enough public support until the telegraph companies uniformly doubled the tariff for a standard twenty-word message in 1865. This move rendered both the powers and the intentions of the existing telegraph cartel clearly visible,[38] and affronted several groups of important customers, in particular the merchant community and the press.[39] These groups now started to campaign for a reform of the system in the form of nationalizing the

[34] Ibid., 56. [35] Roberts, 'Distant Writing', 40–3.

[36] David Hochfelder, 'A Comparison of the Postal Telegraph Movement in Great Britain and the United States, 1866–1900', *Enterprise & Society* 1 (2000), 740.

[37] Ibid., 741.

[38] Perry, 'The Rise and Fall of Government Telegraphy in Britain', 417–18.

[39] Ira J. Cohen, 'Toward a Theory of State Intervention: The Nationalization of the British Telegraphs', *Social Science History* 4, no 2 (1980), 173–4.

entire sector.[40] Their ideas were favourably greeted by several influential administrators in the General Post Office – most prominently by Frank Ives Scudamore, second secretary to the Postmaster General, who had already made a name in the context of the establishment of the Post Office Savings Bank and the sale of life insurance and annuities by the Post Office earlier in the decade.[41] Still within the year 1865, the pressure for reform had become so high that Postmaster General Lord Stanley commissioned Scudamore to look into the state of the telegraph companies and the potential for nationalization. This Scudamore did with unsurpassable zeal and dedication – 'his energy knew no bounds', a colleague reported.[42] In 1866, he submitted a comprehensive report to the Treasury on the basis of which nationalization was eventually decided on[43] – and enacted with the Telegraph Act of 1868.[44] The Post Office eventually took over the operation of the telegraphs in February 1870.[45]

The takeover had severe financial ramifications. Scudamore's report had been overoptimistic regarding both the costs of the acquisition of the telegraphs and the potential earnings from operating the system. Accordingly, Scudamore significantly exceeded the funds allocated for the nationalization and eventually also caused a major public scandal by diverting and misusing funds from Post Office Savings Bank deposits.[46] While the profitability of the telegraph system was limited, nationalization brought a significant expansion of public access to the network. The cost of sending messages dropped massively and the number of messages sent doubled over two years. While the network under the companies had structurally concentrated on the profitable urban areas and often neglected the less central regions,[47] the system was now extended 'by 40,000 new miles of wire'.[48] Telegraphy had now become a public good in

[40] Hochfelder, 'A Comparison of the Postal Telegraph Movement in Great Britain and the United States, 1866–1900', 741.

[41] Perry, 'The Rise and Fall of Government Telegraphy in Britain', 419.

[42] Charles R. Perry, 'Frank Ives Scudamore and the Post Office Telegraphs', *Albion: A Quarterly Journal Concerned with British Studies* 12, no 4 (1980), 353.

[43] House of Commons Parliamentary Papers, C. 202, 'Electric Telegraphs. Return to an Order of the Honourable the House of Commons, Dated 3 April 1868; – for, Copy "of Reports to the Postmaster General by Mr. Scudamore upon the Proposal for Transferring to the Post Office the Control and Management of the Electric Telegraphs throughout the United Kingdom"', 1867–1868.

[44] Act of the Parliament of the United Kingdom, 31 & 32 Vict. c. 110, 'An Act to Enable Her Majesty's Postmaster General to Acquire, Work and Maintain Electric Telegraphs', 1868.

[45] Hochfelder, 'A Comparison of the Postal Telegraph Movement in Great Britain and the United States, 1866–1900', 743.

[46] Perry, 'Frank Ives Scudamore and the Post Office Telegraphs', 360.

[47] See map in Kieve, *The Electric Telegraph: A Social and Economic History*, 75.

[48] Perry, 'Frank Ives Scudamore and the Post Office Telegraphs', 356.

the best sense of the word, so that by 1880 almost thirty million messages were sent and received per year.[49]

7.3 The British telegraph network structure in 1868

Apart from these beneficial effects regarding public network access, the nationalization of domestic telegraphy is also a rare stroke of luck for the historian. Preparing for the takeover, Scudamore gathered all sorts of information on the state of the British telegraph system and initiated a number of comprehensive surveys of the network – some of which have survived in the archives. One particularly valuable survey was conducted in June 1868. Printed forms were sent to all stations of the three principal telegraph companies (at least, returns survive only for the Electric, the Magnetic and the UK). The clerk in charge at each station was requested to complete the form, filling in information such as the station's position in the telegraphic circuits of the United Kingdom, its opening hours, rent paid and – maybe most importantly – the average weekly traffic handled by the station. Regarding analysis of the British telegraph network structure in 1868, this provides information about the number and paths of existing telegraph lines. More importantly, however, the forms list clearly with which other places a particular station was in direct communication. Taken together for all evaluated stations, this highlights the hubs in the network just as it reveals the peripheral regions. To have access to such detailed structural data is already exceptional in itself. In addition, however, the structural analysis can then be contrasted with the actual use of the network. Each evaluated station also submitted information about the average number of messages sent, received and transmitted per week in June 1868. Such station-by-station use data is only rarely available – and if it is, then it is usually only for smaller units of observation such as one particular city or, as will be seen in the next chapter, much smaller networks (in terms of connections, not territory). For a well-developed domestic network such as the British one in 1868, such detailed use data is the absolute exception.

The circuit forms that were returned to the General Post Office from the telegraph stations were bound and filed. Although part of the British National Archives catalogue, the files are currently held at the British Telecom archives on High Holborn in London. All forms filed in POST

[49] ITU Archives, Bureau international des administrations télégraphiques, 'Statistique générale de la télégraphie', 1880.

81/51–55,[50] POST 81/12–13[51] and POST 81/77[52] were photographed at the archives. The information contained in the forms was then entered into a spreadsheet. All in all, information for 992 stations in the Electric network, 366 in the Magnetic network and 137 in the UK network were assessed, making a total of 1,495 stations in England, Wales and Scotland for which detailed use data is available.[53] As the forms contain detailed information about the circuits on which a particular station is located and list all other stations on these circuits, structural information is available for another 333 stations for which no individual survey forms are accessible. Therefore structural data is available for 1,828 stations in total. Of course, this is not the total number of telegraph stations open to the public in Great Britain at the time of observation. A report submitted to the House of Commons in July 1868 puts the total number of stations open at 3,381.[54] This number includes all stations in Ireland as well as the stations of the London & Provincial Telegraph Company (82) and the Universal Private Telegraph Company (24). Most importantly, however, some of the bigger railway companies' stations feature in this report but were not evaluated in the original survey. The most important of these are the South Eastern Railway (113); the London, Brighton and South Coast Railway (104); and the London, Chatham and Dover Railway (50), all of which are also represented separately in Table 7.1 as they had no contracts with the telegraph companies. Only two of the stations of the North British

[50] These contain the Electric's circuit returns. British Telecom Archives, POST 81/51, 'Electric and International Telegraph Co Circuit Returns – Metropolitan and "A" and "B"', 1868; British Telecom Archives, POST 81/52, 'Electric and International Telegraph Co Circuit Returns, "C" to "H"', 1868; British Telecom Archives, POST 81/53, 'Electric and International Telegraph Co Circuit Returns, "I" to "O"', 1868; British Telecom Archives, POST 81/54, 'Electric and International Telegraph Co Circuit Returns, "P" to "T"', 1868; British Telecom Archives, POST 81/55, 'Electric and International Telegraph Co Circuit Returns, and Scotland "U" to "Y"', 1868.

[51] These contain the Magnetic's circuit returns. British Telecom Archives, POST 81/12, 'British and Irish Magnetic Telegraph Co (formerly the English Telegraph Company) Circuit Returns – Metropolitan and "A" to "M"', 1868; British Telecom Archives, POST 81/13, 'British and Irish Magnetic Telegraph Co (formerly the English Telegraph Company) Circuit Returns "N" to "Z" and Scotland and Ireland', 1868.

[52] This contains the UK's circuit returns. British Telecom Archives, POST 81/77, 'United Kingdom Electric Telegraph Company, Circuit Returns from Offices in the Metropolitan, English and Scottish Districts', 1868.

[53] Telegraph stations in Ireland have not been considered here.

[54] House of Commons Parliamentary Papers, 416, 'Electric Telegraphs. Returns of the Names of All Railway Companies in the United Kingdom Which Construct or Use Electric Telegraphs as Part of Their Undertaking; of the Number of Miles of Telegraph, Both Authorised and Constructed, and of the Number of Stations and Places Communicating with Such Telegraphs; and, of the Places of Connection, and the Length of Each Submarine Telegraph Connected with any Place in the United Kingdom', 1867–1868, 14.

Railway were evaluated in the survey (of a total of 116), but it seems that practically all Caledonian stations were considered in the original survey. Most of these omissions can clearly be seen in Map 7.1, which shows the location of all stations included in the original survey (black circles) as well as those which were included in the circuit data (grey rectangles). It is clearly visible that almost no stations – apart from the big town offices operated by the telegraph companies themselves – are located in Kent and Sussex (where the South Eastern; the London, Brighton and South Coast; and the London, Chatham and Dover railways operate). Similarly, in Scotland, Lothian, the Borders and Fife, and the western Highlands do not show the stations operated by the North British Railway. All these regions have, therefore, not been represented properly in either the structural or the use analysis undertaken here. If the stations belonging to these railway companies, and the stations in Ireland, are deducted from the total number of stations open in the United Kingdom, this study covers approximately 70 per cent of all company and railway stations included in the survey. For more than 80 per cent of those, both structural and use data is available. Considering the size and density of the British network at the time of observation, this is an exceptionally high sample rate and secures a high validity of the results obtained.

Map 7.2 depicts all of the 2,458 individual connections that were considered in this study – regardless of the operating company. It visualizes the same gaps in the data that are already highlighted in Map 7.1. In addition, however, it neatly shows the core regions of telegraphic development – namely in and around London, the strongly urbanized areas of northern England (around Liverpool, Manchester, Newcastle and West Yorkshire) and around the principal cities of Scotland. In Maps 7.3–7.5 the networks of the three principal firms (and their associated railway companies) are visualized separately. These maps are instructive regarding the regional focuses of the companies. Connections operated by the Electric and the various railway companies with which it had contracts practically covered all of Great Britain but clearly converged on London (Map 7.3). The British metropolis stood at the very core of the Electric network with connections radiating in all directions – save for the south-east, for which, as pointed out above, there is no data available. The Electric network also seems to have been particularly dense around the industrial centres of northern England and to the south-west of London. And judging from the visualization in Map 7.3 alone, almost all of England between London and the industrial north seems to have been reasonably well serviced either by the Electric itself or the various associated railway companies such as, for instance, the London and South Western, the London and North Western, the Great Western, the North

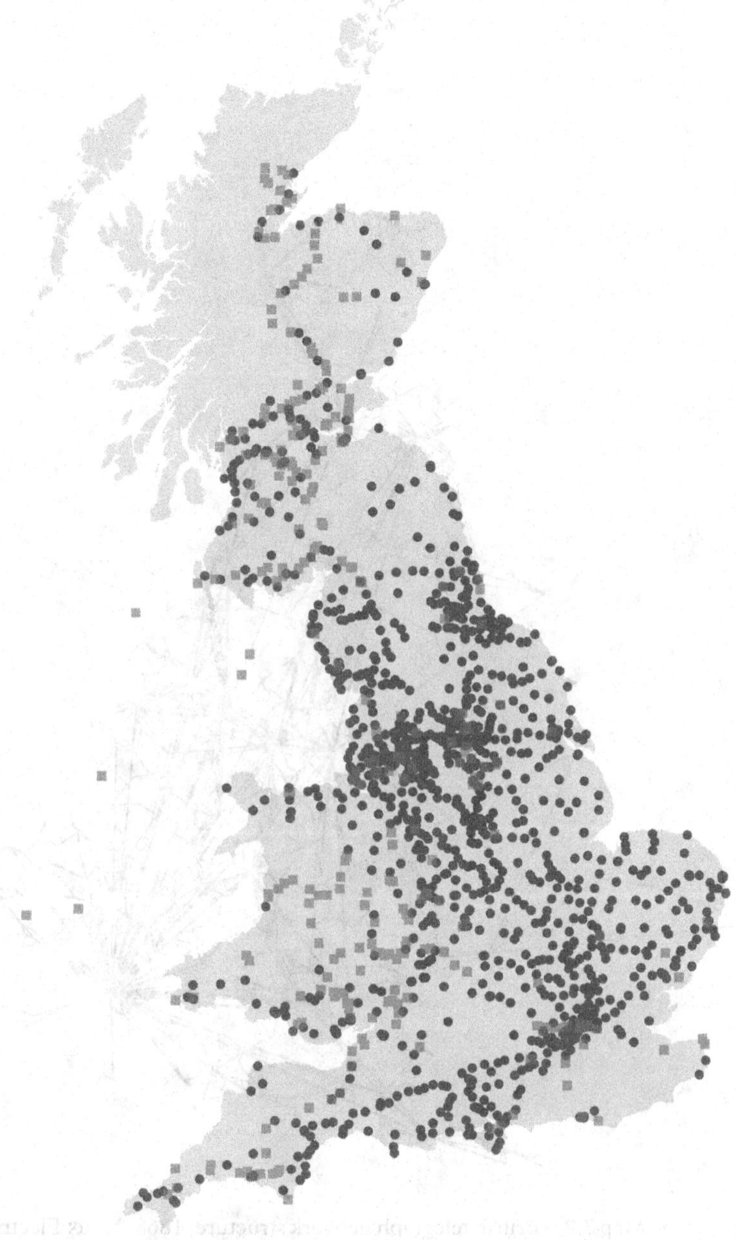

Map 7.1 Telegraph stations included in the 1868 circuit returns directly (black circles) or indirectly (grey rectangles).

Map 7.2 British telegraph network structure, 1868. Note: Electric lines are shown as solid; Magnetic lines as dashed; UK lines as dotted.

Map 7.3 Electric network structure, 1868.

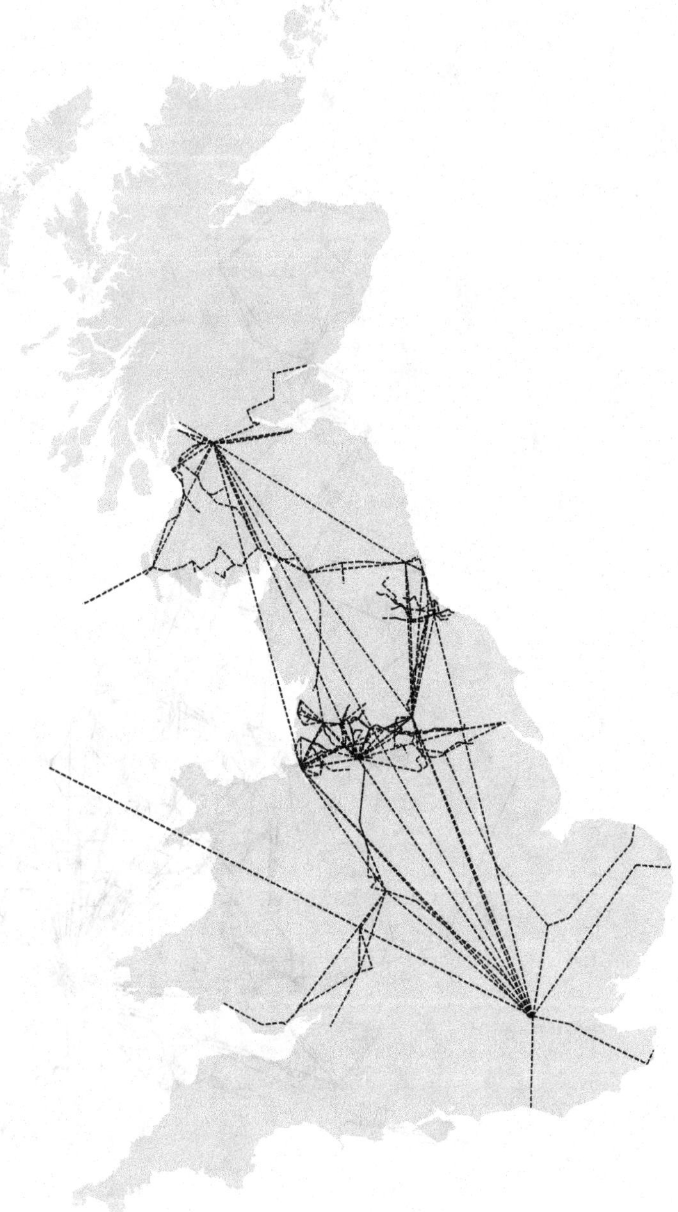

Map 7.4 Magnetic network structure, 1868.

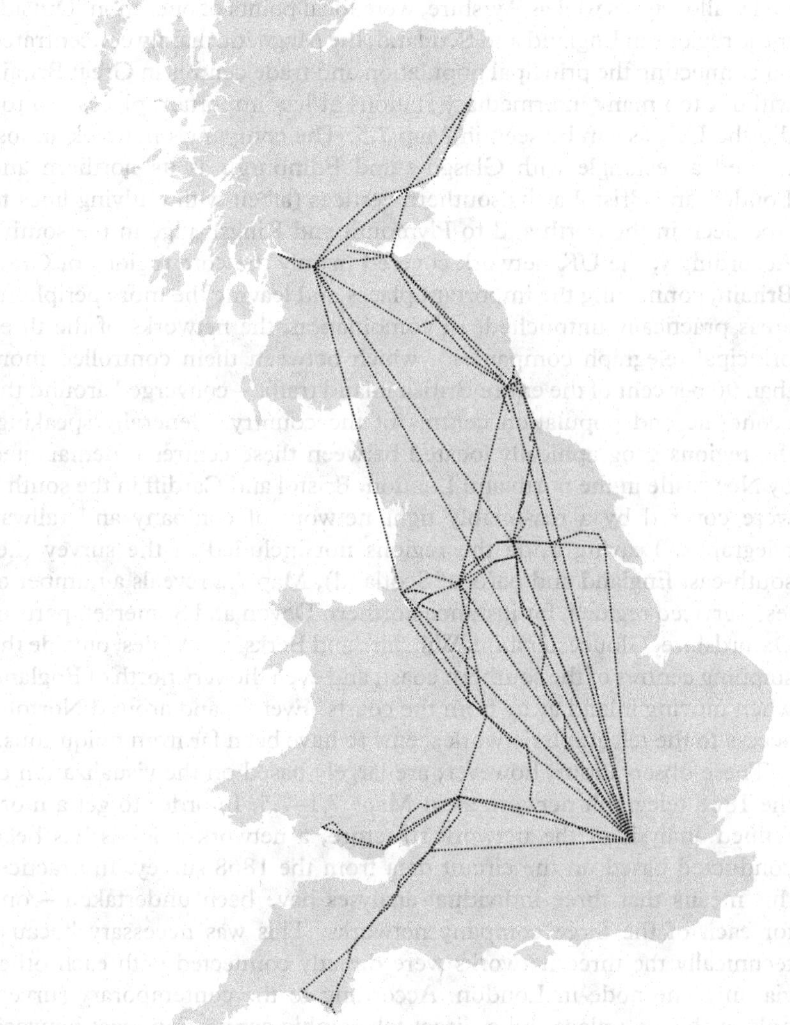

Map 7.5 The UK company's network structure, 1868.

Staffordshire and the Midland railways. Of course, the Magnetic connections also have one centre in London, but in addition the company network is particularly tight in and around Merseyside, Greater Manchester, Lancashire and Yorkshire, as well as in and around Tyne and Wear and Durham (Map 7.4). Its co-operation with the Lancashire and Yorkshire and the North Eastern railway companies emphasizes the Magnetic's concentration on the industrial north of England. In Scotland, Dumfries and Galloway, as well as Ayrshire, were focal points of operation. Outside these regions in England and Scotland, the Magnetic mainly concentrated on connecting the principal population and trade centres in Great Britain without too many intermediary stations at less important places. So too did the UK, as can be seen in Map 7.5. The company's network almost formed a rectangle with Glasgow and Edinburgh as its northern and London and Bristol as its southern vertices (albeit with outlying lines to Aberdeen in the north and to Plymouth and Kingsbridge in the south). Accordingly, the UK network covered mainly the core regions of Great Britain, connecting the important places and leaving the more peripheral areas practically untouched. In combination, the networks of the three principal telegraph companies – which between them controlled more than 90 per cent of the entire British inland traffic – converged around the economic and population centres of the country. Generally speaking, the regions geographically located between these centres – demarcated by Newcastle in the north and London, Bristol and Cardiff in the south – were covered by a reasonably tight network of company and railway telegraphs. Leaving aside the regions not included in the survey (i.e. south-east England and parts of Scotland), Map 7.2 reveals a number of less-serviced regions, for instance northern Devon and Somerset; parts of Oxfordshire, Gloucestershire, Wiltshire and Berkshire; Wales, outside the shipping centres of the southern coast; and even the very north of England when moving inland away from the coasts. Even in and around Norfolk, access to the telegraph network seems to have been far from ubiquitous.

These observations, however, are largely based on the visualization of the 1868 telegraph network as in Maps 7.1–7.5. In order to get a more refined analysis of the network structure, a network analysis has been conducted based on the circuit data from the 1868 survey. In practice, this means that three individual analyses have been undertaken – one for each of the three company networks. This was necessary because technically the three networks were directly connected with each other via only one node in London. According to the contemporary survey, only at this one place did a direct telegraphic connection exist between the individual company networks. Of course, in most principal towns the offices of the three companies were in very close proximity so that there were touching points between the networks, but as a general rule a message was kept within the own company's network whenever possible. This means that an analysis of the entire British inland network would produce flawed results as the barriers of exchange between the networks could not be considered in the analysis. Therefore all three networks have been evaluated separately as to the centrality of their network nodes. Four centrality measures have been computed: Freeman *degree*, *closeness*, *betweenness* and Bonacich *eigenvector*. Of these, only three measures will be presented and discussed in the following as the closeness values for all three networks were very near.[55] This emphasizes the tightness of the networks but allows for no further interpretation. Farness and closeness values have, therefore, not been included in the following.

The *degree* centrality analysis confirms the central role of London in the Electric network (see Table A.20 in the Appendix for a list of degree values for all three important companies). The Electric headquarters (usually called Central; sometimes featuring under its old name and location, Lothbury) reaches an unrivalled degree value of 343. Coming second, London Shoreditch can only score 38 per cent of this value. London Stratford (sixteenth) and London Waterloo (twenty-ninth) also feature among the top nodes of the network. Just like Shoreditch, these two were important railway stations from which railway lines radiated to the south-west, the north and the north-east. Of course, the principal industrial centres of the north also occupied nodal positions in the Electric network as can be seen in the presence of, for instance, Manchester (fifth and fourteenth), Carlisle (tenth), Newcastle (eleventh and twenty-fourth) or the northern railway hub York (fourth and sixth). The presence of nodes such as Derby (third), Birmingham (seventh), Peterborough (eighth) or Rugby (twelfth) shows that the regions between London and the industrial north were also well served by the Electric and its associates. Southampton (ninth) was the most central town south of London. Scotland does not occupy a particularly central position in the Electric network. The surprisingly high rankings of the Scottish towns of Perth and Inverness must, unfortunately, be attributed to a statistical distortion stemming from their placement in unusually long telegraphic circuits criss-crossing the Highlands. The many stations in these circuits

[55] To illustrate, the highest farness value in the Electric network is 1,061,204 (nCloseness: 0.172). The lowest is 1,065,866 (nCloseness: 0.171). This amounts to a marginal difference of 4,662 between the closest and the furthest node in the Electric network. The corresponding values for the Magnetic network are 2,558,363 (nCloseness: 0.071) and 2,559,681 (nCloseness: 0.071). For the UK network they are 3,067,633 (nCloseness: 0.060) and 3,068,194 (nCloseness: 0.060).

Table 7.2 *Percentage of telegraphic traffic (in weekly messages) handled by British telegraph stations, 1868.*

Stations		Traffic	
Abs.	%	Abs.	%
15	1	115,654	41
75	5	186,720	67
149	10	218,265	78
298	20	247,363	88
373	25	255,957	91
746	50	274,669	98

Source: see Map 7.1

led to slightly inflated values in the network analysis. While both Inverness and Perth were, indeed, regional telegraphic hubs, their role in the entire network is exaggerated in our evaluation. This leaves Glasgow (twenty-fifth) as the most central Scottish node and confirms the peripheral position of Scotland in the Electric network. These findings are visualized in the circles in Map 7.6.

The Magnetic had a different regional focus. Together with the principal office in Manchester, it was the Glasgow town office that exhibited the highest *degree* centrality in the Magnetic network. The company headquarters in Threadneedle Street in the City of London came only third. With only very few exceptions – such as Threadneedle Street (third), the Glasgow offices (first and nineteenth) or Birmingham New Street office (fifteenth) – almost all top-ranking nodes were located in the industrial north of England. Of the top twenty nodes, three could be found in Manchester (second, fourth and ninth), two in Liverpool (eighth and eighteenth) and one each in Bolton (fifth), Preston (sixth), Leeds (seventh), Darlington (tenth), Wakefield (eleventh) and Newcastle (thirteenth). Salford (twelfth), Mirfield (fourteenth), Sowerby Bridge (sixteenth) and Todmorden (seventeenth) were smaller towns in the area but also occupied central positions in the Magnetic network. Judging from the number and position of Scottish telegraph offices in the ranking, Scotland played a more central role in the operations of the Magnetic than it did in those of the Electric. In Map 7.7, the results of the degree analysis are visualized with circles. The map clearly shows a concentration of big circles in the industrial north of England, along with further focal points in London and Glasgow, while the rest of England, Wales and Scotland housed only nodes of limited centrality.

Map 7.6 Freeman degree, Freeman betweenness and Bonacich eigenvector centrality in the Electric telegraph network, 1868. Note: Circles represent degree; rectangles represent betweenness; crosses represent eigenvector.

Map 7.7 Freeman degree, Freeman betweenness and Bonacich eigenvector centrality in the Magnetic telegraph network, 1868. Note: Circles represent degree; rectangles represent betweenness; crosses represent eigenvector.

In the UK network, the company headquarters at Gresham House in London rank highest in degree and occupied a central hub position. While the principal offices in Leeds (second), Manchester (third) and Newcastle (fourth) followed suit and emphasized the importance of the English north in the UK network, towns such as Gloucester (fifth), Nottingham (seventh) and Glasgow (ninth) also featured among the top ten degree nodes. Together with stations in Birmingham (eleventh), Cardiff (twelfth), Oxford (fourteenth) and Edinburgh (eighteenth) – all of them in the top twenty – their good scores illustrate that the company also concentrated on the telegraphic supply of the principal towns in the English Midlands and in Scotland. While there was, of course, a strong presence in the north of England in Lancashire and Yorkshire, this was far less pronounced in the UK network than it was in that of the Magnetic. Also, judging from the degree measure, the headquarters at Gresham House seem to have played a more central role here than Threadneedle Street did in the Magnetic network. This can also be seen in the visualization of the results in Map 7.8.

The second network analysis measure to be discussed here is *betweenness* (see Table A.21 in the Appendix for all three companies). In general, the results of the betweenness analysis correspond closely with the degree values. In the case of the Electric network, the pivotal role of the company headquarters is immediately obvious. Coming second, the company's principal office in Manchester reached only 30 per cent of London Central's betweenness score. Only five more town offices at Edinburgh (third), York (fourth), Birmingham (fifth), Glasgow (sixth) and Southampton (seventh) reach a double-figure percentage in this regard. The town office at Crewe occupied thirtieth position out of almost a thousand Electric stations considered in the analysis – and it reached a meagre 3 per cent of London Central's betweenness. All this clearly confirms the centrality of the London headquarters, through which almost all domestic telegraphic traffic in the Electric network had to pass at one stage or another. If they were not located on the same circuit, chances were that the shortest connection between two nodes in the network went through Central, which was therefore the all-important hub in the system (followed by an only regionally significant hub at Manchester Central). The distribution of rectangles in Map 7.6 visualizes the powerful position of London in the Electric telegraph network and shows that the few existing regional hubs were subordinate to the London headquarters.

The case is different regarding the Magnetic network. Here, the top nodes were much closer together in terms of betweenness. The town office at Glasgow (second) and headquarters at Threadneedle Street

Map 7.8 Freeman degree, Freeman betweenness and Bonacich eigenvector centrality in the UK company's telegraph network, 1868. Note: Circles represent degree; rectangles represent betweenness; crosses represent eigenvector.

(third), of course, occupied important hub positions, but the table is led by the Leeds town office. The principal Magnetic offices at Manchester (fourth) and Liverpool (fifth) reached 74 per cent and 56 per cent respectively of the Leeds value. Together with Bolton (sixth), Darlington (seventh), Newcastle (eighth), Shildon (ninth) and Preston (tenth), eight out of the top ten betweenness nodes in the Magnetic network were located in the north of England. With Birmingham (nineteenth), only one station in the English Midlands region can be found among the top thirty nodes. In addition to Glasgow, three more Scottish nodes exhibited considerable betweenness values – Dumfries (twelfth), Stranraer (seventeenth) and Castle Douglas (twenty-third). As visualized in the rectangles in Map 7.7, the Magnetic network was, therefore, less dependent on a single node through which most of the traffic had to pass. Several stations functioned as central hubs here. Most of these switches, however, were located in and around the industrial north of England, with particularly important centres in Leeds, Manchester and Liverpool. The station at Threadneedle Street in London was, of course, also an important hub, but fulfilled this function alongside several others.

The UK network was again more centralized in terms of the betweenness of its nodes. The principal London station at Gresham House scored highest here and was the central hub of the network. At some distance, it was followed by offices in Newcastle (second), Gloucester (third) and Glasgow (fourth), which reached 37 per cent, 32 per cent and 30 per cent respectively of the headquarters' betweenness. This shows that centralization was considerable but not as pronounced as in the Electric network. Also, the geographical distribution of network hubs was relatively even, with the top four nodes located in London, the north of England, the English Midlands and Scotland. This can also be seen in the location of the top thirty nodes, including northern English cities such as Leeds (fifth) and Manchester (sixth); English Midlands cities such as Birmingham (eighth); Scottish cities such as Dundee (tenth) and Edinburgh (eleventh); southern English cities such as Bristol (seventh), Plymouth (thirteenth) and Exeter (seventeenth); and Welsh cities such as Cardiff (sixteenth) and Swansea (eighteenth). As Map 7.8 depicts, a clear transactional centre is discernible in London, while other secondary hubs were relatively evenly distributed throughout Great Britain.

As has been pointed out in previous chapters, the Bonacich eigenvector measure identifies a node as central in a network if it is strongly connected to other central nodes.[56] Following this approach, the British capital,

[56] Bonacich, 'Factoring and Weighting Approaches to Status Scores and Clique Identification'; Bonacich, 'Power and Centrality'. A good example of the fruitful

London, occupied the central position in the Electric telegraph network of 1868 (see Table A.22 in the Appendix for all three companies). Central and Shoreditch clearly led the table. They were followed by Lowestoft (third) and Colchester (fourth) – stations which were centrally located on the important circuit to the continental mainland cities of Amsterdam (fifth) and Emden (seventh). The metropolitan station at Stratford (sixth) was closely connected to this pivotal circuit and was located on several important circuits radiating to the north and north-east of London. With already much lower eigenvector values, towns such as Chelmsford (eighth), Ipswich (tenth), Broxbourne (eleventh) or Norwich (twelfth) also represented the region to the north and north-east of the capital that was relatively closely connected to the principal stations of the network. The remainder of the top thirty-one eigenvector nodes were almost evenly distributed throughout England. Cardiff, at position 28, is the first Welsh city in the ranking. Edinburgh, the first Scottish city in the eigenvector ranking, comes in at position 77. The visualization of these results as crosses in Map 7.6 confirms that London itself and the stations en route to the Continent were extraordinarily well placed in the Electric network. Outside this principal telegraphic route, eigenvector centrality was relatively evenly spread out across England, with distinct gaps in Wales and Scotland.

In the Magnetic network, the company headquarters at Threadneedle Street in London rank only twenty-third in terms of their eigenvector centrality. Apart from Glasgow (twenty-first), all other Magnetic nodes in the top thirty can be found in the north of England, particularly around Manchester (first, second, and fourth), Liverpool (twelfth and sixteenth) and Leeds (fourteenth). As the distribution of crosses in Map 7.7 shows, the regional focus here was really very narrow and concentrated almost exclusively on the territory around the aforementioned cities. The case was, again, slightly different regarding the UK network. Here, Gresham House (second) in London was closely connected to other important telegraphic centres and, accordingly, scored high in eigenvector centrality. Almost all other stations in the top twenty, however, – with the notable exceptions of Nottingham (eleventh) and Glasgow (twentieth) – were located in the northern industrial region of England. But, as Map 7.8 shows, these northern nodes were much more dispersed than in the case of the Magnetic. This is a hint that the UK network in the north of England had more cross-regional connections than did the Magnetic

employment of eigenvector measures can be found in Junho H. Choi, George A. Barnett and Bum-Soo Chon, 'Comparing World City Networks: A Network Analysis of Internet Backbone and Air Transport Intercity Linkages', *Global Networks* 6, no 1 (2006).

network and was also better linked with the central station in London. Also, several nodes in the English Midlands maintained close connections either to the north (e.g. Nottingham) or to London (e.g. Birmingham, Leamington and Oxford).

To summarize, the Electric telegraph network of the late 1860s was strictly centralized, with the all-important hubs in and around the City of London. Access to the network was, however, relatively evenly distributed throughout Great Britain. Stations closely connected to the pivotal route between London and the Continent occupied an especially privileged position in the network. The Magnetic, on the other hand, had developed a clear regional focus on the north of England, with London and Glasgow as further centres of activity. While these latter two performed quite well in the degree and betweenness analyses, the eigenvector values reveal how tight and cross-connected the Magnetic network was around the northern hubs of Manchester, Liverpool and Leeds. The UK network seems to have been more centralized than that of the Magnetic but less than that of the Electric. Especially in terms of betweenness, London occupied a crucial place in the network but was supported by regional centres spread across all England. The UK network was, therefore, multicentred, with important focuses on London, the north of England, the English Midlands and some places in Scotland. It is striking that large parts of south-western and north-western England, Wales and the more remote parts of Scotland were largely neglected by all three companies. All three networks mainly focused on the urban regions of Great Britain and did not prioritize the provision of telegraphic services to the more rural areas.

7.4 British telegraph network use, 1868

In addition to the structural data discussed in the previous section, the circuit returns filed under POST 81/51–55, POST 81/12–13 and POST 81/77 also contain information on the average number of messages handled per week in the year 1868. As already pointed out above, 1,494 returned survey forms have survived in the archives and usually contain traffic information. This amounts to 81.7 per cent of the 1,828 stations for which the survey provides structural data. The geographic distribution of stations for which traffic data exists can be seen in Map 7.1. The circuit return forms normally provide information on the average number of messages sent, received and transmitted by the station in question. Only in a few cases was this category left blank on the form – usually when the form dealt with a government station (for instance the telegraph station at the Admiralty in London) or when a line was exclusively used for railway service telegrams (for instance the line along the 'mineral' railway between Shildon, Durham and Upleatham in North Yorkshire). All other forms provide detailed traffic information. Interestingly, however, a number of forms dealing with very important stations – for instance in Manchester, Liverpool and Leeds – have not been included in the survey files. Structural information regarding these stations can easily be reconstructed by consulting the forms of the neighbouring stations in the various circuits. Information on the traffic handled by these stations is harder to obtain. Fortunately, a digest of the principal results of the survey, focusing on the telegraphic apparatus and the staff associated with the individual stations, has been compiled from the original survey data.[57] This file also provides some information on the messages transacted in the evaluated stations but does not break down the numbers into the sent, received and transmitted categories. Drawing on this source, the aggregate traffic data for the most important missing stations in Manchester and Liverpool has been reconstructed. Traffic information for several other stations, however, remains obscure. Mostly, the stations concerned are relatively minor and it is reasonable to assume that they handled very small numbers of telegrams. But at least for three other important cities no traffic information is available at all. The forms for Leeds (West Yorkshire), Bolton (Greater Manchester) and Preston (Lancashire) are missing in the original survey. What is more, the sheets in the digest that would contain the aggregate data for these places have been removed from the file, as can be seen from the page numbering. At this point in time, we can only assume that the circuit returns for the principal stations in these cities became relevant to the system administrators at a later date and were accordingly removed and filed elsewhere. Regarding the accuracy of this study, the non-existence of information for these three cities has to be critically considered.

Together with the data retrieved from the survey digest, traffic information for 1,492 stations is available (with government and railway service stations already deducted). All in all, 280,061 messages were in one form or another handled per week at the time of the survey. As can be seen in Table 7.2, this total traffic of the system was very unevenly distributed among the network nodes. Some 1 per cent of all stations – equalling the top fifteen telegraph bureaus in terms of throughput – handled 41 per cent of all traffic. The top 149 stations (10 per cent of all those evaluated) already handled 78 per cent of all messages. Extending this to the 746 busiest stations, i.e. to the upper half of the entire list, 274,669 messages

[57] British Telecom Archives, POST 82/303, 'Telegraphs. Return of Persons Employed; Wages; Average Weekly Messages', 1869–1872.

were handled by these stations. This means that 50 per cent of the stations saw 98 per cent of the telegraphic traffic. Of all 1,492 stations, 964 transacted fifty messages or less per week. These figures indicate how unevenly telegraphic traffic was distributed in the system and how little use the smaller stations outside the urban centres actually saw. Among those, only forty-one stations saw weekly traffic in four- or five-digit numbers – starting with Electric's London Central and ending with the Magnetic town office in Hull. Among these forty-one stations, only sixteen different towns or cities are found. With the possible exception of Shrewsbury and Epsom (which produced most of its traffic at the Grand Stand during races), all of these are among the principal cities of the United Kingdom or at least occupy strategically and economically important positions (such as Southampton and Plymouth). Among the top hundred stations, no less than twenty-seven metropolitan stations can be found. Manchester has nine of its stations in this group. Liverpool manages six and Glasgow four.[58]

In order to render these figures more comparable to each other and to allow for the visualization of the geographic distribution of telegraphic traffic, the information on individual telegraph stations has been combined and added up for the respective towns and cities. Many smaller places in Great Britain had only one telegraph office (if any at all), which was often located at the railway station, while most of the bigger towns featured at least a town and a railway office (sometimes one each for each telegraph company). The principal population centres, on the other hand, usually had around ten or more stations (considering the offices of all companies and those at the various railway stations) that were evaluated and often many more that were not included in the survey. Aiming at a town-to-town (rather than station-to-station) comparison, the figures for all stations within a particular town need to be added up. In terms of the average weekly telegraphic traffic handled, only thirty-one places in Great

58 Ranking ninety-first, Keith in Banffshire is the only node among the top hundred stations that was not located in densely populated, urban areas. One might speculate whether there has been a mistake (deliberate or not) in filling out the survey form. Keith was located on five different circuits – several of them intermediary circuits between Aberdeen and Inverness – and this could explain the higher-than-usual numbers of transmitted messages, i.e. messages handed from one circuit to another. And Keith was the telegraphic gateway to the harbour and lighthouse at Lossiemouth and handled the traffic originating there. It should, however, be doubted whether this already suffices to explain a volume of 515 weekly messages. Rather untypically, the clerk-in-charge had also put on the circuit form three signal circuits, which were most probably used only for railway service telegrams. Following the very same logic, it might be a possible explanation that these service telegrams were also included in the message count (despite the going practice). But this, of course, remains a mere guess.

Britain saw more than 1,000 messages per week at all – and among those Epsom and Newmarket can only be found because the survey also included the messages transacted at the only temporarily open racecourse offices (see Table A.23 in the Appendix). London, solitarily, leads the table, with 87,049 messages handled per week in all metropolitan offices in 1868. This equals 31.1 per cent of the entire British domestic traffic. Manchester and Liverpool follow at a safe distance, transacting 29,568 and 23,639 messages weekly, respectively. After a further significant gap, Glasgow still manages a five-digit number of telegrams. Birmingham and Newcastle are the final two places with more than 5,000 messages weekly. Southampton, Bristol, Hull and Edinburgh complete the top ten. Practically all places in the top fifty either were important centres of population (and industry) or occupied some core role in terms of access to the sea (such as Southampton, Plymouth, Newport or Greenock). This geographical distribution of telegraphic traffic as evaluated by the 1868 survey is visualized in Map 7.9.

Even if put in relation to contemporary population numbers, similar regional telegraphic focuses remain. Map 7.10 depicts the density of telegraphic communication per head in Great Britain. The population census of 1871 has been used as reference and the original parish figures have been added up to census-district level (or registration-county level in the case of Scotland). In Map 7.10 proportionality has been discarded for the sake of interpretability. The areas shaded the darkest grey are those twenty-eight districts with a ratio of twenty or more weekly messages per 1,000 people living there. The foremost among those is, of course, the City of London, with more than 974 messages per 1,000 head. It is followed by the districts of Manchester (167), Liverpool (101) and Taunton (101). Other districts included here are usually those that house high-traffic cities such as Bristol, Hull, Southampton or Cardiff. The horse-racing centres at Epsom, Newmarket and Stockbridge can also be found here. By far the biggest number of census districts, however, exhibit ratios of significantly below twenty weekly messages per 1,000 inhabitants. For those, a proportional gradient of different shades of grey has been applied. Districts with a density below one weekly message per 1,000 inhabitants have not been shaded at all. Again, a concentration of traffic density becomes apparent in the north of England. Big parts of the Midlands and southern England, as well as of Wales, are white and therefore exhibit extremely low ratios of telegraphic communication per head. In the north of England, however, most of the districts are shaded, some even in darker grey. This region surely constituted one focal point of telegraph use, even in relation to its relatively high population density.

Map 7.9 Distribution of telegraphic traffic in the British telegraph network, 1868.

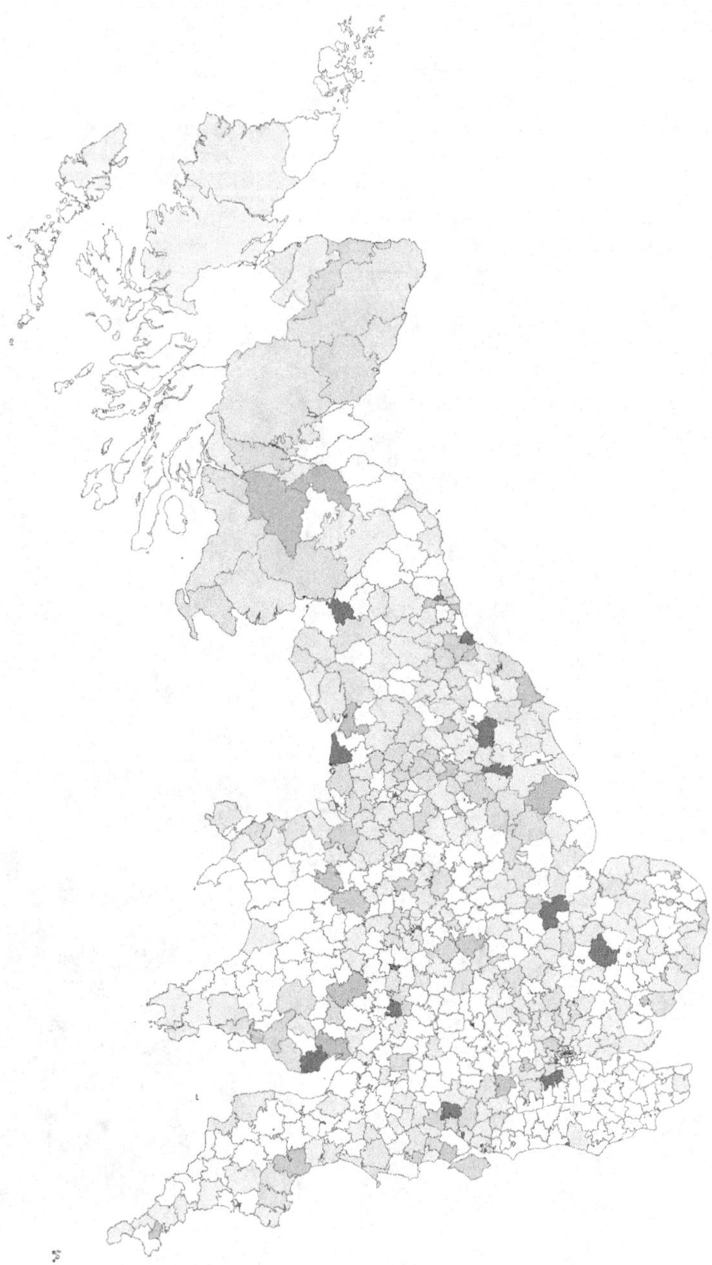

Map 7.10 Density of telegraphic traffic per head in Great Britain, 1868. Note: The darker the grey, the higher the density. Districts with twenty or more messages per thousand inhabitants are the darkest shade.

In general, the evaluation of the telegraphic traffic data confirms the results of the structural analysis conducted in the previous section. Of course, there is a correlation between the structural centrality or non-centrality of a station, a city or a region and the demand for telegraphic communication there. On the one hand, structures do respond to demand or perceived demand. On the other hand, existing structure can at times also instigate use. What is remarkable, however, is the fact that the already rather drastic division between structurally well-developed regions and the system periphery is even more pronounced in terms of system use. Here, the centres in London, the north of England and some individually important cities at strategic positions can hardly be evaluated within the same scale as the smaller towns and villages in more rural settings. Structurally, the 1868 telegraph network under the companies focused primarily on the important centres of population, industry and administration. Less-important regions could, however, not be completely ignored as the quality and attraction of a network to some part also rests in the possibility of reaching a maximum of nodes in a maximum of geographical locations. The actual use of the system, however, shows how focused on the urban centres the network really was and how strongly the demand for telegraphic communication was intertwined with the existence of a large populace on the one hand and, even more importantly, the economic necessity to communicate with partners in remote places on the other. While the structure of the network itself would have made it possible for the inhabitants of many a small town or village to partake in superregional business, this seems to have been the case only very rarely. Access to the system did not automatically create demand.

7.5 London at the centre

The results presented in this chapter so far have impressively emphasized the centrality of the capital, London, in the British domestic telegraph network. Earlier chapters showed that the metropolis occupied a similar position regarding the expanding global telecommunication network of the nineteenth century. This role as communication hub and control centre is clearly visible in the various structural network analyses that have been conducted in this book. In terms of the actual use of the system, London's extraordinary position becomes even more pronounced. Almost a third of all the British inland telegraph messages either originated or terminated in, or passed through, London at one point in their lives. Therefore late nineteenth-century London was not merely the administrative centre of the British Empire and the finance and trade centre of

Figure 7.1 *Punch* cartoon showing a woman hanging her washing on a telegraph wire.

the evolving global economy. On top of this and, of course, closely entangled with it, the metropolis was also the single most important node in the national, supranational and global telecommunication networks of the day. It thus merits a closer and more detailed look at its internal telegraphic development.[59]

Figure 7.1 is taken from *Punch's Almanack* for this was the District for 1862.[60] Beneath the general title 'Positive Fact, of Course' a subtitle reads, 'A Message comes off on Mrs. Bluebag's Linen, which she is Hanging, as usual, on the Telegraph Wires'. The cartoon itself has been drawn by an anonymous artist and shows a woman standing on a stool on the rooftop of a house. In front of her, a piece of linen is already hanging on the telegraph wires sporting the message 'Mr. Coddle to Mrs. Coddle HOME to DINNER at 6 30'. The caricature is playing on the – for contemporaries often still mysterious – fact that electric impulses

[59] See also Wenzlhuemer, 'Metropolitan Telecommunication'; Wenzlhuemer, 'London in the Global Telecommunication Network of the Nineteenth Century'.

[60] 'Positive Fact, of Course', *Punch's Almanack* 42 (January–June 1862), v.

transmitted over telegraph wires then somehow rematerialized as letters on a piece of paper. Hanging her washing on the wires, Mrs Bluebag seems to have intercepted a message sent by Mr Coddle to his wife. Of course, the triviality of the message displayed on the linen is part of the satirical edge of the caricature, as is the omnipresence of overhead wires in London in the second half of the nineteenth century. Mainly responsible for this was the District, founded in 1859 to provide telegraphic services to the British metropolis. Unlike the big three telegraph companies, the District relied practically exclusively on overhead wires, and therefore 'was subject to much public criticism due to its ugly overhead iron lines protruding on posts above roof-tops, which, as every station had a single wire connecting to its hub office, led to a great mass of wires in the City centre, and to its general poor performance'.[61] Public criticism, it seems, was strong enough even to qualify the subject for the attention of *Punch*.

While the District was not famous for its smooth operations and inconspicuous wiring, it did at least bring telegraphic connectivity to those parts of London that were mostly neglected by the three principal telegraph companies of the country. A newspaper report originally published in the *London Review* on this very topic in early 1863 was so widely received that as far away as Australia the *Perth Gazette and Independent Journal of Politics and News* reprinted the piece in its edition of 31 July 1863. The article, entitled 'Town Telegraphs', opens with the following passage:

> Whilst this metropolis [i.e. London] and all other parts of the civilized world have long been put in speedy connection by means of the electric telegraph, the three millions of people living within the Post-office radius have until very lately been denied the use of this necessary of life. This fact is the more strange inasmuch as the dealings of the great public are much more with their immediate neighbours than with those who live at a distance. Yet while any one could be put in instant communication with the mountaineers of Switzerland or the Tyrol, he had not the means of talking across the town with his own wife or servants at Hampstead. Like some pious missionaries, in looking too much abroad we had overlooked the needs of home. However, the pedestrian who makes his way along the streets, on looking up, discovers that the town is being gradually wired in overhead like the cage of the polar bear at the Zoological Gardens, must have discovered that this omission is in rapid progress of being corrected.[62]

[61] Roberts, 'Distant Writing', 35. For an interesting discussion of the telegraphic 'topography' of London, see Francis Celoria, 'Early Victorian Telegraphs in London's Topography, History and Archaeology', in *Collectanea Londiniensia: Studies in London Archaeology and History Presented to Ralph Merrifield*, ed. Joanna Bird, Hugh Chapman and John Clark, London and Middlesex Archaeological Society, Special Paper No 2 (London: London and Middlesex Archaeological Society, 1978).

[62] 'Town Telegraphs', *Perth Gazette and Independent Journal of Politics and News*, 31 July 1863, 4.

Of course, London and its principal telegraph stations occupied essential roles in the networks of the big three companies. As has been seen, the London headquarters were the central hub of the Electric and UK networks, without which the entire network would not have been able to function. In the case of the Magnetic, the centrality was distributed more evenly within the system, with the headquarters in Threadneedle Street still representing one of the irreplaceable network nodes. Therefore the metropolitan stations were of central importance in all three networks, but the stations themselves were very unevenly distributed across the metropolis. Map 7.11 shows the position of all London telegraph stations in the

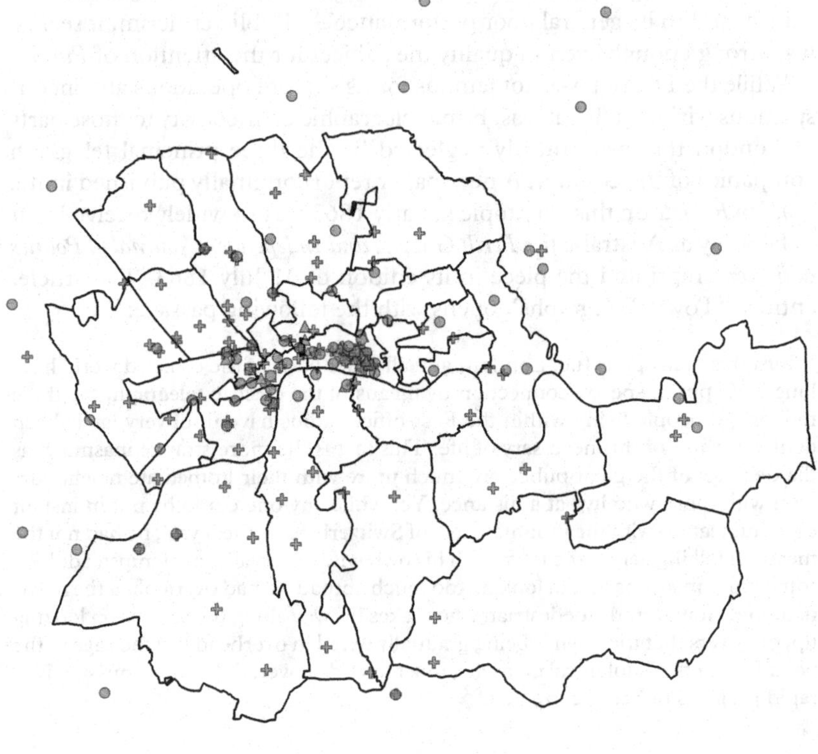

Map 7.11 Distribution of telegraph stations in London, 1868. Note: Circles represent Electric stations; rectangles represent Magnetic stations; crosses represent District stations.

year 1868. Regarding the Electric, the Magnetic and the UK, the map draws on the 1868 station survey. The District, which had in 1867 been renamed the London & Provincial Telegraph Company, had not been included in this survey. Information on the location of its stations, therefore, comes from Scudamore's initial report and in all likelihood captures the situation of early 1866.[63] The map depicts each company's stations in different symbols. It can be seen that the operations of the Magnetic (rectangles) and the UK (triangles) almost exclusively focused on the administrative and financial centre of London in and around the City of London and the West End. The distribution of Electric telegraph stations (circles) in general exhibited the same regional concentration. But the railway companies operating in and around London were mostly associated with the Electric and therefore provided telegraphic services outside the very city centre at their railway stations.[64] All in all, however, this could only slightly cushion the structural concentration of the telegraph companies on the City, Westminster and the Strand. The distribution of the District stations (crosses), on the other hand, seems to be much more even. In comparison with the other three companies this is beyond doubt true. After all, it was the provision of telegraph services to London that the District had identified as its niche and this encompassed an operational radius larger than the Square Mile and the West End. But even the District sported a strong geographical focus on the financial and administrative centres of London. The concentration of telegraph stations within the small area of the City communicationally dwarfs the rest of the metropolis – even regarding the operations of the District.

Unfortunately, the London & Provincial Telegraph Company either was not covered by the 1868 circuit survey or no records of the survey have survived in the archives. Therefore there is no information on this company's circuits or its stations' traffic that could meaningfully be compared with the data for the other three companies. This has to be taken into account when interpreting Map 7.12, which visualizes the circuit returns for Electric, Magnetic and UK metropolitan stations and retraces the structure of the telegraph network in and around London in 1868. The map

63 House of Commons Parliamentary Papers, C. 202, 'Electric Telegraphs. Return to an Order of the Honourable the House of Commons, Dated 3 April 1868; – for, Copy "of Reports to the Postmaster General by Mr. Scudamore upon the Proposal for Transferring to the Post Office the Control and Management of the Electric Telegraphs throughout the United Kingdom"', 1867–1868, 111–14.

64 Accordingly, the lack of company-coloured dots in the southeast of London stems from the unwillingness of the principal railways operating in this area to enter into contracts with the telegraph companies. As already explained above, these railway companies are not included in the 1868 survey.

Map 7.12 British telegraph network structure. Close-up of London, 1868. Note: Electric lines are shown as solid; Magnetic lines as dashed; UK lines as dotted.

impressively shows how clearly the telegraphic connections out of London (but also those within the metropolis) centred on the City, while the other districts remained almost untouched by these circuits. As pointed out above, the map does not depict London & Provincial circuits due to problems of comparability. Referring to the principal course of the District connections of some years earlier, Jeffrey Kieve has shown that, of course, the District's circuits also converged on the City at Cannon Street, while, however, the less central districts were also serviced.[65] The District became

[65] Kieve, *The Electric Telegraph: A Social and Economic History*, 60–1.

the telegraph company of choice for customers who, for instance, wanted to order seats at the opera or bought perishable foodstuffs at the fish and poultry wholesale markets at Billingsgate and Leadenhall.[66] Its comparatively cheap rates promoted intra-city use of the telegraph for a variety of subjects ranging from household matters to business organization and generally made the telegraph system accessible to a wider public in London.

Despite the efforts and good capacity utilization of the District/London & Provincial, the use of and access to the telegraph system still was very much centred on the City of London and the West End. As Table 7.1 shows, the London & Provincial forwarded 183,304 telegrams throughout the financial year of 1868. Broken down to the weekly average, this amounts to about 3,500 messages sent per week. Taken together, the London stations of the Electric, the Magnetic and the UK forwarded more than 23,000 messages in the same time. Distributing these 3,500 weekly messages evenly among the 101 District stations that have been considered in Maps 7.11 and 7.12, each station (statistically, not realistically) would forward a little less than thirty-five telegrams per week. Compared to the top London stations (almost all of which can be found in the City, in the West End or at an important railway terminus) this is marginal – especially as it is reasonable to assume that the London & Provincial traffic was not evenly distributed among all stations but had itself a focus on, for instance, the company headquarters at Cannon Street or the markets at Leadenhall and Billingsgate (all of which were located in the City of London). While the company did, of course, contribute to making the telegraph more accessible outside the very city centre, the financial and administrative districts still handled by far most of the telegraphic traffic of London. Map 7.13 visualizes how pronounced this use concentration actually was around the year 1868. The shading gradient in the map refers to the message density per head in the different districts. The total numbers of messages handled by all Electric, Magnetic and UK stations in each district have been added up and put in relation to the respective population numbers (taken from the 1871 census). The figures displayed in the map give the number of messages transacted per week and per 10,000 inhabitants. The City of London sports such a high value that the shading gradient has been calculated with the Strand value as the top value. All other districts should, therefore, be seen as depicted in relation to the Strand rather than to the City, which bursts all scales.[67] It is, of

[66] Ibid., 59.

[67] Again, the zero density in south-eastern districts should be attributed to the fact that the 1868 survey did not cover the railways serving the south-east of England. Therefore their stations have not been included in this map (as in several others).

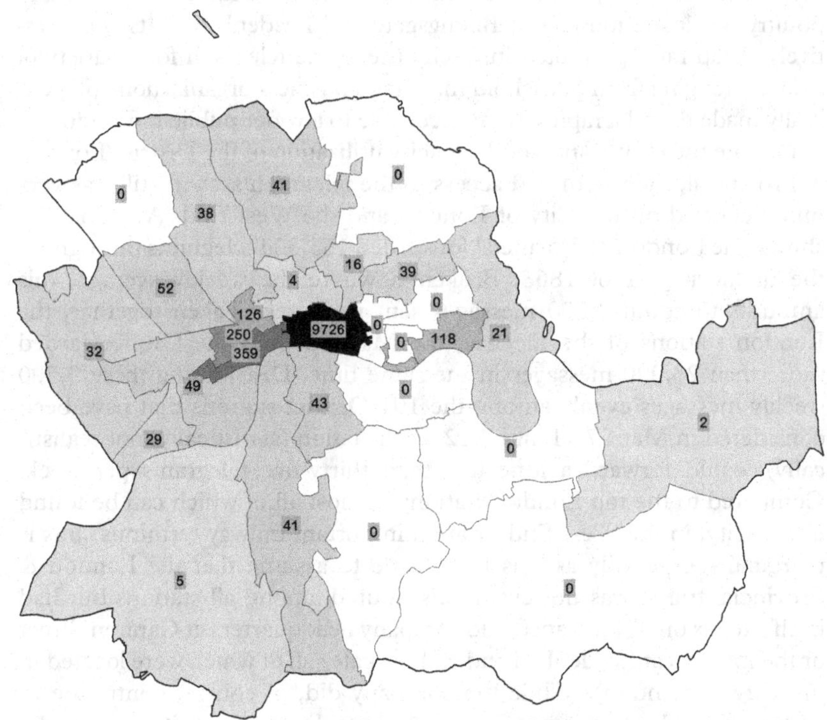

Map 7.13 Density of telegraphic traffic per head in London, 1868. Note: The darker the grey, the higher the density. The City of London is black.

course, true that the population numbers of the City were decreasing throughout the nineteenth century, but still its population density in 1871 was on average almost twice as high as that of the whole of the rest of London. Accordingly, it is not the fact that more and more people were moving out of the City to make way for new businesses that explains the exorbitant ratio of 9,726 weekly messages per 10,000 inhabitants as a form of statistical distortion due to low population figures. This was not yet the case in the middle of the nineteenth century. Nevertheless, this shows that the telegraph mainly – at times almost exclusively – catered to (imperial) administration and (high) finance, the best parts of which were physically located in the City and the West End. Both structurally and from a telegraph-use perspective, these core districts of London stood at the very centre of the local, the national and the global telegraph network of the day, while other districts – in direct comparison with the core – saw only very little telegraphic traffic.

Throughout the nineteenth century, a communicational divide ripped through the city.[68] As can be seen from the enthusiasm for the District's efforts in the *Perth Gazette*, this divide was extremely pronounced up to the early 1860s. But as this section has tried to show, the services of the District brought only partial remedy. The principal hubs of the telegraphic traffic of London, Great Britain and actually the world firmly stayed in the City of London. All the big telegraph companies were focused on this spot and devoted much of their efforts to providing services for the business clientele there. Within a few years – i.e. with the opening of the Indo-European line and the Red Sea cable to India – it would, on good days, take only a reported twenty-eight minutes to send a telegram from London to Calcutta.[69] Intra-London telegraphic exchanges could, however, be painstakingly slow at times, as the *Punch* caricature in Figure 7.2 suggests. Published in 1863, the drawing with the title 'The District Telegraph. Invaluable to the Man of Business' shows two businessmen in their office on Fleet Street, one saying to the other, 'What an age we live in! Talk of the introduction of Steam or of Gas! Just look at the Facilities afforded us by Electricity. It is now Six o'clock, and we are in Fleet Street, and this Message was only sent from Oxford Street yesterday afternoon at

[68] Translated into the times of broadband digital communication via fibre-optic cables, this communicational divide within London still exists. The first 'tale of the networked metropolis' that Stephen Graham and Simon Marvin offer in their book *Splintering Urbanism* clearly illustrates this: 'The fast-growing US telecommunications firm WorldCom/MCI recently built an optic fibre network covering only the core of central London. Only 125 km long, it carries fully 20 per cent of the whole of the United Kingdom's international telecommunications traffic. This is only one of a rapidly emerging global archipelago of urban optic fibre grids concentrated in the urban cores of the world's fifty financial capitals in Asia, Europe, Australasia, and North and South America. Such networks serve no other places. A widening global web of transoceanic and transcontinental fibre networks interconnects these high capacity urban grids, which are carefully located to serve the most communications-intensive international firms. However, whilst the cores of global financial centre spaces reach out to the globe with unprecedented power, increasing efforts are being made to "filter" their connections with their host cities. In London, for example, the so-called "ring of steel" supports electronic surveillance systems and armed guards on every entry point into the financial district. Cars entering have their number plates read automatically. Stolen cars are detected within three seconds. And the potential for the facial recognition of drivers, by linking automatically with digitised photographs on national licence records, exists in the system and has already been tested.' Stephen Graham and Simon Marvin, *Splintering Urbanism: Networked Infrastructures, Technological Mobilities and the Urban Condition* (London: Routledge, 2001), 2.

[69] Hence the tile of Hans Pieper's work: Hans Pieper and Kilian Kuenzi, *In 28 Minuten von London nach Kalkutta: Aufsätze zur Telegrafiegeschichte aus der Sammlung Dr. Hans Pieper im Museum für Kommunikation, Bern*, Schriftenreihe des Museums für Kommunikation, Bern (Zurich: Chronos, 2000).

THE DISTRICT TELEGRAPH.

INVALUABLE TO THE MAN OF BUSINESS.

First Partner (to Second ditto). "WHAT AN AGE WE LIVE IN! TALK OF THE INTRODUCTION OF STEAM OR OF GAS! JUST LOOK AT THE FACILITIES AFFORDED US BY ELECTRICITY. IT IS NOW SIX O'CLOCK, AND WE ARE IN FLEET STREET, AND THIS MESSAGE WAS ONLY SENT FROM OXFORD STREET YESTERDAY AFTERNOON AT THREE!"

Figure 7.2 *Punch* cartoon showing two men in a Fleet Street office discussing a telegram.

Table 7.3 *Examples for high delivery times of intra-London messages, 1879.*

To	From	Duration
Piccadilly Circus	Euston Square	20 minutes
	Parliament Street	24 minutes
	Paddington	21 minutes
	Stock Exchange	nearly an hour
	St Pancras	more than half an hour
South Audley Street	*average*	13 minutes
	Victoria Station	38 minutes
	Hyde Park Square	23 minutes
Paddington office	Vere Street	24 minutes
	Cornhill	25 minutes
	Langham Hotel	26 minutes
	Stock Exchange	26 minutes
	Westminster Palace Hotel	28 minutes
	Waterloo Station	30 minutes
Branch office near South Kensington Museum	St James's Street	27 minutes
	Regent Street	28 minutes
	Wood Street (City)	30 minutes
	Cornhill	35 minutes
	Duke Street	35 minutes
	Hyde Park Square	35 minutes
	Vigo Street	36 minutes
	Brixton	39 minutes
	Mark Lane	32 and 53 minutes
	Temple Bar	51 minutes
	Charles Street	57 minutes

Source: British Telecom Archives, POST 82/209, 'Reports by Mr. F. E. Baines, the Surveyor General for Telegraphs. Quarterly Report of the Surveyor-General for Telegraph Business to the Secretary, 14 January 1879'.

Three!'[70] Precisely because the title refers to the company by name, it seems that the District and its efforts to telegraphically develop more of London than its very core had only been half-successful. One and a half decades later, and with the British inland telegraphs nationalized for almost ten years, the speed and quality of intra-city communication seem to have improved considerably, but it still did not work seamlessly.

[70] 'The District Telegraph. Invaluable to the Man of Business', *Punch, or the London Charivari* 44, no 10 (January 1863), 20.

In his quarterly report of January 1879, Frederick E. Baines, the surveyor-general for telegraph business, stated,

> Looking at a return before me of Metropolitan messages delivered from the Branch Office at Picadilly [*sic*] Circus, I see in numerous instances messages received in ten and even in seven minutes from distant parts of London. Such messages would be enveloped in 2 or 3 minutes and, the local delivery at the Picadilly [*sic*] Circus Office being very circumscribed, would probably be delivered in 5 or 6 minutes more. Hence a total time occupied not exceeding a quarter of an hour or so would imply such celerity as would necessarily give a great stimulus to Metropolitan telegraphy.[71]

Sounding generally satisfied with these results, Baines also refers, however, to the fact that in many cases delivery still took significantly longer. He went on:

> But at the risk of making these remarks too long I must point to the fact that while the average time occupied in the wire transmission, as shown by three returns from the Western District now before me, is from 13 to 16 minutes – a period not too great if it were never exceeded – there are many cases in which the maximum rises to a very much higher figure.[72]

Baines also included a table (reproduced in Table 7.3) exhibiting several delivery time samples. These suggest that twenty years after the founding of the London District Telegraph Company and almost a decade after the nationalization of the telegraph system (for which one of the principal arguments had been the improvement of public service), delivery times for messages within London could still at times surpass those of intercontinental messages.

[71] British Telecom Archives, POST 82/209, 'Reports by Mr. F. E. Baines, the Surveyor General for Telegraphs. Quarterly Report of the Surveyor-General for Telegraph Business to the Secretary', 14 January 1879.

[72] Ibid.

8 The British Indian telegraph network

8.1 1857 and the telegraph

On 29 September 1897, the *Daily News* printed a short piece on the Indian Uprising, which forty years earlier had been in full swing. Under the heading 'How the Electric Telegraph Saved India', the article commemorated the contribution of the novel technology – and in particular that of a teenage telegraph signaller at Delhi – to putting down the 'mutiny'.

There is a third claimant [to the title Saviour of India – after Viceroy Lord Lawrence and John Nicholson], Mr. William Brendish, the signaller boy at the Delhi telegraph office in 1857, who on the 11th May (a day after the outbreak at Meerut) sent the messages partly founded on bazaar 'gup,' which gave the Punjab men, and the Commander-in-Chief at Simla, the first vague news of the mutiny and its murderous work. The electric telegraph, said Montgomery – one of that great school – has saved India. Said Sir Herbert Edwardes, 'that message,' sent by 'that little boy,' was, 'I do not hesitate to say, the means of the salvation of the Punjab.' It enabled Montgomery, and the commanding officer at Lahore to disarm the native troops before the news of the revolt reached the barracks; and to flash their warning over the lines to Peshawar. According to one version of the story, the telegraph boy had just finished the last click of his message when the Sepoys burst into the office and killed him. But young William Brendish not only escaped in good time, but is still living, having retired from the Indian Service with a special pension, and a flattering acknowledgement of his services from the Governor-General.[1]

Of course, what Robert Montgomery, the judicial commissioner of the Punjab,[2] meant when he said that the telegraph 'has saved India' (and what the *Daily News* meant when quoting him) was that it had saved India for rather than from the British.[3] A similar attitude towards the potential uses of the telegraph in India also transpires from a statement by

[1] 'How the Electric Telegraph Saved India', *Daily News*, 29 September 1897, 6.
[2] Deep Kanta Lahiri Choudhury, '"1857" and the Communication Crisis', in *Rethinking 1857*, ed. Sabyasachi Bhattacharya (Delhi: Orient Longman, 2007), 262.
[3] Headrick, 'A Double-Edged Sword', 53; Headrick, *The Invisible Weapon*, 52.

Lord Dalhousie made five years before the uprising and quoted in Deep Kanta Lahiri Choudhury's article on the communication crisis of the year 1857. In 1852, Dalhousie had called the project of creating a telegraph system in India a 'national experiment'. As Choudhury argues, Dalhousie 'was not referring to India as a nation. He meant that it was a national investment for Britain and an experiment in empire. India was to be the empty space for the enactment of the telegraph experiment'.[4] From these quotes it becomes apparent that the introduction of telegraphy to India needs to be seen in a larger imperial context. Questions of administration, security and control were far more important than they ever were regarding the British inland telegraph system. In the latter case, not only had the Admiralty held on to their semaphores for quite some time and shown little interest in the new technology, it had also needed private railway companies, betting men and, of course, the trading community to create a demand for telegraphic communication in the first place. While, in the course of time, the Admiralty and other government departments developed an interest in telegraphy and acquired a number of lines for their exclusive use, the aspect of administration and control was never very prominent in the British inland system, which was mainly geared to serving a business clientele (or the railways for their own purposes). This was different in India, where the sheer geographic size of the colony posed a significant challenge to the British administrators. Here, aspects of efficient administration and imperial control clearly informed Dalhousie's and the East India Company Court of Directors' decision to invest in an Indian telegraph system.[5] The route of the first Indian telegraph line, finished in 1855, from Saugor Island via Diamond Harbour to Calcutta and on via 'the key military cantonments in upper and central India until Peshawar',[6] and the fact that 'Dalhousie even had a line built to the hill station of Ootacamund, where he spent the hot season of 1855',[7] illustrate clearly how important strategic and administrative considerations were in the design of the system. Less well known, however, is the fact that the needs of the business community (and the potential profit to be made from this) had, of course, never been completely absent in the deliberations of the men behind the network.

4 Choudhury, '"1857" and the Communication Crisis', 263.

5 Headrick, 'A Double-Edged Sword', 52–3; Headrick, *The Invisible Weapon*, 52–3.

6 Deep Kanta Lahiri Choudhury, '"Beyond the Reach of Monkeys and Men"? O'Shaughnessy and the Telegraph in India circa 1836–56', *Indian Economic and Social History Review* 37, no 3 (2000), 348.

7 Headrick, *The Invisible Weapon*, 52.

William O'Shaughnessy[8] – an army surgeon with a long-standing interest in telegraphy and eventually the first Superintendent of Electric Telegraphs in India – had proposed to build the very first stretch of the first line from Calcutta to Chinsurah as he was convinced that

> [a] very large return would, in the opinion of the mercantile gentlemen consulted, be made from Mizrapore and mercantile and banking establishments of Muttra, and the Marwaree shroffs. The newspapers of Upper India would also contribute . . . I would consider it highly probable that these items with the amount above specified (Rs. 8 for 480 words for Calcutta and Bombay) would pay a large sum beyond the yearly expenditure and leave the telegraph eighteen hours available in the day for the use of the government without charge.[9]

O'Shaughnessy's words aptly sum up Dalhousie's and the East India Company's view on the purpose of telegraphy in India: of course, fostering commerce in the colony and generating revenue with the help of the telegraph would not hurt and must surely be included in one's considerations, but most importantly the new means of communication must be at the immediate disposal of the government whenever need arises. Contrary to O'Shaughnessy's plans, John Bethune, a member of the Governor-General's Council, put forward that before being extended to Agra, a line to Chinsurah would not attract much commercial traffic. As an alternative first step, Bethune suggested to telegraphically connect Diamond Harbour with Calcutta in order to provide the Calcutta merchants with swift shipping information. This plan was eventually followed and the stretch from Calcutta to the coast where the Hooghly meets the Bay of Bengal became the first non-experimental telegraph line in India.[10] This choice and the deliberations of both O'Shaughnessy and Bethune clearly illustrate that economic considerations were, of course, not absent in designing and building the Indian telegraph system. Its principal purpose nevertheless rested in enhancing the administration of and ultimately control over the subcontinent. In view of the sheer size of the territory and the large distances that needed to be covered, telegraphic communication promised even higher gains in administrative efficiency than it did in smaller entities. Contrary to what had happened, for instance, in the United Kingdom or the United States, the telegraph was introduced in

[8] For more information on O'Shaughnessy, see Choudhury, 'Beyond the Reach of Monkeys and Men?'; Saroj Ghose, 'William O'Shaughnessy: An Innovator and Entrepreneur', *Indian Journal of History of Science* 29, no 1 (1994); Gorman, 'Sir William O'Shaughnessy, Lord Dalhousie, and the Establishment of the Telegraph System in India'.

[9] Home Department, Public Proceedings, 4 April 1850, No 48, Report 1, quoted in Choudhury, 'Beyond the Reach of Monkeys and Men?', 348–9.

[10] Ibid., 349.

British India practically on government initiative and, at least initially, as a government monopoly. While its economic potential was not unimportant, the origins of the Indian telegraph system therefore need to be interpreted within a larger imperial context in which questions of administration, strategy and control set the general tone. In this context, it is all the more surprising that the system realized during the mid-1850s could not rightly be called a network. Governmental attention rested on the main line between Calcutta and Peshawar (following the general course of the Grand Trunk Road) and on a second route from Madras to Bombay connecting with the first line at Agra.[11] Additional loop lines and cross-connections had long been suggested by experts but had not been realized when crisis struck in 1857. There were only singular connections without backup options. 'The lack of a link between Calcutta and Madras and the absence of circuits or duplicate lines made the system inherently vulnerable.'[12]

The story of the telegraph in the Indian Uprising, therefore, has two rather different sides. On the one hand, there is the imperial narrative popularized in the accounts of British colonial officials and spread by English-language newspapers in both the United Kingdom and the colonies. This is the tale of how the telegraph 'has saved India'. As the *Daily News* article at the opening of this chapter shows, this version of the story emphasized the role of the initial telegram that alerted the British and enabled them to prepare themselves for the outbreak of hostilities. On the other hand, however, most of the important nodes in the rudimentary Indian telegraph network were easily put out of operation during the uprising and the system proved to be vulnerable to the point of uselessness.[13] Accordingly, when the rebellion was eventually put down, the British had learned a double lesson as regards telegraphy in India. First, of course, the technology had proved its potential and it could, indeed, be very useful in times of crisis. Second, however, in order to guarantee such usefulness throughout a crisis, the network had to be improved, extended and cross-linked. As a consequence, as Choudhury points out, after 1857 'the principle of alternate and duplicate lines was adopted in every case, in India, as well as internationally'.[14]

[11] Saroj Ghose, 'Commercial Needs and Military Necessities: The Telegraph in India', in *Technology and the Raj: Western Technology and Technical Transfers to India 1700–1947*, ed. Roy MacLeod and Deepak Kumar (New Delhi, Thousand Oaks and London: Sage Publications, 1995), 157.

[12] Choudhury, '"1857" and the Communication Crisis', 267.

[13] Ghose, 'Commercial Needs and Military Necessities', 166–8; Choudhury, '"1857" and the Communication Crisis', 267.

[14] Choudhury, '"1857" and the Communication Crisis', 267.

The experiences of 1857–8, therefore, gave a great boost to telegraphic development within India and led to the extension of the network in terms of both the length of lines and the number of stations.[15] This will be discussed in more detail in the following section. Such an extension and improvement of the service seems to have been overdue not only regarding security issues but also from a public perspective. On 7 October 1858, *The Times* published a substantial article by its special correspondent in India, William Howard Russell. The piece carried the title 'The English Raj in India' and had been finished at Simla on 17 August 1858, only about two months after the last substantial part of the uprising had been put down at Gwalior. Russell – who had been in Lucknow during the siege and would later publish his Indian diaries[16] – first discussed the old and new attitudes of British administrators towards 'disinherited or ousted rajahs' before he paid very detailed attention to the current state of the Indian telegraph system. About halfway through his article, Russell changed the topic in a rather abrupt manner:

> To return to our own affairs, ere I close this letter, the Indian electric telegraph system is in a most imperfect and unsatisfactory state. For the purposes of Government and for the transmission of depatches [*sic*] it is, perhaps, adequate enough, and its utility during the recent campaigns was beyond all price or praise, but even for those purposes it sometimes failed. Posts hastily erected fell or were blown down, and interruptions occurred, which were, however, rapidly remedied by the activity of the European officers of the department. Admitting its uses as a Government machine, it must, however, be fairly stated that as far as the public are concerned the electric telegraph in India is conducted with such utter indifference to good faith that it is practically a swindle, and nothing else or less. They take your money, receive your message, and there is an end of the transaction. The Indian papers teem with groans on this score, but their indulgence in scurrilous personality and their habit of universal aggression and attack have, with some most able

15 And they also provided additional motivation for the laying of submarine cables as a message transmitted via the short-lived 1858 transatlantic cable successfully cancelled the transhipment of Canadian troops to India when the uprising had already been brought under control. This emphasized the geostrategic potential of submarine telegraphy and gave an additional boost to initiatives in this field (see Chapter 2). Odlyzko, 'History of Communications and Its Implications for the Internet', 38; Headrick, *The Invisible Weapon*, 18; Scholl, 'The Global Communication Industry', 200.

16 William Howard Russell, *My Diary in India, in the Year 1858–9. Vol. 1* (London: Routledge, Warne and Routledge, 1860); Russell, *My Diary in India, in the Year 1858–9. Vol. 2* (London: Routledge, Warne and Routledge, 1860). Russell was interested in and very well acquainted with telegraphy. As a war correspondent in the Crimean he had reported from the scene by means of telegrams. In 1865, Russell was commissioned to write a book about the laying of the Atlantic telegraph cable. He was onboard the *Great Eastern* during the telegraph expedition in order to get a first-hand impression. The resulting book was richly illustrated by Robert Dudley. William Howard Russell, *The Atlantic Telegraph* (London: Day & Son Limited, 1866).

and honourable exceptions, utterly destroyed the influence of their representations with the Government and the public, if it ever existed.[17]

A little further on Russell then referred to his own experiences with the Indian telegraph system and gave the following case:

About a month ago I sent a message from Umballah to Calcutta. As I received no reply I wrote to the gentleman respecting its subject matter, and he, in his answer a fortnight after, said, – 'I have received no telegraph message from you. It is, no doubt, on the road, and will turn up some time or other.' Another message to Calcutta I have traced from Umballah to Delhi, beyond which there is no sign of its existence, and the gentleman who honours the country by accepting his salary for the charge of that station has not deigned to reply to an inquiry which I sent him weeks ago as to the fate of a telegram destined for a much longer career.[18]

In the remainder of the report, Russell then moved on to discuss the Indian postal service as an alternative to sending telegrams but pointed out that the post was also not free of deficiencies. He closed the section on the telegraph and postal system in India by saying that every week 'some 20 or 30 complaints appear in the various Indian papers respecting delay in the post and in the telegraph'.[19]

While the size and capacity of the Indian telegraph network started to grow substantially in 1858, Russell's report confirms that for the general public the system worked only imperfectly and was anything but reliable. Therefore it seems that the local commercial classes, for instance, could not use and benefit from the network to the same extent as their European counterparts. This was not for lack of interest, though, as the case of a 'telegraph fraud' occurring in India illustrates. Quoting from the *Bombay Gazette* of 27 February 1861, *Lloyd's Weekly Newspaper* on 31 March 1861 reported on 'The Telegraph Frauds in India', where a few 'speculators in opium have caused messages to be most grossly falsified whilst passing through the wires between Galle and Bombay'. Apparently, two telegraph signallers, George Pecktall and William Allen, who had both been dismissed from service in the Indian telegraph office, had been approached by shady speculators and hired to find a way to interfere with the telegraph system. Pecktall and Allen obliged, somehow managed to obtain a battery and signalling apparatus, 'and proceeded to a spot in the immediate vicinity of the village Beebee chawaddee, about four or five miles off at the foot of the Katruj Ghaut, over which the telegraph wire from Sattar passes'. There, they cut the telegraph wire and inserted their own apparatus into the circuit, which enabled them to intercept messages and forward them in falsified form. The messages concerned dealt with

[17] 'The English Raj in India', *The Times*, 7 October 1858, 9. [18] Ibid., 9. [19] Ibid., 9.

opium prices and 'enormous sums of money were alleged to be made by the parties in the secret'.[20] Despite the fact that the telegraph line had been temporarily disrupted and that suspiciously high profits were made, the fraud was only discovered when full information on opium prices reached Bombay by steamer from Galle.[21]

This episode illustrates how inexperienced in telegraphic matters the Indian mercantile community still was in the early 1860s. But it also draws attention to the general deficits of the telegraph system itself. First, the fact that the fraud remained undetected until the arrival of the steamer testifies to the prevailing lack of alternative routes and cross-links in the Indian telegraph system via which confirmation or rejection of the forged telegrams could have been obtained. Second, the distances covered by the lines were so great that the network was practically unmanageable. Years after the experiences of the Indian Uprising, it was still easy to interfere with the wires without being detected. Third, a notorious shortness of competent and sufficiently trained signallers and clerks further enhanced the unmanageability of the system and made the hiring of unqualified or otherwise unreliable staff a not uncommon feature. This was such a pronounced problem that even the director general of telegraphs in India, Daniel George Robinson, did not fail to notice it in his administration report for the 1862–3 year (which was compiled only in 1866). Here, Robinson commented on the many new provisions in 'the code, which is to define the duties, salaries, responsibilities, and rights of the different officers of the department', and went on to say that these

> changes, all tending to make the officers and signallers of the department feel they are sure of considerate and liberal treatment, have already done an immensity of good. The scarcity of signallers that a year since bid fair to stop work altogether, no longer exists. Many of those officers who had left are anxious to rejoin the department.[22]

Of course, Robinson's report drew attention to the improvement of the situation, but in doing so also made clear how problematic the matter had been around 1860 and 1861.

[20] 'The Telegraph Frauds in India', *Lloyd's Weekly Newspaper*, 31 March 1861, 2.

[21] In the 'Abstracts from the Annual Reports of the Superintendents of Circles for the Year 1862–63', reference was made to the case. 'On the 24th of January 1863, George Pectall [*sic*] . . . incautiously made some admission as to the party who bribed William Allen and himself to cut the wire in February 1861. With the assistance of the Police, it was ascertained that one Nim Chund Melap Chund, a Marwarree Merchant, was the instigator, and he was convicted in the High Court and sentenced on the 6th April to two years' imprisonment with hard labour.' British Library, Oriental Collections, IOR/V/24/4284, 'Administration Report of the Indian Telegraph Department for 1862–63', 1863.

[22] Ibid., 4.

In addition to the changes in the code for signallers and officers, the department also improved their policy towards complaints. Robinson was, again, slightly overoptimistic when he stated that

> it is gratifying to learn [from the officer in charge of the check and complaint office] that there is considerable improvement in the accuracy as well as speed with which messages are now transmitted; were it otherwise, it may fairly be presumed that the number of complaints would have very materially increased, since complaints are now encouraged, instead of remaining months unanswered; replies are now promptly rendered, and when demanded, every satisfaction is given as far as the rules of the department admit. So far, indeed, from resisting or deprecating complaints, the administration is grateful to any person who supplies information of any kind which may facilitate the detection and correction of faults of commission or omission, or in any way facilitate or improve the efficiency of the department.[23]

Again, the references to the situation now allegedly overcome – i.e. to the practice of 'resisting or deprecating complaints' – is telling about the state of affairs in the telegraph department in the late 1850s and early 1860s. While Robinson himself – at least in his reports – was absolutely positive that things were improving quickly, the public for some time would not concur in this view, as can, for instance, be seen in both the content and the tone of the following article. On Thursday, 20 October 1864, the *Friend of India* – published in Calcutta and one of the forerunners of *The Statesman* – reported on the state of the telegraph system in India. The substantial article opened with the following lines:

> It is a curious fact that the two public departments which in Europe and America have been wrought to the highest possible state of perfection are, in India, peculiarly conspicuous for defective administration and consequent inefficacy in the service of the public. The two departments to which we allude are the Post Office and the Telegraph.[24]

At the time of writing, of course, only the postal affairs were managed by government departments in either the United States or the United Kingdom. In 1864, the telegraph systems in both countries were still in private hands. That the article nevertheless refers to 'public departments' emphasizes the belief that it was the duty of whoever ran the postal and telegraph networks to provide a service to the public. Regarding the management of the Indian telegraph system, which had been under government management from its inception, there seemed to be room for improvement, in the opinion of the writer:

> It may seem scarcely fair to institute a comparison between the working of the telegraph lines in Europe and the administration of the telegraph department in

[23] Ibid., 5. [24] 'The Government Telegraph', *Friend of India*, 20 October 1864, 1175.

India; for, in the one case, there is private management and a vast number of competing lines, and, in the other, governmental administration and an entire absence of competition. But these facts can scarcely be set forth by the Indian government in excuse for the shortcomings of its own department, for we have, at all events, a right to expect that such experience as may be derived from the practice of home institutions shall be applied, so far as differences of local peculiarities will permit, in India. As far as we have been able to discover, this is not done in the instance to which we are now alluding. On the contrary, we have little hesitation in asserting that of all the departments of the Indian government in this country that of the Telegraph is the most mismanaged. This is saying a good deal.[25]

The author moved on to say that there was 'a good deal of hard work done in the principal offices of the department, but it is, for the most part, work in the wrong direction'. He eventually came to the condemning

conclusion that, taking it all in all, the telegraph department is about as thoroughly bad as it well can be. The plant is bad, the organization defective, the directing power misapplied. The result is failure. We do not know of a single line in India that can be really depended upon. For commercial purposes the telegraph in India is practically of no value.[26]

The last two lines point at the heart of the problem. In order to become a valuable instrument for investors and merchants, the telegraph needed to be reliable. Investments, sales and purchases could not be made on a potentially imperfect information basis. While speed in transmission was, of course, an important asset for the business community, it helped little if there was a constant uncertainty as to whether a telegraphic message actually reached its destination. The reasons for the unreliability of the system were manifold and could be found, among other factors, in the unsuitable technical specifications of the system itself, the at times extreme climatic conditions and the only basic training of signallers and clerks that often did not suffice to guarantee a smooth working of the communication process. In order to justify the condemning conclusion reached, the author of 'The Government Telegraph' then provided an example of the doubtful working of the telegraph system that referred precisely to the last factor:

A few days ago a gentleman had occasion to despatch a telegram from one of the most important stations in the North-West. The clerk in charge of the office was a native; and, from the importance of the station, it might have been expected that he would at least have been an intelligent native. The message was clearly and legibly written upon the usual form. This is what the clerk did with it. He counted the words and stated the cost of the message. But when, at the sender's suggestion, he tried to read it he could not do so. It was read over to him, but still he failed to comprehend

[25] Ibid., 1175. [26] Ibid., 1175.

it, and it was not until it had been thrice repeated to him that he was able, even imperfectly, to spell over the words of the message. This is an incident that would be scarcely worth recording except that it serves as a practical illustration of the inefficient instruments through which the telegraph is worked. Here, in charge of one of the most important offices in the country, was a man who whether you judged of him by his education, or by his speech, or by his knowledge of the English language, would not be admitted as a common writer into any mercantile office in Calcutta. Now, if we consider that the chief requisite of a signal clerk in the telegraph is a complete acquaintance with the language in which messages are transmitted we may, from this, come to some understanding of the numerous delays, errors, omissions, and blunders, that so constantly occur on the Indian lines.[27]

From the tone and choice of words in which this example is related to the reader, it seems not completely unreasonable to assume that the author might have entertained some prejudice against the intellectual capabilities of the native Indian population that informed his opinion on the employment of native clerks in the telegraph department. Therefore the entire example should be interpreted with caution, allowing for the possibility that the matter might well have been exaggerated. On the other hand, the central problem identified in the example – an only rudimentary knowledge of the English language – could, of course, seriously hamper the smooth working of the system when occurring on a larger scale. And around the time of writing the article for the *Friend of India* this problem seemed, indeed, to have peaked.

8.2 The growth of the Indian Telegraph Department network

In the following years, however, Robinson's small reforms appear to have yielded first results. Hiring competent and well-trained telegraphers gradually became easier and the quality of the service started to improve. In the administration report for the 1870–1 year, Robinson proudly stated that '[s]ix years ago, signallers in sufficient numbers were not obtainable. It even was difficult to retain the services of those we had; now, the demands for admission are so far in excess of our wants that we can afford to be particular'.[28] In the preceding paragraph, he had already found only the warmest words for those selected and in the service of the department:

Our signalling staff is in truth the backbone of our Telegraph Establishment. According to the evidence given before Parliament in 1866, the Indian signalling

[27] Ibid., 1175.

[28] British Library, Oriental Collections, IOR/V/24/4284, 'Administration Report of the Indian Telegraph Department for 1867–68 to 1870–71', 1871, 12.

staff was then deplorably ignorant and thoroughly incompetent. The status of education was then decidedly low, but that the lads only needed stimulus and opportunity to profit by instruction is manifested by the discontinuance of complaints, and the universal admission that the signallers work is now done very well. I have now little fault to find with them. I believe that the Government now possesses a thoroughly reliable body of signallers, contented, generally well conducted, and far better educated than is usual with men of their class.[29]

This significant improvement in the training and in the motivation of the staff is also reflected by the department's records on transmission errors and complaints by the public. The administration report also contained figures that depict development between 1867 and 1871 in these two fields.[30] The number of errors occurring in the transmission of telegrams in the Indian inland system decreased from 4,526 in 1867–8 to 2,938 two years later, while the total number of messages dispatched grew from 337,022 to 499,946 in the same period. Relatively speaking, this marks a drop in the percentage of errors from 1.342 to 0.587. In 1870–1, the number of errors increased significantly again and reached a percentage of 0.81. Robinson, however, was very keen to point out that 'this is due to the scrutiny in the Check Office having, under better management, become much more searching, and not to any real falling off in efficiency'.[31] This, of course, explains the pronounced increase in errors in 1870–1, but it also casts some doubt on the accuracy of the figures for the previous years, as the responsible officers seem to have applied rather slack quality standards in their search for errors. The number of complaints by the public, however, confirms the general development of the quality of service. Regarding the Indian inland system, the number of complaints peaked in 1868–9 at 618 and then fell significantly to only 312 in 1870–1. Given the rising number of total messages, this amounts to a drop from 0.18 per cent to 0.06 per cent of all paid messages and indicates real improvement in terms of the quality of the service.

The above-mentioned rise in the total number of messages handled already hints at the fast growth of the Indian telegraph system that had begun in the late 1850s. Regarding the structure of the network, the experience of 1857–8 brought about a quick expansion of the system.[32] Both the lengths of lines and wires and the number of telegraph offices increased substantially directly after 1858 and sustained a reasonable growth rate thereafter. By 1860–1, the Indian state telegraph system had

[29] Ibid., 12. [30] Ibid., 54–5. [31] Ibid., 54.

[32] British Library, Oriental Collections, IOR/V/24/4288, 'Administration Report of the Indian Telegraph Department for 1900–1901', 1901, 8–9.

reached a total length of almost 18,000 kilometres of line and only a few hundred kilometres more of wire. Messages could be posted at 145 telegraph stations in the colony. In the following decades, the network grew mostly continuously at rates that usually were in the range between 2 per cent and 5 per cent annually. Every few years this equilibrium was punctuated by an explosive expansion of the system. The 1864–5 administrative year, for instance, brought about an increase in the lengths of lines and wires, as well as in the number of stations, of more than 12 per cent. Here, the network was expanded particularly in the Bengal, Bombay and Madras 'circles', completing lines, for instance, from Titalya to Gowhatty, from Ajmere to Deesa, or from Mercara to Mangalore.[33] During the late 1860s, the length of lines in operation saw little expansion, but the length of wires and the number of stations grew pronouncedly. The capacity of parts of the network increased accordingly and access became easier. Another example can be found in the 1871–2 year, during which telegraph lines increased by almost 10 per cent in length compared to the previous year, while the length of telegraph wires increased by almost 25 per cent. During this year, 'between Bombay and Madras a thoroughly good line ha[d] been erected along the Railway, providing perfect communication for the through traffic between the cables'. And furthermore, '[t]he construction of a line along the Chord Line of the East Indian Railway ha[d] shortened the distance between Calcutta and Bombay and Kurrachee – a great desideratum – and has rendered communication between these important places secure'.[34] Another similar surge in expansion occurred a few years later in 1879–80, when the length of lines grew by 14 per cent and that of wires by more than 20 per cent. From the early 1880s onwards, the network then started to grow much faster on average, sporting annual growth rates of up to 8 or 9 per cent for several consecutive years. At the same time, access to the system improved significantly through the introduction of combined postal and telegraph offices. This measure led to a more than doubling of the number of offices in the three years between 1882–3 and 1885–6. Growth rates in all structural categories remained high throughout the rest of the nineteenth century. By 1900–1, the Indian telegraph system consisted of more than 88,000 kilometres of line, most of which contained more than just one wire and therefore supported a total of 293,189 kilometres of wire. Almost

[33] British Library, Oriental Collections, IOR/V/24/4284, 'Administration Report of the Indian Telegraph Department for 1862–63, 1863–64, 1864–65, and 1865–66', 1866, 37–8.

[34] British Library, Oriental Collections, IOR/V/24/4284, 'Administration Report of the Indian Telegraph Department for 1871–72', 1872, 6.

2,000 postal or telegraph stations were now open to the public and provided access to the system. This accounts for a continuous structural growth of the Indian telegraph network in the four decades after the Indian Uprising – even if the network could not compare by far with those of the telegraphically well-developed countries in Europe and North America.[35]

Regarding the use of the system, reliable and comparable data becomes available from 1866–7 onwards. It seems that Robinson's optimism about the steady improvement of the service in the late 1860s and 1870s was reflected in customers' rising trust in the system (see Table A.24 in the Appendix).[36] Throughout this period, the number of paid inland messages grew substantially at rates between 12 and 21 per cent annually. Almost all of this growth was generated in the private sector and not by state use of the telegraph. Generally, this development continued throughout the nineteenth century (leaving aside a few exceptional years with no or minimal growth). In the 1900–1 administrative year, about 5.5 million paid inland messages were transacted by Indian Telegraph Department offices and forwarded over its wires.

Given its modest origins in the 1850s and 1860s, this number constitutes a remarkable expansion of the use of the network. In comparison with European or North American networks, however, the use rate is meagre. In the same period, the French system handled more than seven times the number of telegrams, Western Union in the United States more than eleven times and the British government telegraph more than fourteen times.[37] Considering the size of the territory and of the population of the subcontinent, it becomes very clear that the telegraph in India catered to a very select part of the populace.

Starting in the 1867–8 administrative year, the Indian Telegraph Department's reports also contain information on average transmission times between the principal cities of the subcontinent. On practically all important connections, transmission times significantly improved in the closing years of the 1860s.[38] While in 1867–8 it took almost eighteen hours on average for a telegram posted in Calcutta to reach Karachi, the

[35] ITU Archives, Bureau international des administrations télégraphiques, 'Statistique générale de la télégraphie', 1900.

[36] British Library, Oriental Collections, IOR/V/24/4288, 'Administration Report of the Indian Telegraph Department for 1900–1901', 1901, 8–9.

[37] See Wenzlhuemer, 'The Development of Telegraphy, 1870–1900'.

[38] British Library, Oriental Collections, IOR/V/24/4284, 'Administration Report of the Indian Telegraph Department for 1867–68 to 1870–71', 1871; British Library, Oriental Collections, IOR/V/24/4284, 'Administration Report of the Indian Telegraph Department for 1872–73', 1873; British Library, Oriental Collections, IOR/V/24/4286,

average transmission time on this central route had dropped to just under two hours only four years later. Another five years on, such a message reached its destination in less than one hour. Improvements of a similar magnitude can be found on practically all other major lines, such as the Calcutta–Bombay, the Calcutta–Madras, the Bombay–Karachi or the Bombay–Madras routes. Transmission times along all these lines dropped massively between 1867 and 1871. This, again, confirms the beneficial effect of Robinson's adjustments in the service.

From about the mid-1870s onwards, transmission times continued to shrink throughout the remainder of the century but at an altogether much lower (and sometimes temporarily reversing) rate. But then there was a sudden rise of transmission times on practically all routes in the 1899–1900 year. Communication times between many major cities again reached lamentable values of between thirty and more than sixty minutes in this year, and thus roughly equalled the average of the mid-1880s. However, this increase does not indicate an abrupt deterioration of the service but rather stems from the coincidence of two unrelated factors. First, it had been 'the practice in previous years to calculate the maxima [*sic*] time intervals on messages transmitted by the direct routes only. From the beginning of the year 1898–99, the time intervals on messages transmitted by alternative routes on account of pressure of traffic on direct routes have also been taken into account'.[39] As telegraphic traffic in India was not particularly high during the 1898–9 administrative year, these changes in the statistical method are not directly reflected in the average transmission times for this year. Due to the lack of traffic pressure, alternative routes rarely had to be used. In the following year, however, inland traffic practically exploded and grew by more than 15 per cent. The number of state telegrams increased significantly due to 'the arrangements necessary for the despatch of the Indian Contingent to South Africa' and the mobilization of the force in this regard.[40] At about the same time, private inland telegrams also multiplied around 'the middle of August, when probably the failure of the rains in certain parts of India had been realised [and] speculation in the prices of grain became acute, causing an exceptional increase in traffic'.[41] Both these events led to rising traffic pressure on the main routes and therefore to an increased resorting to alternative routes. In combination with the change in the statistical

'Administration Report of the Indian Telegraph Department for 1880–81', 1881; British Library, Oriental Collections, IOR/V/24/4288, 'Administration Report of the Indian Telegraph Department for 1899–1900', 1900.

[39] British Library, Oriental Collections, IOR/V/24/4288, 'Administration Report of the Indian Telegraph Department for 1899–1900', 1900, 21.

[40] Ibid., 6–7. [41] Ibid., 7.

method, this brought about the significant surge in transmission times for the 1899–1900 administrative year. This episode, however, also testifies to the fact that by the end of the nineteenth century, India was eventually hosting a generally reliable and cross-linked telegraph system that could cope with exploding traffic numbers when need arose. In the three decades leading up to 1900, the network had been systematically expanded and technically improved. Access had been facilitated for private customers and, accordingly, network use had grown continuously throughout this period.

8.3 Indian Telegraph Department network structure in 1871–1872

Despite the sustained growth of the British Indian telegraph network in the late nineteenth century, both its structural density and the degree of telegraph use in India was minuscule when compared to most European countries or the United States. British India lagged far behind in terms of lines and stations per unit of area and also regarding the number of telegrams transacted per head. For instance, British India reached only about 9 per cent of the European average density of lines per unit of area and 1 per cent of stations per unit of area in the year 1870. In the same year, the number of inland messages transacted per inhabitant amounted to only 1 per cent, while foreign messages per head were rounded down to 0 per cent of the corresponding European average.[42] This significant lag in development can only be explained by looking at both the geographical and the demographical preconditions as well as at the purpose of the network. First, of course, the sheer size of the subcontinent and its large population both posed a formidable challenge to constructing a tight network of sufficient length that was accessible at many telegraph stations. To some extent, this distorted the per-area and the per-head measures and led to overly low figures in these categories when compared to a European average. Second, and even more importantly, the telegraph in British India was an imperial endeavour born out of the demands (and fears) of colonial administrators. Therefore it catered primarily to the needs of a very small group of officials, soldiers, merchants, financiers and newsmen who were by no means equally distributed throughout the subcontinent. The British Indian telegraph network therefore had not been designed to spread evenly across the colony. From its beginnings, it concentrated mainly on the important administrative and business centres and connected these with each other. While such a focus on the

[42] See Wenzlhuemer, 'The Development of Telegraphy, 1870–1900'.

centres is, of course, quite common in the European context as well (as has been seen in previous chapters), in British India the communicational gap between the few centres and the hinterland is much more pronounced than, for instance, in Europe in general or in Great Britain in particular.

In late nineteenth-century India, the telegraph only very rarely left the central axes of communication in order to reach out into the less-central regions. This can be seen both in the structure of the network and in its use figures. While the next section will be concerned with the latter, the former is the subject of this section. In the following, a network analysis of the British Indian telegraph network as it stood in the 1871–2 administrative year will be conducted. This particular time of observation has been selected for three reasons. First, the Indian Telegraph Department network reached a first stable working state in the early 1870s. By this time, the overall structure of the network had been laid out and the most urgent improvements had been made. While the following decades would bring further gradual development, a level of reasonable manageability and reliability had been achieved by that time. Second, the time of observation is reasonably close to 1868 – the only year for which comprehensive network information for the British telegraph system is available. The following analysis is, therefore, chronologically close enough to the study conducted in the previous chapter to allow for a direct comparison of the two cases. Third, sufficiently accurate and cross-referenced data is available for this year that renders a structural as well as a use analysis possible. In combination with use data for the 1872–3 administrative year, the structural data can be contrasted with individual information on foreign and inland traffic as well as on the total traffic split into sent, received and transmitted categories – all within an observational period of two years.

The data, which informs the following network analysis as well as the use study in the next section, stems from the administrative reports published by the Indian Telegraph Department. Therefore it covers only the government-run part of the British Indian telegraph network. However, private railway lines operating in the subcontinent also maintained telegraph lines along their railway tracks. While co-operation and the interchange of messages between the various railway companies seems to have worked quite well, this was more problematic between the government and the railway systems. In the combined administrative report for the years 1867–8, 1868–9, 1869–70 and 1870–1, Robinson comments on this point in the following words:

> The extravagance of having two lines of telegraph on the opposite sides of the same Railway when one would suffice, and the absurdity of the two systems, both

supported out of Indian Revenues, competing against each other for the favor of the public, instead of being combined together to serve the public in the best possible manner, are too obvious to require any lengthened demonstration, indeed, so obvious that one would suppose that, considering the intimate relations that exist in this country between the Government and the Railway, there would be less difficulty in effecting their removal than in almost any other part of the world. Not so, however, although all over Europe and in England since its telegraphs have come under State management, the Railways carry messages for the public only as agents for or as servants of the State, and only over those short lengths which are not provided with a Government Telegraph, in this country the vested interest of the Companies, and the impatience of control of the agents and representatives of the two great Companies, have effectually resisted the arrangement of this important question.[43]

As becomes clear from this statement, two practically independent telegraph systems with only very little contact co-existed in British India. Message exchange between them was absolutely minimal. The administration report for the 1871–2 year gives the number of messages transferred in both directions. Altogether, only 19,528 messages were handed from the railway telegraph operators to the government telegraph officers during that year. And even fewer than that, just 13,305 telegrams, were transferred in the other direction. In the case of the former, this amounts to 2.8 per cent of all messages posted at government stations in that year. Regarding the latter, it is 1.9 per cent of all messages received at government stations.[44] Contact and, thus, division of labour between the two systems were, indeed, minimal. Both networks were largely isolated from each other. And, as Robinson in the first sentence of the above extract indicated, the two systems mostly ran parallel to each other in geographical terms as well. Map 8.1 depicts both the Indian Telegraph Department lines existing in 1871–2 and the railway lines operating in British India by 1875–6. Completed government lines are shown solid, while railway lines are dashed for private companies and dotted for state railways. As can clearly be seen, the state telegraph and the railway network were almost completely congruent. At times, the railway lines diverted slightly from the telegraphs as they called at more and smaller intermediary stations. And in South India the railways, indeed, catered to a region that had largely been bypassed by the state telegraph. Yet, all in all, the two systems worked along the same axes and provided telegraphic communication to the same cities and regions. Due to both the isolation and the congruence

[43] British Library, Oriental Collections, IOR/V/24/4284, 'Administration Report of the Indian Telegraph Department for 1867–68 to 1870–71', 1871, 16.
[44] British Library, Oriental Collections, IOR/V/24/4284, 'Administration Report of the Indian Telegraph Department for 1871–72', 1872, 35.

of the two systems, an analysis of only one of them – in this case of the government telegraph network as compatible data exists only here – does make sense and produces valid results.

In the structural analysis of the Indian Telegraph Department network existing in 1871–2, 268 stations and their connections have been considered. The information on their position in the various government circuits has been extracted from Annexure III of the Administration Report of the Indian Telegraph Department for the Year 1871/72, entitled 'Classification and Description of the Lines of Telegraph in India, British Burmah, and Ceylon, as They Stood on the 31st March 1872'.[45] The connections between these 268 government stations have been entered into a data matrix which forms the basis for a social network analysis looking at the degree, betweenness and eigenvector centrality measures. The visualization of the government and railway telegraph network in Map 8.1 already quite clearly suggests that the structure of the British Indian telegraph system in the early 1870s differed quite markedly from that of contemporary Western networks, for instance the British network discussed in some detail in the previous chapter. While the British network centred quite pronouncedly on London – and to a lesser extent on the industrial north of England – the British Indian network seems to have had no obvious centre. It featured clearly discernible circuits and communicational axes but had practically no cross-connections between these. The distribution of degree centrality within the network confirms this preliminary visual analysis.

Calcutta is the only node in the network with a degree value (48) significantly higher than those following (see Table A.25 in the Appendix). Bombay, Madras, Barrackpore, Agra, Allahabad and Raneegunge all exhibit values in the range between thirty-five and thirty. Ranks nine (Nynee) to nineteen (Bezwarrah) still feature degree values between twenty-six and twenty. From there it is a very gradual decline to the town of Sylhet, which still has a degree of ten and ranks 120th. For comparison, London Central in Electric's network exhibits a degree value of 343. These results testify to the fact that the telegraphic circuits in India do not branch out much, concentrate on their principal routes and – most importantly – have almost no cross-connections between each other. There are only few alternative routes or direct circuits in the system. As visualized by the circles in Map 8.2, degree centrality is also relatively evenly distributed across the subcontinent, with centres at the eastern coast (Calcutta, Barrackpore, Madras), the western coast (Bombay) and

[45] Ibid., Annexure III.

inland (Agra, Allahabad). While Calcutta occupies a *primus inter pares* position, it does not have values high enough to qualify as the single hub or gatekeeper of telegraphic traffic in India. The degree analysis confirms that there was no central switch, no control station in the British Indian system. Rather, this function was relatively well distributed among the colonial centres.

The results of the betweenness analysis further support the above findings. The five nodes with the highest betweenness values are all among the top degree nodes as well (see Table A.26 in the Appendix). Interestingly, however, the inland towns of Allahabad (22.9 per cent)

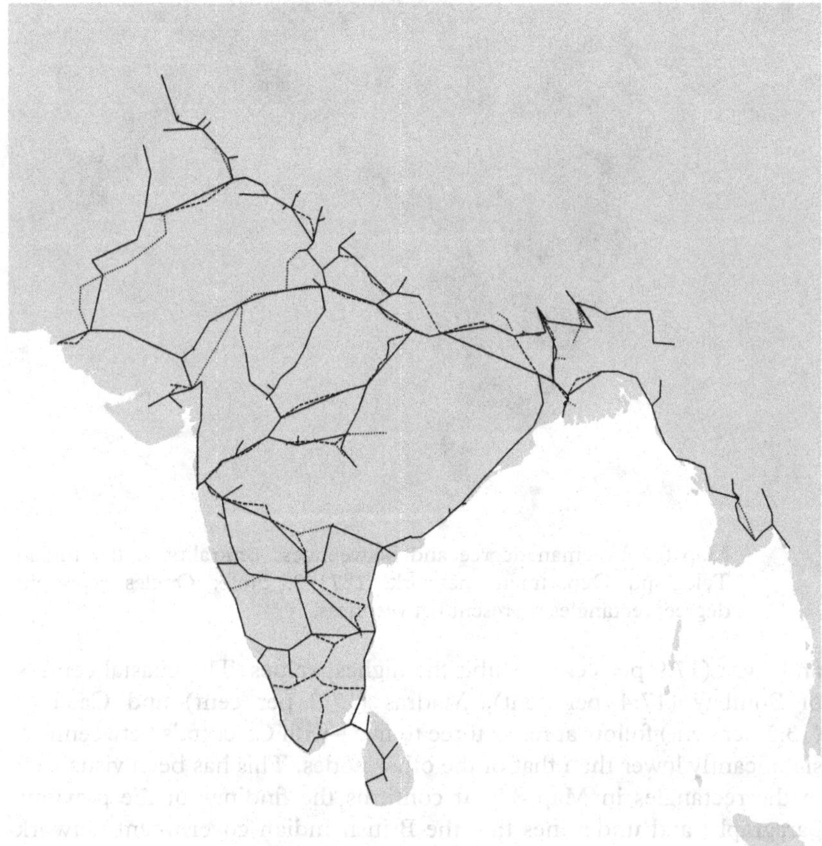

Map 8.1 Telegraph lines of the Indian Telegraph Department (1871–2) and railway lines (1875–6) operating in British India. Note: Government telegraph lines are shown as solid; private railway lines as dashed; state railway lines as dotted.

Map 8.2 Freeman degree and betweenness centrality in the Indian Telegraph Department network, 1871–2. Note: Circles represent degree; rectangles represent betweenness.

and Agra (17.9 per cent) exhibit the highest values. The coastal centres of Bombay (17.4 per cent), Madras (17.2 per cent) and Calcutta (13.5 per cent) follow at ranks three to five – with Calcutta's betweenness significantly lower than that of the other nodes. This has been visualized in the rectangles in Map 8.2. It confirms the findings of the previous paragraphs and underlines that the British Indian government network knew no central switch and featured no single gateway or control centre. The even distribution of betweenness in the network shows that the network structure was quite balanced. While there were almost no cross-connections between circuits, the few alternative routes available were connected in a decentralized and geographically spread-out fashion that increased the durability of the network at least in a modest way. Several nodes shared responsibility in the British Indian network.

The Bonacich eigenvector centrality measure produced data of only limited usefulness. With 46.4 per cent normalized eigenvector, Calcutta ranks highest, followed by Barrackpore (37.6 per cent) and Raneegunge (26.2 per cent). All the following towns are nodes on the Calcutta–Moulmein circuit and seem to potentiate themselves statistically. The British Indian telegraph network was comparably tight around Calcutta, and the city sat at the centre of a number of important connections. Therefore the eigenvector centrality of Calcutta is plausible. The high values of the Calcutta–Moulmein stations, however, seem to be a statistical oddity.

8.4 Indian Telegraph Department network use in 1872–1873

The findings discussed in the previous section clearly confirm that the British Indian government telegraph network did not emerge as an answer to the real or perceived needs of the public – a public, of course, that consisted mainly of people with an interest in business – as it did, for instance, in the United Kingdom. There, the telegraph network structure obviously reflected the perspective of a thriving business community that placed London at the centre and then needed a seemingly endless number of direct connections all across the country. In the case of British India, the network structure mirrored a more specific administrative purpose and exhibited a design developed on the drawing board rather than shaped by market forces. Such a design fulfilled the interests of the colonial government in the most economical way possible. As was seen in the first section of this chapter, these interests, from the very beginnings of the system, also encompassed the needs of the merchants and financiers operating out of the principal cities of the subcontinent who were crucially important to the British administrators. At the same time, however, concentration on the principal cities and important communication axes also limited the capacity, durability and attractiveness of a network system that thrived on the existence of cross-connections, alternative routes and ready access. At the time of observation in the early 1870s (and for a long time thereafter), the biggest parts of British India and its populace remained completely untouched by the telegraph. The already existing gap between centre and periphery, urban and rural India, therefore, widened with the increasing use of the telegraph. Active market participation outside the population centres became even harder when market information travelled over the wire. In short, the British Indian telegraph network of the nineteenth century was designed with the needs and demands of a very small elite community of colonial administrators and mostly white businesspeople in mind and clearly reflected this in its structure.

While the British Indian telegraph network of the late nineteenth century strongly concentrated on connecting the principal centres of the subcontinent, and thereby further enhanced a prevailing integration gap within the colony, the network in itself – as has been shown above – had no particular control centre, no central switch or gateway comparable to the role of London in the United Kingdom's network of the time. The examination of the available network use data presented below, however, produces different results. Network use was by no means evenly distributed within the system but rather concentrated in and around a handful of metropolises in British India – namely Bombay, Calcutta and Madras, as well as, to a smaller degree, Karachi and Rangoon. This section draws on two different sets of information on telegraphic traffic in the British Indian network. The government department's administration report for 1871–2 lists 217 telegraph stations according to the administrative division they belonged to. The list contains information on the number of telegrams sent, received or transmitted at each individual station.[46] In the report published one year later, Appendix H consists of a 'List of Offices arranged according to the number of paid Sent Messages during the year 1872–73' that contains 212 telegraph stations with data on the inland and foreign messages sent from there.[47] In combination, these two data sets allow for a relatively refined and differentiated analysis of telegraphic traffic and its distribution within the British Indian system in the early 1870s.

The distribution of messages sent and received within the British Indian state network is very similar (see Table A.27 in the Appendix).[48] In both cases, Bombay and Calcutta handled by far the largest portion of traffic. Madras ranks third and is followed at some distance by Karachi and Rangoon. At Bombay, 120,638 telegrams were posted in 1871–2 and 88,579 were received. For Calcutta, the corresponding figures are 89,171 and 83,582. This means that, taken together, the two cities account for 29.9 per cent of all telegrams sent from all 217 British Indian government stations included in the list and for 24.1 per cent of all messages received there. The top twenty nodes within the network

[46] Ibid., 26–33.
[47] British Library, Oriental Collections, IOR/V/24/4284, 'Administration Report of the Indian Telegraph Department for 1872–73', 1873, 49–51.
[48] British Library, Oriental Collections, IOR/V/24/4284, 'Administration Report of the Indian Telegraph Department for 1871–72', 1872, 26–33.

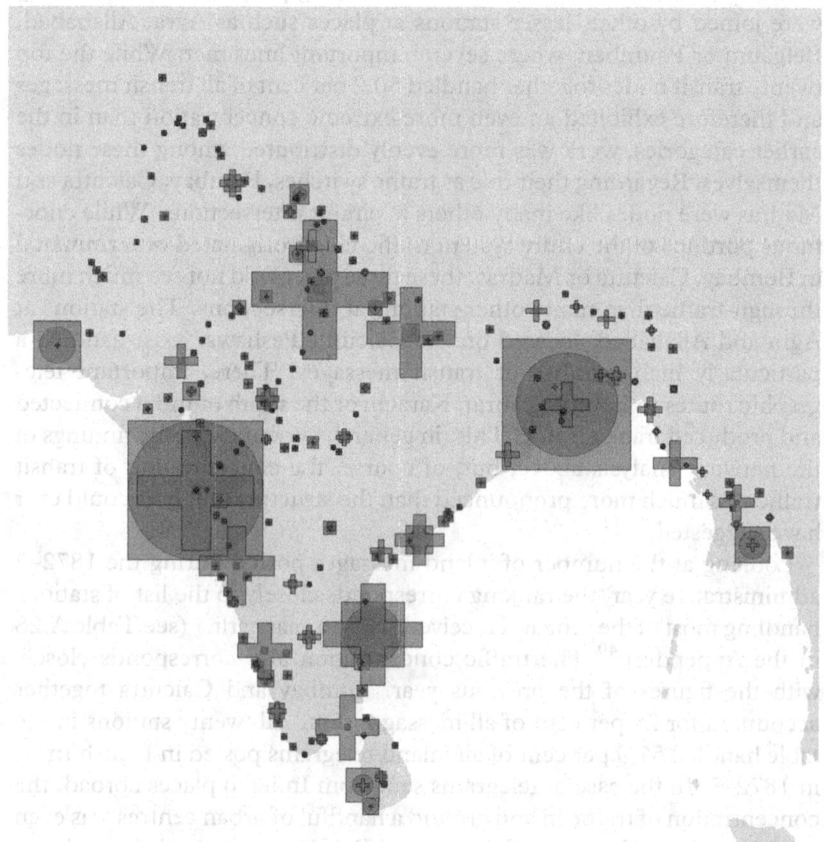

Map 8.3 Messages sent, received and transmitted at stations in the Indian Telegraph Department network, 1871–2. Note: Circles represent sent messages; rectangles represent messages received; crosses represent messages transmitted.

together account for 61.7 per cent of all sent messages and for 57.2 per cent of all received. Map 8.3 visualizes this traffic concentration in and around the principal cities of the subcontinent. This imbalance was especially pronounced regarding the posting of telegrams, while at least a slightly higher proportion of messages was delivered to places outside the principal metropolises. All in all, however, a disproportionately high percentage of the total traffic in the network originated or terminated in three or four important cities. Often standing at the intersection of two or more telegraphic routes, these cities also saw much of the transit traffic between different circuits. For these switching purposes, however, they were joined by other, lesser stations at places such as Agra, Allahabad, Belgaum or Paumben, where several important lines met. While the top twenty transit nodes together handled 80.2 per cent of all transit messages and therefore exhibited an even more extreme concentration than in the earlier categories, work was more evenly distributed among these nodes themselves. Regarding their role as traffic switches, Bombay, Calcutta and Madras were nodes like many others at circuit intersections. While enormous portions of the entire system traffic either originated or terminated in Bombay, Calcutta or Madras, these three places did not see much more through-traffic than many other stations at intersections. The stations at Agra and Allahabad, located on the Calcutta–Peshawar axis, handled a particularly high number of transit messages. There, important telegraphic routes to Bombay, Surat, Karachi or the south of India connected and produced transit traffic. This, in general, concurs with the findings of the network analysis above, but, of course, the concentration of transit traffic was much more pronounced than the structural analysis could ever have suggested.

Looking at the number of inland messages posted during the 1872–3 administrative year, the ranking corresponds closely to the list of stations handling most of the sent and received traffic a year earlier (see Table A.28 in the Appendix).[49] The traffic concentration also corresponds closely with the figures of the previous year. Bombay and Calcutta together accounted for 28 per cent of all messages sent. All twenty stations in the table handled 57.9 per cent of all inland telegrams posted in British India in 1872–3. In the case of telegrams sent from India to places abroad, the concentration of traffic in and around a handful of urban centres was even more pronounced. Again, Calcutta and Bombay easily lead the table. In these two places, 9,989 and 7,301 respectively of the 25,849 telegrams sent abroad originated. Taken together, this accounts for 66.9 per cent of the total. The top twenty nodes handled 95.3 per cent of all the messages to destinations outside India. Outside the principal centres of the subcontinent, practically no foreign telegraphic traffic was handled. Map 8.4 displays the number of telegrams sent inland and abroad in correct proportions and reveals that only a minuscule part of the entire traffic handled by the British Indian telegraph system was destined for places abroad.

In short, both inland and foreign telegraphic traffic in British India was highly concentrated around only a very small number of principal

[49] British Library, Oriental Collections, IOR/V/24/4284, 'Administration Report of the Indian Telegraph Department for 1872–73', 1873, 49–51.

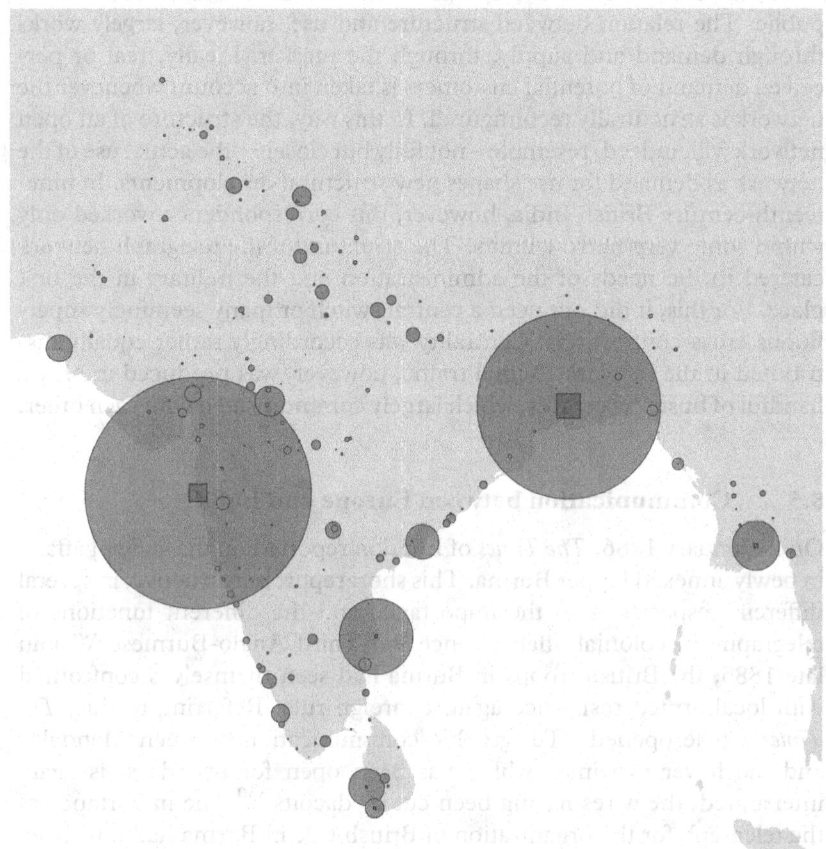

Map 8.4 Inland and foreign paid telegrams sent from stations in the Indian Telegraph Department network, 1872–3 (in proportion). Note: Circles represent inland messages; rectangles represent foreign messages.

administrative and business centres. Network traffic was, therefore, anything but equally distributed within the system. Unlike, for instance, the case of the British telegraph system, network structure and network use patterns did not correspond much with each other. While the structure – which presents the theoretical maximum potential of the network – knew no real centre or single privileged gateways, network use clearly revolved around only a few places and revealed the position of the key switches in the system. This non-correspondence between structure and use also stems from the fact that the British Indian telegraph system had been purposely designed with the specific needs of a small colonial elite in mind, and therefore could not respond much to the demands of the wider public. The relation between structure and use, however, largely works through demand and supply, through the market. Ideally, real or perceived demand of potential customers is taken into account whenever the network is structurally reconfigured. In this way, the structure of an open network will, indeed, resemble – not fully but closely – the actual use of the network as demand for use shapes new structural developments. In nineteenth-century British India, however, this correspondence worked only within some very narrow limits. The structure of the telegraph network catered to the needs of the administration and the military in the first place. For this, it did not need a central switch or many seemingly superfluous cross-connections. Centrality was accordingly rather equally distributed in the network. Actual traffic, however, was produced in only a handful of business centres, which largely communicated with each other.

8.5 Communication between Europe and India

On 21 January 1886, *The Times* of London reported on the state of affairs in newly annexed Upper Burma. This short report is instructive, in several different respects, as to the importance and the different functions of telegraphy in colonial affairs. Since the Third Anglo-Burmese War in late 1885, the British troops in Burma had seen themselves confronted with local armed resistance against foreign rule. Referring to this, *The Times* article opened, 'Telegraphic communication between Mandalay and the lower province, which has been open for two days, is again interrupted, the wires having been cut by dacoits.'[50] The importance of the telegraph for the organization of British rule in Burma had thus been duly noticed by the local resistance movement. Furthermore, the article itself was based on a correspondent's report from Mandalay posted there on 19 January. Communication between Burma and London therefore worked quickly and enabled a stable and reasonably up-to-date flow of information to the British public. And the interest of just this public was certainly aroused more than usual by the further contents of the article, which would eventually trigger a whole flurry of telegraphic interchange between London, Calcutta, Rangoon and Mandalay. The article ended with the following passage:

> The Rev. Mr. Colbeck, the representative in Mandalay of the Society for the Propagation of the Gospel, has addressed a public protest to the Chief Commissioner against a recent attempt by the Provost-Marshal to procure

[50] 'Burmah', *The Times*, 21 January 1886, 5.

testimony against other persons from a Burman while he was covered by the presented rifles of a firing party. Mr. Colbeck, who has long been resident in Burmah, declares that such proceedings cannot fail to bring shame and discredit upon our name, nation, and religion.

The ghastly scenes which constantly recur in executions carried out by the Provost-Marshal constitute grave public scandals. The Provost-Marshal, who is an ardent amateur photographer, is desirous of securing views of the persons executed at the precise moment when they are struck by the bullets. To secure this result, after the orders, 'Ready,' 'Present,' have been given to the firing-party, the Provost-Marshal fixes his camera on the prisoners, who at times are kept waiting for some minutes in that position. The officer commanding the firing party is then directed by the Provost-Marshal to give order to fire at the moment when he exposes his plate.

So far no satisfactory negative has been obtained, and the experiments are likely to be continued. These proceedings take place before a crowd of mixed nationalities, and cannot fail to have a demoralizing effect on both soldiers and spectators.[51]

This caused a public stir in England and almost immediately led to questions in the House of Commons. In the Commons sitting of 25 January, the Secretary of State for India, Lord Randolph Churchill, answered several questions referring to the treatment of Burmese prisoners under martial law and to the conduct of Provost-Marshal Willoughby Wallace Hooper. Among other things, Churchill said,

With regard to the Questions asked me on Friday, I am sorry to say that the information in my possession is far from satisfactory. The Viceroy telegraphs to me that it is clear that the Provost Marshal has proceeded in a most unjustifiable manner; at any rate, in one case. That alludes to the case where evidence was sought to be extorted by placing a prisoner apparently under the fire of soldiers. The Viceroy says he has telegraphed to General Prendergast directing that if a prima facie case is made out against the Provost Marshal on either of the counts mentioned, he and other officers implicated are to be suspended from their functions, and, if proved to be guilty, to be visited with the severest penalty. Mr. Bernard telegraphs from Rangoon to the Viceroy that he is still investigating or asking for information at Mandalay as to the allegations with regard to the Provost Marshal photographing prisoners under execution.[52]

The telegrams, which the Secretary of State referred to, formed only a small part of the somewhat hectic communication between London, Calcutta, Rangoon and Mandalay that had unfolded after the report in *The Times*. The entire telegraphic exchange was later compiled as a parliamentary paper presented to the House of Commons and has, therefore, survived in its full length. Only a day after *The Times* article had been

[51] Ibid., 5.
[52] Hansard, vol. 302, cols. 314–17. 'House of Commons Debate', 25 January 1886.

published, Churchill had grasped the seriousness of the situation and telegraphed the viceroy at Calcutta:

'Times' yesterday reports Mandalay, 19th January, grave scandals at military executions in Burma through Provost-Marshal photographing prisoners at moment of execution . . . Please report circumstances at once, and, if in any degree true, gravest and most immediate action must be taken . . . Questions now pending in Parliament. These reports are creating a very unfavourable impression.[53]

Again a day later, on 23 January 1886, the viceroy sent a telegram each to Chief Commissioner Bernard at Rangoon and Lieutenant-General Prendergast in Mandalay. An extract of the former reads,

I cannot believe that proceedings so contrary to what was proper and desirable should have taken place. Am telegraphing to General Prendergast in same sense. You will not fail to comprehend extreme gravity of foregoing subject. Effect upon public opinion in England, in Europe, and in India, if such transactions should have taken place, cannot fail to be most disastrous.[54]

Between 22 January and 1 March 1886, twenty telegrams were exchanged between the different parties involved in order to establish the exact facts of Hooper's alleged misconduct, to do some damage control and to prepare a formal court of inquiry into the matter.[55] Eventually, the court of inquiry held at Mandalay on 19 March 1886 came to the opinion that the 'conduct of Colonel Hooper ... has deservedly met with public condemnation. It reflects discredit on the army to which he belongs, and is damaging to the character of the British Administration in India'. Nevertheless, taking into account that Hooper 'had already suffered severely from the consequences of his actions', the former provost-marshal got away with nothing but a public reprimand.[56]

This episode is telling in many different ways. Most obviously, it highlights the ruthlessness with which the British in Burma acted against those whom they perceived and denounced as dacoits. Furthermore, the scandal around Provost-Marshal Hooper drew public attention to questions of morality and ethics regarding the application of a relatively new technology (in this particular case, photography). Most relevant to the purpose of this study, however, is the illustration of several of the different functions that the telegraph fulfilled in the context of communication between Europe and Asia, between the imperial metropolis and the colony. First, telegraphic communication had long become a routine feature of military

[53] House of Commons Parliamentary Papers, C. 4690, 'Burmah, No 2 (1886). Telegraphic Correspondence Relating to Military Executions and Dacoity in Burmah', 1886, 7.
[54] Ibid., 7. [55] Ibid., 7.
[56] 'The Charges against Colonel Hooper', *The Times*, 8 September 1886, 3.

and other strategic operations. The compilation of telegrams later published as a parliamentary paper shows that there existed a regular flow of information from Burma – sometimes via India – to England. Until the publicization of Hooper's questionable practices in *The Times* article, these messages were unidirectional updates on the situation in Burma sent from Asia to Europe only. The telegraph was, accordingly, used in a routine fashion to inform the higher echelons of colonial administration (in this case either in Calcutta or directly in London) about the strategic situation on the spot. Second, the telegraph could, of course, be deployed as an administrative tool. The Secretary of State's message from 22 January constituted the first message in the exchange sent in the other direction and changed the nature of the communication. The telegrams changed in tone, contents and purpose. The technology was now used to make urgent inquiries and to swiftly implement policies. It was employed in a mainly administrative fashion and provided the only means to resolve the issue – and its implications on public opinion back in England – fast and efficiently. This is all the more true as, third, reports about such grievances in the colonies also reached the British papers, and thus the British public, by telegraph. The original report in *The Times* was published only two days after the correspondent had dispatched his views in Mandalay. The flow of news between the imperial metropolis and the colonies also used the telegraph as a medium.[57]

Of course, telegraphy could also be employed in communication between Asia and Europe in ways not covered by the above episode. By far the biggest proportion of telegraphic traffic was produced not by governments or the press but by private persons, most of whom belonged to the business community. During the 1888–9 administrative year, for instance, state messages accounted for only about 2.6 per cent of messages sent via the lines of the Indo-European Telegraph Department (IETD). Press telegrams – including those of *The Times* of London handled under a special agreement – made up another 2.2 per cent. The remaining (rounded) 95.3 per cent of messages were labelled 'Commercial and Private'.[58] From the early 1870s onwards, all these telegrams between Europe and India could be sent over three different routes. Since 1865, it had been possible to communicate with India over a landline through Turkey that connected with the Indo-European Telegraph Department's cables at Fao (Al-Faw) near Basra. From

[57] For more background on this, see Bonea, 'The Medium and Its Message'.

[58] British Library, Oriental Collections, IOR/V/24/4290, 'Administration Report of the Indo-European Telegraph Department for 1892–93', 1893, 21.

there, the cable reached Karachi in several legs.[59] The so-called Turkish line, however, was notoriously slow and unreliable and,[60] in the eyes of the British administration, had the additional drawback of passing through territory not under direct British control. Relief came in 1870, when within only three months two new alternative routes to India were opened to the public. In January, the Indo-European Telegraph Company (IETC) inaugurated its landline service from London via Prussia and Russia to Tehran.[61] In Persia, the line connected with the system of the Indo-European Telegraph Department – with which it has often been confused due to the similarity of the names. While the IETD was operated by the British Indian government, the IETC was a private company led by Siemens. In March 1870, John Pender's British Indian Submarine Telegraph Company completed its cable connection between Suez and Bombay. In June, the Falmouth, Gibraltar and Malta Telegraph Company linked up with this connection and direct submarine cable communication between Great Britain and India became possible (with only a short stretch of landline between Alexandria and Suez in the circuit). Both these new lines presented serious competition to the slow and inefficient Turkish line and attracted much traffic immediately. Only two years after its opening, the Siemens line handled at least twice, sometimes up to five times, the monthly traffic of the Turkish line (see Table A.29 in the Appendix).[62] From April 1873, the administration reports of the IETD also contain figures for the Suez cable's traffic, and thus a fuller picture of the monthly telegraphic exchange between Europe and India emerges. By that time, the share of the Turkish line had dropped to under 10 per cent and the cable already handled a little more traffic than the

[59] Harris, 'The Persian Gulf Submarine Telegraph of 1864'; Farajollah Ahmadi, 'Linking India with Britain: The Persian Gulf Cables, 1864–1907' (unpublished PhD thesis, University of Exeter, 2003).

[60] See the statistics on average transmission times via Turkey, Tehran and the submarine cable given in the administration reports, for instance British Library, Oriental Collections, IOR/V/24/4289, 'Administration Report of the Indo-European Telegraph Department for 1873–74', 1874; British Library, Oriental Collections, IOR/V/24/4289, 'Administration Report of the Indo-European Telegraph Department for 1882–83', 1883; British Library, Oriental Collections, IOR/V/24/4290, 'Administration Report of the Indo-European Telegraph Department for 1889–90', 1890.

[61] Elisabeth Bühlmann, *La Ligne Siemens: La construction du télégraphe Indo-Européen 1867–1870* (Frankfurt a. M.: Peter Lang, 1999); Margot Fuchs, 'The Indo-European Telegraph System 1868–1931: Politics and Technical Change', *Berichte zur Wissenschaftsgeschichte* 13 (1990); Andre Karbelashvili, 'Europe–India Telegraph "Bridge" via the Caucasus', *Indian Journal of History of Science* 26, no 3 (1991).

[62] British Library, Oriental Collections, IOR/V/24/4289, 'Administration Report of the Indo-European Telegraph Department for 1873–74', 1874; British Library, Oriental Collections, IOR/V/24/4289, 'Administration Report of the Indo-European Telegraph Department for 1878–79', 1879.

landline. During the following years, Turkish line traffic further decreased, while the two other routes shared the remaining message volume in fluctuating but mostly equal proportions. The traffic figures also highlight the interdependence of the three routes. Between November 1875 and February 1876, for instance, traffic via both Turkey and Tehran increased explosively due to an interruption of the submarine cable connection. Between May and August 1877, service on the Siemens line was disrupted and more than 90 per cent of all Euro-Indian telegrams were transmitted via the Red Sea cable. Although owned and run by completely different entities, the different parts of the communication system depended very much on each other and reacted sensitively to all sorts of events and disturbances along their routes.

By the 1870s India had become well connected with Europe. The communication system was reasonably stable due to the existence of several fallback options. And, as can be seen in Map 5.2, the network was immediately extended further to the east. Another one of Pender's companies – the British Indian Extension Telegraph Company – opened cables from Madras via Penang to Singapore already in 1870. The British Australian Telegraph Company extended the connection to Batavia in the same year and on to Port Darwin in Australia in 1871. A connection to Shanghai and Hong Kong was inaugurated in that year as well. And Rangoon was linked with Penang in 1877. These are just a few examples of the growth of the global telegraph network to the east, in the course of which India developed into a veritable hub of telegraphic traffic between Europe and Australasia. Data in the 'Administration Report of the Indian Telegraph Department for the Year 1872–73' already reflects this development. The statistics on inland and foreign messages sent from India contain further information on international transit traffic that has not been discussed above (again, see Table A.28 in the Appendix). Accordingly, during the 1872–3 administrative year, the principal government telegraph station at Bombay handled 11,327 transit messages from Europe to what has been called the Far East. The station at Karachi transacted 2,049 such telegrams. And Madras saw 14,256 transit messages from the Far East to Europe.[63] Table 8.1 shows how telegraphic traffic was distributed between the Indo-European Telegraph Department's Persian Gulf cables (connecting with the Turkish line and the Indo-European Telegraph Company's route) and Pender's submarine cable system through the Red Sea. The submarine cable attracted a bigger share of the total traffic between Europe and India towards the end

[63] British Library, Oriental Collections, IOR/V/24/4284, 'Administration Report of the Indian Telegraph Department for 1872–73', 1873, 49–51.

Table 8.1 *Indo-European and Far East telegraphic traffic, 1873–4 to 1878–9.*

	Red Sea line		Persian Gulf line	
Year	Between India and Europe	Far East traffic	Between India and Europe	Far East traffic
1873–4	25,123	24,863	24,255	3,992
1874–5	31,608	23,892	31,761	4,354
1875–6	29,408	17,200	41,210	9,213
1876–7	56,862	23,977	37,415	4,950
1877–8	86,637	50,838	23,494	2,602
1878–9	81,605	56,549	27,799	3,655

Source: British Library, Oriental Collections, IOR/V/24/4289, 'Administration Report of the Indo-European Telegraph Department for 1873–74', 1874; British Library, Oriental Collections, IOR/V/24/4289, 'Administration Report of the Indo-European Telegraph Department for 1878–79', 1879.

of the 1870s. Regarding messages to and from the Far East, however, its position was unrivalled from its very opening. Table 8.1 shows that only a small share of the Far East traffic went through the Persian Gulf cables at all. In 1872, the individual companies operating the submarine connection between Europe and India had been merged to form the Eastern Telegraph Company. Likewise, a year later the companies controlling the extensions to the east of India had been united to create the Eastern Extension, Australasia and China Telegraph Company. The two co-operated closely and thus provided a direct connection in which telegrams did not need to be interchanged between differently owned companies. This was efficient and convenient for the customer and therefore attracted the biggest part of the Far East traffic, which was growing substantially throughout the 1870s and the following decades. Until the opening of the cross-connection between Africa and Australia via the Cocos Islands in 1901, practically all the telegraphic traffic between Europe and Africa in the west and East and South East Asia as well as Australia in the east had to pass through India at one point in time. The British colony had, therefore, become one of the central switches in the global telegraph network of the nineteenth century.

9 Conclusion

9.1 Information, knowledge and cultural practices

On 30 August 1847, *The Times* of London reported extensively about the judicial enquiries into a case of poisoning. Mary Hutchings, the forty-eight-year-old wife of John Hutchings, a cooper in Her Majesty's Victualling Yard at Deptford, died after a lengthy and painful struggle on the evening of Sunday, 22 August. From the witness accounts and the postmortem examination – which were both described in meticulous and sometimes unsavoury detail in the article – it was established that the deceased had died of arsenic poisoning. Sixteen-year-old Thomas Hutchings, son of John and Mary, had kept a bottle of arsenic in a locked drawer in his bedroom for the purpose of poisoning rats and cats. In the course of the enquiries, it was established that his father had broken open the drawer and taken the arsenic under the pretence of keeping it out of reach of his wife.[1] Other, more direct evidence against John Hutchings was scarce. Nevertheless, it was decided to put him to trial. According to *The Times* article, the responsible coroner said to Hutchings,

> [I]t is my painful duty, after a most patient investigation into the whole of the evidence, to inform you that the jury, by the solemn oath they have taken, have agreed unanimously on a verdict of wilful murder against you, and that you will be forthwith committed to Newgate to stand your trial on this most serious charge.[2]

On 20 September 1847, the trial took place and, judging from the court record, little new evidence was produced. Nevertheless, John Hutchings was found guilty of wilful murder and sentenced to death.[3] On the day of the execution at Maidstone Gaol, however, a remarkable incident took place that found its way into the *London Anecdotes* on telegraphy. Under

[1] 'Another Case of Poisoning', *The Times*, 30 August 1847, 7. [2] Ibid., 7.

[3] Old Bailey Proceedings Online (www.oldbaileyonline.org), t18470920-2217, 'Proceedings of the Central Criminal Court. Trial of John Hutchings', 20 September 1847, 167–81.

the heading 'The Telegraph the Messenger of Death' the following was related there:

On Thursday, the 2nd of October, 1847, a man named Hutchings was to have been executed for murder at Maidstone; but just before the appointed hour, the Government sent a message by the South Eastern Telegraph to stay the execution for two hours. This was virtually looked on as a reprieve; and regarding all the circumstances of the case, everybody in Maidstone considered that the man's sentence had been commuted. The sheriff was busily engaged in examining the exact character of the communication, with a view, no doubt, of satisfying himself that, in acting on the order of the electric telegraph, he was not exceeding his duty. Perplexed as to the proper course to be adopted, the sheriff, in his trepidation, commenced by the electric telegraph a correspondence with the Home Office, to the effect that he waited for further orders.[4]

The Times also reported on the incident. The order to stay the execution for two hours had apparently come directly from the Home Office. 'It seems that the Under Secretary of State had been in conference with a gentleman who had interested himself in the case, and a re-examination of the evidence was humanely determined on; pending the consultation the Under Secretary ordered the temporary respite.'[5] The sheriff at Maidstone Gaol most probably knew about the scarcity of non-circumstantial evidence in the case, which also explains the re-examination of the matter on very short notice. Due to the brevity of the telegraphic message and the lack of background information, he was understandably confused. Only a few years after the opening of the first commercial telegraph lines in the United Kingdom, to receive such a request by telegram was more than just unusual. He was, accordingly, unsure as to the proper course of action. The sheriff found himself in a state of insecurity and abeyance and had no practical information to act on apart from the rudimentary message and, of course, the many connotations that the use of the telegraph in such a case carried. *The Times* article said, 'An extraordinary sensation was created in Maidstone; it was generally believed that the man would not be hanged. The Sheriff delayed the execution the full time of two hours, and did not get the second mandate, ordering the execution, until after the expiration of the time.'[6]

The delay of a second message from the Home Office offering clarification and clear orders had two reasons. First, it 'was in consequence of the wires being engaged in transmitting a message from the Sheriff to the Home-office, so that the Secretary of State's order could not pass through until the Sheriff's conversation had ended'.[7]

[4] New Anecdote Library, ed., *The London Anecdotes*, 14.
[5] 'The Electric Telegraph', *The Times*, 8 October 1847, 8. [6] Ibid., 8. [7] Ibid., 8.

The telegram that occupied the line was probably the sheriff's enquiry as to the next steps. Most of the delay, however, stemmed from another problem. Apparently, the re-examination had not lasted very long and '[s] hortly after the transmission of the order deferring the execution for two hours, a messenger from the Home-office conveyed to the railway the Secretary of State's order that the law was to take its course, and that the culprit was to be at once executed'.[8] The telegraph clerk at the London Bridge terminus of the South Eastern Railway, however, hesitated to forward the message to Maidstone. He was aware that sending the message would lead to John Hutchings's immediate execution and wanted 'to know whether the authority for sending such a message was sufficient'.[9] Both *The Times* article and the anecdote collection state that out of sheer coincidence James McGregor, the chairman of the South Eastern Railway, happened to be at the terminus at precisely the time and was alarmed to the matter:

> The messenger from the Home-office could not be certain that the order for Hutchings's execution was signed by the Home Secretary, although it bore his name, and accordingly Mr. Macgregor [*sic*], with great judgment and humanity, instantly decided that it was not a sufficient authority on such a momentous matter.[10]

McGregor sent James Walter, his chief superintendent, to Downing Street in order to see Sir Denis Le Marchant, the Under Secretary of State for the Home Department. Walter informed Le Marchant

> that the railway company, in being required to deal with such a matter as a man's execution, must have the signature of the order affixed in the presence of the responsible officer; that the second telegraphic message was in fact a death warrant; and that Mr. Walter must have undoubted evidence of its correctness. It is stated that on Mr. Walter drawing the attention of the Secretary of State to the fact that the transmission of such a message was, in effect, to make him the sheriff, the conduct of the railway company in requiring unquestionable evidence and authority was warmly approved. The proper signature was affixed in Mr. Walter's presence, and the telegraph then conveyed to the sad criminal news that the suspension of the awful sentence was only temporary. Hutchings was executed soon after it reached Maidstone.[11]

In the anecdote collection, the exchange between Walter and Le Marchant is described with a similar emphasis on the matter of proof of authority. Here, Walter explained 'that in a matter involving such awful consequences, it became his duty to see the order for execution signed, and that without evidence of this kind the railway authorities would not be

[8] Ibid., 8. [9] *The London Anecdotes*, 14. [10] 'The Electric Telegraph', 8. [11] Ibid., 8.

justified in instructing the sheriff'.[12] It is in this very context that this unedifying episode is particularly revealing. It is an example of the uneasiness, the confusion and the frictions that can at times result from the use of a new technology in a specific setting. Telegraphic communication offered many distinct advantages to its users, most of which had to do with the swiftness of information transmission. Especially in the early days of telegraphy, the use of the new technology, therefore, had the connotation of urgency and exceptional circumstances – particularly if used on comparatively short hauls such as from London to Maidstone. At the same time, if the advantages of swift telegraphic communication were to be realized, the disadvantages of the technology had to be accepted as well. This is how the rationale of a technology unfolds. The telegraph does not lend itself readily to the transmission of substantial background reports nor does it convey any traditional certificate of authority such as a signature or a seal. Accordingly, when the telegraph was used in a situation that required both background and authentication, frictions occurred and new procedures and practices emerged in order to compensate for the frictional loss. In the case at hand, the signing of the message in Walter's presence was such a new procedure of authentication.

This example shows how difficult it could be to integrate new technologies into existing cultural systems. In the case of the telegraph, this was particularly true regarding established systems of information and knowledge. The technology stood right at the interface between these two. The technological rationale of the telegraph, therefore, had a strong bearing on the relation between information and knowledge. In the above case, the lack of necessary proof of authenticity constituted a formidable obstacle in the translation between information and knowledge. This translation process was, however, also affected and transformed by the need for and prevalence of brevity in telegrams. A widely used booklet of guidelines about the composition of telegrams said,

> Naturally, there is a right way and a wrong way of wording telegrams. The right way is economical, the wrong way, wasteful. If the telegram is packed full of unnecessary words, words which might be omitted without impairing the sense of the message, the sender has been guilty of economic waste.[13]

Both the transmission time and the cost of a telegram increased with its length and, therefore, being concise was important. Such rewards for brevity naturally impacted on the language used in telegrams. As was

[12] *The London Anecdotes*, 14.

[13] Nelson E. Ross, *How to Write Telegrams Properly* (Girard, KS: Haldeman-Julius Publications, 1928).

seen in Chapters 1 and 2 on the basis of the telegraphic exchanges at John Pender's telegraphic soirée, frequent users of the new technology adapted quickly to the new requirements. Their messages were short to the point of impoliteness even when limitations of time and money were not given. Of course, such messages were usually not perceived as impolite as everyone involved in sending and receiving telegrams knew about their conversational limitations. Conciseness was considered more important than the established protocol, which was suspended for telegrams.[14]

The need for brevity, together with a certain desire for secrecy, also led to the emergence of elaborate code systems. One widespread way of employing such codes in telegraphic communication could be found in the use of code books. These contained an extensive list of artificial words which usually had very elaborate meanings. In the well-known *ABC Telegraphic Code*, for instance, the word *Aigulet* translated as 'Is not likely to affect you in any manner'[15] and *Bluster* meant 'The boxes were delivered in bad order.'[16] In this way, very complex messages could be packed into only a few words so that transmission was swift and relatively cheap. Especially in international business, the use of such codes was an everyday practice. But the excessive use of codes and abbreviations also fostered misunderstandings either due to mistakes in the encoding and decoding process or due to misspellings in the transmission.[17] However, telegraphic misunderstandings did not only occur when elaborate and very abstract code systems were employed. To a certain degree, they were an everyday feature of telegraphic communication facilitated by the decontextualization and skeletonizing that telegrams had to suffer. While not many concrete examples of such faulty messages survive in the archives,[18] the

[14] Ross's manual of style in telegrams did, however, mention one proposal to further increase brevity that was not adopted: 'A man high in American business life has been quoted as remarking that elimination of the word "please" from all telegrams would save the American public millions of dollars annually. Despite this apparent endorsement of such procedure, however, it is unlikely that the public will lightly relinquish the use of this really valuable word. "Please" is to the language of social and business intercourse what art and music are to everyday, humdrum existence. Fortunes might be saved by discounting the manufacture of musical instruments and by closing the art galleries, but no one thinks of suggesting such a procedure. By all means let us retain the word "please" in our telegraphic correspondence.' Ibid.

[15] William Clauson-Thue, *ABC Universal Commercial Electric Telegraphic Code (Fourth Edition). Specially Adapted for the Use of Financiers, Merchants, Shipowners, Brokers, Agents, &c* (London: Eden Fisher, 1881), 13.

[16] Ibid., 41. [17] See, for instance, Choudhury, 'Of Codes and Coda, 135–6.

[18] Some of the rare examples can be found in the station memoranda circulated at the Eastern's hub station at Porthcurno. In several of these notes, the managing director pointed to the confusion that could arise from confounding, for instance, 'hold' and 'sold' or 'Calicut' and 'Calcutta' and eventually even issued a memo asking Morse operators to stop 'guessing' at what the content of a message could be. Cable & Wireless Archive,

abundance of anecdotes about telegraphic miscommunication is a reliable signifier of their everyday occurrence. For instance, in Chapter 4 reference was made to a popular contemporary story in which a telegram posted as 'I tea with Mrs — in Dover Street. Stay for me' reached its recipient as 'I flee with Mr — to Dover straight. Pray for me.'[19] Another anecdote played on the political ramifications such miscommunications could have. While the historical accuracy of the account is unfortunately impossible to confirm, the anecdote entitled 'A Telegraphic Blunder' shall nevertheless be reproduced in its full extent here:

> During the mania for the dethronement of kings, subsequent to the French Revolution of 1848, when for a time, almost every post brought tidings of 'change perplexing nations,' it was related in the papers of the day that the King of Prussia had abdicated. The news not being confirmed, it was speedily discovered to be erroneous. An ingenious provincial editor thus accounts for the mistake: – The magnetic interpreter at the office of the electric telegraph is a politician, and considerably interested in foreign affairs. Late events have considerably excited him, and news from France has been so extraordinary, that there is not anything which his excited mind does not anticipate on the first word of communication. The telegraph, after due warning, the other day, said, 'The – King – of – Prussia' – The reader turned pale, and thought of the morning paper that had offered the highest price for early and exclusive intelligence. The dial proceeded – 'The – King – of – Prussia – has – gone – to – Pot – ' In another minute, the communication was on its way to the newspaper-office. Not long after, however, the dial was again agitated, and then came 's – dam.' Making it read thus – 'The King of Prussia has gone to Potsdam.'[20]

The problems with authentication, the transformation of the language and the many misunderstandings (substantiated by the abundance of anecdotes concerning this matter) highlight only some of the frictions that occurred with the expansion of use of the telegraph. They are all in one way or another a consequence of the dematerialization of information flows that constitutes the key quality of electric telegraphy, as was argued in Chapter 2. The telegraph encoded information in electric impulses and sent them along a conductor to the receiving apparatus, where these impulses were decoded again. While, of course, many tangible objects such as telegraph cables, telegraph apparatuses or even telegraph operators were involved in this process, the information itself was dematerialized and

DOC/ETC/7/15/4, 'Porthcurno Station Correspondence. Memorandum to Staff Ln Inst', 9 September 1878; Cable & Wireless Archive, DOC/ETC/7/33, 'Letters and Memo's re Traffic Matters. Including Prospectus'es of Several Early Cable Companies. 1883–1896', 15 January 1879; Cable & Wireless Archive, 1998–44, 'Memorandum to Morse Staff', 1879.

[19] 'Tales of the Telegraph', 127. [20] *The London Anecdotes*, 116–17.

could, therefore, be transmitted with opportunities and limitations very different from those of the movement of solid matter. This resulted in a hitherto unimaginable increase of information transmission speed especially over longer distances. The increase in speed has usually been identified as the single most important improvement made possible by telegraphy. In this respect, it is, however, important to distinguish between the absolute and the relative gain in the speed of communication. It is the latter that rendered electric telegraphy so important in nineteenth-century globalization processes. The movements of trains and ships could now be controlled and co-ordinated from the centre. The flow of information had been detached from that of people and objects. This was what made telegraphy so attractive to its users and what let them accept the various disadvantages that non-material communication entailed.

9.2 Structures and use

In its issue of 6 April 1872, *Punch* published a cartoon depicting two British farmers inspecting a telegraph line (Figure 9.1). The caricature by Charles Keene was entitled 'Pursuit o' Knowledge!' and sported the following text:

> *First Agricultural* (quite a year after our branch had been opened) 'What be they Post-es vur, Mas'r Sam'l?'
>
> *Second Ditto* (Wag of the village) 'Why, to carry the Telegraft Woires, Gearge!'
>
> *First Ditto* 'What be the Woires vur, then?'
>
> *Second Ditto* 'What be the Woires Fur? Why, to hold up the Post-es, sart'n'y, Gearge.'!!![21]

About thirty years after the building of the first public telegraph lines in the United Kingdom, the satirical cartoon mainly alluded to the apparent ignorance of the British rural population as to the virtues and the functioning of a modern device such as the telegraph. It thereby served as a reminder of how concentrated the British telegraph system was on the urban centres of the country. But the joke of the 'wag of the village' also illustrates a particular feature of telegraphy that must, indeed, have been confusing for many contemporaries who were less acquainted with the practicalities of electric communication. The infrastructure of the telegraph network (at least in the case of overland lines) was clearly visible to every observer in the form of telegraph poles, wires and – occasionally – stations. The traffic within the network, however, remained invisible to the casual onlooker. Carts on roads or trains on rails could be observed

[21] 'Pursuit o' Knowledge', *Punch, or the London Charivari* 62, no 6 (April 1872), 139.

PURSUIT O' KNOWLEDGE!

First Agricultural (*quite a Year after our Branch had been Opened*). "What be they Post-es vur, Mas'r Sam'l?"

Second Ditto (*Wag of the Village*). "Why, to carry the Telegraft Woires, Gearge!"

First Ditto. "What be the Woires vur, then?"

Second Ditto. "What be the Woires Fur? Why, to hoold up the Post-es, sart'n'y, Gearge." ! ! !

Figure 9.1 *Punch* cartoon showing two British farmers discussing telegraph poles.

moving and using the infrastructures built for their movement. The electric impulses passing through the telegraph wires could not be seen. Even if this was in all likelihood not the intended message of the cartoon, it was the imperceptibility of any actual function of the poles and wires that informed the dialogue of the two farmers. The structures that criss-crossed the country seemed to have no discernible purpose.

Interestingly, the invisibility of the telegraph network use also poses a formidable problem when shifting to the historian's perspective. Information on the traffic occurring in telegraph networks can only rarely be found in the archives. And if such data exists, it usually does not contain information about the traffic on particular routes but only about the throughput of individual network nodes. Despite these difficulties, this study has tried to access and prepare network use data whenever possible and relate it to the corresponding structural data on telegraph networks. This is essential as network use, of course, forms the interface between the actors and the structures in telegraphic communication. Telegraph structures provide the foundations for telegraphic communication. The actors act within a framework defined, among other factors, by these structures. But then structures also represent an abstract ideal that does not have to be realized fully. Therefore only the study of both network structures and network use allows researchers to trace the interplay between people and network technologies.

Structural and use data have been examined in several different contexts in this study. The Bureau international des administrations télégraphiques at irregular intervals compiled lists of existing and working submarine cables – the so-called 'Nomenclatures des cables formant le réseau sous-marin du globe'. These lists allow for an analysis of the growth of the international (mostly submarine) telegraph network that connected the national networks on a global scale. After an experimental phase that lasted roughly until 1865, cable-laying received a boost from the successful working of the Persian Gulf cables and the transatlantic cable. Seen from Europe, telegraphic trunk connections started to head eastwards to South Asia, South East Asia, East Asia and Australia; and westwards to North America. When the pace of expansion started to slow down around 1880, this central east–west axis had been amended with connections to South America and along the African east coast to the Cape Colony. By about 1890, all major world regions had been integrated into the global telegraph network. From then on, the focus of expansion rested primarily on the establishment of cross-connections between the different parts of the system, culminating in the transpacific cables opened in 1902 and 1903. By far the greatest part of the global submarine telegraph network was financed and operated by British firms. The structure and growth patterns of the network therefore to a great extent reflected the changing dynamics of British imperial and business interests. In the concluding section of Chapter 5 I tried to base this observation on a sound empirical footing by correlating the growth of the cable network with the development of British trade with different parts of the world. Altogether, the results of this attempt remained inconclusive. In some cases, a clear connection between the intensity of trade and the connectivity of a place could be revealed. In other cases, however, no such interrelation whatsoever could be detected. At the current state of research, the reasons behind this inconclusiveness can only be guessed at.

Together, the national telegraph networks and the international trunk connections formed the global telegraph network. Due to the non-existence of a coherent data set containing information on the entire global network of the late nineteenth century, several network analyses have been conducted in the framework of this study. They probe the structural condition of the global telegraph system from different vantage points and at different points in time. In combination, their shared results gain validity. Two social network analyses focus exclusively on the structure of the European telegraph network in 1906 and 1923 as information on direct telegraphic circuits is only available for these cases. The results are mutually confirmatory. The European network was very tightly integrated, but only a very small number of important metropolises occupied the central positions in the system. Places such as London, Paris, Berlin and Vienna maintained the highest number of direct connections to other nodes and controlled most of the traffic flow. A number of cities in the Netherlands, Belgium and Switzerland emerged as network nodes of quite some importance. While not in the league of the international metropolises, places such as Amsterdam, Antwerp, Rotterdam, Brussels, Zurich and Basle stood at the centre of a reasonable amount of telegraphic connections. These cities were not particularly well placed as regards control over the information flow, but they were in close contact with the important controlling hubs. These findings emphasize the existence of a number of European communication centres of a second order that merit some more attention in future studies on the subject. Three more network analyses probe the structure of the global telegraph network in the years 1881, 1892 and 1902. Substituting analytical depth for geographical breadth, these studies generally confirm the centrality of cities such as London, Paris and Berlin in the global communication web. And they draw attention to the important gatekeeping role of the nodes at the submarine cable landing sites, such as Cape Canso, Brest, Funchal, Penzance, Lisbon, Gibraltar, Malta and Aden, to name but a few. Eventually, they emphasize the centrality of Europe and the North

American East Coast in the global telegraph network and visualize the above-mentioned east–west submarine cable axis and the nodes therein as the vital backbone of the global communication system.

In two cases, very detailed studies of national telegraph networks were undertaken. Especially in the case of Great Britain, the existence of fairly comprehensive data on both the structure and the traffic of the network made an in-depth analysis possible. It can be shown that the three private company networks evaluated for the year 1868 had very different structural focuses. In all cases, however, the urban areas, and especially the metropolis, London, stood at the centre of attention. It was in these regions that the networks grew extremely tight and cross-linked. Regarding the biggest network, operated by the Electric & International Telegraph Company and the various associated railway companies, basic connectivity to the system was provided in most (but not all, by far) rural areas as this, of course, increased the general attractiveness of the network. Most other companies, however, concentrated either on densely populated regions such as the industrial north of England or London or mainly provided intercity connections. This disproportional concentration on the urban areas of Great Britain was even more pronounced regarding the actual traffic in the system. The pivotal role of London as the central hub of the system became very clearly discernible here. Only 1 per cent – fifteen, in absolute numbers – of all evaluated stations saw 41 per cent of the network traffic in 1868. All of these fifteen nodes were stations in London, Manchester, Liverpool, Glasgow and Southampton. The rural areas produced and received practically no telegraphic traffic at all. A comparison between the British network and the second case study, British India, showed that the respective network structures strongly reflected the different origins of the telegraph systems. While the British network evolved practically without government interference and on private initiative alone, the British Indian network was a state-planned affair. Accordingly, the Indian telegraph system concentrated on regional and superregional centres. It knew no central hub and practically no cross-connections between the main routes of communication. And, even more so than in Great Britain, telegraphic traffic was produced and consumed almost exclusively in the principal cities of the subcontinent.

9.3 Global spaces

In his instructive article on telegraphy and public participation in financial markets, David Hochfelder reproduces a 1903 cartoon showing 'a businessman unwilling to forgo his stock quotations even while on vacation, suggesting the psychological power and ubiquity of the ticker'.[22] The drawing depicts a well-dressed man standing in the spacious garden of his country house holding a newspaper and a ticker tape in his hands. Next to him is a stock ticker apparatus. The lawn is littered with old newspapers and ticker tapes. Sitting in the shadow of a tree, the female secretary is typing on a typewriter, while two telegraph boys are taking a nap and another man is speaking on the telephone which is attached to the tree. The caption reads, 'Mr. A. Merger Hogg is taking a few days' much-needed rest at his country home.'[23] The cartoon alludes to a pair of developments that contemporaries of the late twentieth and early twenty-first century know very well and often think to be exclusive features of life in their historical period: the perceived acceleration of time and the shrinking of global space. These are two widespread notions about life in the so-called information age, but in colloquial usage they are rarely associated with nineteenth-century processes of globalization. And yet the perceptions of actors entangled in these historical globalization processes were strikingly similar, as the cartoon reflects. Contemporary observers found a number of terms to refer to the transformation of both time and space that they witnessed. To some, the changes seemed dramatic enough to justify the claim that currently the 'annihilation of time and space' was taking place.[24] Looking at such processes both in the past and in the present, scholars have introduced such notions as the 'convergence of space and time', 'time–space distanciation', 'space–time compression' or the 'disempowerment of space' to describe the development from an analytical perspective.[25] However, it was argued in Chapter 2 that none of these concepts can do justice to either the historical or the more current transformations in time and space perceptions.

Regarding the alleged annihilation of time by the telegraph, it was demonstrated that the acceleration of information transmission facilitated exactly the opposite development, which could at times culminate in a quasi-essentialization of time. The shrinking of communication times emphasized the importance of even minuscule time differences and

[22] Hochfelder, 'Where the Common People Could Speculate', 337.

[23] Charles Dana Gibson, *The Gibson Book: A Collection of the Published Works of Charles Dana Gibson* (New York, 1970), quoted in Hochfelder, 'Where the Common People Could Speculate', 337.

[24] Morus, 'The Nervous System of Britain', 456–63; Stein, 'Reflections on Time, Time–Space Compression and Technology', 108.

[25] Janelle, 'Spatial Reorganization'; Giddens, *A Contemporary Critique of Historical Materialism. Volume 1: Power, Property and the State*; Giddens, *The Constitution of Society*; Harvey, 'Between Space and Time: Reflections on the Geographical Imagination'; Stein, 'Reflections on Time, Time–Space Compression and Technology', 106; Sonnemann, 'Die Ohnmacht des Raums und der uneingestandene Fehlschlag der Zeitentmachtung', 21; quoted in Läpple, 'Essay über den Raum', 162.

required an even faster and more immediate handling of the transmitted information. The connection of stock exchanges by telegraph can serve as a principal example here. Trade at these exchanges now took place almost in real time and fortunes could be made or lost within hitherto insignificant time spans. Faster international and intercontinental communication also made the standardization of timekeeping a necessity. At the International Meridian Conference, taking place in Washington in 1884, first steps towards a global standardization of time were taken and an international time-zone system was established. Thus differences between various local times (beyond the fixed time-zone difference) were avoided that had hitherto often made it difficult for the participants in a communication process to establish a clear chronology of the exchange. To know when exactly a particular message had been posted was, of course, crucial to actors in global business and international politics alike. This is illustrated by an example related by Deep Kanta Lahiri Choudhury in his work on the 1908 Telegraph General Strike in India. Here, the signallers on strike did forward telegrams but omitted the date and time of their posting, thus rendering many messages practically worthless.[26] Time, therefore, was certainly not annihilated with the emergence of a global telegraph network. The opposite is the case.

And the same can be said for space. Neither geographic nor any other form of space was done away with. It is, of course, true that electric telegraphy loosened the connection between the geographic and the communicational distance between two places. Until information flows were dematerialized, information was commonly transported attached to a material carrier. The duration of the physical movement of such a carrier was usually a function of the geographic distance between origin and destination.[27] With the emergence of a global telegraph network, this association became much less compelling. Even telegrams normally needed more time to travel over longer distances than they needed on shorter hauls, but the correlation between the two factors was distinctly less pronounced than before. Instead, the structure of the network now replaced geographic distance as the principal factor in this context. Communication structure had become the defining moment in a space formed by global communication. Network structures, however, were never even, and thus connectivity was never uniformly distributed in a

[26] Choudhury, 'Treasons of the Clerks', 312; Choudhury, 'India's First Virtual Community and the Telegraph General Strike of 1908', in *Uncovering Labour in Information Revolutions, 1750–2000*, ed. Aad Blok and Gregory Downey (Cambridge: Cambridge University Press, 2003), 66.

[27] It is needless to say that other factors such as topography or network structure played an important role as to how such geographic distances could actually be negotiated.

network. Ergo, the space created on the basis of such structures could not be without its centres and peripheries. Space had not been annihilated; it had merely been amended and transformed, substituting one dividing factor for another.

In order to accommodate these changes conceptually in the perception of both time and space, this study suggests a strictly relative understanding of space. As explained in detail in Chapter 2, space is merely the sum of the relations between its various constituents. And as the relations between different people or objects can be of very different kinds, many different spaces co-exist. Some of these spaces do have a direct relation with time when the kind of relation constituting the space is time-based. If, for instance, the time it takes to communicate between two places is the constituting relation, time becomes a shaping factor for this space. Other spaces have no time component apart from the fact, of course, that they exist in time. From such an analytical perspective, space was, therefore, not annihilated in the globalization processes of the nineteenth century. On the contrary, new spaces were created while existing ones were transformed and reshaped. All these spaces are denser between some of their objects than they are between others. They are uneven. Accordingly, a shrinking of global space can only be diagnosed for some of the many existing spaces, and even then only for parts of them while other parts are – at least in relative terms – further apart. The understanding of space suggested in the present study is actor-centred. It is not an objective concept employing a third-person perspective. It needs an inside perspective. Space becomes discernible only through the eyes of an actor or object within this space. In this actor or object, the many different spaces (in the plural) converge to form an individual perception of space (in the singular).

For many actors involved in nineteenth-century globalization, such a perception of global space was transformed by the availability of telegraphic communication. This is illustrated by several different examples throughout this study. In the good-humoured letter of complaint that opens Chapter 5, the anonymous writer commented on the respective positions of Calcutta and Fernando Po in relation to London.[28] It is very apparent that his perception of global space was influenced less by geographic distances than by questions of communication and economic relevance – both of which depended, among other factors, on the availability of telegraphic facilities. Similar insights can be gained from several of the private letters of Eustace Alban Kenyon (Chapter 6). In a letter to his sister written in Ellore in 1891, he said that after finishing his work and disbanding his

[28] 'The Post Office and the Telegraphs', 6.

working party, he is afraid to receive a telegram ordering him to continue his work immediately.[29] As he travelled from Ellore to Calcutta along existing telegraph lines, he was permanently at his superiors' beck and call, expecting new orders at any time. The closeness, and thus connectedness, to the telegraph network, therefore, had immediate bearings on Kenyon's perceptions of space and time. A similar such instance can be found in the writings of Lieutenant Commander Hellmuth von Mücke (see Chapter 4), who was informed by the British telegraph staff at Direction Island that back in Germany the Iron Cross had been bestowed on him.[30] Several thousand miles removed from his home country, somewhere halfway between Sri Lanka and Australia, in the Indian Ocean, von Mücke happened to be at one of the central global information hubs. The access he gained to the telegraph network courtesy of the British telegraphists made him part of a different space that did not reflect geographic distances but informational density. These examples show how the different spaces relevant to an actor converge in the person in order to form their individual perspective and horizon.

Looking out of London, or more specifically the City of London, the transformation of global communication space throughout the second half of the nineteenth century is traced in Chapter 5 and related to the growth of the global telegraph network. While communication times had been decreasing for some time before as well, this development gained considerable momentum with the expansion of the telegraph network. Especially along the axis from the North American East Coast via London and Europe in general and on to South Asia, communication space started to condense around 1870 at hitherto impossible rates. In the remaining decades of the nineteenth century, this axis was continually expanded both westwards and eastwards. South America and Africa were also connected to the global telegraph network, but their communication with London seems to have been less stable and reliable than that along the east–west axis. By 1900 at the latest, the telegraph network had been developed to a degree where global communication space had been almost completely detached from geographic or navigational space.

9.4 Conclusion and outlook

Summing up, it can safely be said that the growth of a global telegraph network in the nineteenth century had a decisive impact on the event and

[29] Cambridge South Asian Archive, Centre of South Asian Studies, University of Cambridge, Kenyon (E. A.) Papers, Kenyon, 'Letter to Tizie', 9 March 1891.

[30] Mücke, *The 'Ayesha'*, 3–6.

action horizons of the historical actors connected or unconnected to this network. Individual perceptions of global space and time depended heavily on an actor's physical, economic and cultural position in the network. In short, it depended on network access. The structural condition of the network played a significant role in this respect. On the one hand, the structure mirrors – at least to a degree – the purposes and intentions of its creators. On the other hand, it is itself a prerequisite for network access. The structure of the global telegraph network, therefore, had great influence on the shape of global communication space – a form of space that was immensely important for people involved in globalization processes.

This study has for the first time successfully reconstructed the structural conditions of the nineteenth-century telegraph network. It has contrasted these ideal conditions with the actual use of the structures and has identified and analysed numerous examples of the interdependence between structures and actors. The study has also highlighted the cultural context in which the use of telegraphy was embedded. Neither the invention nor the application of the new technology was a neat story of technological advancement and progress. Rather, the telegraph operated within a socially and culturally defined framework with continually shifting boundaries. What was communicated and how was constantly negotiated between the historical actors and the rationale of the telegraph. And these negotiations, as has been seen, were not without friction. In order to grasp analytically the relationship between actors and technologies, structures and networks, the study has also developed a conceptual framework that provides the heuristic tools for this endeavour. It is hoped that these tools will be adopted and adapted for use outside the initial scope of this study.

In other regards, however, the study could only provide a first impetus for further research necessary to advance our understanding of the concrete negotiation processes that local actors faced in nineteenth-century globalization. In this respect, micro-studies are needed that trace the actions and perceptions of a particular actor or a group of actors regarding global telegraphic communication. Partly due to the perceived ephemeral nature of telegrams, only few of them survive in the archives. It should be the task of future studies to locate such surviving collections of telegrams and to work directly with a large number of them in order to create a larger source basis. In this way, questions regarding the actual contents of telegrams can be asked, encompassing, of course, an interest in what kind of information cannot be found in there. Such an increased (also quantitatively increased) focus on the telegrams themselves will also for the first time allow for the reconstruction of the actual routes of communication, as only they contain information on both the sender and the recipient. So far, the statistical information available has only helped to identify structural and use centres and peripheries in communication networks. The principal routes of communication, however, have remained untraceable. Directly working with a larger number of telegrams would also allow for more refined studies of the transformation of language in the age of telegraphy. And it could highlight more instances in which individual historical actors acted against the technological rationale of the telegraph. Eventually, such telegrams will need to be embedded in their cultural context and examined regarding their role in established cultural practices. Here, possible questions could focus on the difficulties arising from the replacement of an established technique (such as letter writing) by a new and largely untested one that provided many new possibilities but on the other hand rendered other practices impossible. Such studies of telegraphy should furthermore be contrasted with research on other historical processes of medial transformation – for instance the transition from parchment to paper or, of course, from analogue to digital communication. It is of central importance that future studies investigating these questions employ neither a purely structural nor a purely cultural-constructivist approach. This book has tried to show that structures and actors can only be understood in correspondence with each other.

This text closes with the reproduction of a telegraphic exchange in a British imperial setting right in the midst of the First World War. The correspondence was related by Lord Edward Cecil in his well-known book *The Leisure of an Egyptian Official*,[31] in which he described his life as an influential office-holder in British-controlled Egypt. The account is amusing and at the same time highlights several of the problems that occur when a new technology, with all its possibilities, is squeezed into an existing administrative system. The new tool is not fit for many purposes. Misunderstandings occur. Much efficiency is lost. In the exchange related by Cecil, these frictions escalate to a point of profound absurdity. Despite the exact dating of the correspondence, it has not been possible to confirm its historical authenticity. The corresponding documents could not be located in the archives. While this is no positive evidence that Cecil made up the exchange of telegrams, this is what we have to assume for the moment. However, we should ask ourselves what practical experiences in the realm of telegraphic communication impressed Cecil to come up with such a fabricated exchange. As this communication stood at the very beginning of the investigations that inform this book and triggered much of the research interest behind the study, it seems only fitting to close with it.

[31] Edward Cecil, *The Leisure of an Egyptian Official* (London: Century Publishing, 1984).

AN OFFICIAL CORRESPONDENCE, 1916

January 1st. F.O. to Cairo.

101. Greek Prime Minister wishes to import grain. Can you do this?

January 4th. Cairo to F.O.

416. Your 101 not understood. Where does he want to import? Is it into Egypt?

January 8th. F.O. to Cairo.

103. Greek Prime Minister wishes to import grain into Greece. Can you do this?

January 11th. Cairo to F.O.

420. Your 103. We have done it several times.

January 12th. F.O. to Cairo.

108. Regret copy mislaid. What is gist of my 103? If possible, repeat.

January 14th. Cairo to F.O.

Regret copy to your 103 mislaid here. Believe it concerned Greek Prime Minister.

January 16th. F.O. to Cairo.

108. Greek Prime Minister wishes to import grain into Greece. Can you do this?

January 19th. Cairo to F.O.

428. Your 108. We have imported grain into Greece several times. It was believed to go to the German Army.

January 22nd. F.O. to Cairo.

112. Your 428. If you import grain to Greek Prime Minister, can you suggest measures to prevent its reaching the German Army? Would Prime Minister's personal guarantee be sufficient?

January 24th. Cairo to F.O.

430. Your 112. Which Prime Minister's guarantee do you suggest? Prefer M. Briand, if still in office.

January 27th. F.O. to Cairo.

114. Your 430. We alluded to Greek Prime Minister. Please let me have your views as soon as possible, as matter is urgent and delay to be avoided.

February 8th. Cairo to F.O.

435. Your 114. To avoid delay, suggest the personal guarantee in writing of Greek Prime Minister countersigned by British Consul at Piræus, with documentary assent of British Government and approval Director General Customs Administration, Alexandria.

February 10th. F.O. to Cairo.

118. Your 435. Have agreed to accept joint and several guarantee of King of Greece, Archimandrite and Greek Prime Minister, countersigned by leading British merchant at Piræus, Mr. Carl Sonnenschein. How much can you send?

February 13th. Cairo to F.O.

440. Your 118. Will reply as soon as possible, but some delay inevitable, as uncertain what Department of the Egyptian Government deals with these questions. Have so far unsuccessfully inquired of Main Drainage, Public Instruction, War Office, Agriculture, Public Works and Wakf. Will wire again later.

March 23rd. Cairo to F.O.

150. Regret delay answering your 118. Matter very complicated. Your 487. Naval authorities object export of seed, as many seeds contain oil suitable for submarines. Can you arrange with Admiralty?

March 26th. F.O. to Cairo.

495. Your 150. Have arranged with Admiralty. Seed will be escorted by two destroyers.

March 28th. F.O. to Cairo.

499. My 495. Have ascertained seed question less important than at first considered. Greek Prime Minister has written explaining seed is needed for his favourite parrot, who is of great age and delicate. Two pounds of selected will be sufficient. Please obtain and send. Admiralty consider escort unnecessary under circumstances.

March 31st. Cairo to F.O.

161. Your 499. Am obtaining seed at once. Can you inform me of approximate size of parrot, as understand from inquiries that there is a direct relation between size of birds and size of food seeds?

April 7th. F.O. to Cairo.

506. Your 161. Stop seed.

April 8th. Cairo to F.O.

165. Your 506. Seed stopped.

April 12th. F.O. to Cairo.

510. Your 165. As information has reached me that the Greek Prime Minister's parrot died last week of indigestion, no further action in matter is necessary.[32]

[32] Ibid., 211–16.

Appendix

Table A.1 *Number and length of government submarine telegraph cables, 1877.*

	Cables	Length of cable		Length of wire	
Government	Abs.	Abs. (km)	%	Abs. (km)	%
Austria	25	160	1.94	179	1.69
British India: Indian Administration	2	111	1.35	111	1.05
British India: Indo-European Tel. Depart.	6	3,187	38.74	3,187	30.05
Denmark	29	188	2.28	620	5.85
Dutch Indies	1	104	1.26	104	0.98
France	26	1,246	15.15	1,246	11.75
Germany	21	276	3.36	494	4.66
Greece	2	6	0.08	6	0.06
Italy	12	404	4.92	410	3.86
Japan	11	133	1.61	133	1.25
Netherlands	18	68	0.83	102	0.96
New Zealand	1	37	0.45	37	0.35
Norway	193	432	5.25	432	4.07
Russia	3	116	1.41	131	1.23
Spain	6	525	6.38	625	5.89
Sweden	4	42	0.51	42	0.39
Turkey	11	265	3.22	270	2.55
United Kingdom	49	927	11.27	2,478	23.36
Total	**420**	**8,227**	**100.00**	**10,607**	**100.00**

Note: Length is given in kilometers here. In the sources, nautical miles are used.
Source: 'Nomenclature des câbles formant le réseau sous-marin du globe dressée d'après des documents officiels par le Bureau international des administrations télégraphiques', *Journal télégraphique* 3, no 29 (1877), 590.

Table A.2 *Number and length of private submarine telegraph cables, 1877.*

		Cables	Length of cable		Length of wire	
Business seat	Company	Abs.	Abs. (km)	%	Abs. (km)	%
	Vereinigte Deutsche Telegraphen-Ges.	2	417	0.38	1,667	1.42
Berlin	Hamburg-Helgolander Telegraphen-Ges.	1	59	0.05	59	0.05
	Berlin total	**3**	**476**	**0.43**	**1,726**	**1.47**
Buenos Aires	River Plate Telegraph Company	1	59	0.05	119	0.10
Copenhagen*	Great-Northern Telegraph Company	13	7,606	6.90	7,814	6.66
La Valetta*	Mediterranean Extension Telegraph Co.	3	367	0.33	367	0.31
Lima*	West Coast of America Telegraph Company	6	3,092	2.80	3,092	2.64
	Submarine Telegraph Company	10	1,483	1.34	6,883	5.87
	Scilly Telegraph Company	1	50	0.05	50	0.04
	Direct Spanish Telegraph Company	3	1,386	1.26	1,386	1.18
	Black-Sea Telegraph Company	1	676	0.61	676	0.58
	Indo-European Telegraph Company	1	15	0.01	44	0.04
	Eastern Telegraph Company	39	26,859	24.35	26,942	22.97
	Eastern Ext. Australasia and China Telegraph Company	9	13,670	12.40	13,670	11.65
London	Anglo-American Telegraph Company	17	22,808	20.68	22,808	19.44
	Direct United States Cable Company	2	5,630	5.11	5,630	4.80

Table A.2 *(cont'd)*

Business seat	Company	Cables	Length of cable		Length of wire	
		Abs.	Abs. (km)	%	Abs. (km)	%
	Brazilian Submarine Telegraph Company	3	7,160	6.49	7,160	6.10
	Cuba Submarine Telegraph Company	3	1,741	1.58	1,741	1.48
	West India and Panama Telegraph Company	19	7,352	6.67	7,352	6.27
	Central American Telegraph Company	2	2,000	1.81	2,000	1.70
	Western and Brazilian Telegraph Company	9	6,945	6.30	6,945	5.92
	London total	**119**	**97,774**	**88.66**	**103,288**	**88.05**
New York	International Ocean Telegraph Company	4	907	0.82	907	0.77
	Total	**149**	**110,282**	**100.00**	**117,312**	**100.00**

Notes: Length is given in kilometers here. In the sources, nautical miles are used.

* And an additional business seat in London.

Source: 'Nomenclature des câbles formant le réseau sous-marin du globe dressée d'après des documents officiels par le Bureau international des administrations télégraphiques', *Journal télégraphique* 3, no 29 (1877), 576–81.

Table A.3 *Average communication times in days between London and ports in selected world regions, 1850–1900.*

Region		1850		1860			1870			1880			1890			1900		
		Av	Med	Av	Med	AAG Av	Av	Med	AAG Av	Av	Med	AAG Av	Av	Med	AAG Av	Av	Med	AAG Av
	Atlantic Coast	6.5	6.0	5.5	4.0	1.6	7.7	7.0	− 3.4	2.8	2.0	9.5	1.2	1.0	8.2	1.8	2.0	− 4.3
	North Sea Coast	6.2	4.0	3.4	3.0	5.8	3.8	3.0	− 1.1	n.a.	n.a.	n.a.	n.a.	n.a.	n.a.	1.7	2.0	n.a.
Europe	Baltic Sea	9.8	9.0	5.5	5.0	5.6	5.5	5.5	0.1	2.7	3.0	6.8	n.a.	n.a.	n.a.	2.3	1.0	n.a.
	W Mediterranean	11.1	11.0	6.7	6.5	4.9	7.9	7.0	− 1.6	2.2	2.0	11.9	1.5	1.0	4.0	1.8	1.0	− 1.8
	E Mediterranean	16.6	17.0	9.9	11.0	5.0	8.6	8.0	1.4	2.7	3.0	10.8	1.4	1.0	6.7	1.9	2.0	− 3.5
	Black Sea	22.6	17.0	n.a.	n.a.	n.a.	n.a.	n.a.	n.a.	3.5	3.0	n.a.	n.a.	n.a.	n.a.	1.5	1.0	n.a.
	US East Coast	17.3	16.0	15.0	14.0	1.4	8.1	3.0	6.0	2.2	2.0	12.2	1.7	1.0	2.8	2.0	2.0	− 1.8
North America	Canada East Coast	20.1	19.0	16.3	14.0	2.1	13.2	15.0	2.0	3.1	3.0	13.4	2.5	2.0	2.3	2.6	2.0	− 0.4
	US West Coast	n.a.	n.a.	n.a.	n.a.	n.a.	7.4	3.0	n.a.	2.8	2.0	9.1	2.3	2.0	2.0	2.4	2.0	− 0.2
Caribbean		29,2	28.0	20.3	20.0	3.6	19.6	22.0	0.3	3.1	2.0	16.7	3.4	3.0	− 0.8	2.8	2.5	1.9
Central America	East Coast	n.a.	n.a.	n.a.	n.a.	n.a.	34.0	35.0	n.a.	n.a.	n.a.	n.a.	n.a.	n.a.	n.a.	2.5	3.0	n.a.
South America	South East Coast	49.3	52.5	45.0	36.0	0.9	30.5	34.0	3.8	4.3	4.0	17.9	6.4	4.0	− 4.1	3.1	3.0	6.8
	North East Coast	35.1	37.0	24.6	22.0	3.5	28.1	28.0	− 1.3	20.0	23.5	3.3	3.7	3.5	15.5	3.8	4.0	− 0.2
	South West Coast	n.a.	n.a.	n.a.	n.a.	n.a.	42.5	42.5	n.a.	n.a.	n.a.	n.a.	5.8	3.0	n.a.	3.1	3.0	6.1
	North West Coast	n.a.	n.a.	n.a.	n.a.	n.a.	n.a.	n.a.	n.a.	n.a.	n.a.	n.a.	6.9	4.0	n.a.	n.a.	n.a.	n.a.
Arabian Peninsula		n.a.	n.a.	n.a.	n.a.	n.a.	7.9	3.0	n.a.	1.8	1.5	13.6	1.7	2.0	0.5	1.2	1.0	3.9
	West	n.a.	n.a.	n.a.	n.a.	n.a.	11.0	3.0	n.a.	2.1	2.0	15.5	1.4	1.0	4.1	2.3	1.5	− 5.2
South Asia	East	44.6	43.0	43.0	37.0	0.4	9.6	4.0	13.9	1.8	2.0	15.2	1.4	1.0	2.6	1.8	2.0	− 2.2

Table A.3 *(cont'd)*

Region		1850		1860			1870			1880			1890			1900		
		Av	Med	Av	Med	AAG Av	Av	Med	AAG Av	Av	Med	AAG Av	Av	Med	AAG Av	Av	Med	AAG Av
South East Asia	West	55.6	52.0	n.a.	n.a.	n.a.	22.0	18.0	n.a.	4.8	2.0	14.0	1.8	2.0	9.5	2.2	2.0	− 2.3
	East	n.a.	n.a.	n.a.	n.a.	n.a.	43.3	47.5	n.a.	n.a.	n.a.	n.a.	3.0	2.0	n.a.	2.3	2.0	2.5
East Asia	China	63.9	61.0	56.2	54.0	1.3	34.0	27.5	4.9	2.2	2.0	23.9	1.5	1.0	4.1	2.2	2.0	− 4.0
	Japan	n.a.	n.a.	n.a.	n.a.	n.a.	53.6	52.5	n.a.	n.a.	n.a.	n.a.	2.4	2.0	n.a.	2.9	2.0	− 2.0
	South	64.0	65.0	47.2	41.5	3.0	43.8	41.5	0.7	3.3	2.0	22.8	5.0	2.0	− 4.3	2.9	3.0	5.3
Africa	North West Coast	52.8	52.5	35.0	33.0	4.0	n.a.	n.a.	n.a.	n.a.	n.a.	n.a.	n.a.	n.a.	n.a.	3.5	4.0	n.a.
	Canaries & Madeira	n.a.	n.a.	25.4	13.0	n.a.	16.2	14.0	4.4	2.0	2.0	18.9	2.2	2.0	− 0.7	2.3	2.0	− 0.5
	St Helena & Ascension	50.0	49.0	34.0	32.0	3.8	n.a.	n.a.	n.a.	n.a.	n.a.	n.a.	n.a.	n.a.	n.a.	2.5	2.0	n.a.
Australia	East Coast	114.9	114.0	53.8	53.5	7.3	41.1	40.0	2.7	2.5	2.0	24.3	1.8	1.0	3.5	1.8	1.0	0.1
	West Coast	n.a.	n.a.	n.a.	n.a.	n.a.	n.a.	n.a.	n.a.	n.a.	n.a.	n.a.	2.0	2.0	n.a.	1.0	1.0	6.7
	New Zealand	n.a.	n.a.	n.a.	n.a.	n.a.	n.a.	n.a.	n.a.	1.8	2.0	n.a.	1.3	1.0	3.4	1.0	1.0	2.2
Indian Ocean		70.6	68.0	n.a.	n.a.	n.a.	n.a.	n.a.	n.a.	n.a.	n.a.	n.a.	16.0	16.0	n.a.	n.a.	n.a.	n.a.

Source: 'Ship News', 'Latest Shipping Intelligence' and 'Mail & Shipping Intelligence', in *The Times* of London. Samples for the years 1850, 1860, 1870, 1880, 1890 and 1900.

Table A.4 *Annual growth of British trade with selected world regions, 1863–71.*

Country or colony			1863	1864	1865	1866	1867	1868	1869	1870	1871
Foreign											
Japan	Exp.	Grwth.	105	29	76	23	28	− 4	0	8	4
		Abs.	0.13	0.67	1.65	1.56	1.69	1.22	1.60	1.78	1.75
	Imp.	Grwth.	− 7	− 6	− 7	− 28	− 45	− 33	− 16	− 15	51
		Abs.	1.28	1.42	0.61	0.27	0.32	0.18	0.17	0.10	0.11
Portugal: Madeira	Exp.	Grwth.	2	15	− 3	6	2	4	1	8	85
		Abs.	0.07	0.09	0.07	0.09	0.08	0.08	0.09	0.09	0.09
	Imp.	Grwth.	− 4	− 11	22	24	21	17	24	12	4
		Abs.	0.02	0.02	0.02	0.03	0.05	0.05	0.05	0.06	0.09
United States of America	Exp.	Grwth.	19	21	− 2	13	7	3	2	13	4
		Abs.	19.70	20.17	25.17	31.84	24.12	23.80	26.79	31.31	38.69
	Imp.	Grwth.	− 5	− 2	10	16	14	14	6	6	11
		Abs.	19.57	17.92	21.62	46.85	41.05	43.06	42.57	49.80	61.13
British possessions											
Arabia: Aden	Exp.	Grwth.	32	25	8	8	15	31	− 12	23	8
		Abs.	0.05	0.03	0.05	0.06	0.08	0.08	0.06	0.11	0.07
	Imp.	Grwth.	0	6	− 1	− 91	238	198	697	23	73
		Abs.	0.00	0.00	0.00	0.00	0.00	0.00	0.00	0.00	0.03
Australia	Exp.	Grwth.	12	4	− 5	7	− 2	− 9	0	10	3
		Abs.	13.64	12.92	14.17	14.62	10.36	13.06	14.38	10.74	11.11
	Imp.	Grwth.	6	11	13	10	4	6	5	4	7
		Abs.	7.16	10.04	10.27	11.42	12.88	12.57	12.15	14.07	14.52
British Guiana	Exp.	Grwth.	− 1	8	6	9	− 7	4	− 3	11	1
		Abs.	0.58	0.89	0.81	0.79	0.68	0.75	0.73	0.93	0.89
	Imp.	Grwth.	0	− 1	− 1	2	− 8	− 3	− 4	− 2	3
		Abs.	1.51	1.91	1.71	1.69	1.50	1.65	1.21	1.47	1.41

Table A.4 *(cont'd)*

Country or colony			1863	1864	1865	1866	1867	1868	1869	1870	1871
British North America	Exp.	Grwth.	6	20	0	4	3	6	− 1	11	5
		Abs.	5.53	6.27	5.72	7.70	6.73	5.57	5.91	7.58	9.11
	Imp.	Grwth.	− 4	− 5	− 5	− 4	3	6	7	6	12
		Abs.	8.17	6.85	6.35	6.87	6.77	6.77	7.73	8.52	9.29
British West India Islands	Exp.	Grwth.	3	10	− 7	− 7	− 11	6	− 4	13	4
		Abs.	2.98	2.94	2.13	2.13	1.84	2.01	2.06	2.66	2.41
	Imp.	Grwth.	− 1	2	− 1	− 5	− 9	− 3	4	3	− 1
		Abs.	6.27	7.16	5.16	4.64	4.37	4.92	4.78	4.47	5.57
Hong Kong	Exp.	Grwth.	3	14	7	9	9	23	− 7	11	11
		Abs.	1.56	1.77	1.59	2.47	2.56	2.31	2.25	3.57	3.02
	Imp.	Grwth.	− 6	3	1	− 19	− 60	− 28	7	56	26
		Abs.	1.29	2.88	0.77	0.28	0.18	0.24	0.28	0.28	0.37
India (excl. transit through Egypt)	Exp.	Grwth.	8	8	7	− 1	− 2	6	− 4	− 3	− 1
		Abs.	20.82	20.75	18.83	20.67	22.85	22.27	18.51	20.09	19.01
	Imp.	Grwth.	− 1	8	− 4	− 9	− 10	− 8	− 4	6	0
		Abs.	48.43	52.30	37.40	36.90	25.49	30.07	33.25	25.09	30.74
Straits Settlements	Exp.	Grwth.	23	14	9	0	17	9	− 7	10	1
		Abs.	1.52	1.23	1.51	2.04	2.13	1.63	1.83	2.41	2.07
	Imp.	Grwth.	1	− 3	− 9	2	3	4	11	19	11
		Abs.	1.83	2.07	2.16	1.61	1.43	2.05	2.31	2.55	2.70

Source: House of Commons Parliamentary Papers, 3723, 'Annual Statement of the Trade and Navigation of the United Kingdom with Foreign Countries and British Possessions in the Year 1865', 1866; House of Commons Parliamentary Papers, C. 437, 'Annual Statement of the Trade and Navigation of the United Kingdom with Foreign Countries and British Possessions in the Year 1870', 1871.

Table A.4 *Annual growth of British trade with selected world regions, 1872–80.*

Country or colony			1872	1873	1874	1875	1876	1877	1878	1879	1880
Foreign											
	Exp.	Grwth.	0	19	− 9	9	9	13	11	1	5
Japan		Abs.	2.15	1.88	1.36	2.59	2.19	2.46	2.91	3.00	3.81
	Imp.	Grwth.	36	18	30	23	2	− 4	5	1	0
		Abs.	0.18	0.56	0.57	0.38	0.66	0.73	0.63	0.45	0.53
	Exp.	Grwth.	− 18	29	25	− 1	− 36	− 30	− 6	− 8	6
Portugal: Madeira		Abs.	0.11	0.43	0.28	0.11	0.11	0.10	0.08	0.09	0.09
	Imp.	Grwth.	5	4	2	− 4	− 1	− 2	2	− 5	4
		Abs.	0.08	0.07	0.07	0.07	0.10	0.07	0.07	0.06	0.08
	Exp.	Grwth.	11	− 1	− 8	− 16	− 17	− 5	5	4	20
United States of America		Abs.	45.91	36.70	32.24	25.06	20.23	19.89	17.53	25.52	37.95
	Imp.	Grwth.	11	6	4	7	5	5	9	6	2
		Abs.	54.66	71.47	73.90	69.59	75.90	77.83	89.15	91.82	107.08
British possessions											
	Exp.	Grwth.	64	− 17	49	8	2	2	− 31	26	2
Arabia: Aden		Abs.	0.11	0.14	0.35	0.20	0.19	0.15	0.13	0.34	0.14
	Imp.	Grwth.	309	106	43	29	16	2	11	9	3
		Abs.	0.01	0.03	0.19	0.27	0.25	0.22	0.18	0.21	0.39
	Exp.	Grwth.	5	16	12	10	0	− 3	1	5	2
Australia		Abs.	15.48	19.23	20.67	21.22	19.47	21.50	21.53	17.96	18.75
	Imp.	Grwth.	9	8	9	6	4	3	5	4	3
		Abs.	15.63	17.26	18.55	20.56	21.96	21.73	20.86	21.96	25.66
	Exp.	Grwth.	14	− 7	10	− 4	− 2	− 7	4	− 10	6
British Guiana		Abs.	1.00	0.91	1.13	0.85	0.97	0.97	0.84	0.72	0.86
	Imp.	Grwth.	9	6	13	10	1	3	2	− 5	1
		Abs.	1.36	1.84	1.85	1.91	2.50	2.28	1.93	2.21	2.12

Table A.4 *(cont'd)*

Country or colony			1872	1873	1874	1875	1876	1877	1878	1879	1880
British North America	Exp.	Grwth.	20	3	− 1	− 4	− 7	− 8	− 1	− 4	5
		Abs.	11.32	9.37	10.21	9.68	8.03	8.26	7.03	6.12	8.52
	Imp.	Grwth.	9	3	3	5	− 4	− 3	6	0	− 3
		Abs.	9.13	11.73	11.86	10.21	11.02	12.04	9.53	10.45	13.39
British West India Islands	Exp.	Grwth.	4	0	− 2	− 3	− 6	− 1	− 2	− 3	5
		Abs.	2.69	2.67	2.40	2.42	2.23	2.16	2.05	2.22	2.38
	Imp.	Grwth.	− 2	4	− 5	− 2	− 2	2	− 4	− 3	− 2
		Abs.	5.08	4.64	4.34	5.41	4.40	4.65	4.22	4.86	4.45
Hong Kong	Exp.	Grwth.	9	0	2	8	− 6	− 1	0	− 2	− 2
		Abs.	3.10	3.61	3.91	3.84	3.26	3.65	3.04	3.13	3.97
	Imp.	Grwth.	18	28	25	19	7	9	1	− 5	− 7
		Abs.	0.94	0.78	0.75	1.15	1.36	1.90	1.17	1.33	1.25
India (excl. of transit through Egypt)	Exp.	Grwth.	5	3	5	10	− 1	− 1	8	− 2	5
		Abs.	19.49	22.31	25.43	25.60	23.68	26.62	24.66	22.71	32.03
	Imp.	Grwth.	− 1	3	0	− 2	− 2	− 4	0	2	6
		Abs.	33.68	29.89	31.20	30.14	30.03	31.22	27.47	24.70	30.12
Straits Settlements	Exp.	Grwth.	16	− 10	8	− 1	− 7	− 1	1	5	− 2
		Abs.	2.53	2.17	2.81	2.09	2.07	2.41	1.88	2.18	2.46
	Imp.	Grwth.	2	4	0	− 5	− 6	0	4	8	12
		Abs.	3.51	3.46	2.60	3.15	2.64	2.72	2.54	2.57	3.70

Note: Growth in % based on five-year moving averages; absolute numbers are in £million.

Sources (contd): House of Commons Parliamentary Papers, C. 1571, 'Annual Statement of the Trade of the United Kingdom with Foreign Countries and British Possessions for the Year 1875', 1876; House of Commons Parliamentary Papers, C. 2920, 'Annual Statement of the Trade of the United Kingdom with Foreign Countries and British Possessions for the Year 1880', 1881.

Table A.5 *Freeman degree centrality in the European Telegraph Network, 1906.*

	Degree	
No.	Node	Degree
1	London (Londres)	45
2	Berlin	37
3	Wien (Vienne)	34
4	Paris	33
5	Hamburg	20
6	Budapest	18
7	Milano (Milan)	16
8	Anvers	15
9	Cöln (Cologne)	15
10	Amsterdam	14
11	Basel (Bâle)	13
12	München (Munich)	13
13	Göteborg (Gothembourg)	12
14	Zágráb	12
15	Frankfurt/Main	12
16	Sarajevo	11
17	Krakau (Cracovie)	11
18	Bucuresti (Bucarest)	10
19	Emden	10
20	Roma (Rome)	10
21	Innsbruck	10
22	Kattowitz	9
23	Triest	9
24	Arendal	9
25	Bruxelles	9
26	Fredericia	9
27	Kjöbenhavn (Copenhague)	9
28	Genève	9
29	Rotterdam	9
30	Marseilles	8
31	Gibraltar	8
32	Öresund	8
33	Sofia	8
34	Varsovie	8
35	Breslau	8
36	Czernowitz	8
37	Le Havre	8
38	Prag (Prague)	8

Note: All placenames reflect the language, spelling etc. in the original source.
Source: ITU Archives, Bureau international des administrations télégraphiques, 'Liste des communications télégraphiques internationales directes du régime européen. Annexe à la carte des communications télégraphiques du régime européen – édition 1906', 1906.

Table A.6 *Freeman betweenness centrality in the European telegraph network, 1906.*

		Betweenness	
No.	Node	Betweenness	nBetweenness
1	Wien (Vienne)	44471.262	22.374
2	Berlin	34883.98	17.55
3	Paris	25068.402	12.612
4	London (Londres)	17776.352	8.943
5	Budapest	14206.766	7.148
6	Breslau	12474.142	6.276
7	Milano (Milan)	10688.358	5.377
8	München (Munich)	9858.125	4.96
9	Sarajevo	9577.891	4.819
10	Dresden	8623.071	4.338
11	Königsberg	7632.583	3.84
12	Hamburg	7542.363	3.795
13	Krakau (Cracovie)	7369.183	3.707
14	Cöln (Cologne)	7009.58	3.527
15	Varsovie	6393.587	3.217
16	Bucuresti (Bucarest)	6276.779	3.158
17	Emden	5570.503	2.803
18	Genève	5382.297	2.708
19	Innsbruck	5378.987	2.706
20	Metz	5302.785	2.668
21	Bordeaux	5140.167	2.586
22	Prag (Prague)	5046.236	2.539
23	Danzig	4780	2.405
24	Vigo	4731.53	2.38
25	Chur (Coire)	4581.939	2.305
26	St. Pétersbourg	4558.744	2.294
27	Roma (Rome)	4462.905	2.245
28	Czernowitz	4343	2.185
29	Constantinople	4335.837	2.181
30	Strassburg	4326.333	2.177
31	Alexandrow	4326	2.176
32	Oppeln	4311	2.169
33	Marseilles	3981.664	2.003
34	Anvers	3914.618	1.969
35	Basel (Bâle)	3864.857	1.944
36	Ratibor	3847	1.935
37	Splügen	3840	1.932
38	Riga	3789.529	1.907
39	Sofia	3761.565	1.892
40	Salzburg	3684.057	1.853

Note: All placenames reflect the language, spelling etc. in the original source.
Source: ITU Archives, Bureau international des administrations télégraphiques, 'Liste des communications télégraphiques internationales directes du régime européen. Annexe à la carte des communications télégraphiques du régime européen – édition 1906', 1906.

Table A.7 *Bonacich eigenvector in the European telegraph network, 1906.*

		Eigenvector	
No.	Node	Eigenvector	nEigenvector
1	London (Londres)	− 0.445	− 62.929
2	Berlin	− 0.342	− 48.352
3	Paris	− 0.296	− 41.929
4	Wien (Vienne)	− 0.222	− 31.424
5	Hamburg	− 0.214	− 30.238
6	Budapest	− 0.207	− 29.218
7	Amsterdam	− 0.203	− 28.746
8	Frankfurt/Main	− 0.189	− 26.773
9	Cöln (Cologne)	− 0.174	− 24.601
10	Anvers	− 0.172	− 24.353
11	Milano (Milan)	− 0.171	− 24.158
12	Rotterdam	− 0.168	− 23.716
13	Emden	− 0.151	− 21.289
14	Roma (Rome)	− 0.15	− 21.237
15	Bruxelles	− 0.142	− 20.07
16	Zurich	− 0.121	− 17.087
17	Basel (Bâle)	− 0.116	− 16.438
18	Genova (Gênes)	− 0.111	− 15.706
19	Le Havre	− 0.1	− 14.195
20	Bucuresti (Bucarest)	− 0.099	− 13.962
21	München (Munich)	− 0.093	− 13.177
22	Varsovie	− 0.087	− 12.286
23	Liverpool	− 0.083	− 11.799
24	Krakau (Cracovie)	− 0.081	− 11.437
25	Odessa	− 0.077	− 10.933
26	Prag (Prague)	− 0.075	− 10.61
27	Göteborg (Gothembourg)	− 0.072	− 10.232
28	Arendal	− 0.072	− 10.226
29	Innsbruck	− 0.062	− 8.736
30	Lille	− 0.061	− 8.567
31	Marseilles	− 0.061	− 8.566
32	Bordeaux	− 0.059	− 8.329
33	Ostende	− 0.056	− 7.922
34	Lyon	− 0.055	− 7.775
35	Bremen (Brême)	− 0.055	− 7.773
36	Strassburg	− 0.053	− 7.479
37	Stockholm	− 0.049	− 6.972
38	Zágráb	− 0.046	− 6.494
39	Lowestoft	− 0.045	− 6.327
40	Constantinople	− 0.044	− 6.2

Note: All placenames reflect the language, spelling etc. in the original source.
Source: ITU Archives, Bureau international des administrations télégraphiques, 'Liste des communications télégraphiques internationales directes du régime européen. Annexe à la carte des communications télégraphiques du régime européen – édition 1906', 1906.

Table A.8 *Freeman degree centrality in the European telegraph network, 1923.*

Degree		
No.	Node	Degree
1	London	69
2	Paris	58
3	Berlin	50
4	Wien	41
5	Budapest	30
6	Amsterdam	23
7	Danzig	21
8	Hamburg	21
9	Praha	20
10	Anvers	20
11	Bruxelles	20
12	Rotterdam	18
13	Malta	17
14	Frankfurt	16
15	Marseilles	15
16	Milano	14
17	Gibraltar	14
18	Warschau	14
19	München	14
20	Zurich	13
21	Basel	12
22	Trieste	11
23	Köln	10
24	Penzance	10
25	Waterville	10
26	Fredericia	10
27	Düsseldorf	9
28	Katowice	9
29	Beograd	9
30	Königsberg	9
31	Thessaloniki	9
32	Carcavelos	9
33	Kjöbenhavn	9
34	Breslau	9
35	Strasbourg	9
36	Stockholm	9
37	Riga	9

Note: All placenames reflect the language, spelling etc. in the original source.

Source: ITU Archives, Bureau international de l'Union télégraphique, 'Carte schématique des grandes communications télégraphiques internationales du régime européen', 1923.

Table A.9 *Freeman betweenness centrality in the European telegraph network, 1923.*

		Betweenness	
No.	Node	Betweenness	nBetweenness
1	Berlin	8434.273	20.408
2	Paris	8296.616	20.075
3	London	8204.229	19.852
4	Wien	4983.795	12.059
5	Praha	3462.52	8.378
6	Budapest	3381.937	8.183
7	Hamburg	2319.863	5.613
8	Fredericia	2079.51	5.032
9	Danzig	2018.054	4.883
10	Marseilles	1998.448	4.836
11	Gibraltar	1956.103	4.733
12	Malta	1716.444	4.153
13	Roma	1659.672	4.016
14	Beograd	1599.634	3.871
15	Thessaloniki	1459	3.53
16	München	1282.23	3.103
17	Dresden	1271.256	3.076
18	Le Havre	1268.666	3.07
19	Fayal	1210	2.928
20	Brest	1197.683	2.898
21	Milano	1159.954	2.807
22	Trieste	1159.318	2.805
23	Zakynthos	1134.396	2.745
24	Basel	1114.059	2.696
25	Katowice	1081.076	2.616
26	Warschau	1011.425	2.447
27	Rotterdam	1006.408	2.435
28	Zurich	997.097	2.413
29	Bucuresti	984.375	2.382
30	Penzance	977	2.364
31	Riga	933.599	2.259
32	Madrid	886.583	2.145
33	Breslau	761.386	1.842
34	Geneve	756.304	1.83
35	Waterville	753.317	1.823
36	Flensburg	735	1.778
37	Bruxelles	655.575	1.586
38	Stockholm	557.446	1.349
39	Bern	540.178	1.307
40	Carcavelos	538.759	1.304

Note: All placenames reflect the language, spelling etc. in the original source.
Source: ITU Archives, Bureau international de l'Union télégraphique, 'Carte schématique des grandes communications télégraphiques internationales du régime européen', 1923.

Table A.10 *Bonacich eigenvector in the European telegraph network, 1923.*

Eigenvector		
No.	Node	nEigenvector
1	Paris	− 49.974
2	Berlin	− 45.439
3	London	− 39.414
4	Wien	− 34.743
5	Anvers	− 30.808
6	Hamburg	− 28.881
7	Praha	− 28.817
8	Bruxelles	− 28.446
9	Amsterdam	− 28.032
10	Frankfurt	− 27.411
11	Rotterdam	− 26.077
12	Zurich	− 22.689
13	Köln	− 22.237
14	Budapest	− 20.883
15	München	− 20.063
16	Düsseldorf	− 19.722
17	Milano	− 17.978
18	Basel	− 16.885
19	Warschau	− 14.671
20	Strasbourg	− 13.958
21	Fredericia	− 12.938
22	Leipzig	− 12.741
23	Gravenhage	− 11.898
24	Bern	− 11.838
25	Saarbrücken	− 11.615
26	Le Havre	− 11.338
27	Danzig	− 10.713
28	Kristiania	− 10.077
29	Trieste	− 10.012
30	Bucuresti	− 10.005
31	Beograd	− 9.791
32	Bratislava	− 9.629
33	Kjöbenhavn	− 9.627
34	Roma	− 9.588
35	Brno	− 9.51
36	Zagreb	− 9.407
37	Dresden	− 9.258
38	Innsbruck	− 9.143
39	Stockholm	− 8.714
40	Bremen	− 8.564

Note: All placenames reflect the language, spelling etc. in the original source.
Source: ITU Archives, Bureau international de l'Union télégraphique, 'Carte schématique des grandes communications télégraphiques internationales du régime européen', 1923.

Table A.11 *Freeman degree in the global telegraph network, 1881, 1892 and 1902.*

1881		1892		1902	
Node	Degree	Node	Degree	Node	Degree
Paris	14	London	15	Wien (Vienne)	16
London	12	Paris	14	London	15
Wien	12	Wien (Vienne)	14	Paris	14
Marseilles	11	Berlin	13	Budapest	14
Berlin	10	Cape Canso (CAN)	11	Cape Canso (CAN)	14
Lyon	10	Marseilles	10	Berlin	13
St. Louis (US)	9	Lyon	10	Dublin	12
Cincinnati (US)	9	Dublin	10	St. Louis (US)	12
St. Pierre (CAN)	8	Budapest	10	Marseilles	12
Bruxelles	8	Cincinnati (US)	9	Gibraltar	11
Halle (GER)	8	Breslau (GER)	9	New York	11
Chicago	7	Memphis	9	Rio de Janeiro	11
La Havane	7	Lublin (RUS)	9	Pernambuco (BRA)	11
Newcastle (UK)	7	Lisboa	9	Breslau (GER)	10
München	7	Malte	9	Lublin (RUS)	10
Basel	7	St. Louis (US)	9	Lisboa	10
Dublin	7	Saratow (RUS)	9	Malte	10
Mexico	7	Halle (GER)	9	Mariinsk (RUS)	10
Madras	7	La Havane	9	Chicago	10
Alger (ALG)	7	Varsovie (RUS)	9	Montreal (CAN)	10
St. Paul (US)	7			Minsk (RUS)	10
Constantinople	7			Lyon	10
Malte	7				
Stockholm	7				

Note: All placenames reflect the language, spelling etc. in the original source.
If the location of a place could be unclear, country code has been added in brackets.
Source: ITU Archives, Bureau international des administrations télégraphiques, 'Carte des communications télégraphiques du régime extra-européen', 1881; ITU Archives, Bureau international des administrations télégraphiques, 'Carte des communications télégraphiques de régime extra-européen', 1892; ITU Archives, Bureau international des administrations télégraphiques, 'Cartes des communications télégraphiques du régime extra-européen', 1902

Table A.12 *Freeman betweenness in the global telegraph network, 1881, 1892 and 1902.*

1881		1892		1902	
Node	nBetweenn.	Node	nBetweenn.	Node	nBetweenn.
Alexandrie	30.509	Lisboa	36.145	Aden	44.794
Lisboa	28.479	Malte	34.406	Malte	44.221
Malte	27.435	Alexandrie	31.715	Alexandrie	42.256
Brest (F)	23.553	Gibraltar	30.834	Suez	39.691
St. Pierre (CAN)	23.451	Cape Canso (CAN)	26.119	Gibraltar	38.969
Gibraltar	23.203	Penzance (UK)	24.779	Penzance (UK)	38.19
Penzance (UK)	22.761	New York	23.989	Bombay	31.334
Boston	22.309	Wladikawkas (RUS)	21.043	Cape Canso (CAN)	27.632
Le Caire	21.599	Petrowsk (RUS)	20.901	Poona (IND)	23.494
Tantah (EGY)	21.136	Khabarowka (RUS)	20.654	Dhond (IND)	22.793
Aden	20.701	Puerto Grande (VER)	19.361	Sholapur (IND)	22.769
Suez	19.985	Funchal (MAD)	18.677	Penang	22.323
Bombay	17.476	Pernambuco (BRA)	18.463	Madras	22.173
Albany (US)	16.082	Lattàquié (TUR)	17.964	Shahabad (IND)	22
Exeter (UK)	12.094	Alep (TUR)	17.886	New York	21.584
London	12.039	Tiflis (RUS)	17.834	Guntakal (IND)	21.427
Cape Cod (US)	10.808	Diarbekir (TUR)	17.426	Singapore	20.891
Duxbury (US)	10.808	Urfa (TUR)	17.195	Zanzibar (TAN)	20.578
Funchal (MAD)	10.731	Larnaca (TUR)	17.074	Kantara (EGY)	20.167
Puerto Grande (VER)	10.66	Nagasaki	16.959	Le Caire	19.912

Notes: All placenames reflect the language, spelling etc. in the original source.
If the location of a place is unclear, the country code has been added in brackets.
Source: ITU Archives, Bureau international des administrations télégraphiques, 'Carte des communications télégraphiques du régime extra-européen', 1881; ITU Archives, Bureau international des administrations télégraphiques, 'Carte des communications télégraphiques de régime extra-européen', 1892; ITU Archives, Bureau international des administrations télégraphiques, 'Cartes des communications télégraphiques du régime extra-européen', 1902

Table A.13 *External messages sent, received and transmitted, 1860. Indexed with selected European average = 100.*

	Sent		Received		Transmitted	
1860	Abs.	p. pop. (indexed)	Abs.	p. pop. (indexed)	Abs.	p. pop. (indexed)
Austria–Hungary	95,356	45	84,123	37	42,754	17
Belgium	45,278	159	49,921	161	50,404	153
Denmark	23,651	151	23,865	140	23,441	129
France	151,885	70	204,743	87	52,288	21
Germany*	183,456	81	196,361	80	193,031	74
Netherlands	59,348	295	65,700	300	90,319	388
Norway	12,526	140	13,408	137	0	0
Portugal	8,513	39	7,711	33	0	0
Romania†	n.a.	n.a.	n.a.	n.a.	n.a.	n.a.
Russia	49,131	10	49,340	10	0	0
Spain	18,264	19	19,650	19	9,532	9
Sweden	18,362	79	19,679	78	15,146	56
Switzerland‡	n.a.	n.a.	n.a.	n.a.	26.967	154

Notes:
* 'Germany' means Bavaria, Baden, North German Confederation and Württemberg. Therefore the figures for external messages are inflated.
† Not included in Selected European Average in all categories of external messages.
‡ Not included in Selected European Average in external messages sent and received.
Source: ITU Archives. Bureau International des Administrations Télégraphiques, 'Statistique générale de la télégraphie dans les différents pays de l'ancien continent', 1849–1869.

Table A.14 *Average annual growth rates of external traffic, 1860–1910.*

	1860–70			1870–80			1880–90			1890–1900			1900–10		
1860–1910	St.	Rec.	Trs.	St.	Rec.	Trs.	St.	Rec.	Trs.	St.	Rec.	Trs.	St.	Rec.	Trs.
Austria	n.a.	n.a.	n.a.	5	7	−5	5	7	−5	5	7	−5	4	4	7
Belgium	19	18	11	7	8	9	7	8	9	7	8	9	4	4	2
British India	n.a.	n.a.	n.a.	13	13	36	13	13	36	13	13	36	8	8	0
Denmark	15	14	17	5	7	11	5	7	11	5	7	11	5	5	4
France	18	14	n.a.	7	6	n.a.	7	6	n.a.	7	6	n.a.	3	3	5
Germany*	22	23	15	3	2	−3	3	2	−3	3	2	−3	4	5	7
Great Britain and Ireland	n.a.	n.a.	n.a.	n.a.	n.a.	n.a.	n.a.	n.a.	n.a.	n.a.	n.a.	n.a.	4	4	2
Hungary	n.a.	n.a.	n.a.	24	24	n.a.	24	24	n.a.	24	24	n.a.	6	6	−1
Italy	n.a.	n.a.	n.a.	6	6	2	6	6	2	6	6	2	4	3	1
Japan	n.a.	n.a.	n.a.	n.a.	n.a.	n.a.	n.a.	n.a.	n.a.	n.a.	n.a.	n.a.	8	10	n.a.
Luxembourg	n.a.	n.a.	n.a.	n.a.	n.a.	n.a.	n.a.	n.a.	n.a.	n.a.	n.a.	n.a.	2	2	n.a.
Netherlands	16	15	9	6	7	−1	6	7	−1	6	7	−1	4	4	1
Norway	20	21	n.a.	6	7	−17	6	7	−17	6	7	−17	n.a.	n.a.	n.a.
Portugal	12	13	n.a.	10	11	22	10	11	22	10	11	22	n.a.	n.a.	n.a.
Romania	n.a.	n.a.	n.a.	5	5	−2	5	5	−2	5	5	−2	6	6	17
Russia	16	16	n.a.	9	8	8	9	8	8	9	8	8	7	8	10
Spain	15	16	19	n.a.	n.a.	n.a.	n.a.	n.a.	n.a.	n.a.	n.a.	n.a.	6	5	5
Sweden	17	17	12	7	7	7	7	7	7	7	7	7	4	4	9
Switzerland	n.a.	n.a.	15	7	7	9	7	7	9	7	7	9	5	5	6

Note: * In 1860, ‘Germany’ means Bavaria, Baden, the North German Confederation and Württemberg.
Source: ITU Archives, Bureau international des administrations télégraphiques, ‘Statistique générale de la télégraphie dans les différents pays de l’ancien continent’, 1849–1869; ITU Archives, Bureau international des administrations télégraphiques, ‘Statistique générale de la télégraphie dans les différents pays de l’ancien continent’, 1870; ITU Archives, Bureau international des administrations télégraphiques, ‘Statistique générale de la télégraphie’, 1880; ITU Archives, Bureau international des administrations télégraphiques, ‘Statistique générale de la télégraphie’, 1890; ITU Archives, Bureau international des administrations télégraphiques, ‘Statistique générale de la télégraphie’, 1900; ITU Archives, Bureau international de l’Union télégraphique, ‘Statistique générale de la télégraphie’, 1910.

Table A.15 *External messages sent, received and transmitted, 1870. Indexed with selected European average = 100.*

	Sent		Received		Transmitted	
1870	Abs.	p. pop. (indexed)	Abs.	p. pop. (indexed)	Abs.	p. pop. (indexed)
Austria	472,471	64	435,275	58	638,177	124
Belgium	248,961	151	258,485	154	147,848	129
Denmark	94,413	155	92,307	149	108,071	255
France	791,842	61	765,356	58	n.a.	n.a.
Germany	1,394,626	108	1,573,620	120	759,154	84
Great Britain and Ireland*	n.a.	n.a.	n.a.	n.a.	n.a.	n.a.
Greece	6,477	13	9,727	19	0	0
Hungary	63,449	13	67,133	14	0	0
Italy	263,596	32	280,307	33	181,550	32
Netherlands	251,191	201	264,878	209	216,072	249
Norway	78,377	127	89,549	143	18,332	43
Portugal	25,780	20	25,742	19	15,944	18
Romania	73,885	43	71,737	41	14,240	12
Russia	216,104	8	226,371	8	31,016	2
Spain	77,013	13	83,967	14	53,626	14
Sweden	86,522	61	90,753	63	47,050	48
Switzerland	197,032	230	190,620	219	109,554	184
Outside Europe						
British India	29,792	0	28,129	0	4,408	0

Note: * Railway lines not included. Figure for size of British population given in the 'Statistique générale' of 1870 was clearly incorrect. Figure from 1871 has been used.

Source: ITU Archives, Bureau international des administrations télégraphiques, 'Statistique générale de la télégraphie dans les différents pays de l'ancien continent', 1870.

Table A.16 *External messages sent, received and transmitted, 1880. Indexed with selected European average = 100.*

	Sent		Received		Transmitted	
1880	Abs.	p. pop. (indexed)	Abs.	p. pop. (indexed)	Abs.	p. pop. (indexed)
Austria	772,924	55	848,124	57	378,324	40
Belgium	500,282	142	535,383	145	356,724	150
Bosnia–Herzegovina	2,680	4	2,387	3	0	0
Bulgaria	23,464	18	22,268	17	3,023	4
Denmark	156,817	125	176,164	133	311,413	365
France	1,582,234	67	1,413,256	57	397,840	25
Germany	1,909,400	66	1,996,454	66	569,006	29
Great Britain and Ireland	1,907,168	87	1,642,997	71	356,746	24
Greece	29,398	28	33,428	30	40,581	56
Hungary	555,799	57	599,056	58	99,981	15
Italy	474,260	26	487,383	26	211,980	17
Luxembourg	23,095	177	21,163	154	14	0
Netherlands	460,087	178	518,249	191	189,032	108
Norway	144,171	121	169,484	136	2,682	3
Portugal	68,649	25	70,402	25	114,366	62
Romania	120,060	37	120,471	36	11,867	5

Russia	496,955	9	500,126	8	68,346	2
Serbia	27,382	25	27,896	25	1,289	2
Spain*	n.a.	n.a.	n.a.	n.a.	n.a.	n.a.
Sweden	170,705	59	186,411	61	93,108	47
Switzerland	383,247	213	370,640	196	262,333	215
Outside Europe						
Algeria	137,431	63	120,512	52	0	0
Brazil	7,275	1	1,928	0	880	0
British India	103,832	1	95,266	1	98,655	1
Cochinchina	4,867	5	4,925	5	0	0
Dutch Indies	16,016	1	15,265	1	26,837	3
Egypt	9,764	3	7,811	2	1,899	1
Japan	12,040	1	12,115	1	0	0
New Zealand	13,227	43	11,265	35	0	0
Victoria	4,271	8	5,232	9	0	0
Western Union	n.a.	n.a.	n.a.	n.a.	n.a.	n.a.

Note: * Not included in selected European average in all categories of external message.

Source: ITU Archives, Bureau international des administrations télégraphiques, 'Statistique générale de la télégraphie', 1880.

Table A.17 *External messages sent, received and transmitted, 1890. Indexed with selected European average = 100.*

	Sent		Received		Transmitted	
1890	Abs.	p. pop. (indexed)	Abs.	p. pop. (indexed)	Abs.	p. pop. (indexed)
Austria	1,733,394	79	1,831,080	76	743,832	47
Belgium	952,846	169	1,030,827	167	667,499	165
Bosnia–Herzegovina	54,679	44	47,302	35	67,572	76
Bulgaria	65,157	22	54,050	17	40,544	19
Denmark	254,450	127	297,930	135	396,019	274
France	2,783,148	79	2,631,246	68	1,265,848	50
Germany	3,401,681	75	3,790,641	76	1,015,153	31
Great Britain and Ireland	3,667,054	105	3,208,299	84	755,576	30
Greece	76,410	37	81,090	36	118,545	80
Hungary	783,159	49	855,931	49	260,932	23
Italy	708,122	26	792,931	26	125,560	6
Luxembourg	36,034	185	33,294	156	8	0
Netherlands	708,938	168	887,550	192	503,912	166
Norway	240,480	130	283,446	140	1	0
Portugal	144,368	36	155,390	36	373,733	131
Romania	183,324	39	161,214	32	43,948	13
Russia	695,836	7	745,679	7	153,197	2
Serbia	46,869	23	55,985	26	19,989	14

Spain	485,460	30	506,250	28	106,678	9
Sweden	286,551	65	316,966	65	190,352	60
Switzerland	591,196	220	628,457	213	510,473	263
Outside Europe						
Algeria	35,079	10	25,713	7	0	0
British India	158,865	1	140,115	1	190,656	1
Cochinchina	7,963	3	9,238	3	9,578	6
Cuba	33,639	22	33,043	20	58,508	54
Dutch Indies*	31,110	1	32,195	1	65,541	3
Japan	n.a.	n.a.	n.a.	n.a.	n.a.	n.a.
New Zealand	21,272	35	26,005	38	0	0
Philippines	9,837	2	11,448	2	0	0
Porto-Rico	6,776	9	5,411	7	4,442	8
South Australia	3,903	13	6,526	19	56,637	257
The Senegal	3,430	n.a.	2,561	n.a.	0	n.a.
Tunisia	92,198	67	83,122	55	0	0
Victoria	n.a.	n.a.	n.a.	n.a.	n.a.	n.a.
Western Union	n.a.	n.a.	n.a.	n.a.	n.a.	n.a.

Notes: All placenames reflect the language, spelling etc. in the original source.

* Railway and private messages not included.

Source: ITU Archives, Bureau international des administrations télégraphiques, 'Statistique générale de la télégraphie', 1890.

Table A.18 *External messages sent, received and transmitted, 1900. Indexed with selected European average = 100.*

	Sent		Received		Transmitted	
1900	Abs.	p. pop. (indexed)	Abs.	p. pop. (indexed)	Abs.	p. pop. (indexed)
Austria	2,501,944	80	2,639,280	78	1,240,092	63
Belgium	1,393,943	171	1,414,296	161	550,338	108
Bosnia–Herzegovina	124,548	66	106,353	52	137,292	117
Bulgaria	67,151	15	69,459	14	45,335	16
Denmark	394,799	134	460,641	145	648,771	353
France	3,373,740	73	3,291,671	66	1,122,610	39
Germany	4,882,643	72	5,956,613	82	1,442,997	34
Great Britain and Ireland	5,177,861	105	4,423,287	83	1,111,318	36
Hungary	1,252,352	60	1,212,938	54	363,168	28
Italy	1,052,907	28	1,190,083	29	102,234	4
Luxembourg	70,761	249	61,451	201	0	0
Montenegro	9,754	27	9,383	24	1,607	7
Netherlands	1,033,939	166	1,233,552	184	326,471	84
Norway	389,130	151	446,143	160	1	0
Portugal	196,345	32	214,102	33	665,166	176
Romania	275,748	43	242,627	35	59,565	15
Russia	1,182,719	8	1,255,660	8	213,222	2
Spain	502,192	23	561,201	24	114,250	8

Sweden	417,051	68	472,165	71	364.255	95
Switzerland	835,941	210	858,430	200	677.817	273
Outside Europe						
Algeria	35,044	6	24,505	4	0	0
Angola	127	0	151	0	0	0
Brazil	21,394	1	21,214	1	1,170	0
British India	206,939	1	210,236	1	482,802	2
Cochinchina	29,228	6	28,176	5	14,534	5
Dutch Indies	51,994	1	52,310	1	188,874	7
Japan	234,284	4	238,416	4	3,972	0
Natal	30,658	43	34,124	44	0	0
New Caledonia	2,730	37	2,940	37	0	0
New South Wales	491,301	299	506,787	286	161,187	157
New Zealand	63,309	64	59,267	56	0	0
Portuguese Indies	2,958	4	4,702	6	0	0
The Senegal	7,129	5	2,413	2	0	0
Tunisia	205,714	114	190,144	98	0	0
Victoria	n.a.	n.a.	n.a.	n.a.	n.a.	n.a.
Western Union	n.a.	n.a.	n.a.	n.a.	n.a.	n.a.

Source: ITU Archives, Bureau international des administrations télégraphiques, 'Statistique générale de la télégraphie', 1900.

Table A.19 *External messages sent, received and transmitted, 1910. Indexed with selected European average = 100.*

	Sent		Received		Transmitted	
1910	Abs.	p. pop. (indexed)	Abs.	p. pop. (indexed)	Abs.	p. pop. (indexed)
Austria	3,758,858	80	3,820,084	74	2,456,173	77
Belgium	2,001,353	162	2,085,957	154	672,940	80
Bosnia–Herzegovina	216,300	84	204,608	72	160,745	91
Bulgaria	174,489	25	174,626	22	16,848	3
Denmark	635,957	140	749,733	151	987,994	320
France	4,684,052	72	4,614,939	65	1,776,729	40
Germany	7,506,290	70	9,578,470	82	2,967,970	41
Great Britain and Ireland	7,569,000	102	6,691,000	83	1,325,000	26
Greece	107,805	25	197,804	42	117,503	40
Hungary	2,266,528	66	2,130,548	57	324,952	14
Italy	1,534,563	28	1,602,952	27	116,725	3
Luxembourg	87,286	203	77,056	164	0	0
Netherlands	1,472,431	152	1,795,004	169	364,109	55
Romania	479,109	42	452,306	36	282,525	36
Russia	2,253,883	9	2,618,527	10	574,861	3
Serbia	109,128	23	113,105	22	155,885	48
Spain	911,748	30	941,075	28	178,247	9
Sweden	636,385	70	732,016	74	872,841	141

Switzerland	1,341,951	217	1,421,426	210	1,212,070	288
Outside Europe						
Algeria	71,078	8	50,575	5	0	0
Bolivia*	n.a.	n.a.	n.a.	n.a.	n.a.	n.a.
British India	465,860	1	446,133	1	505,101	1
Cochinchina	36,056	1	35,171	1	34,302	1
Dutch Indies	121,013	2	123,511	2	75,143	2
Japan	520,901	6	594,384	7	0	0
New South Wales	932,841	345	965,869	326	386,216	210
New Zealand	122,860	70	115,282	60	0	0
Queensland	11,898	12	9,699	9	191,729	286
Siam	37,616	3	50,781	4	63,024	8
South Australia	16,615	25	18,208	25	223,260	487
Tasmania	151,290	491	164,017	486	0	0
The Senegal	22,450	12	15,170	7	0	0
Tunisia	309,994	98	293,387	85	0	0
Union of South Africa	134,328	15	118,955	12	16,582	3
Victoria	814,718	381	921,834	394	125,408	86
Western Australia	17,220	36	13,162	25	0	0

Note: * Data for 1910 not available. Data for 1909 has been used.

Source: ITU Archives, Bureau international de l'Union télégraphique, 'Statistique générale de la télégraphie', 1910.

Table A.20 *Freeman degree centrality in the Electric, Magnetic and UK telegraph networks, 1868.*

Electric			Magnetic			UK		
Station	Degree	Index	Station	Degree	Index	Station	Degree	Index
LDN Central	343	100	Glasgow Town	66	100	LDN Gresham House	48	100
LDN Shoreditch	131	38	Manchester Chief	66	100	Leeds	37	77
Derby Railway	129	38	LDN Threadneedle St	62	94	Manchester Main	36	75
York Town	118	34	Manchester Hunts Bank	60	91	Newcastle Queen St	34	71
Manchester Central	115	34	Bolton	50	76	Gloucester	19	40
York Railway	108	31	Preston	50	76	Middlesbro	18	38
Birmingham Central	93	27	Leeds Town	43	65	Nottingham	18	38
Peterboro GNR	91	27	Liverpool Central	41	62	Liverpool Central	17	35
Southampton	91	27	Manchester Victoria	40	61	Glasgow Exchg. Sq	17	35
Carlisle Citadel Station	89	26	Darlington Railway	39	59	Sunderland	16	33
Newcastle Town	87	25	Wakefield Railway	35	53	Birmingham	16	33
Rugby	87	25	Salford	34	52	Cardiff Bute Street	15	31
Lancaster	86	25	Newcastle Town	33	50	Wakefield	14	29
Manchester London Road	84	24	Mirfield	33	50	Oxford	13	27
Perth	81	24	Birmingham New St	32	48	Stockton-on-Tees	13	27
LDN Stratford	79	23	Sowerby Bridge	32	48	West Hartlepool	13	27
Leicester Rail	79	23	Todmorden	32	48	Hull Town	13	27
Birmingham New St Rlwy.	77	22	Liverpool Tithebarn St	31	47	Edinboro	13	27

Bletchley	77	22	Glasgow Railway	31	47	Hartlepool Town	13	27
Norwich Thorp	77	22	Carlisle Town	30	45	Hanley	13	27
Retford	70	20	Blackburn Railway	29	44	Thirsk	12	25
Inverness	68	20	Shildon	28	42	Bristol	12	25
Lowestoft	68	20	Blue Pits	27	41	Leamington	12	25
Newcastle Railway	67	20	Accrington Railway	27	41	Sheffield	12	25
Glasgow Buchanan Street	64	19	Stockton-on-Tees Rlwy.	26	39	Exeter	11	23
Motherwell	63	18	Middlesbro Railway	25	38	Ashton-under-Lyne	11	23
Cambridge Railway	62	18	Wigan	25	38	Uxbridge	10	21
Hitchin	61	18	Stockton-on-Tees Town	23	35	Deddington	10	21
LDN Waterloo	61	18	Preston-on-Tees Jctn.	23	35	Huddersfield	10	21
Hull Railway	60	17	Paisley	22	33	Woodstock	10	21
Cardiff Docks	58	17	Rochdale Railway	21	32	Wheatley	10	21
Carnforth	58	17	Ripon	21	32	Newport Dock Street	10	21
Bristol Exchange	56	16	Arthington	20	30	Warrington	10	21
Leamside	56	16	Leeds Railway	20	30	Tetsworth	10	21
Milford Junction	56	16	Ormskirk	19	29	Dundee Cowgate	10	21
Stirling	55	16	Doncaster	19	29	Southam	10	21
Bishopstoke	54	16	Ayr	19	29	Wycombe	10	21
Carstairs	54	16	Castle Douglas	19	29	Runcorn	10	21
Hull Town	54	16	Halifax	19	29	Banbury	10	21
Normanton Junction	54	16				Wolverhampton	9	19
Norwich Town	54	16						

Source: see Map 7.1

Table A.21 *Freeman betweenness centrality in the Electric, Magnetic and UK telegraph networks, 1868.*

Electric			Magnetic			UK		
Station	Betwn.	Index	Station	Betwn.	Index	Station	Betwn.	Index
LDN Central	494,398	100	Leeds Town	23,602	100	LDN Gresham House	6,376	100
Manchester Central	148,063	30	Glasgow Town	19,909	84	Newcastle Queen St	2,341	37
Edinboro Commercial	90,941	18	LDN Threadneedle St	17,872	76	Gloucester	2,009	32
York Town	80,992	16	Manchester Chief	17,467	74	Glasgow Exchange Sq	1,899	30
Birmingham Central	74,510	15	Liverpool Central	13,130	56	Leeds	1,852	29
Glasgow Royal Exchange	68,205	14	Bolton	9,327	40	Manchester Main	1,669	26
Southampton	62,257	13	Darlington Railway	9,173	39	Bristol	1,621	25
Liverpool Central	45,505	9	Newcastle Town	8,088	34	Birmingham	1,137	18
Perth	32,545	7	Shildon	6,275	27	Liverpool Central	1,029	16
Derby Railway	32,008	6	Preston	6,057	26	Dundee Cowgate	731	11
Lancaster	31,239	6	Carlisle Town	5,699	24	Edinboro	629	10
Newcastle Town	30,857	6	Dumfries Town	5,280	22	Hull Town	467	7
Inverness	29,756	6	Wakefield Railway	4,792	20	Plymouth Town	426	7
Peterboro GNR	28,112	6	Darlington Town	4,452	19	Nottingham	403	6
Carlisle Citadel Station	26,619	5	Manchester Hunts Bank	4,416	19	Sunderland	319	5
Leeds Town	23,303	5	Doncaster	4,338	18	Cardiff Bute Street	299	5
Bristol Exchange	21,975	4	Stranraer	4,217	18	Exeter	298	5

Cardiff Docks	21,309	4	West Hartlepool Town	3,646	15	Swansea Central	288	5
Worcester Town	21,309	4	Birmingham New Street	3,523	15	Oxford	174	3
Plymouth Town	20,993	4	Sowerby Bridge	3,263	14	Newport Dock Street	151	2
Stirling	20,959	4	Sunderland	3,164	13	Aberdeen Unicn St	148	2
Hull Town	19,617	4	Wigan	3,159	13	Kingsbridge	148	2
Oswestry	17,597	4	Castle Douglas	3,127	13	Hanley	139	2
Leicester Rail	16,764	3	Middlesbro Railway	3,127	13	Sheffield	87	1
Aberdeen Commercial	16,638	3	Stockton-on-Tees Rlwy.	3,041	13	Leamington	82	1
Gloucester Rail	16,504	3	Leeds Railway	2,993	13	Runcorn	51	1
Rugby	16,344	3	Todmorden	2,883	12	Warrington	51	1
Penrith	16,090	3	Liverpool Tithebarn St	2,782	12	LDN Stock Exchange	49	1
Whitehaven	15,608	3	Halifax	2,687	11	Ashton-under-Lyne	35	1
Crewe	15,079	3	Huddersfield Railway	2,322	10	Hawick	34	1

Source: see Map 7.1

Table A.22 *Bonacich eigenvector centrality in the Electric, Magnetic and UK telegraph networks, 1868.*

Electric			Magnetic			UK		
Station	Eigenvector	Index	Station	Eigenvector	Index	Station	Eigenvector	Index
LDN Central	73,107	100	Manchester Hunts Bank	56,728	100	Leeds	53,242	100
LDN Shoreditch	63,948	87	Manchester Victoria	46,156	81	LDN Gresham House	45,952	86
Lowestoft	49,892	68	Bolton	34,222	60	Manchester Main	44,04	83
Colchester Town	47,991	66	Manchester Chief	33,204	59	Newcastle Queen St	38,375	72
Amsterdam	33,494	46	Salford	32,811	58	Middlesbro	33,891	64
LDN Stratford	21,175	29	Blue Pits	28,184	50	Sunderland	33,29	63
Emden	16,747	23	Preston	28,002	49	Hartlepool Town	27,767	52
Chelmsford	14,659	20	Sowerby Bridge	27,879	49	Stockton-on-Tees	27,767	52
Colchester Railway	13,994	19	Todmorden	27,122	48	West Hartlepool	27,767	52
Ipswich Town	13,589	19	Mirfield	25,897	46	Wakefield	25,097	47
Broxbourne	13,447	18	Wakefield Railway	25,352	45	Nottingham	24,552	46
Norwich Thorp	12,371	17	Liverpool Central	23,218	41	Thirsk	23,933	45
Witham	11,591	16	Rochdale Railway	19,191	34	Hull Town	21,916	41
Manningtree	11,473	16	Leeds Town	18,73	33	Huddersfield	18,92	36
Ipswich Railway	10,423	14	Blackburn Railway	18,182	32	Sheffield	18,066	34
Waltham	9,512	13	Liverpool Tithebarn St	17,057	30	Liverpool Central	17,344	33
Liverpool Central	9,12	12	Fleetwood	15,795	28	Bradford Market St	16,174	30

Bishopstortford	8,51	12	Blackpool	15,148	27	Ashton-under-Lyne	13,741	26
Bristol Exchange	8,35	11	Wigan	14,526	26	Bradford Wells Street	13,559	25
Birmingham Central	7,997	11	Miles Platting	14,174	25	Glasgow Exchange Sq	13,454	25
Ely	7,98	11	Glasgow Town	13,282	23	Birmingham	13,353	25
Manchester Central	7,89	11	Normanton	13,109	23	South Shields	12,726	24
Norwich Town	7,822	11	LDN Threadneedle St	12,979	23	Hunslet	10,998	21
LDN Euston	7,808	11	Halifax	11,812	21	Halifax	9,177	17
LDN Waterloo	7,491	10	Pendleton	11,704	21	Rochdale	9,177	17
Southampton	7,486	10	Dewsbury	11,231	20	Leamington	9,058	17
Cambridge Rail	7,286	10	Accrington Railway	11,138	20	Edinboro	8,674	16
Cardiff Docks	7,145	10	Bury East Lanc	10,875	19	Borobridge	8,65	16
Rugby	6,256	9	Darwen	10,721	19	Knaresboro	8,65	16
LDN Dalston	6,192	8	Blackburn Town	10,481	18	Oxford	8,65	16
Wolverton	6,016	8	Radcliffe	10,31	18	Wetherby	8,65	16

Note: All placenames reflect the language, spelling etc. in the original source.

Source: see Map 7.1

Table A.23 *Top 50 British cities according to weekly messages handled, 1868.*

		Messages	
No	Station	Abs.	%
1	London	87,049	31.1
2	Manchester	29,568	10.6
3	Liverpool	23,639	8.4
4	Glasgow	12,851	4.6
5	Birmingham	7,585	2.7
6	Newcastle	5,197	1.9
7	Southampton	4,788	1.7
8	Bristol	4,591	1.6
9	Hull	4,514	1.6
10	Edinborough	4,229	1.5
11	Cardiff	3,840	1.4
12	Bradford	2,259	0.8
13	Plymouth	2,147	0.8
14	Brighton	2,109	0.8
15	York	1,902	0.7
16	Leith	1,669	0.6
17	Epsom	1,657	0.6
18	Sheffield	1,543	0.6
19	Dundee	1,523	0.5
20	Sunderland	1,398	0.5
21	Carlisle	1,368	0.5
22	Nottingham	1,365	0.5
23	Aberdeen	1,324	0.5
24	Exeter	1,293	0.5
25	Gloucester	1,255	0.4
26	Newport	1,184	0.4
27	Swansea	1,077	0.4
28	Shrewsbury	1,070	0.4
29	Newmarket	1,050	0.4
30	Derby	1,012	0.4
31	Hereford	1,000	0.4
32	Greenock	975	0.3
33	Wakefield	970	0.3
34	Peterborough	917	0.3
35	Blackburn	848	0.3
36	Grimsby	817	0.3
37	Halifax	802	0.3
38	Leicester	768	0.3
39	Middlesbrough	768	0.3
40	Norwich	760	0.3
41	Huddersfield	755	0.3
42	Chester	751	0.3

Table A.23 (*cont'd*)

No	Station	Messages	
		Abs.	%
43	Portsmouth	723	0.3
44	Worcester	676	0.2
45	Rochdale	666	0.2
46	Yarmouth	629	0.2
47	West Hartlepool	600	0.2
48	Ipswich	576	0.2
49	Wolverhampton	563	0.2
50	Oldham	549	0.2

Source: see Map 7.1; and British Telecom Archives, POST 82/303, 'Telegraphs. Return of Persons Employed; Wages; Average Weekly Messages 1869–1872'.

Table A.24 *Telegraphic traffic growth in the Indian Telegraph Department network, 1866–7 to 1900–1.*

	Paid inland messages			
	Abs.			
Year	State	Private	Total	Growth in %
1866–7	29,444	239,422	268,866	
1867–8	41,306	269,638	310,944	15.7
1868–9	40,615	333,856	374,471	20.4
1869–70	39,403	415,215	454,618	21.4
1870–1	37,606	472,735	510,341	12.3
1871–2	52,512	523,023	575,535	12.8
1872–3	57,448	548,846	606,294	5.3
1873–4	65,339	592,243	657,582	8.5
1874–5	77,226	658,522	735,748	11.9
1875–6	89,111	707,136	796,247	8.2
1876–7	99,003	874,348	973,351	22.2
1877–8	123,834	1,046,120	1,169,954	20.2
1878–9	209,544	964,307	1,173,851	0.3
1879–80	290,622	1,037,330	1,327,952	13.1
1880–1	313,648	1,032,710	1,346,358	1.4
1881–2	245,836	1,035,137	1,280,973	− 4.9
1882–3	253,731	1,189,437	1,443,168	12.7
1883–4	226,840	1,236,140	1,462,980	1.4
1884–5	286,966	1,364,814	1,651,780	12.9
1885–6	382,732	1,527,990	1,910,722	15.7
1886–7	452,277	1,683,758	2,136,035	11.8
1887–8	537,193	1,860,390	2,397,583	12.2
1888–9	441,375	2,115,863	2,557,238	6.7
1889–90	493,442	2,191,645	2,685,087	5.0
1890–1	552,436	2,365,028	2,917,464	8.7
1891–2	661,904	2,627,408	3,289,312	12.7
1892–3	604,124	2,837,513	3,441,637	4.6
1893–4	598,226	3,031,993	3,630,219	5.5
1894–5	585,571	3,231,555	3,817,126	5.1
1895–6	603,366	3,491,571	4,094,937	7.3
1896–7	599,890	3,786,938	4,386,828	7.1
1897–8	860,382	4,107,270	4,967,652	13.2
1898–9	659,304	4,036,510	4,695,814	− 5.5
1899–00	702,055	4,700,753	5,402,808	15.1
1900–1	805,216	4,744,179	5,549,395	2.7

Source: British Library, Oriental Collections, IOR/V/24/4288, 'Administration Report of the Indian Telegraph Department for 1900–1901', 1901, Appendix D, 8–9.

Table A.25 *Freeman Degree centrality in the Indian Telegraph Department network, 1871–2.*

No.	Place	Degree	nDegree
1	Calcutta	48	5.993
2	Bombay	35	4.37
3	Madras	34	4.245
4	Barrackpore	33	4.12
5	Agra	31	3.87
6	Allahabad	30	3.745
7	Raneegunge	30	3.745
8	Nynee	26	3.246
9	Belgaum	25	3.121
10	Lahore	25	3.121
11	Kurrachee	24	2.996
12	Sealdah	24	2.996
13	Callian	23	2.871
14	Kureli	22	2.747
15	Paumben	22	2.747

Note: All places spelled as in the original source.
Source: British Library, Oriental Collections, IOR/V/24/4284, 'Administration Report of the Indian Telegraph Department for 1871–72', 1872, Appendices, Annexure III.

Table A.26 *Freeman betweenness centrality in the Indian Telegraph Department network, 1871–2.*

No.	Place	Between	nBetween
1	Allahabad	8,127.841	22.888
2	Agra	6,386.478	17.985
3	Bombay	6,175.882	17.391
4	Madras	6,117.602	17.227
5	Calcutta	4,793.806	13.499
6	Lahore	4,513.806	12.711
7	Kurrachee	3,260.259	9.181
8	Sealdah	2,990	8.42
9	Paumben	2,716.618	7.65
10	Talla Manaar	2,590.099	7.294
11	Toondla	1,878.26	5.289
12	Galle	1,818.266	5.12
13	Allyghur	1,618.931	4.559
14	Poona	1,597.794	4.499
15	Raneegunge	1,581.23	4.453

Note: All places spelled as in the original source.
Source: British Library, Oriental Collections, IOR/V/24/4284, 'Administration Report of the Indian Telegraph Department for 1871–72', 1872, Appendices, Annexure III.

Table A.27 *Number of messages sent, received and transmitted at Indian Telegraph Department stations, 1871–2.*

Messages sent			Messages received			Messages transmitted		
Division	Offices	Abs.	Division	Offices	Abs.	Division	Offices	Abs.
Bombay	Bombay	120,638	Bombay	Bombay	88,579	Bengal	Agra	82,488
Bengal	Calcutta	89,171	Bengal	Calcutta	83,582	Bombay	Bombay	71,015
Madras	Madras	48,310	Madras	Madras	39,823	Madras	Madras	59,431
Sind	Kurrachee	28,814	Sind	Kurrachee	28,704	Bengal	Allahabad	52,434
British Burmah	Rangoon	21,103	British Burmah	Rangoon	20,390	Bombay	Belgaum	44,924
Ganjam	Coconada	15,765	Ceylon	Colombo	19,543	Madras	Paumben	36,680
Ceylon	Colombo	14,920	Ganjam	Coconada	15,293	Malabar Cst.	Mercara	31,225
Indore	Indore	10,518	Bengal	Agra	13,340	Ganjam	Coconada	27,926
Ceylon	Galle	10,364	Indore	Indore	10,822	Bengal	Calcutta	24,792
Punjab	Simla	8,935	Punjab	Simla	9,892	Arracan	Akyab	24,754
Malabar Coast	Cochin	8,087	Bengal	Allahabad	8,970	Br. Burmah	Padeng	19,081
Malabar Coast	Calicut	7,929	Punjab	Lahore	8,670	Rajpootana	Deesa	18,371
Punjab	Delhi	7,283	Bombay	Ahmedabad	8,553	Punjab	Meerut	17,206
Bengal	Agra	6,560	Ceylon	Galle	8,121	Punjab	Lahore	13,663
Punjab	Lahore	6,391	Malabar Cst.	Calicut	7,952	Dacca	Chittagong	12,482
Bengal	Cawnpore	6,297	Punjab	Delhi	7,933	Ganjam	Cuttack	11,926
Bombay	Poona	5,990	Malabar Cst.	Cochin	7,445	Indore	Indore	11,654
Bengal	Allahabad	5,928	Madras	Pondicherry	7,209	Bangalore	Bangalore	11,597
Bombay	Ahmedabad	5,477	Bombay	Poona	6,489	Madras	Bezwarrah	10,771
Madras	Pondicherry	5,408	Bengal	Cawnpore	6,433	Bengal	Sahabgunge	10,286

Note: All places spelled as in the original source.

Source: British Library, Oriental Collections, IOR/V/24/4284, 'Administration Report of the Indian Telegraph Department for 1871–72', 1872, Appendix A, 26–33.

Table A.28 *Number of inland and foreign paid messages sent from Indian Telegraph Department stations, 1872–3.*

Inland		Foreign	
Office	Messages	Office	Messages
Bombay	93,839	Calcutta	9,989
Calcutta	75,694	Bombay*	7,301
Madras	30,881	Rangoon	1,733
Rangoon	19,964	Madras†	1,431
Colombo	15,014	Galle	1,159
Coconada	13,958	Colombo	1,073
Indore	12,277	Akyab	339
Kurrachee	10,874	Pondicherry	279
Simla	7,950	Simla	212
Galle	7,867	Coconada	190
Cochin	7,546	Kurrachee‡	185
Ahmedabad	6,817	Moulmein	154
Lahore	6,669	Tellicherry	99
Hyderabad	6,588	Chittagong	95
Cawnpore	6,158	Kandy	81
Calicut	6,117	Negapatam	70
Agra	5,927	Governor of Bombay's Office	68
Allahabad	5,790	Poona	63
Delhi	5,671	Lahore	62
Poona	5,461	Calicut	60

Notes: All places spelled as in the original source.
* Exclusive of 11,327 transit messages from Europe to the Far East and 14,044 messages from Europe to India.
† Exclusive of 14,256 transit messages from the Far East to Europe and 3,438 messages from the Far East to India.
‡ Exclusive of 2,049 transit messages from Europe to the Far East and 7,131 messages from Europe to India.
Source: British Library, Oriental Collections, IOR/V/24/4284, 'Administration Report of the Indian Telegraph Department for 1872–73', 1873, Appendix H, 49–51.

Table A.29 *Monthly telegraphic traffic between Europe and India, April 1872 to September 1875.*

		Turkey		Tehran		Suez	
Month	Year	Abs.	%	Abs.	%	Abs.	%
April	1872	300	n.a.	1,608	n.a.	n.a.	n.a.
May	1872	333	n.a.	953	n.a.	n.a.	n.a.
June	1872	420	n.a.	883	n.a.	n.a.	n.a.
July	1872	476	n.a.	1,089	n.a.	n.a.	n.a.
August	1872	450	n.a.	1,015	n.a.	n.a.	n.a.
September	1872	506	n.a.	918	n.a.	n.a.	n.a.
October	1872	459	n.a.	1,051	n.a.	n.a.	n.a.
November	1872	438	n.a.	1,158	n.a.	n.a.	n.a.
December	1872	441	n.a.	1,218	n.a.	n.a.	n.a.
January	1873	429	n.a.	1,444	n.a.	n.a.	n.a.
February	1873	372	n.a.	1,429	n.a.	n.a.	n.a.
March	1873	387	n.a.	1,447	n.a.	n.a.	n.a.
April	1873	357	9.0	1,578	40.0	2,010	51.0
May	1873	264	7.3	1,392	38.3	1,983	54.5
June	1873	252	8.4	1,120	37.5	1,616	54.1
July	1873	274	9.0	1,016	33.4	1,752	57.6
August	1873	223	7.2	1,371	44.2	1,507	48.6
September	1873	275	8.1	1,348	39.6	1,783	52.3
October	1873	217	6.5	1,827	54.5	1,311	39.1
November	1873	237	5.6	1,789	42.6	2,169	51.7
December	1873	236	4.7	2,540	50.5	2,256	44.8
January	1874	258	3.9	2,860	43.7	3,427	52.4
February	1874	208	3.5	2,781	47.1	2,919	49.4
March	1874	234	3.6	3,835	59.4	2,390	37.0
April	1874	188	3.2	3,043	52.3	2,584	44.4
May	1874	195	3.7	2,938	55.5	2,162	40.8
June	1874	229	4.5	2,707	53.4	2,132	42.1
July	1874	187	3.7	2,834	56.6	1,985	39.7
August	1874	161	3.3	2,267	47.0	2,398	49.7
September	1874	189	3.8	2,501	50.4	2,269	45.8
October	1874	206	4.1	2,250	44.5	2,604	51.5
November	1874	267	5.2	2,359	45.8	2,525	49.0
December	1874	220	3.9	2,755	48.9	2,662	47.2
January	1875	199	3.1	2,705	42.1	3,515	54.8
February	1875	149	2.4	2,756	45.1	3,204	52.4
March	1875	172	2.4	3,365	47.4	3,568	50.2
April	1875	188	3.0	2,920	46.5	3,175	50.5
May	1875	177	3.1	2,527	44.3	2,998	52.6
June	1875	124	2.3	2,463	45.2	2,860	52.5
July	1875	158	3.0	2,389	45.3	2,722	51.7
August	1875	184	3.6	2,458	48.0	2,474	48.4
September	1875	180	3.5	2,041	39.3	2,966	57.2

Source: British Library, Oriental Collections, IOR/V/24/4289, 'Administration Report of the Indo-European Telegraph Department for 1873–74', 1874; British Library, Oriental Collections, IOR/V/24/4289, 'Administration Report of the Indo-European Telegraph Department for 1878–79', 1879.

Table A.29 *(cont'd) Monthly telegraphic traffic between Europe and India, October 1875 to March 1879.*

Month	Year	Turkey		Tehran		Suez	
		Abs.	%	Abs.	%	Abs.	%
October	1875	191	3.5	2,702	49.4	2,581	47.2
November	1875	335	5.2	4,318	67.2	1,771	27.6
December	1875	721	11.3	5,404	84.4	275	4.3
January	1876	1037	10.5	8,575	86.5	298	3.0
February	1876	450	5.4	4,306	51.6	3,592	43.0
March	1876	349	4.2	4,238	51.2	3,696	44.6
April	1876	281	3.8	3,330	45.6	3,696	50.6
May	1876	272	3.4	3,398	42.3	4,358	54.3
June	1876	252	3.5	2,838	40.0	4,011	56.5
July	1876	268	3.5	2,816	36.3	4,669	60.2
August	1876	321	4.1	3,286	42.0	4,226	54.0
September	1876	266	3.5	3,108	40.5	4,294	56.0
October	1876	305	3.8	3,630	45.0	4,129	51.2
November	1876	345	3.9	3,809	43.4	4,614	52.6
December	1876	377	4.3	2,435	27.9	5,902	67.7
January	1877	271	2.8	3,446	36.2	5,796	60.9
February	1877	300	3.2	4,028	42.8	5,084	54.0
March	1877	312	2.9	4,366	40.6	6,083	56.5
April	1877	304	3.0	4,147	40.5	5,793	56.6
May	1877	552	5.7	1,713	17.7	7,400	76.6
June	1877	742	8.9	63	0.8	7,524	90.3
July	1877	590	7.1	50	0.6	7,679	92.3
August	1877	559	7.0	550	6.9	6,890	86.1
September	1877	369	4.5	1,738	21.3	6,046	74.2
October	1877	357	3.8	2,076	22.0	6,993	74.2
November	1877	248	2.5	2,102	21.3	7,535	76.2
December	1877	316	3.4	1,780	19.0	7,275	77.6
January	1878	253	2.4	2,234	20.9	8,177	76.7
February	1878	619	5.9	2,151	20.6	7,670	73.5
March	1878	320	3.1	2,263	22.1	7,655	74.8
April	1878	260	2.7	2,366	24.8	6,916	72.5
May	1878	239	2.4	2,379	24.1	7,242	73.4
June	1878	224	2.7	2,403	29.0	5,661	68.3
July	1878	251	2.8	2,868	31.6	5,944	65.6
August	1878	276	3.1	2,492	28.2	6,056	68.6
September	1878	243	2.8	2,202	25.5	6,183	71.7
October	1878	342	3.5	2,482	25.4	6,939	71.1
November	1878	328	3.5	2,511	26.5	6,630	70.0
December	1878	340	3.8	1,867	20.6	6,856	75.6
January	1879	340	3.3	2,304	22.3	7,669	74.4
February	1879	362	3.6	2,382	23.8	7,273	72.6
March	1879	339	3.0	2,724	24.1	8,236	72.9

Bibliography

ARCHIVED DOCUMENTS

British Library, General Reference Collection, Shelfmark 8761.b.62, 'Souvenir of the Inaugural Fête [Held at the house of Mr. John Pender], in Commemoration of the Opening of Direct Submarine Telegraph with India', 23 June 1870.

British Library, Oriental Collections, IOR/V/24/4284, 'Administration Report of the Indian Telegraph Department for 1862–63', 1863.

British Library, Oriental Collections, IOR/V/24/4284, 'Administration Report of the Indian Telegraph Department for 1862–63, 1863–64, 1864–65, and 1865–66', 1866.

British Library, Oriental Collections, IOR/V/24/4284, 'Administration Report of the Indian Telegraph Department for 1867–68 to 1870–71', 1871.

British Library, Oriental Collections, IOR/V/24/4284, 'Administration Report of the Indian Telegraph Department for 1871–72', 1872.

British Library, Oriental Collections, IOR/V/24/4284, 'Administration Report of the Indian Telegraph Department for 1872–73', 1873.

British Library, Oriental Collections, IOR/V/24/4286, 'Administration Report of the Indian Telegraph Department for 1880–81', 1881.

British Library, Oriental Collections, IOR/V/24/4288, 'Administration Report of the Indian Telegraph Department for 1899–1900', 1900.

British Library, Oriental Collections, IOR/V/24/4288, 'Administration Report of the Indian Telegraph Department for 1900–1901', 1901.

British Library, Oriental Collections, IOR/V/24/4289, 'Administration Report of the Indo-European Telegraph Department for 1873–74', 1874.

British Library, Oriental Collections, IOR/V/24/4289, 'Administration Report of the Indo-European Telegraph Department for 1878–79', 1879.

British Library, Oriental Collections, IOR/V/24/4289, 'Administration Report of the Indo-European Telegraph Department for 1882–83', 1883.

British Library, Oriental Collections, IOR/V/24/4290, 'Administration Report of the Indo-European Telegraph Department for 1889–90', 1890.

British Library, Oriental Collections, IOR/V/24/4290, 'Administration Report of the Indo-European Telegraph Department for 1892–93', 1893.

British Telecom Archives, POST 33/1997, 'Anglo-Australian Beam Service. Proposal Chess Match between House of Commons and Australian Commonwealth House of Representatives', 25 June 1926.

British Telecom Archives, POST 33/2000, 'Registered Telegraphic Addresses. Firms with Similar Names or Businesses, etc. Memorandum Agile (Electrodes) Limited to General Post Office', 9 October 1933.

British Telecom Archives, POST 33/2000, 'Registered Telegraphic Addresses. Firms with Similar Names or Businesses, etc. Letter from the Controller Central Telegraph Office to the Secretary General Post Office', 17 November 1933.

British Telecom Archives, POST 33/2000, 'Registered Telegraphic Addresses. Firms with Similar Names or Businesses, etc. Letter from Controller Central Telegraph Office to A. Arc Limited', 8 December 1933.

British Telecom Archives, POST 33/2000, 'Registered Telegraphic Addresses. Firms with Similar Names or Businesses, etc. Letter from A. Arc Limited to Controller Central Telegraph Office', 12 December 1933.

British Telecom Archives, POST 33/2000, 'Registered Telegraphic Addresses. Firms with Similar Names or Businesses, etc. Letter from Agile (Electrodes) Limited to the Telegraph & Telephone Department General Post Office', 5 October 1934.

British Telecom Archives, POST 81/12, 'British and Irish Magnetic Telegraph Co (formerly the English Telegraph Company) Circuit Returns – Metropolitan and "A" to "M"', 1868.

British Telecom Archives, POST 81/13, 'British and Irish Magnetic Telegraph Co (formerly the English Telegraph Company) Circuit Returns "N" to "Z" and Scotland and Ireland', 1868.

British Telecom Archives, POST 81/51, 'Electric and International Telegraph Co Circuit Returns – Metropolitan and "A" and "B"', 1868.

British Telecom Archives, POST 81/52, 'Electric and International Telegraph Co Circuit Returns, "C" to "H"', 1868.

British Telecom Archives, POST 81/53, 'Electric and International Telegraph Co Circuit Returns, "I" to "O"', 1868.

British Telecom Archives, POST 81/54, 'Electric and International Telegraph Co Circuit Returns, "P" to "T"', 1868.

British Telecom Archives, POST 81/55, 'Electric and International Telegraph Co Circuit Returns, and Scotland "U" to "Y"', 1868.

British Telecom Archives, POST 81/77, 'United Kingdom Electric Telegraph Company, Circuit Returns from Offices in the Metropolitan, English and Scottish Districts', 1868.

British Telecom Archives, POST 82/70, 'List of Codes and Telegraph Stations in the United Kingdom', 1876.

British Telecom Archives, POST 82/71, 'List of Codes and Telegraph Stations in the United Kingdom', 1882.

British Telecom Archives, POST 82/72, 'List of Codes and Telegraph Stations in the United Kingdom', 1885.

British Telecom Archives, POST 82/73, 'List of Codes and Telegraph Stations in the United Kingdom', 1889.

British Telecom Archives, POST 82/181, 'Re-arrangement of the Metropolitan Telegraph System', 1869.

British Telecom Archives, POST 82/209, 'Reports by Mr. F. E. Baines, the Surveyor General for Telegraphs. Quarterly Report of the Surveyor-General for Telegraph Business to the Secretary', 14 January 1879.
British Telecom Archives, POST 82/303, 'Telegraphs. Return of Persons Employed; Wages; Average Weekly Messages', 1869–72.
Cable & Wireless Archive, 1998–44, 'Memorandum to Morse Staff', 1879.
Cable & Wireless Archive, DOC/CW/7/15, 'Commercial Pacific Cable Company 1934 to 1935', 1934/35.
Cable & Wireless Archive, DOC/E&ATC/7/1, 'Correspondence regarding censorship. 1914 to 1918', 1914–18.
Cable & Wireless Archive, DOC/EEACTC/1/13, Minute Book No 5, 'Eastern Extension Company. Minute Books of the Board', 29 January 1896.
Cable & Wireless Archive, DOC/ETC/7/15/4, 'Porthcurno Station Correspondence. Memorandum to Staff Ln Inst', 9 September 1878.
Cable & Wireless Archive, DOC/ETC/7/15/9, 'Porthcurno Station Correspondence. Return of Number of Errors made during February 1879', 7 July 1879.
Cable & Wireless Archive, DOC/ETC/7/15/11, 'Porthcurno Station Correspondence. Return of Number of Errors made during March 1879', 31 July 1879.
Cable & Wireless Archive, DOC/ETC/7/33, 'Letters and Memo's re Traffic Matters. Including Prospectus'es of Several Early Cable Companies. 1883–1896', 15 January 1879.
Cable & Wireless Archive, DOC/I&IC/1/9, 'Imperial and International Communications Ltd., Report of the Directors. 1929 to 1933', 1929–33.
Cable & Wireless Archive, exhibited in display window at the Porthcurno Telegraph Museum, 'Porthcurno Station Correspondence. Return of Number of Errors made during April 1879', 14 August 1879.
Cable & Wireless Archive, exhibited in display window at the Porthcurno Telegraph Museum, 'Porthcurno Station Correspondence. Return of Number of Errors made during May 1879', 18 September 1879.
Cambridge South Asian Archive, Centre of South Asian Studies, University of Cambridge, Kenyon (E. A.) Papers, Kenyon, Eustace Alban, 'Letter to Mary', 9 July 1885.
Cambridge South Asian Archive, Centre of South Asian Studies, University of Cambridge, Kenyon (E. A.) Papers, Kenyon, Eustace Alban, 'Letter to Mother', 1 February 1885.
Cambridge South Asian Archive, Centre of South Asian Studies, University of Cambridge, Kenyon (E. A.) Papers, Kenyon, Eustace Alban, 'Letter to Tizie', 9 March 1891.
ITU Archives, Bureau international de l'Union télégraphique, 'Carte schématique des grandes communications télégraphiques internationales du régime européen', 1923.
ITU Archives, Bureau international de l'Union télégraphique, 'Statistique générale de la télégraphie', 1910.
ITU Archives, Bureau international des administrations télégraphiques, 'Carte des communications télégraphiques du régime extra-européen', 1881.
ITU Archives, Bureau international des administrations télégraphiques, 'Carte des communications télégraphiques de régime extra-européen', 1892.

ITU Archives, Bureau international des administrations télégraphiques, 'Cartes des communications télégraphiques du régime extra-européen', 1902.

ITU Archives, Bureau international des administrations télégraphiques, 'Liste des communications télégraphiques internationales directes du régime européen. Annexe à la carte des communications télégraphiques du régime européen – édition 1906', 1906.

ITU Archives, Bureau international des administrations télégraphiques, 'Statistique générale de la télégraphie dans les différents pays de l'ancien continent', 1849–69.

ITU Archives, Bureau international des administrations télégraphiques, 'Statistique générale de la télégraphie dans les différents pays de l'ancien continent', 1870.

ITU Archives, Bureau international des administrations télégraphiques, 'Statistique générale de la télégraphie', 1880.

ITU Archives, Bureau international des administrations télégraphiques, 'Statistique générale de la télégraphie', 1890.

ITU Archives, Bureau international des administrations télégraphiques, 'Statistique générale de la télégraphie', 1900.

National Archives, BT 41/225/1269, 'English and Irish Magnetic Telegraph Company', 1844–*c.*1860.

National Archives, BT 41/321/1847, 'International Telegraph Company', 1844–*c.*1860.

National Archives, BT 41/88/501, 'British Electric Telegraph Company', 1844–*c.*1860.

National Archives, CAB 16/14, 'Standing Sub-committee of the Committee of Imperial Defence. Submarine Cable Communication in Time of War. Report with Table and Appendices', December 1911.

National Archives, RAIL 236/718/22, 'Inhabitants of Tattershall for Installation of Telegraph Communication at Tattershall instead of Dogdyke. Letter Francis P. Cockshott to Earl Fortescue', 2 October 1867.

National Archives, RAIL 236/718/22, 'Inhabitants of Tattershall for Installation of Telegraph Communication at Tattershall instead of Dogdyke. Letter Seymour Clarke to James Banks Stanhope', 7 October 1867.

National Archives, RAIL 236/718/22, 'Inhabitants of Tattershall for Installation of Telegraph Communication at Tattershall instead of Dogdyke. Memorial', 1867.

National Archives, T 1/15916, 'Telegraph Service at Newmarket Race Meetings: Transport for Telegraphists and Provision of Improved Accommodation. Letter John Manners, GPO, to Treasury', 5 February 1879.

Old Bailey Proceedings Online (www.oldbaileyonline.org), t18470920–2217, 'Proceedings of the Central Criminal Court. Trial of John Hutchings', 20 September 1847.

HANSARD AND PARLIAMENTARY PAPERS

Hansard. vol. **302** cols. 314–17, 'House of Commons Debate', 25 January 1886.

House of Commons Parliamentary Papers, 416, 'Electric Telegraphs. Returns of the Names of All Railway Companies in the United Kingdom Which

Construct or Use Electric Telegraphs as Part of Their Undertaking; of the Number of Miles of Telegraph, Both Authorised and Constructed, and of the Number of Stations and Places Communicating with Such Telegraphs; and, of the Places of Connection, and the Length of Each Submarine Telegraph Connected with any Place in the United Kingdom', 1867–8.

House of Commons Parliamentary Papers, 3723, 'Annual Statement of the Trade and Navigation of the United Kingdom with Foreign Countries and British Possessions in the Year 1865', 1866.

House of Commons Parliamentary Papers, C. 202, 'Electric Telegraphs. Return to an Order of the Honourable the House of Commons, Dated 3 April 1868; – for, Copy "of Reports to the Postmaster General by Mr. Scudamore upon the Proposal for Transferring to the Post Office the Control and Management of the Electric Telegraphs throughout the United Kingdom"', 1867–8.

House of Commons Parliamentary Papers, C. 304, 'Telegraphs. Report by Mr. Scudamore on the Re-organization of the Telegraph System of the United Kingdom', 1871.

House of Commons Parliamentary Papers, C. 437, 'Annual Statement of the Trade and Navigation of the United Kingdom with Foreign Countries and British Possessions in the Year 1870', 1871.

House of Commons Parliamentary Papers, C. 1571, 'Annual Statement of the Trade of the United Kingdom with Foreign Countries and British Possessions for the Year 1875', 1876.

House of Commons Parliamentary Papers, C. 1584, 'Report to the Secretary of State for India in Council on Railways in India for the Year 1875–76', 1876.

House of Commons Parliamentary Papers, C. 2920, 'Annual Statement of the Trade of the United Kingdom with Foreign Countries and British Possessions for the Year 1880', 1881.

House of Commons Parliamentary Papers, C. 4690, 'Burmah, No 2 (1886). Telegraphic Correspondence Relating to Military Executions and Dacoity in Burmah', 1886.

House of Commons Parliamentary Papers, C. 9247, 'Pacific Cable Committee. Report, Minutes of Proceedings, &c.', 1899.

House of Commons Parliamentary Papers, Cd. 1056, 'Cable Communications Report of the Inter-departmental Committee on Cable Communications', 1902.

NOMENCLATURES

'Les communications sous-marines du globe', *Journal télégraphique* **3**, no 12 (1875), 224–8.

'Nomenclature des cables formant le réseau sous-marin du globe dressée d'après des documents officiels par le Bureau international des administrations télégraphiques', *Journal télégraphique* **3**, no 29 (1877), 575–90.

'Nomenclature des cables formant le réseau sous-marin du globe dressée d'après des documents officiels par le Bureau international des administrations télégraphiques', *Journal télégraphique* **7**, no 5 (1883), 113–35.

'Nomenclature des cables formant le réseau sous-marin du globe dressée d'après des documents officiels par le Bureau international des administrations télégraphiques', *Journal télégraphique* **11**, no 4 (1887), 97–126.

'Nomenclature des cables formant le réseau sous-marin du globe dressée d'après des documents officiels par le Bureau international des administrations télégraphiques', *Journal télégraphique* **13**, no 9 (1889), 213–43.
'Nomenclature des cables formant le réseau sous-marin du globe dressée d'après des documents officiels par le Bureau international des administrations télégraphiques', *Journal télégraphique* **16**, no 4 (1892), 97–131.
'Nomenclature des cables formant le réseau sous-marin du globe dressée d'après des documents officiels par le Bureau international des administrations télégraphiques', *Journal télégraphique* **18**, no 10 (1894), 277–316.
'Nomenclature des cables formant le réseau sous-marin du globe dressée d'après des documents officiels par le Bureau international des administrations télégraphiques', *Journal télégraphique* **21**, no 11 (1897), 265–311.
'Nomenclature des cables formant le réseau sous-marin du globe dressée d'après des documents officiels par le Bureau international des administrations télégraphiques', *Journal télégraphique* **25** (1901), 121–71.
'Nomenclature des cables formant le réseau sous-marin du globe dressée d'après des documents officiels par le Bureau international des administrations télégraphiques', *Journal télégraphique* **27** (1903), 1–56.

OTHER DOCUMENTS

Act of the Parliament of the United Kingdom, 31 & 32 Vict. c. 110, 'An Act to Enable Her Majesty's Postmaster General to Acquire, Work and Maintain Electric Telegraphs', 1868.
Documents de la Conférence télégraphique internationale de Vienne, Vienna: Imprimerie impériale et royale de la cour et de l'état, 1868.
Documents diplomatiques de la Conférence télégraphique internationale de Paris, Paris: Imprimerie impériale, 1865.
The India List and India Office List for 1905 Compiled from Official Records by Direction of the Secretary of State for India in Council, London: Harrison and Sons, 1905.

NEWSPAPER ARTICLES AND CARICATURES

'Another Case of Poisoning', *The Times*, 30 August 1847.
'The Arrival of the Simla at Marseilles Presents', *The Times*, 4 April 1857.
'Australia', *The Times*, 4 April 1857.
'Burmah', *The Times*, 21 January 1886.
'The Calcutta Telegraph', *The Times*, 19 February 1869.
'The Charges against Colonel Hooper', *The Times*, 8 September 1886.
'The District Telegraph. Invaluable to the Man of Business', *Punch, or the London Charivari* **44**, no 10 (January 1863).
'The Electric Telegraph', *The Times*, 8 October 1847.
'The English Raj in India', *The Times*, 7 October 1858.
'The Enthusiastic Meeting Which Yesterday', *The Times*, 30 November 1892.
'How the Electric Telegraph Saved India', *Daily News*, 29 September 1897.
'The Government Telegraph', *Friend of India*, 20 October 1864.

'Latest Intelligence. The United States', *The Times*, 8 January 1867.
Lloyd's List, 25 August 1858.
'Positive Fact, of Course', *Punch's Almanack* **42** (January–June 1862).
'The Post Office and the Telegraphs', *The Times*, 7 December 1870.
'Pursuit o' Knowledge', *Punch, or the London Charivari* **62**, no 6 (April 1872).
'The Rhodes Colossus Striding from Cape Town to Cairo', *Punch, or the London Charivari* **103**, no 10 (December 1892).
'The Salt-Hill Murder. Execution of John Tawell', *The Times*, 29 March 1845.
'Ship News', *The Times*, 24 August 1858.
'Shipping Intelligence', *The Times*, 25 August 1858.
'Suspected Murder at Salt-Hill', *The Times*, 3 January 1845, 7.
'Tales of the Telegraph', *Chambers's Journal of Popular Literature, Science and Arts* no 843 (1880).
'Telegraph between England and India', *The Times*, 17 March 1860.
'The Telegraph Frauds in India', *Lloyd's Weekly Newspaper*, 31 March 1861.
'Town Telegraphs', *Perth Gazette and Independent Journal of Politics and News*, 31 July 1863.

SOFTWARE

Forestry GIS (fGIS) Version 2005.09.13. University of Wisconsin.
MapWindow GIS: Open Source Programmable Geographic Information System Tools Version 4.8 RC1. Idaho State University, Pocatello.
UCINET for Windows: Software for Social Network Analysis Version 6.288. Analytic Technologies, Cambridge, MA.

ARTICLES AND BOOKS

Adams, J. M. 'Development of the Anglo-Indian Telegraph', *Engineering Science and Education Journal* **6**, no 4 (1997), 140–48.
Ahmadi, Farajollah. 'Linking India with Britain: The Persian Gulf Cables, *1864–1907*' (unpublished PhD thesis, University of Exeter, 2003).
Ahvenainen, Jorma. *The European Cable Companies in South America before the First World War*. Helsinki: Finnish Academy of Science and Letters, 2004.
Ahvenainen, Jorma. *The Far Eastern Telegraphs: The History of Telegraphic Communications between the Far East, Europe and America before the First World War*. Helsinki: Finnish Academy of Science and Letters, 1981.
Ahvenainen, Jorma. 'The International Telegraph Union: The Cable Companies and the Governments', in *Communications under the Seas: The Evolving Cable Network and Its Implications*, edited by Bernard Finn and Daqing Yang. Cambridge, MA, London: The MIT Press, 2009, 61–79.
Ahvenainen, Jorma. *The History of the Caribbean Telegraphs before the First World War*. Helsinki: Finnish Academy of Science and Letters, 1996.
Ahvenainen, Jorma. 'The Role of Telegraphs in the 19th Century Revolution of Communications', in *Kommunikationsrevolutionen: Die neuen Medien des 16. und 19. Jahrhunderts*, edited by Michael North. Cologne: Böhlau, 1995, 73–80.

Ahvenainen, Jorma. 'Telegraphs, Trade and Policy. The Role of the International Telegraphs in the Years 1870–1914', in *Commercial and Financial Services*, edited by Ranald C. Michie. Oxford and Cambridge, MA: Basil Blackwell, 1994, 505–15.

Allain, Jean-Claude. 'Strategic Independence and Security of Communications: The Undersea Telegraph Cables', in *Nationhood and Nationalism in France: From Boulangism to the Great War 1889–1918*, edited by Robert Tombs. London and New York: HarperCollinsAcademic, 1991, 267–78.

Andrews, Melodie. '"What the Girls Can Do": The Debate over the Employment of Women in the Early American Telegraph Industry', *Essays in Economic and Business History* **8** (1990), 109–20.

Aschoff, Volker. *Aus der Geschichte der Nachrichtentechnik*. Opladen: Westdeutscher Verlag, 1974.

Aschoff, Volker. *Aus der Geschichte der Telegraphen-Codes*. Opladen: Westdeutscher Verlag, 1981.

Aschoff, Volker. *Nachrichtentechnische Entwicklung in der ersten Hälfte des 19. Jahrhunderts. Volume 2: Geschichte der Nachrichtentechnik*. Berlin, Heidelberg, New York, London, Paris and Tokyo: Springer, 1987.

Aschoff, Volker. *Paul Schilling von Canstatt und die Geschichte des elektromagnetischen Telegraphen*. Munich, Oldenbourg and Duesseldorf: VDI-Verlag, 1977.

Baark, Erik. *Lightning Wires: The Telegraph and China's Technological Modernization, 1860–1890*, Contributions in Asian Studies. Westport, CT: Greenwood Press, 1997.

Baia Curioni, Stefano, and Luca Fantacci. 'Telegraphy and New Financial Procedures', in *Communication and Its Lines: Telegraphy in the 19th Century among Economy, Politics and Technology*, edited by Andrea Giuntini. Prato: Istituto di studi storici postali onlus, 2004, 83–98.

Barton, Ellen L. 'The Grammar of Telegraphic Structures: Sentential and Nonsentential Derivation', *Journal of English Linguistics* **26**, no 1 (1998), 37–67.

Barton, Roger Neil. 'Brief Lives: Three British Telegraph Companies 1850–56', *International Journal for the History of Engineering & Technology* **80**, no 2 (2010), 183–98.

Barton, Roger Neil. 'New Media: The Birth of Telegraphic News in Britain 1847–68', *Media History* **16**, no 4 (2010), 379–406.

Basse, Dieter. *Wolff's Telegraphisches Bureau 1849 bis 1933: Agenturpublizistik zwischen Politik und Wirtschaft, Kommunikation und Politik*. Munich and New York: K. G. Saur, 1991.

Bayly, Christopher A. *Empire and Information: Intelligence Gathering and Social Communication in India, 1780–1870*. New York: Cambridge University Press, 1996.

Beauchamp, Ken G. *History of Telegraphy, IEE History of Technology Series*. London: Institution of Electrical Engineers, 2001.

Bektas, Yakup. 'Displaying the American Genius: The Electromagnetic Telegraph in the Wider World', *British Journal for the History of Science* **34**, no 2 (2001), 199–232.

Bektas, Yakup. 'The Sultan's Messenger: Cultural Constructions of Ottoman Telegraphy, 1847–1880', *Technology and Culture* **41**, no 4 (2000), 669–96.

Bell, Duncan S. A. 'Dissolving Distance: Technology, Space, and Empire in British Political Thought, 1770–1900', *Journal of Modern History* 77, no 3 (2005), 523–62.

Belliger, Andréa, and David J. Krieger. 'Einführung in die Akteur-Netzwerk-Theorie', in *ANThology: Ein einführendes Handbuch zur Akteur-Netzwerk-Theorie*, edited by Andréa Belliger and David J. Krieger. Bielefeld: transcript, 2006, 13–50.

Beyrer, Klaus. 'Die optische Telegraphie als Beginn der modernen Telekommunikation', in *Vom Flügeltelegraphen zum Internet: Geschichte der modernen Telekommunikation*, edited by Hans-Jürgen Teuteberg and Cornelius Neutsch. Stuttgart: Franz Steiner Verlag, 1998, 14–26.

Beyrer, Klaus, and Birgit-Susann Mathis, eds. *So weit das Auge reicht: Die Geschichte der optischen Telegrafie*. Karlsruhe: Braun, 1995.

Blok, Aad, and Gregory Downey, eds. *Uncovering Labour in Information Revolutions, 1750–2000*. Cambridge: Cambridge University Press, 2003.

Blondheim, Menahem. *News over the Wires: The Telegraph and the Flow of Public Information in America, 1844–1897*. Cambridge, MA: Harvard University Press, 1994.

Blondheim, Menahem. 'Rehearsal for Media Regulation: Congress versus the Telegraph-News Monopoly, 1866–1900', *Federal Communications Law Journal* **56**, no 2 (2004), 299–328.

Blondheim, Menahem. '"Slender Bridges" of Misunderstanding: The Social Legacy of Transatlantic Cable Communications', in *Atlantic Communications: The Media in American and German History from the Seventeenth to the Twentieth Century*, edited by Norbert Finzsch and Ursula Lehmkuhl. Oxford, New York: Berg, 2004, 153–69.

Bonacich, Phillip. 'Factoring and Weighting Approaches to Status Scores and Clique Identification', *Journal of Mathematical Sociology* **2** (1972), 113–20.

Bonacich, Phillip. 'Power and Centrality: A Family of Measures', *American Journal of Sociology* **92**, no 5 (1987), 1170–82.

Bonea, Amelia. 'The Medium and Its Message: Reporting the Austro-Prussian War in the *Times of India*', in *Historical Social Research – Historische Sozialforschung. Global Communication: Telecommunication and Global Flows of Information in the Late 19th and Early 20th Century*, edited by Roland Wenzlhuemer. Cologne: Center for Historical Social Research, 2010, 167–87.

Boyce, Robert. 'Imperial Dreams and National Realities: Britain, Canada and the Struggle for a Pacific Telegraph Cable, 1879–1902', *English Historical Review* **115**, no 460 (2000), 39–70.

Boyce, Robert. 'The Origins of Cable and Wireless Limited, 1918–1939: Capitalism, Imperialism, and Technical Change', in *Communications under the Seas: The Evolving Cable Network and Its Implications*, edited by Bernard Finn and Daqing Yang. Cambridge, MA and London: The MIT Press, 2009, 81–114.

Boyce, Robert. 'Submarine Cables as a Factor in Britain's Ascendancy as a World Power, 1850–1914', in *Kommunikationsrevolutionen: Die neuen Medien des 16. und 19. Jahrhunderts*, edited by Michael North. Cologne: Böhlau, 1995, 81–99.

Brendecke, Arndt. *Imperium und Empirie: Funktionen des Wissens in der Spanischen Kolonialherrschaft*. Cologne, Weimar and Vienna: Böhlau, 2009.

Brittain, James E. 'Scanning the Past: Morse and the Telegraph', *Proceedings of the IEEE* **79** (1991), 591–2.

Britton, John A., and Jorma Ahvenainen. 'Showdown in South America: James Scrymser, John Pender, and United States–British Cable Competition', *Business History Review* **78** (2004), 1–27.

Brodie, Robert N. '"Take a Wire, Like a Good Fellow": The Telegraph in the Canon', *Baker Street Journal: An Irregular Quarterly of Sherlockiana* **41**, no 3 (1991), 148–52.

Bühlmann, Elisabeth. *La ligne Siemens: La construction du télégraphe indo-européen 1867–1870.* Frankfurt a. M.: Peter Lang, 1999.

Buschauer, Regine. *Mobile Räume: Medien- und diskursgeschichtliche Studien zur Tele-Kommunikation.* Bielefeld: transcript, 2010.

Carey, James W. *Communication as Culture: Essays on Media and Society*, edited by David Thorburn, Media and Popular Culture: A Series of Critical Books. Boston: Unwin Hyman, 1989.

Carey, James W. 'Technology and Ideology: The Case of the Telegraph', *Prospects: An Annual of American Cultural Studies* **8** (1983), 303–25.

Carré, Patrice A. 'From the Telegraph to the Telex: A History of Technology, Early Networks and Issues in France in the 19th and 20th Centuries', *Flux* **11** (1993), 17–31.

Carrington, Peter J., John Scott and Stanley Wasserman. *Models and Methods in Social Network Analysis.* Cambridge: Cambridge University Press, 2005.

Castells, Manuel. *End of Millennium.* Malden: Blackwell 1998.

Castells, Manuel. 'Epilogue: Informationalism and the Network Society', in *The Hacker Ethic and the Spirit of the Information Age*, edited by Pekka Himanen, 155–78. New York: Random House, 2001.

Castells, Manuel. *The Informational City: Information Technology, Economic Restructuring, and the Urban–Regional Process.* Oxford: Basil Blackwell, 1989.

Castells, Manuel. 'Informationalism, Networks, and the Network Society: A Theoretical Blueprint', in *The Network Society: A Cross-Cultural Perspective*, edited by Manuel Castells. Cheltenham and Northampton: Edward Elgar, 2004, 3–45.

Castells, Manuel. *The Power of Identity.* Malden: Blackwell, 1997.

Castells, Manuel. *The Rise of the Network Society.* Malden: Blackwell 1996.

Cecil, Edward. *The Leisure of an Egyptian Official.* London: Century Publishing, 1984.

Celoria, Francis. 'Early Victorian Telegraphs in London's Topography, History and Archaeology', in *Collectanea Londiniensia: Studies in London Archaeology and History Presented to Ralph Merrifield*, edited by Joanna Bird, Hugh Chapman and John Clark. London: London and Middlesex Archaeological Society, 1978, 415–35.

Chiles, James R. 'The Cable under the Sea', *American Heritage of Invention & Technology* **3** (Fall 1987), 34–41.

Choi, Junho H., George A. Barnett, and Bum-Soo Chon. 'Comparing World City Networks: A Network Analysis of Internet Backbone and Air Transport Intercity Linkages', *Global Networks* **6**, no 1 (2006), 81–99.

Choudhury, Deep Kanta Lahiri. '"Beyond the Reach of Monkeys and Men"? O'Shaughnessy and the Telegraph in India circa 1836–56', *Indian Economic and Social History Review* **37**, no 3 (2000), 331–59.

Choudhury, Deep Kanta Lahiri. '"1857" and the Communication Crisis', in *Rethinking 1857*, edited by Sabyasachi Bhattacharya. Delhi: Orient Longman, 2007, 261–82.

Choudhury, Deep Kanta Lahiri. 'India's First Virtual Community and the Telegraph General Strike of 1908', in *Uncovering Labour in Information Revolutions, 1750–2000*, edited by Aad Blok and Gregory Downey. Cambridge: Cambridge University Press, 2003, 45–71.

Choudhury, Deep Kanta Lahiri. 'Of Codes and Coda: Meaning in Telegraph Messages, circa 1850–1920', in *Historical Social Research – Historische Sozialforschung. Global Communication: Telecommunication and Global Flows of Information in the Late 19th and Early 20th Century*, edited by Roland Wenzlhuemer. Cologne: Center for Historical Social Research, 2010, 127–39.

Choudhury, Deep Kanta Lahiri. *Telegraphic Imperialism: Crisis and Panic in the Indian Empire, c.1830–1920*. Basingstoke: Palgrave Macmillan, 2010.

Choudhury, Deep Kanta Lahiri. 'Treasons of the Clerks: Sedition and Representation in the Telegraph General Strike of 1908', in *Beyond Representation: Colonial and Postcolonial Constructions of Indian Identity*, edited by Crispin Bates. Oxford and New York: Oxford University Press, 2006, 300–21.

Clauson-Thue, William. *ABC Universal Commercial Electric Telegraphic Code (Fourth Edition). Specially Adapted for the Use of Financiers, Merchants, Shipowners, Brokers, Agents, &c.* London: Eden Fisher, 1881.

Coates, Vary T., and Bernard Finn. *A Retrospective Technology Assessment: Submarine Telegraphy – The Transatlantic Cable of 1866*, edited by Program of Policy Studies in Science and Technology. San Francisco: San Francisco Press, 1979.

Codding, George A., and Anthony M. Rutkowski. *The International Telecommunication Union in a Changing World*. Dedham, MA: Artech House, 1982.

Coe, Lewis. *The Telegraph: A History of Morse's Invention and Its Predecessors in the United States*. Jefferson and London: McFarland, 1993.

Coe, Lewis. *Wireless Radio: A Brief History*. Jefferson and London: McFarland, 1996.

Cohen, Ira J. 'Toward a Theory of State Intervention: The Nationalization of the British Telegraphs', *Social Science History* **4**, no 2 (1980), 155–205.

Compaine, Benjamin M. *The Digital Divide: Facing a Crisis or Creating a Myth?* Cambridge, MA and London: MIT Press, 2001.

Cookson, Gillian. 'The Transatlantic Telegraph Cable', *History Today* **50**, no 3 (2000), 7.

Cookson, Gillian. *The Cable: The Wire That Changed the World*. Stroud: Tempus, 2003.

Cookson, Gillian. 'Submarine Cables: Novelty and Innovations 1850–1870', *Transactions of the Newcomen Society* **76**, no 2 (2006), 207–20.

Craypo, Charles. 'The Impact of Changing Corporate Structure and Technology on Telegraph Labour, 1870–1978', *Journal of the American Statistical Association* (1997), 283–305.

Cryle, Denis. 'Peripheral Politics? Antipodean Interventions in Imperial News and Cable Communication (1870–1912)', in *Media and the British Empire*, edited by Chandrika Kaul. Basingstoke and New York: Palgrave Macmillan, 2006, 174–89.

David, Paul A. 'Clio and the Economics of QWERTY', *American Economic Review* **75**, no 2 (1985), 332–7.

David, Paul A. 'Path Dependence: A Foundational Concept for Historical Social Science', *Cliometrica: The Journal of Historical Economics and Econometric History* **1**, no 2 (2007), 145–75.

Davies, Peter N. 'The Impact of Improving Communications on Commercial Transactions: Nineteenth-Century Case Studies from British West Africa and Japan', *International Journal of Maritime History* **14**, no 1 (2002), 225–38.

Davin, Anna. 'Women Telegraphists and Typists', in *Women in Industry and Technology: From Prehistory to the Present Day*, edited by Amanda Devonshire and Barbara Wood. London: Museum of London, 1996, 213–23.

Dawson, Keith. 'Electromagnetic Telegraphy: Early Ideas, Proposals, and Apparatus', *History of Technology* **1** (1976), 113–41.

De Cogan, Donard. 'Dr E. O. W. Whitehouse and the 1858 Trans-Atlantic Cable', *History of Technology* **10** (1985), 1–15.

De Cogan, Donard. 'Ireland, Telecommunications and International Politics, 1866–1922', *History Ireland* **1** (1993), 34–9.

De Cogan, Donard, and Dominic De Cogan. 'Private Enterprise and State Control in Trans-Atlantic Telegraph (The Early Period)', in *Communication and Its Lines: Telegraphy in the 19th Century among Economy, Politics and Technology*, edited by Andrea Giuntini. Prato: Istituto di studi storici postali onlus, 2004, 24–32.

Degele, Nina. *Einführung in die Techniksoziologie*. Munich: Wilhelm Fink Verlag, 2002.

Dibner, Bern. *The Atlantic Cable*. Norwalk, CT: Burndy Library, 1959.

Dodge, Martin, and Rob Kitchin. *Atlas of Cyberspace*. Harlow: Addison-Wesley, 2001.

Dodge, Martin, and Rob Kitchin. *Mapping Cyberspace*. New York: Routledge, 2000.

Döring, Jörg, and Tristan Thielmann, eds. *Spatial Turn: Das Raumparadigma in den Kultur- und Sozialwissenschaften*. Bielefeld: transcript, 2008.

Downey, Gregory *Telegraph Messenger Boys: Labor, Technology, and Geography, 1850–1950*. New York: Routledge, 2002.

Du Boff, Richard B. 'Business Demand and the Development of the Telegraph in the United States,1844–1860', *Business History Review* **54**, no 4 (1980), 459–79.

Du Boff, Richard B. 'The Rise of Communications Regulation: The Telegraph Industry, 1844–1880', *Journal of Communication* **34**, no 3 (1984), 52–66.

Du Boff, Richard B. 'The Telegraph and the Structure of Markets in the United States, 1845–1890', in *Commercial and Financial Services*, edited by Ranald C. Michie. Oxford and Cambridge, MA: Basil Blackwell, 1994, 253–77.

Du Boff, Richard B. 'The Telegraph in Nineteenth-Century America: Technology and Monopoly', *Comparative Studies in Society and History* **26**, no 4 (1984), 571–86.

Early, Julie English. 'Technology, Modernity, and "the Little Man": Crippen's Capture by Wireless', *Victorian Studies* **39**, no 3 (1996), 309–37.

Edgerton, David. 'From Innovation to Use: Ten Eclectic Theses on the Historiography of Technology', *History and Technology* **16** (1999), 111–36.

Ejrnæa, Mette, and Karl Gunnar Persson. 'The Gains from Improved Market Efficiency: Trade before and after the Transatlantic Telegraph', *European Review of Economic History* **14**, no 3 (2010), 361–81.

Ejrnæa, Mette, Karl Gunnar Persson, and Søren Rich. 'Feeding the British: Convergence and Market Efficiency in the Nineteenth-Century Grain Trade', *Economic History Review* **61**, no S1 (2008), 140–71.

Emirbayer, Mustafa, and Jeff Goodwin. 'Network Analysis, Culture, and the Problem of Agency', *American Journal of Sociology* **99**, no 6 (1994), 1411–54.

Ewing, Thomas E. '"A Most Powerful Instrument for a Despot": The Telegraph as a Transnational Instrument of Imperial Control and Political Mobilization in the Middle East', in *The Nation State and Beyond*, edited by Isabella Löhr and Roland Wenzlhuemer. Heidelberg: Springer, forthcoming.

Ferderer, J. Peter. 'Advances in Communication Technology and Growth of the American Over-the-Counter Markets, 1876–1929', *Journal of Economic History* **68**, no 2 (2008), 1–34.

Field, Alexander J. 'French Optical Telegraphy, 1793–1855: Hardware, Software, Administration', *Technology and Culture* **35**, no 2 (1994), 315–47.

Field, Alexander J. 'The Magnetic Telegraph, Price and Quantity Data, and the New Management of Capital', *Journal of Economic History* **52**, no 2 (1992), 401–13.

Field, Alexander J. 'The Telegraphic Transmission of Financial Asset Prices and Orders to Trade: Implications for Economic Growth, Trading Volume, and Securities Market Regulation', in *Research in Economic History*, edited by Alexander J. Field. Stamford and London: JAI, 1998, 145–84.

Finn, Bernard. 'Submarine Telegraphy: A Study in Technical Stagnation', in *Communications under the Seas: The Evolving Cable Network and Its Implications*, edited by Bernard Finn and Daqing Yang. Cambridge, MA and London: The MIT Press, 2009, 9–24.

Finzsch, Norbert, and Ursula Lehmkuhl, eds. *Atlantic Communications: The Media in American and German History from the Seventeenth to the Twentieth Century*. Oxford and New York: Berg, 2004.

Fletcher, Paul. 'The Uses and Limitations of Telegrams in Official Correspondence between Ceylon's Governor General and the Secretary of State for the Colonies, circa 1870–1900', in *Historical Social Research – Historische Sozialforschung. Global Communication: Telecommunication and Global Flows of Information in the Late 19th and Early 20th Century*, edited by Roland Wenzlhuemer. Cologne: Center for Historical Social Research, 2010, 90–107.

Flichy, Patrice. 'The Birth of Long Distance Communication: Semaphore Telegraphs in Europe (1790–1840)', *Réseaux* **1**, no 1 (1993), 81–101.

Föcking, Marc. 'Drei Verbindungen: Lyrik. Telefon. Telegrafie 1900–1913 (Liliencron. Altenberg. Apollinaire)', in *Die schönen und die nützlichen Künste: Literatur, Technik und Medien seit der Aufklärung*, edited by Knut Hickethier and Katja Schumann. Munich: Fink 2007, 167–80.

Fone, John F. 'Signalling from Norwich to the Coast in the Napoleonic Period', *Norfolk Archaelogy* **42** (1996), 356–61.

Foreman-Peck, James. 'Competition, Co-operation and Nationalisation in the Nineteenth Century Telegraph System', *Business History* **31**, no 3 (1989), 81–101.

Freeman, Linton C. 'Centrality in Networks: I. Conceptual Clarification', *Social Networks* **1**, no 3 (1979), 215–39.

Freeman, Linton C. *The Development of Social Network Analysis: A Study in the Sociology of Science*. Vancouver: Empirical Press, 2004.

Freeman, Linton C. 'The Gatekeeper, Pair-Dependency and Structural Centrality', *Quality and Quantity* **14** (1980), 585–92.

Freeman, Linton C. *Social Network Analysis. 4 vols*. London: Sage Publications, 2007.

Freeman, Linton C. 'Social Network Analysis: Definition and History', in *Encyclopedia of Psychology*, edited by A. E. Kazdan. New York: Oxford University Press, 2000, 350–1.

Freeman, Linton C., Douglas R. White, and A. Kimball Romney, eds. *Research Methods in Social Network Analysis*. Fairfax: George Mason University Press, 1989.

Freezee, Walter D. 'The First Trans-Atlantic Cable', *Journal of the Washington Academy of Science* **68** (1978), 3–13.

Friedewald, Michael. 'Funkentelegrafie und deutsche Kolonien: Technik als Mittel imperialistischer Politik', in *Kommunikation in Geschichte und Gegenwart: Vorträge der Jahrestagung der Georg-Agricola-Gesellschaft 2001 in München*, ed. Kai Handel (Freiberg/Sachsen: Georg-Agricola-Gesellschaft, 2002), 51–68.

Fuchs, Margot. 'The Indo-European Telegraph System 1868–1931: Politics and Technical Change', *Berichte zur Wissenschaftsgeschichte* **13** (1990), 157–66.

Gabler, Edwin. *The American Telegrapher: A Social History, 1860–1900*. New Brunswick: Rutgers University Press, 1988.

Galbraith, John S. *Crown and Charter: The Early Years of the British South Africa Company*. Berkeley, Los Angeles and London: University of California Press, 1974.

Garbade, Kenneth D., and William L. Silber. 'Technology, Communication and the Performance of Financial Markets: 1840–1975', *Journal of Finance* **33**, no 3 (1978), 819–32.

Ghose, Saroj. 'Commercial Needs and Military Necessities: The Telegraph in India', in *Technology and the Raj: Western Technology and Technical Transfers to India 1700–1947*, edited by Roy MacLeod and Deepak Kumar. New Delhi, Thousand Oaks and London: Sage Publications, 1995, 153–76.

Ghose, Saroj. 'William O'Shaughnessy: An Innovator and Entrepeneur', *Indian Journal of History of Science* **29**, no 1 (1994), 9–22.

Gibson, William. *Neuromancer*. New York: Ace, 1984.

Giddens, Anthony. *The Constitution of Society*. Cambridge: Polity Press, 1984.

Giddens, Anthony. *A Contemporary Critique of Historical Materialism. Volume 1: Power, Property and the State*. London: Macmillan, 1981.

Giuntini, Andrea. 'The Power of Cables: Submarine Communication in the Mediterranean', in *Communication and Its Lines: Telegraphy in the 19th Century among Economy, Politics and Technology*, edited by Andrea Giuntini. Prato: Istituto di studi storici postali onlus, 2004, 59–82.

Goheen, Peter G. 'The Impact of the Telegraph on the Newspaper in Mid-Nineteenth Century British North America', *Urban Geography* **11**, no 2 (1990), 107–29.

Gordon, John Steele. *A Thread across the Ocean: The Heroic Story of the Transatlantic Cable*. London: Simon & Schuster, 2002.

Gorman, Mel. 'Sir William O'Shaughnessy, Lord Dalhousie, and the Establishment of the Telegraph System in India', *Technology and Culture* **12**, no 4 (1971), 581–601.

Gould, Peter. 'Dynamic Structures of Geographic Space', in *Collapsing Space and Time: Geographic Aspects of Communications and Information*, edited by Stanley D. Brunn and Thomas R. Leinbach. Hammersmith: HarperCollinsAcademic, 1991, 3–30.

Graham, Stephen, and Simon Marvin. *Splintering Urbanism: Networked Infrastructures, Technological Mobilities and the Urban Condition*. London: Routledge, 2001.

Griset, Pascal. *Entreprise, technologie et souverainité: Les télécommunications transatlantiques de la France, XIX–XXe siècles, edited by Institut d'Histoire de l'Industrie*. Paris: Éditions rive droite, 1996.

Griset, Pascal. 'France and the Adoption of the Electric Telegraph: An Achievement without a Real Future', in *Communication and Its Lines: Telegraphy in the 19th Century among Economy, Politics and Technology*, edited by Andrea Giuntini. Prato: Istituto di studi storici postali onlus, 2004, 99–109.

Griset, Pascal. 'Je t'aime, moi non plus: The Development of Atlantic Submarine Cables and the Complexity of the French–American Dialogue, 1870–1960', in *Communications under the Seas: The Evolving Cable Network and Its Implications*, edited by Bernard Finn and Daqing Yang. Cambridge, MA and London: The MIT Press, 2009, 159–82.

Harris, Christina Phelps. 'The Persian Gulf Submarine Telegraph of 1864', *Geographical Journal* **135**, no 2 (1969), 169–90.

Hartmann, Frank. *Globale Medienkultur: Technik, Geschichte, Theorien*. Vienna: WUV/UTB, 2006.

Harvey, David. 'Between Space and Time: Reflections on the Geographical Imagination', *Annals of the Association of American Geographers* **80**, no 3 (1990), 418–34.

Harvey, David. *The Condition of Postmodernity: An Enquiry into the Origins of Cultural Change*. Cambridge, MA and Oxford: Blackwell, 1990.

Harvey, David. *Social Justice and the City*. Baltimore: Johns Hopkins University Press, 1973.

Harvey, Ross. 'A "Sense of Common Citizenship"? Mrs Potts of Reefton, New Zealand, Communicates with the Empire', in *Media and the British Empire*, edited by Chandrika Kaul. Basingstoke and New York: Palgrave Macmillan, 2006, 190–204.

Headrick, Daniel R. 'A Double-Edged Sword: Communications and Imperial Control in British India', in *Historical Social Research – Historische Sozialforschung. Global Communication: Telecommunication and Global Flows of Information in the Late 19th and Early 20th Century*, edited by Roland Wenzlhuemer. Cologne: Center for Historical Social Research, 2010, 51–65.

Headrick, Daniel R. *The Invisible Weapon: Telecommunications and International Politics, 1851–1945*. New York: Oxford University Press, 1991.

Headrick, Daniel R. 'Radio versus Cable: International Telecommunications before Satellites' (1991), http://history.nasa.gov/SP-4217/ch1.htm.

Headrick, Daniel R. 'Strategic and Military Aspects of Submarine Telegraph Cables, 1851–1945', in *Communications under the Seas: The Evolving Cable Network and Its Implications*, edited by Bernard Finn and Daqing Yang. Cambridge, MA and London: The MIT Press, 2009, 185–207.

Headrick, Daniel R. *The Tentacles of Progress: Technology Transfer in the Age of Imperialism, 1850–1940*. New York and Oxford: Oxford University Press, 1988.

Headrick, Daniel R. *The Tools of Empire: Technology and European Imperialism in the Nineteenth Century*. New York: Oxford University Press, 1981.

Headrick, Daniel R. *When Information Came of Age: Technologies of Knowledge in the Age of Reason and Revolution, 1700–1850*. Oxford University Press, 2000.

Headrick, Daniel R., and Pascal Griset. 'Submarine Telegraph Cables: Business and Politics, 1838–1939', *Business History Review* **75**, no 3 (2001), 543–78.

Hearn, Chester G. *Circuits in the Sea: The Men, the Ships, and the Atlantic Cable*. Westport, CT: Praeger, 2004.

Heilbroner, Robert. 'Do Machines Make History?' *Technology and Culture* **8**, no 3 (1967), 335–45.

Hempstead, Colin. 'Representations of Transatlantic Telegraphy', *Engineering Science and Education Journal* **4**, no 6 (1995), 17–25.

Hennig, Richard. *Überseeische Telegraphie und auswärtige Politik*. Berlin: Carl Heymanns Verlag, 1919.

Hills, Jill. *The Struggle for Control of Global Communication: The Formative Century, The History of Communication*. Urbana: University of Illinois Press, 2002.

Hoag, Christopher. 'The Atlantic Telegraph Cable and Capital Market Information Flows', *Journal of Economic History* **66**, no 2 (2006), 342–53.

Hochfelder, David. 'A Comparison of the Postal Telegraph Movement in Great Britain and the United States, 1866–1900', *Enterprise & Society* **1** (2000), 739–61.

Hochfelder, David. 'Constructing an Industrial Divide: Western Union, AT&T, and the Federal Government, 1876–1971', *Business History Review* **76**, no 4 (2002), 705–32.

Hochfelder, David. '"Where the Common People Could Speculate": The Ticker, Bucket Shops, and the Origins of Popular Participation in Financial Markets, 1880–1920', *Journal of American History* **93**, no 2 (2006), 335–58.

Höhler, Sabine. 'Depth Records and Ocean Volumes: Ocean Profiling by Sounding Technology, 1850–1930', *History and Technology* **18**, no 2 (2002), 119–54.

Höhler, Sabine. 'A Sound Survey: The Technological Perception of Ocean Depth, 1850–1930' (paper presented at Transforming Spaces: The Topological Turn in Technology Studies, Darmstadt, 2003).

Holten, Birgitte. '*Telegraphy and Business Methods in the Late 19th Century*' (paper presented at the Cross-Connexions Conference, London, 11–13 November 2005).

Holtorf, Christian. 'Die Modernisierung des nordatlantischen Raumes. Cyrus Field, Taliaferro Shaffner und das submarine Telegraphennetz von 1858', in *Ortsgespräche: Raum und Kommunikation im 19. und 20. Jahrhundert*, edited by Alexander C. T. Geppert, Uffa Jensen and Jörn Weinhold. Bielefeld: transcript, 2005, 157–78.

Holzer, Boris. *Netzwerke*. Bielefeld: transcript, 2006.

Hughes, Thomas. 'The Evolution of Large Technological Systems', in *The Social Construction of Technological Systems*, edited by Wiebe E. Bijker, Thomas P. Hughes and Trevor J. Pinch. Cambridge, MA: MIT Press, 1993, 51–82.

Hugill, Peter J. 'The Geopolitical Implications of Communication under the Seas', in *Communications under the Seas: The Evolving Cable Network and Its Implications*, edited by Bernard Finn and Daqing Yang. Cambridge, MA and London: MIT Press, 2009, 257–77.

Hugill, Peter J. *Global Communications since 1844: Geopolitics and Technology*. Baltimore: Johns Hopkins University Press, 1999.

Huisman, Mark, and Marijtje A. J. van Duijn. 'Software for Social Network Analysis', in *Models and Methods in Social Network Analysis*, edited by Peter J. Carrington, John Scott and Stanley Wasserman. Cambridge: Cambridge University Press, 2005, 270–316.

Hunt, Bruce J. 'Doing Science in a Global Empire: Cable Telegraphy and Electrical Physics in Victorian Britain', in *Victorian Science in Context*, edited by Bernard Lightman. Chicago and London: The University of Chicago Press, 1997, 312–33.

Hunt, Bruce J. 'Michael Faraday, Cable Telegraphy and the Rise of Field Theory', in *History of Technology*, edited by Graham Hollister-Short and Frank A. J. L. James. London and New York: Mansell, 1991, 1–19.

Hunt, Bruce J. 'The Ohm Is Where the Art Is: British Telegraph Engineers and the Development of Electrical Standards', *Osiris* **9** (1994), 48–63.

Hunt, Bruce J. 'Scientists, Engineers and Wildman Whitehouse: Measurement and Credibility in Early Cable Telegraphy', *British Journal for the History of Science* **29**, no 101 (1996), 155–69.

Huurdeman, Anton A. *The Worldwide History of Telecommunications*. New York: John Wiley & Sons, Inc., 2003.

Inglis, Kenneth Stanley. 'The Imperial Connection: Telegraphic Communication between England and Australia, 1872–1902', in *Australia and Britain: Studies in a Changing Relationship*, edited by A. Frederick Madden and Wyndraeth Humphreys Morris-Jones. Sydney: Frank Cass, 1980, 21–38.

Innis, Harold A. *Empire and Communications*. Toronto: Dundurn Press, 2007.

Israel, Paul. *From Machine Shop to Industrial Laboratory: Telegraphy and the Changing Context of American Invention, 1830–1920*, edited by Merritt Roe Smith, *Johns Hopkins Studies in the History of Technology*. Baltimore and London: Johns Hopkins University Press, 1992.

Jacobsen, Kurt. 'The Great Northern Telegraph Company and the British Empire', in *Britain and Denmark: Political, Economic, and Cultural Relations in the 19th and 20th Centuries*, edited by Jørgen Sevaldsen, Bo Boørke and Claus Bjørn. Copenhagen: Museum Tusculanum Press, 2002, 199–230.

Jacobsen, Kurt. 'Small Nation, International Submarine Telegraphy, and International Politics: The Great Northern Telegraph Company, 1869–1940', in *Communications under the Seas: The Evolving Cable Network and Its Implications*, edited by Bernard Finn and Daqing Yang. Cambridge, MA and London: The MIT Press, 2009, 116–57.

James, H. V. 'The London–Yarmouth Telegraph Line 1806–1814', *Norfolk Archaeology* **37** (1978), 126–9.

Janelle, Donald G. 'Spatial Reorganization: A Model and Concept', *Annals of the Association of American Geographers* **59** (1969), 348–64.

Jepsen, Thomas C. 'Women Telegraph Operators on the Western Frontier', *Journal of the West* **35** (1996), 72–80.

Jepsen, Thomas C. 'Women Telegraphers in the Railroad Depot', *Railroad History* **173** (1995), 142–54.

John, Richard R. *Network Nation: Inventing American Telecommunications*. Cambridge, MA and London: The Belknap Press of Harvard University Press, 2010.

John, Richard R. 'Private Enterprise, Public Good? Communications Deregulation as a National Political Issue, 1839–1851', in *Communication and Its Lines: Telegraphy in the 19th Century among Economy, Politics and Technology*, edited by Andrea Giuntini. Prato: Istituto di studi storici postali onlus, 2004, 33–58.

Kallioinen, Mika. 'Information, Communication, Technology, and Business in the Nineteenth Century: The Case of a Finnish Merchant House', *Scandinavian Economic History Review* **102**, no 1 (2004), 19–34.

Kang, Ung. 'The Development of the Telegraph in Korea in the Late 19th Century', *Kagakusi Kenkyu* **30** (1991), 161–69.

Karbelashvili, Andre. 'Europe–India Telegraph "Bridge" via the Caucasus', *Indian Journal of History of Science* **26**, no 3 (1991), 277–81.

Kaschuba, Wolfgang. *Die Überwindung der Distanz: Zeit und Raum in der europäischen Moderne*. Frankfurt a. M.: Fischer Taschenbuch Verlag, 2004.

Kaukiainen, Yrjö. 'Shrinking the World: Improvements in the Speed of Information Transmission, c.1820–1870', *European Review of Economic History* **5**, no 1 (2001), 1–28.

Kaul, Chandrika. 'A New Angle of Vision: The London Press, Governmental Information Management and the Indian Empire, 1900–22', *Contemporary British History* **8**, no 2 (1994), 213–41.

Kaul, Chandrika. *Reporting the Raj: The British Press and India, 1880–1922*. Manchester University Press, 2003.

Kennedy, Paul. M. 'Imperial Cable Communications and Strategy, 1870–1914', *English Historical Review* **86**, no 341 (1971), 728–52.
Kielbowicz, Richard B. 'News Gathering by Mail in the Age of the Telegraph: Adapting to a New Technology', *Technology and Culture* **28**, no 1 (1987), 26–41.
Kielbowicz, Richard B. 'News Gathering by Printers' Exchanges before the Telegraph', *Journalism History* **9** (1982), 42–8.
Kieve, Jeffrey L. *The Electric Telegraph: A Social and Economic History*. Newton Abbot: David & Charles, 1973.
Klein, Maury. 'What Hath God Wrought?' *American Heritage of Invention and Technology* **8** (Spring 1993), 34–43.
Langdale, John. 'Impact of the Telegraph on the Buffalo Agricultural Commodity Market: 1846–1848', *Professional Geographer* **31**, no 2 (1979), 165–9.
Läpple, Dieter. 'Essay über den Raum. Für ein gesellschaftswissenschaftliches Raumkonzept', in *Stadt und Raum: Soziologische Analysen*, edited by Hartmut Häußermann, Detlev Ipsen, Thomas Krämer-Badoni, Dieter Läpple, Marianne Rodenstein and Walter Siebel. Pfaffenweiler: Centaurus-Verlag, 1991, 157–207.
Latour, Bruno. 'On Actor-Network Theory: A Few Clarifications', *Soziale Welt*, no **47** (1996), 369–81.
Latour, Bruno. *Pandora's Hope: Essays on the Reality of Science Studies*. Cambridge, MA and London: Harvard University Press, 1999.
Latour, Bruno. *Reassembling the Social: An Introduction to Actor-Network-Theory*. Oxford: Oxford University Press, 2005.
Latour, Bruno. *Science in Action: How to Follow Scientists and Engineers through Society*. Cambridge, MA: Havard University Press, 1987.
Law, John. 'Notes on the Theory of the Actor-Network: Ordering, Strategy, and Heterogeneity', *Systems Practice* **5**, no 4 (1992), 379–93.
Law, John, and John Hassard, eds. *Actor Network Theory and After*. Oxford: Blackwell Publishing, 1999.
Lefebvre, Henri. *Le production de l'espace*. Paris: Gallimard, 1974.
Lew, Byron, and Bruce Cater. 'The Telegraph, Co-ordination of Tramp Shipping, and Growth in World Trade, 1870–1910', *European Review of Economic History* **10**, no 2 (2006), 147–73.
Löw, Martina. *Raumsoziologie*. Frankfurt a. M.: Suhrkamp, 2001.
Lubrano, Annteresa. *The Telegraph: How Technology Innovation Caused Social Change*. New York: Garland, 1997.
McConnell, Anita. 'The Art of Submarine Cable-Laying: Its Contribution to Physical Oceanography', in *Ocean Sciences: Their History and Relation to Man. Proceedings of the 4th International Congress on the History of Oceanography, 23–29 September 1987*, edited by Walter Lenz and Margaret Deacon. Hamburg: Bundesamt für Seeschiffahrt und Hydrographie, 1990, 467–73.
McConnell, Anita. *No Sea Too Deep: The History of Oceanographic Instruments*. Bristol: Hilger, 1982.
McCormack, Jerusha Hull. 'Domesticating Delphi: Emily Dickinson and the Electro-Magnetic Telegraph', *American Quarterly* **55**, no 4 (2003), 569–601.

McMahon, Peter. 'Early Electrical Communications Technology and Structural Change in the International Political Economy: The Cases of Telegraphy and Radio', *Prometheus* **20**, no 4 (2002), 379–90.

McMahon, Peter. *Global Control: Information Technology and Globalization since 1845*. Cheltenham: Edward Elgar, 2002.

Malecki, Edward. 'The Economic Geography of the Internet's Infrastructure', *Economic Geography* **78**, no 4 (2002), 399–424.

Mann, Michael. 'Telekommunikation in Britisch-Indien (ca.1850–1930). Ein globalgeschichtliches Paradigma', *Comparativ: Zeitschrift für Globalgeschichte und vergleichende Gesellschaftsforschung* **19**, no 6 (2009), 86–112.

Márquez Quevedo, Javier. 'Telecommunications and Colonial Rivalry: European Telegraph Cables to the Canary Islands and Northwest Africa, 1883–1914', in *Historical Social Research – Historische Sozialforschung. Global Communication: Telecommunication and Global Flows of Information in the Late 19th and Early 20th Century*, edited by Roland Wenzlhuemer. Cologne: Center for Historical Social Research, 2010, 108–24.

Martin, Andy. 'Mentioned in Dispatches: Napoleon, Chappe and Chateaubriand', *Modern & Contemporary France* **8**, no 4 (2000), 445–55.

Marx, Karl. *Grundrisse: Foundations of the Critique of Political Economy (Rough Draft)*. Harmondsworth: Penguin Books, 1973.

Marx, Karl, and Friedrich Engels. *Ökonomische Manuskripte 1857/58*. Berlin: Akademie Verlag, 2006.

Massey, Doreen. 'Politics and Space–Time', *New Left Review* **I**, no 196 (1992), 65–84.

Massey, Doreen. *Space, Place and Gender*. Minneapolis: University of Minnesota Press, 1994.

Massey, Doreen. *For Space*. London, Thousand Oaks and New Delhi: Sage, 2005.

Mather, Frederick C. 'The Railways, the Electric Telegraph and Public Order during the Chartist Period, 1837–48', *Journal of The Historical Association* **38**, no 132 (1953), 40–53.

Menke, Richard. 'Telegraphic Realism: Henry James's *In the Cage*', *Modern Language Association* **115**, no 5 (2000), 975–90.

Michie, Ranald C. 'Friend or Foe? Information Technology and the London Stock Exchange since 1700', *Journal of Historical Geography* **23**, no 3 (1997), 304–26.

Michie, Ranald C. 'The London Stock Exchange and the British Securities Market, 1850–1914', *Economic History Review*, New Series **38**, no 1 (1985), 61–82.

Middell, Matthias, and Katja Naumann. 'Global History and the Spatial Turn: From the Impact of Area Studies to the Study of Critical Junctures of Globalization', *Journal of Global History* **5**, no 1 (2010), 149–70.

Mokyr, Joel. 'Technological Inertia in Economic History', *Journal of Economic History* **52**, no 2 (1992), 325–38.

Moody, Andrew J. '"The Harmless Pleasure of Knowing": Privacy in the Telegraph Office and Henry James's "In the Cage"', *Henry James Review* **16**, no 1 (1995), 53–65.

Morus, Iwan R. 'The Electric Ariel: Telegraphy and Commercial Culture in Early Victorian England', *Victorian Studies* **39**, no 1 (1995), 339–78.

Morus, Iwan R. 'The Nervous System of Britain: Space, Time and the Electric Telegraph in the Victorian Age', *British Journal for the History of Science* **33** (2000), 455–75.

Morus, Iwan R. 'Telegraphy and the Technology of Display: The Electricians and Samuel Morse', in *History of Technology*, edited by Graham Hollister-Short and Frank A. J. L. James. London and New York: Mansell, 1991, 20–40.

Mücke, Hellmuth von. *The 'Ayesha': Being the Adventures of the Landing Squad of the 'Emden'*, Boston, MA: Ritter & Company, 1917.

Muley, Gunakar. 'The Introduction of Semaphore Telegraphy in Colonial India', in *Webs of History: Information, Communication and Technology from Early to Post-colonial India*, edited by Amiya Kumar, Dipankar Sinha and Barnita Bagchi. New Delhi: Manohar, 2005, 165–72.

Müller, Carlos Alves. '*Longa Distância: A Evolução dos Sistemas Nacionais de Telecomunicações da Argentina e do Brasil em Conexão com as Telecomunicações Internacionais (1808–2003)*' (PhD thesis, University of Brasília, Instituto de Ciências Sociais), 2007.

Müller, Simone. 'The Transatlantic Telegraphs and the *Class of 1866*: the Formative Years of Transnational Networks in Telegraphic Space, 1858–1884/89', in *Historical Social Research – Historische Sozialforschung. Global Communication: Telecommunication and Global Flows of Information in the Late 19th and Early 20th Century*, edited by Roland Wenzlhuemer. Cologne: Center for Historical Social Research, 2010, 237–59.

Mumford, Lewis. *Technics and Civilization.* San Diego, New York and London: Harcourt Brace & Company, 1963.

Nalbach, Alex. '"Poisoned at the Source"? Telegraphic News Services and Big Business in the Nineteenth Century', *Business History Review* 77, no 4 (2003), 577–610.

Neilson, Keith. 'For Diplomatic, Economic, Strategic and Telegraphic Reasons: British Imperial Defence, the Middle East and India, 1914–1918', in *Far-Flung Lines: Essays on Imperial Defence in Honour of Donald Mackenzie Schurman*, edited by Greg Kennedy and Keith Neilson. London and Portland: Frank Cass, 1997, 103–23.

New Anecdote Library, ed. *The London Anecdotes for All Readers. Part 1: Anecdotes of the Electric Telegraph.* London, 1848.

Nicholls, Jack. 'The Impact of the Telegraph on Anglo-Japanese Diplomacy during the Nineteenth Century', *New Voices* **3**, no 1 (2009), 1–22.

Nickles, David Paull. 'Diplomatic Telegraph in American and German History', in *Atlantic Communications: The Media in American and German History from the Seventeenth to the Twentieth Century*, edited by Norbert Finzsch and Ursula Lehmkuhl. Oxford and New York: Berg, 2004, 135–69.

Nickles, David Paull. 'Submarine Cables and Diplomatic Culture', in *Communications under the Seas: The Evolving Cable Network and Its Implications*, edited by Bernard Finn and Daqing Yang. Cambridge, MA and London: MIT Press, 2009, 209–25.

Nickles, David Paull. 'Telegraph Diplomats: The United States' Relations with France in 1848 and 1870', *Technology and Culture* **40**, no 1 (1999), 1–25.

Nickles, David Paull. *Under the Wire: How the Telegraph Changed Diplomacy*. Cambridge, MA and London: Harvard University Press, 2003.

Noakes, Richard J. 'Telegraphy Is an Occult Art: Cromwell Fleetwood Varley and the Diffusion of Electricity to the Other World', *British Journal for the History of Science* **32**, no 4 (1999), 421–59.

Nonnenmacher, Tomas. 'Law, Emerging Technology, and Market Structure: The Development of the Telegraph Industry, 1838–1868', *Journal of Economic History* **57**, no 2 (1997), 488–90.

Nonnenmacher, Tomas. 'State Promotion and Regulation of the Telegraph Industry, 1845–1860', *Journal of Economic History* **61**, no 1 (2001), 19–36.

Odlyzko, Andrew M. 'History of Communications and Its Implications for the Internet', AT&T Labs, 2000.

Palmer, Allen W. 'Negotiation and Resistance in Global Networks: The 1884 International Meridian Conference', *Mass Communication & Society* **5**, no 1 (2002), 7–24.

Park, Han Woo. 'Hyperlink Network Analysis: A New Method for the Study of Social Structure on the Web', *Connection* **25**, no 1 (2003), 49–61.

Perry, Charles R. 'Frank Ives Scudamore and the Post Office Telegraphs', *Albion: A Quarterly Journal Concerned with British Studies* **12**, no 4 (1980), 350–67.

Perry, Charles R. 'The Rise and Fall of Government Telegraphy in Britain', *Business and Economic History* **26**, no 2 (1997), 416–25.

Peters, John Durham. 'Technology and Ideology: The Case of the Telegraph Revisited', in *Thinking with James Carey: Essays on Communications, Transportation, History*, edited by Jeremy Packer and Craig Robertson. New York, Washington, Bern, Frankfurt a. M., Berlin, Brussels, Vienna and Oxford: Peter Lang, 2006, 137–55.

Pichler, Franz. 'Die Einführung der Morse-Telegraphie in Deutschland und Österreich. Die konstruktive Entwicklung der Apparate', *Elektrotechnik und Informationstechnik* **9** (2006), 402–8.

Pieper, Hans, and Kilian Kuenzi. *In 28 Minuten von London nach Kalkutta: Aufsätze zur Telegrafiegeschichte aus der Sammlung Dr. Hans Pieper im Museum für Kommunikation, Bern, Schriftenreihe des Museums für Kommunikation, Bern*. Zurich: Chronos, 2000.

Pieper, Renate. *Die Vermittlung einer neuen Welt. Amerika im Nachrichtennetz des Habsburgischen Imperiums 1493–1598*, edited by Heinz Durchhardt, Veröffentlichungen des Instituts für europäische Geschichte Mainz, Abteilung für Universalgeschichte. Mainz: Philipp von Zabern, 2000.

Pike, Richard, ed. *Railway Adventures and Anecdotes: Extending over More than Fifty Years*. London: Hamilton, Adams, and Co., and Nottingham: J. Derry, 1884.

Pike, Robert M., and Dwayne R. Winseck. 'The Politics of Global Media Reform, 1907–23', *Media, Culture & Society* **26**, no 5 (2004), 643–75.

Pollard, Tomas. 'Telegraphing the Sentence and the Story: Iconicity in *In the Cage* by Henry James', *European Journal of English Studies* **5**, no 1 (2001), 81–96.

Potter, Simon J. 'Communication and Integration: The British and Dominions Press and the British World, c.1876–1914', *Journal of Imperial and Commonwealth History* **31**, no 2 (2003), 190–206.

Potter, Simon J. *News and the British World: The Emergence of an Imperial Press System, 1876–1922*. Oxford: Oxford University Press, 2003.

Rantanen, Terhi. 'The Globalization of Electronic News in the 19th Century', *Media, Culture & Society* **19**, no 4 (1997), 605–20.

Rantanen, Terhi. *When News Was New*. Malden, Oxford and Chichester: Wiley-Blackwell, 2009.

Read, Donald. *The Power of News: The History of Reuters*. Oxford: Oxford University Press, 1999.

Read, Donald. 'Reuters: News Agency of the British Empire', *Contemporary British History* **8**, no 2 (1994), 195–212.

Reindl, Josef. *Der Deutsch-Österreichische Telegraphenverein und die Entwicklung des deutschen Telegraphenwesens 1850–1871*. Frankfurt a. M.: Peter Lang, 1993.

Reindl, Josef. 'Partikularstaatliche Politik und technische Dynamik: Die drahtgebundene Telegraphie und der Deutsch-Österreichische Telegraphenverein von 1850', in *Vom Flügeltelegraphen zum Internet: Geschichte der modernen Telekommunikation*, edited by Hans-Jürgen Teuteberg and Cornelius Neutsch. Stuttgart: Franz Steiner Verlag, 1998, 27–46.

Roberts, Steven. 'Distant Writing: A History of Telegraph Companies in Britain between 1838 and 1868', http://distantwriting.co.uk/default.aspx, 2007.

Ross, Nelson E. *How to Write Telegrams Properly*. Girard, KS: Haldeman-Julius Publications, 1928.

Russell, William Howard. *The Atlantic Telegraph*. London: Day & Son Limited, 1866.

Russell, William Howard. *My Diary in India, in the Year 1858–9. Volume 1*. London: Routledge, Warne, and Routledge, 1860.

Russell, William Howard. *My Diary in India, in the Year 1858–9. Volume 2*. London: Routledge, Warne, and Routledge, 1860.

Schivelbusch, Wolfgang. *Geschichte der Eisenbahnreise: Zur Industrialisierung von Raum und Zeit im 19. Jahrhundert*. Munich and Vienna: Hanser, 1977.

Schlögel, Karl. *Im Raume lesen wir die Zeit: Über Zivilisationsgeschichte und Geopolitik*. Munich: Hanser, 2003.

Scholl, Lars U. 'The Global Communication Industry and Its Impact on International Shipping before 1914', in *Global Markets: The Internationalization of the Sea Transport Industries since 1850*, edited by David J. Starkey and Gelina Harlaftis. St John's: International Maritime Economic History Association, 1998, 195–215.

Schroer, Markus. *Räume, Grenzen, Orte: Auf dem Weg zu einer Soziologie des Raums*. Frankfurt a. M.: Suhrkamp, 2006.

Schulz-Schaeffer, Ingo. 'Akteur-Netzwerk-Theorie: Zur Koevolution von Gesellschaft, Natur und Technik', in *Soziale Netzwerke: Konzepte und Methoden der sozialwissenschaftlichen Netzwerkforschung*, edited by Johannes Weyer. Munich: Oldenbourg, 2000, 187–211.

Schwarzlose, Richard. 'Early Telegraphic News Dispatches: Forerunners of the AP', *Journalism Quarterly* **51** (1974), 595–601.

Schwarzlose, Richard. 'The Nation's First Wire Service: Evidence Supporting a Footnote', *Journalism Quarterly* **57** (1980), 555–62.

Scott, John. *Social Network Analysis: A Handbook. 2nd ed.* London: Sage Publications, 2000.

Scowen, F. 'Transoceanic Submarine Telegraphy', *Transactions of the Newcomen Society* **48** (1978), 1–10.

Shahvar, Soli. 'Concession Hunting in the Age of Reform: British Companies and the Search for Government Guarantees; Telegraph Concessions through Ottoman Territories, 1855–58', *Middle Eastern Studies* **38**, no 4 (2002), 169–93.

Shahvar, Soli. 'Iron Poles, Wooden Poles: The Electric Telegraph and the Ottoman–Iranian Boundary Conflict, 1863–1865', *British Journal of Middle Eastern Studies* **34**, no 1 (2007), 23–42.

Shahvar, Soli. 'Tribes and Telegraphs in Lower Iraq: The Muntafiq and the Baghdad–Basrah Telegraph Line of 1863–65', *Middle Eastern Studies* **39**, no 1 (2003), 89–116.

Shaw, Donald L. 'News Bias and the Telegraph: A Study of Historical Change', *Journalism Quarterly* **44**, Spring (1967), 3–12.

Silva, Ana Paula. 'Shaping the Portuguese Empire in the 20th Century: The Telegraph and the Radio', *ICON* 7 (2001), 106–22.

Silva, Ana Paula. 'Portugal and the Building of Atlantic Telegraph Networks', *Journal of History of Science and Technology* **2** (2008).

Smith, Merritt Roe, and Leo Marx, eds. *Does Technology Drive History? The Dilemma of Technological Determinism*. Cambridge, MA and London: The MIT Press, 1994.

Soja, Edward W. *Postmodern Geographies: The Reassertion of Space in Critical Social Theory*. London: Verso Books, 1989.

Soja, Edward W. *Thirdspace: Journeys to Los Angeles and Other Real-and-Imagined Places*. Oxford: Basil Blackwell, 1996.

Solymar, Laszlo. 'The Effect of the Telegraph on Law and Order, War, Diplomacy, and Power Politics', *Interdisciplinary Science Review* **25**, no 3 (2000), 203–10.

Solymar, Laszlo. *Getting the Message: A History of Communications*. Oxford: Oxford University Press, 1999.

Sonnemann, Ulrich. 'Die Ohnmacht des Raums und der uneingestandene Fehlschlag der Zeitentmachtung: Zur Aporetik des Staus', in *Zeit-Zeichen: Aufschübe und Interferenzen zwischen Endzeit und Echtzeit*, edited by Georg Christoph Tholen and Michael Scholl. Weinheim: VHC, Acta Humanioria, 1990, 17–28.

Standage, Tom. *The Victorian Internet: The Remarkable Story of the Telegraph and the Nineteenth Century's On-Line Pioneers*. New York: Walker and Co., 1998.

Stein, Jeremy. 'Reflections on Time, Time–Space Compression and Technology in the Nineteenth Century', in *Timespace: Geographies of Temporality*, edited by Jon May and Nigel Thrift. London and New York: Routledge, 2001, 106–19.

Tarrant, Donald R. *Atlantic Sentinel: Newfoundland's Role in Transatlantic Cable Communication*. St John's: Flanker Press, 1999.

Tegge, Andreas. *Die Internationale Telekommunikations-Union: Organisation und Funktion einer Weltorganisation im Wandel*. Baden-Baden: Nomos, 1994.

Tillotson, Shirley. '"We May All Soon Be 'First-Class Men'": Gender and Skill in Canada's Early Twentieth Century Urban Telegraph Industry', *Journal of Canadian Labour Studies* **27** (1991), 97–126.

Tully, John. 'A Victorian Ecological Disaster: Imperialism, the Telegraph, and Gutta-Percha', *Journal of World History* **20**, no 4 (2009), 559–79.

Tunstall, Jeremy, and Michael Palmer. *Media Moguls*. London and New York: Routledge, 1991.

Wasserman, Stanley, and Katherine Faust. *Social Network Analysis: Methods and Applications*. Cambridge: Cambridge University Press, 1994.

Weller, Toni, and David Bawden. 'Individual Perceptions: A New Chapter on Victorian Information History', *Library History* **22**, no 2 (2006), 137–56.

Wenzlhuemer, Roland. 'The Dematerialization of Telecommunication: Communication Centres and Peripheries in Europe, 1850–1920', *Journal of Global History* **2**, no 3 (2007), 345–72.

Wenzlhuemer, Roland. 'The Development of Telegraphy, 1870–1900: A European Perspective on a World History Challenge', *History Compass* **5**, no 5 (2007), 1720–42.

Wenzlhuemer, Roland. 'Editorial: Telecommunication and Globalization in the Nineteenth Century', in *Historical Social Research – Historische Sozialforschung. Global Communication: Telecommunication and Global Flows of Information in the Late 19th and Early 20th Century*, edited by Roland Wenzlhuemer. Cologne: Center for Historical Social Research, 2010, 7–18.

Wenzlhuemer, Roland. 'Globalization, Communication and the Concept of Space in Global History', in *Historical Social Research – Historische Sozialforschung. Global Communication: Telecommunication and Global Flows of Information in the Late 19th and Early 20th Century*, edited by Roland Wenzlhuemer. Cologne: Center for Historical Social Research, 2010, 19–47.

Wenzlhuemer, Roland. '"I had occasion to telegraph to Calcutta": Die Telegrafie und ihre Rolle in der Globalisierung im 19. Jahrhundert', *Themenportal Europäische Geschichte* (2011), www.europa.clio-online.de/2011/Article=513.

Wenzlhuemer, Roland. 'London in the Global Telecommunication Network of the Nineteenth Century', *New Global Studies* **3**, no 1 (2009), Art. 2, 1–32.

Wenzlhuemer, Roland. 'Metropolitan Telecommunication: Uneven Telegraphic Connectivity in 19th-Century London', *Social Science Computer Review* **27**, no 3 (2009), 437–51.

Wenzlhuemer, Roland. 'Telecommunications', in *Encyclopedia of the Age of the Industrial Revolution, 1700–1920*, edited by Christine Rider. Westport, CT: Greenwood, 2007, 432–8.

Wilke, Jürgen. *Grundzüge der Medien- und Kommunikationsgeschichte*. Cologne, Weimar and Vienna: Böhlau, 2008.

Wilke, Jürgen. 'The Telegraph and the Transatlantic Communications Relations', in *Atlantic Communications: The Media in American and German History from the Seventeenth to the Twentieth Century*, edited by Norbert Finzsch and Ursula Lehmkuhl. Oxford and New York: Berg, 2004, 107–34.

Winkler, Jonathan Reed. 'Information Warfare in World War I', *Journal of Military History* **73** (2009), 845–67.

Winseck, Dwayne R. 'Back to the Future: Telecommunications, Online Information Services and Convergence from 1840 to 1910', *Media History* **5**, no 2 (1999), 137–57.

Winseck, Dwayne R., and Robert M. Pike. *Communication and Empire: Media, Markets, and Globalization, 1860–1930*. Durham, NC and London: Duke University Press, 2007.

Winthrop-Young, Geoffrey. 'The Informatics of Revenge: Telegraphy, Speed and Storage in *The Count of Monte Cristo*', *Weber Studies: An Interdisciplinary Humanities Journal* **14**, no 1 (1997), 5–17.

Wobring, Michael. *Die Globalisierung der Telekommunikation im 19. Jahrhundert: Pläne, Projekte und Kapazitätsausbauten zwischen Wirtschaft und Politik*. Frankfurt a. M.: Peter Lang, 2005.

Yang, Daqing. 'Submarine Cables and the Two Japanese Empires', in *Communications under the Seas: The Evolving Cable Network and Its Implications*, edited by Bernard Finn and Daqing Yang. Cambridge, MA and London: The MIT Press, 2009, 227–54.

Yang, Daqing. *Technology of Empire: Telecommunications and Japanese Expansion in Asia, 1883–1945*. Cambridge, MA: Havard University Asia Center, 2010.

Yang, Daqing. 'Telecommunication and the Japanese Empire: A Preliminary Analysis of Telegraphic Traffic', in *Historical Social Research – Historische Sozialforschung. Global Communication: Telecommunication and Global Flows of Information in the Late 19th and Early 20th Century*, edited by Roland Wenzlhuemer. Cologne: Center for Historical Social Research, 2010, 66–89.

Yates, JoAnne. 'The Telegraph's Effect on Nineteenth Century Markets and Firms', *Business and Economic History* **15** (1986), 149–63.

Zhou, Yongming. *Historicizing Online Politics: Telegraphy, the Internet, and Political Participation in China*. Stanford, CA: Stanford University Press, 2006.

Zook, Matthew. 'Being Connected Is a Matter of Geography', *Networker* **5**, no 3 (2001), 13–17.

Zook, Matthew. 'Cyberspace and Local Places: The Urban Dominance of Dot. Com Geography in the Late 1990s', in *The Cybercities Reader*, edited by Stephen Graham. London: Routledge, 2004, 205–11.

Zook, Matthew. 'Hubs, Nodes and Bypassed Places: A Typology of E-commerce Regions in the United States', *Tijdschrift voor economische en sociale geografie* **93**, no 5 (2002), 509–21.

Zook, Matthew. 'Old Hierarchies or New Networks of Centrality? The Global Geography of the Internet Content Market', *American Behavioral Scientist* **44**, no 10 (2001), 1679–96.

Zook, Matthew, Martin Dodge, Yuko Aoyama and Anthony Townsend. 'New Digital Geographies: Information, Communication, and Place', in *Geography and Technology*, edited by Stanley Brunn, Susan Cutter and James W. Harrington. New York: Kluwer Academic Publishers, 2004, 155–76.

Zweig, Stefan. *Sternstunden der Menschheit: Vierzehn historische Miniaturen*. Frankfurt a. M.: S. Fischer, 2009.

Index

Printed in the United States
By Bookmasters

Printed in the United States
By Bookmasters